Handbook of Childhood Death and Bereavement

Charles A. Corr, PhD, is Professor, Department of Philosophical Studies, Southern Illinois University at Edwardsville, a volunteer with Hospice of Madison County in Illinois, and a former Chairperson of the International Work Group on Death, Dying, and Bereavement (1989–1993). Dr. Corr's previous publications with Springer Publishing Company include: *Adolescence and Death* (1986); *Handbook of Adolescent Death and Bereavement* (1996); and four books co-edited with Donna M. Corr. His other publications include: *Helping Children Cope with Death: Guidelines and Resources* (2nd ed., 1984); *Childhood and Death* (1984); *Death and Dying, Life and Living* (1994; co-authored with Clyde M. Nabe and Donna M. Corr); and some 60 book chapters and articles in professional journals. Dr. Corr's professional work has been recognized by: the Association for Death Education and Counseling (ADEC) in an award for Outstanding Personal Contributions to the Advancement of Knowledge in the Field of Death, Dying, and Bereavement (1988) and in its Death Educator Award (1996); Children's Hospice International (CHI) in an award for Outstanding Contribution to the World of Hospice Support for Children (1989) and in its Charles A. Corr Award for Lifetime Achievement (Literature) (1995); and Southern Illinois University at Edwardsville through Research Scholar (1990), Outstanding Scholar (1991), and Kimmel Community Service (1994) awards.

Donna M. Corr, RN, MSN, is Professor, Department of Nursing, St. Louis Community College at Forest Park, St. Louis, Missouri. Donna Corr's publications include 16 book chapters and articles in professional journals, *Death and Dying, Life and Living* (1994; co-authored with Charles A. Corr and Clyde M. Nabe), and four previous books co-edited with Charles A. Corr for Springer Publishing Company: *Hospice Care: Principles and Practice* (1983); *Hospice Approaches to Pediatric Care* (1985); *Nursing Care in an Aging Society* (1990); and *Sudden Infant Death Syndrome: Who Can Help and How* (1991). Springer books edited by Donna and/or Charles Corr have received five separate Book of the Year Awards from the *American Journal of Nursing*.

HANDBOOK
OF Childhood
Death AND
Bereavement

Charles A. Corr, PhD

Donna M. Corr, RN, MSN

Editors

SPRINGER PUBLISHING COMPANY

Springer Publishing Company, Inc.
536 Broadway
New York, NY 10012-3955

Cover design by Tom Yabut
Production Editor: Pamela Lankas

96 97 98 99 00/5 4 3 2 1

Library of Congress Cataloging-in-Publication Data
Handbook of childhood death and bereavement / Charles A.
    Corr, Donna M. Corr, editors.
        p.   cm.
    Includes bibliographical references and index.
    ISBN 0-8261-9320-X
    1. Children and death.   2. Bereavement in children.
  3. Grief in children.   4. Terminally ill children—Psychology.
  5. Children—Counseling of.   I. Corr, Charles A.   II. Corr,
Donna M.
    BF723.D3H36   1996
    155.9'37'083—dc20   96-5016
                                                         CIP

Printed in the United States of America

This book is for
ANDREW MICHAEL RAMSEY
(born January 6, 1994)
and
CHRISTOPHER JAMES CORR
(born July 25, 1994)
who came into our lives as we were working
on the early stages of this project
and who reminded us once again of the joys of
new life, children, parenting, and grandparenting

Contents

Contributors

Joan B. Bacon, M.S.W., is director of "Endings and Beginnings," a children's bereavement support group in St. Louis, Missouri.

John E. Baker, Ph.D., is Instructor in Psychiatry (Psychology) at the Harvard Medical School, Cambridge Hospital, Cambridge, and in private practice in Belmont, Massachusetts.

Sandor B. Brent, Ph.D., is Professor, Department of Psychology, Wayne State University, Detroit, Michigan.

Carolyn L. Butler, M.S., is Co-Director of CHANGES: The Support for People and Pets Program, Veterinary Teaching Hospital, Colorado State University, Fort Collins, Colorado.

Barbara Oberhofer Dane, D.S.W., is Associate Professor, School of Social Work, New York University, New York, New York.

Kenneth J. Doka, Ph.D., is Professor, Graduate Gerontology Program, College of New Rochelle, New Rochelle, New York.

Beverly S. Hatter, M.S.W., is Director, BRIDGES: A Center for Grieving Children, in Tacoma, Washington.

Laurel S. Lagoni, M.S., is Co-Director of CHANGES: The Support for People and Pets Program, Veterinary Teaching Hospital, Colorado State University, Fort Collins, Colorado.

Antoon A. Leenaars, Ph.D., C.Psych., is a clinical psychologist in Windsor, Ontario, Canada, and a faculty member of the Department of Clinical and Health Psychology, Faculty of Social Sciences, University of Leiden, The Netherlands.

Corinne Masur, Psy.D., is in private practice in Philadelphia, Pennsylvania. She is a clinical associate in psychoanalysis at The Philadelphia Psychoanalytic Institute and Society, an Assistant Clinical Professor at Widener University, and President of the Philadelphia Center for Psychoanalytic Education.

Margaret M. Metzgar, M.A., is founder and primary therapist at the Transition and Loss Center in Seattle, Washington.

Kathleen Olympia Nader, D.S.W., is a consultant in traumatic response in private practice in Laguna Hills, California.

Kevin Ann Oltjenbruns, Ph.D., is Associate Professor, Department of Human Development and Family Studies, Colorado State University, Fort Collins, Colorado.

Lillian M. Range, Ph.D., is Professor, Department of Psychology, The University of Southern Mississippi, Hattiesburg, Mississippi.

Elliott J. Rosen, Ed.D., is on the senior faculty of The Family Institute of Westchester, Consulting Psychologist to Jansen Memorial Hospice, and a family therapist in private practice in Scarsdale, New York.

Mary Anne Sedney, Ph.D., is Professor, Department of Psychology, Providence College, Providence, Rhode Island.

Mark W. Speece, Ph.D., is Assistant Professor, Department of Internal Medicine, School of Medicine, Wayne State University, Detroit, Michigan.

S. D. Stahlman, Ph.D., A.C.S.W., is Professor and Director of Social Work Education, Department of Sociology and Social Work, Indiana Wesleyan University, Marion, Indiana.

Tamina Toray, Ph.D., is Assistant Professor, Department of Psychology, Western Oregon State College, Monmouth, Oregon.

Susanne Wenckstern, M.A., is in the Psychological Services Department of the Windsor Board of Education in Windsor, Ontario, Canada.

Barbara C. Zick, M.A., C.M.H.C., is a psychotherapist in private practice in Redmond, Washington.

Preface

This is a book about three principal topics: (a) children who are coping with confrontations with death and dying; (b) children who are coping with confrontations with bereavement; and (c) interventions designed to help these children. The goal of this book is to contribute to an improved understanding of the challenges and tasks that face children who are coping with death, dying, and bereavement, and to guide efforts to assist such children. In its topics, structure, and goals, this book is designed as a companion to *Handbook of Adolescent Death and Bereavement,* edited by Charles A. Corr and David E. Balk (Springer Publishing Co., 1996).

Many books have been published for many different types of audiences about children and death, or children and bereavement. We set out to create a new book to address the most important of those topics in a single volume and to distinguish them clearly from issues related to adolescents. In particular, we wanted to bring forward and synthesize the best insights from research, the literature in this field, and the expertise of our contributors. And we sought to achieve this in way that could serve as a practical resource for professional readers, students, and other interested persons.

Much has changed in recent years in our understanding of childhood and in children's experiences of death, dying, and bereavement. No longer are or should children be treated merely as little adults or confused with adolescents in their thoughts, feelings, and behaviors. Furthermore, growing attention to developmental differences within childhood and to the normative tasks of children's development has been combined with greater appreciation of the non-normative or situational work of coping with loss and grief that is involved for children in confrontations with death and bereavement. In particular, a careful review of the literature on the development of children's understandings of death (of the kind presented here in chapter 2) has revealed that children's concepts of death are more complex than is usually acknowledged and that it is dangerous to oversimplify our account of the development of such concepts in two or three so-called stages.

Topics related to childhood that have sparked growing interest within the past decade include human immunodeficiency virus (HIV) infection and acquired immunodeficiency syndrome (AIDS), suicide and life-threatening behavior, and encounters with traumatic experiences. Each of these topics is new in its reality or in its effects on children in our society. All of these topics, together with issues facing children who are living with life-threatening illness, are examined in detail in Part I in this book.

For bereavement, not so long ago one could encounter in the scholarly literature learned claims that children do not have the capacity to grieve. Or, perhaps more precisely, we were told by some that children did not have the capacity to mourn, that is, to cope with loss and grief. In recent years, we have learned that these were unreliable claims arising from overly narrow ideological perspectives or misapplications to children of theoretical models derived not from bereaved children but from the study of bereaved adults. Today, there is a growing body of research and insight informed by empirical data concerning the distinctive features of children's grief and mourning. The chapters in Part II of this book offer new and helpful information about the current state of knowledge in that field. They also suggest ways in which present insights need to be expanded, enriched, or reexamined in the future.

Finally, especially during the last few years, much has been learned about interventions that are appropriate to the specific needs of children who are coping with death, dying, and bereavement. The chapters in Part III of this book draw together several important ways in which to help such children and their families. These intervention strategies include capitalizing on and strengthening the family's own resources, preparing children in advance to cope with trauma and loss, undertaking constructive programs of postvention or intervention immediately after a traumatic experience, using support groups, and treating bereaved children individually through psychotherapy when their grief is blocked or their mourning complicated.

For each of the chapters that follow, contributors were invited to explore a particular subject area related to death, dying, or bereavement that was important in the lives of contemporary children. To do so, contributors were asked to draw on their own experience in the field in question, existing research, and relevant literature. Many of these contributors have conducted the research or written the literature that is most prominent in their respective fields; all have direct, professional experience with the children whose situations they discuss.

In the development of this book, its editors are indebted to many individuals who have contributed to our insights and understanding in this field of study during the past 20 years. A smaller number of colleagues, consultants, and friends helped to shape our thinking about this particular project and what it needed to include. A distinguished group of contributors found time in their busy schedules to write the chapters that follow. Southern Illinois University at Edwardsville and Saint Louis Community College at Forest Park generously supported this project, as they have supported our separate professional endeavors over an extended period.

In this project, as in five previous books and a wide variety of articles, presentations, and other professional projects, we have enjoyed working together and learning from each other's insights. We hope that readers will find the results of that work helpful in enriching their understanding of children who are coping with death, dying, and bereavement, and in guiding their efforts to improve assistance offered to such children.

CHARLES A. CORR
DONNA M. CORR

I

Death

Chapters 1 and 2 establish a foundation for all that follows in this book. In chapter 1, Charles Corr introduces us to some fundamental understandings of childhood in the form of distinctions between the four basic eras in childhood—infancy, toddlerhood, early childhood, and middle childhood—and some comments on the developmental tasks that characterize each of those eras. With that in mind, Corr then sketches a portrait of children's encounters with death and bereavement in our society. This is accomplished in two ways: (a) through an analysis of demographic data on deaths and death rates in childhood; and (b) through a description of four case examples, each of which illustrates a child's experience with bereavement in one of the four eras in childhood. The results reveal the many interactions that exist between the normative or expected task work of child development, and the nonnormative or unanticipated task work arising from death-related situations in childhood.

In chapter 2, Mark Speece and Sandor Brent review more than 100 English-language studies of children's understanding of death. From this survey and their own independent research, Speece and Brent identify five central components or subconcepts that enter into children's understanding of death: universality, irreversibility, nonfunctionality, causality, and noncorporeal continuation. Recognition of these five key components enables the authors to comment on the definition and validity of the presumed mature adult concept of death toward which children have been thought to be struggling. On this basis, the authors explain limitations in previous research in this area of study, review findings from past research in terms of the major variables that have been studied in relation to the development of children's concepts of death, and show what will be necessary for future research in this field.

Chapters 3 to 5 then discuss encounters with three specific types of death-related experiences that occur during childhood in contemporary American society: HIV infection and AIDS; suicide and life-threatening behavior; and living with life-threatening illness. In Chapter 3, Barbara Dane explores the implications of HIV (human immunodeficiency virus) infection and AIDS (Acquired Immune Deficiency Syndrome) for children. HIV infection and AIDS may strike children directly or they may impact children who are not themselves infected through the deaths of parents, siblings, and other relatives. In either case, children in our society face a growing threat from HIV infection and AIDS, and one that is complicated by issues of stigma, shame, secrecy, fear of disclosure, multiple loss, and survivor's guilt—as Dane illustrates in her analysis of concrete cases and issues arising for health care practitioners and policy makers.

Another uncomfortable topic that has often been ignored or shoved aside in adult thinking about childhood is suicide and life-threatening behavior. In Chapter 4, Lillian Range reports the epidemiological data on attempted and completed suicide in childhood. In particular, Range outlines how children go about attempting or completing suicide, the individual and family variables that are implicated in these behaviors, ways of assessing risk for these behaviors in children, and ways to prevent or mitigate the likelihood of such behavior in children who may be at risk of ending their lives or harming themselves in a serious way.

Finally, in Chapter 5 Kenneth Doka investigates the experiences of children who are living with life-threatening illness and their family members. In the course of their encounters with such an illness, children encounter and respond to a wide variety of losses and challenges. Doka throws light on these experiences through an insightful model of phases and tasks in coping with life-threatening illness and through a series of concrete examples taken from the lives of ill and dying children.

1

Children, Development, and Encounters with Death and Bereavement

Charles A. Corr

In every living species, offspring represent continuity and the promise of the future—for individuals, families or other groups, and the species itself. Among adult humans, it is common to value children highly for who they are and what they symbolize. Frequently, adults also regard children as innocent and unblemished. That is, many adults wish to think of children only in terms of joy, happiness, and the so-called good things of life.

That is not the whole story of childhood. Children can also help acquaint adults in important ways with other aspects of life. This chapter explores interactions between childhood development and encounters with death and bereavement. Topics examined include (a) the meaning of the terms *child* and *childhood;* (b) the difference between normative and nonnormative life events and transitions within childhood; (c) developmental tasks that confront children during four distinct eras in childhood; (d) encounters with death during childhood expressed through a review of numbers of deaths of children and their causes, death rates during childhood, and race and gender as two significant variables in the deaths of children; and (e) encounters with bereavement during childhood illustrated in examples of four different childhood experiences with the death of a significant other. The goal of this chapter is to introduce these topics and prepare the way for more detailed explorations in the chapters that follow concerning interactions between children and issues associated with death and bereavement.

CHILDHOOD AND ITS FOUR PRINCIPAL ERAS

According to *The Oxford English Dictionary* (Simpson & Weiner, 1989), ever since medieval times the term *child* (Old English = *cild*) has been used to designate the offspring of human parents, that is, the unborn or newly born human being, "originally always used in relation to the mother as the 'fruit of the womb'" (Vol. 3, p. 113). Such offspring may be young children, adolescents, or even the adult children of their parents, but the word "child" most properly refers to an individual younger than the age of puberty. Thus, the related term *childhood* is usually employed to identify the portion of the life span from birth to puberty or the beginning of adolescence.

Within childhood as it is typically experienced in most developed societies in the world today, an interval including approximately the first 10 to 12 years of life, it has become customary to think of four basic developmental eras (sometimes called "ages," "periods," or "stages"): infancy, toddlerhood, early childhood or the preschool years, and middle childhood or the school-age years (see Table 1.1). Although the justifications for these divisions are generally obvious, there may be some arbitrariness in the number of eras identified during childhood and in their precise boundaries. For example, some might wish to draw a further distinction between children in the early primary school years and preteenagers. For the most part, however, this book refers to the standard division of four basic developmental eras within childhood.

Clearly, children differ among themselves in many ways. In addition to differences arising from their developmental status, children differ as unique individuals; as boys and girls; as members of different racial, cultural, religious, or economic communities; as a result of divergent life experiences; and in other salient ways. When generalizations about children are offered, it is helpful to keep these many variables in mind and to be cautious (as suggested in the footnote in Table 1.1) about linking developmental eras with chronological ages.

NORMATIVE AND NONNORMATIVE
LIFE EVENTS AND TRANSITIONS

Throughout the human life span, it has become commonplace to distinguish between normative and nonnormative life events and transitions (Baltes, Reese, & Lipsitt, 1980). A *normative life event* is one that is

TABLE 1.1   **Principal Developmental Eras During Childhood**

Era	Age[a]	Predominant issue	Virtue
Infancy	Birth through 12–18 months	Basic trust vs. mistrust	Hope
Toddlerhood	Infancy to 3 years of age	Autonomy vs. shame and doubt	Will or self-control
Early childhood; sometimes called play age or the preschool period	3–6 years	Initiative vs. guilt	Purpose or direction
Middle childhood; sometimes called school age or the latency period	6 years to puberty	Industry vs. inferiority	Competency or skill

Sources: Erikson, 1963.
[a]All chronological ages are approximate.

expected to occur at a certain time, in a certain relationship to other life events, with predictability, and to most if not all of the members of a developmental group or cohort. Because normative life events follow familiar patterns or standards, they lead to expected transitions or turning points in individual development. Entering the school system around the age of 6 years is a familiar example of a normative life transition in the United States and many other developed countries. This transition is the basis for the distinction noted above between preschool and school-age children or early and middle childhood.

As the language itself indicates, *nonnormative life events* are those that are unexpected or unforeseen. Unlike normative life transitions, they occur atypically or unpredictably, with apparently random relationship to other life events, and to some but not all members of a developmental cohort. Because nonnormative life events are characteristically unanticipated, they usually catch children and adults unprepared. Discovering that a child is a prodigy who has the ability to play an advanced piece of classical music or experiencing the accidental death of a pet during childhood are both examples of nonnormative or distinctively personal life events. Such events do occur, and it can be expected that some of them will occur in the lives of some children, but there is no reliable foundation for predicting whether or not, much less when, they will happen in the life of a specific child.

Most of the death-related events discussed in this book do not fall into the category of predictable life events or normative developmental transitions. In societies like the United States, the death of a youngster during childhood or a child's encounter with the death of a parent, sibling, other relative, or friend is not a normative event. Such deaths do occur, but they are better understood as situational occurrences or examples of unanticipated life crises than as normative life transitions. Among all death-related losses, perhaps the death of a child's pet or grandparent would be the most likely to occur, but even these deaths do not rise to the frequency or predictability of normative life transitions during childhood.

Normative life transitions and unanticipated or nonnormative life events do share some common characteristics. Both confront the children who experience them with life crises, and both may evoke coping processes from such children. As life crises or turning points, they present "dangerous opportunities." That is, they offer opportunities for growth and maturation if a child copes with them effectively, but they also represent danger in the form of possible psychological harm to the child, and distorted or unsatisfactory development if the coping response is inappropriate or inadequate. Consequently, it is useful to understand the nature of normative life transitions in childhood as well as the potential implications of unanticipated life events—especially those which may be traumatic in nature—for children. In the case of events related to death and bereavement, it is also helpful for adults to learn how to foster constructive coping processes in childhood, how to minimize unproductive or counterproductive coping, and how to support children as they are engaged in the work of coping.

DEVELOPMENTAL TASKS WITHIN FOUR PRINCIPAL ERAS IN CHILDHOOD

Throughout the human life span, normative life transitions are usually described in terms of developmental tasks. Within childhood, these tasks represent the work which children must undertake to navigate successfully the developmental challenges that confront them. In his well-known analysis of life-span development within childhood (summarized in Table 1.1), Erikson (1963, 1968) described each era within childhood in terms of *a predominant psychosocial issue or central conflict* and in terms of *a leading virtue* that would be achieved in the normal and healthy development of an individual ego. Erikson meant that in each era of their development, children (and other human beings) are confronted by a pair of opposed tendencies or orientations toward life, the self, and other people. The way in which each of these basic tensions or conflicts is resolved has its outcome in a virtue or quality of ego functioning. Successful resolution or integration results in growth or maturation; unsuccessful responses to developmental challenges may stunt or harm maturation and leave unfinished work for later in life.

For example, in his account of *infancy,* Erikson depicted the central conflict as one between basic trust and mistrust. The developmental task in this era of childhood is to develop a sense of basic trust on which the virtue of hope can be founded. In this context, hope means that children believe they can rely on people and the world to fulfill their needs and satisfy their desires. A view of the world as unfriendly or unpredictable might lead to mistrust in children and a self-protective withdrawal. In *toddlerhood,* Erikson described the central conflict as one between autonomy versus shame and doubt. This is a tension between self-regulation and external control. According to Erikson, the primary developmental task for toddlers is to establish their own legitimate autonomy or independence in making decisions and to develop the virtue of will or self-control.

During *early childhood,* Erikson identified the central conflict as one between initiative versus guilt. The developmental task for children in this era is to cultivate their own initiative or desire to take action and pursue goals, and to balance that with the healthy moral reservations that they may have about their plans—a combination of spontaneity and responsibility. Developing this sort of self-regulation promotes the virtue of purpose or direction in a child's life. Finally, for Erikson children in *middle childhood* are confronted with a developmental conflict between industry versus inferiority. Such children face the challenge of developing their capacities to do productive work. The virtue that results from successful resolution of this crisis is competence, which reflects the child's sense of self-esteem rooted in a view of the self as able to master skills and carry out tasks.

It needs to be remembered that human development is multifaceted and that it extends over a relatively long period. Beginning from the successful fertilization of an ovum by a sperm, child development proceeds through a fairly well-recognized set of physical processes related to biological (or anatomical and physiological) development. After birth, physical development includes mastery of large motor and other skills. For example, normally developing children learn to reach out to toys and other objects; to hold their bottles; to roll over, crawl, and walk;

and eventually to perform other activities that involve complex coordination skills.

At the same time, children also experience psychological, social, and spiritual development. In these areas, greatest attention has been given to personality and social development in childhood (represented by the work of Erikson and many others) and to intellectual development (represented by the work of Piaget [1929, 1932] and many others). However, no aspect of child development is a simple process occurring in isolation. For example, Erikson (1963) spoke of the need for "triple bookkeeping," by which he meant that one must consider social context, ego process or identity, and somatic process or constitution in any satisfactory explication of human development. Elsewhere, Erikson (1975, p. 228) described as these variables as the "history, personality, and anatomy" of a developing individual.

Clearly, the full scope of human development during childhood cannot be explored here in all of its complexities. Happily, that need not be attempted in this chapter, because these subjects have been addressed at length by many developmental psychologists (Papalia & Olds, 1996; Zigler & Stevenson, 1993) and other students of childhood (Coles, 1990). Instead, this chapter focuses on ways in which developmental processes (and other factors) can play important roles in determining encounters with death during childhood, and how encounters with bereavement arising from the deaths of significant others may influence a child's subsequent development.

ENCOUNTERS WITH DEATH DURING CHILDHOOD

Children do die. A description of the frequency of such encounters with death and an analysis of the principal features of those encounters will heighten appreciation of the general patterns of childhood deaths. This section describes the demographics of deaths and death rates among children in our society, leading causes of death during different eras of childhood, and two important variables: race and gender. (Note that the data in this chapter are taken from the National Center for Health Statistics [NCHS]; presentation of that data follows NCHS terminology and format [e.g., for racial groupings] and may not always be identical with our earlier usage and our discussion of four eras during childhood.)

Numbers of Deaths and Death Rates Among Children

Table 1.2 provides data based on an advance report of final mortality statistics in the United States for 1992 (Kochanek & Hudson, 1994) for total numbers of deaths and death rates for three age groups in childhood: infants (children younger than 1 year of age); children from 1 to 4 years of age; and children from 5 to 9 years of age. In Table 1.2, these data are given for all races taken together as well as for white children and Black children separately; in addition, data are provided for both sexes together as well as for male children and female children separately.

The most striking feature of these data is that by far the largest number of deaths in childhood occurs during infancy. This is true for all groups of children in our society: all children together, male and female children, and white and Black children. However, the total number of infant deaths in 1992 (34,628) was more than 2,100 less than the total for 1991. Provisional data for 1993 report a reduction to 33,300 infant deaths and an infant mortality rate of 828.8 per 100,000 live births, "the lowest rate ever recorded in the United States" (NCHS, 1994, p. 7).

With these facts in mind, it is especially unfortunate that the United States—the richest country on earth—had an infant mortality rate in 1992 and again in 1993 that is higher than that of 21 other countries around the globe (Wegman, 1994). As Wegman (1994, p. 802) noted, "a major difference between the US and the[se] other countries . . . is that all the others have some form of a national health program offering preventive and therapeutic coverage to their whole populations."

From Table 1.2, it is evident that many more white children died in 1992 in the United States than did Black children. This is not surprising, because whites make up a much larger proportion of the population than do Blacks. What is startling and shocking is that although Blacks constituted less than 13% of the total population in the United States in 1992, they experienced nearly one third of all infant deaths.

This glaring discrepancy between these two racial groups is evident in the fact that Black children have much higher death rates than white children. During infancy, the ratio of Black to white deaths is more than 2.5 to 1. In the case of children beyond infancy, the discrepancy in these death rates lessens, but is still significant. For children 1 to 4 years of age, the ratio declines to 1.9 to 1; for children 5 to 9 years of age, it falls under 1.8 to 1. But even this last figure describes a death rate of nearly 2 to 1 for Black children versus white children in the 5- to 9-year-old age group.

TABLE 1.2 Deaths and Death Rates During Childhood by Age, Race, and Sex: United States, 1992

Age (years)	All races			White children			Black children		
	Both sexes	Male	Female	Both sexes	Male	Female	Both sexes	Male	Female
Deaths									
Under 1	34,628	19,545	15,083	22,164	12,625	9,539	11,348	6,298	5,050
1–4	6,764	3,809	2,955	4,685	2,690	1,995	1,799	965	834
5–9	3,739	2,231	1,508	2,690	1,605	1,085	894	529	365
Death rates (per 100,000 in the population group)									
Under 1	865.7	956.6	770.8	701.8	780.9	618.7	1,786.0	1,957.9	1,609.7
1–4	43.6	48.0	39.0	38.1	42.6	33.3	73.2	77.6	68.7
5–9	20.4	23.7	16.8	18.3	21.3	15.2	32.1	37.5	26.6

Source: Kochanek & Hudson, 1994.

Table 1.2 also indicates that male children in all age and racial groups have notably higher death rates than female children. To be male, Black, and under 1 year of age is most hazardous of all.

The 45,131 deaths experienced by children under 10 years of age is a relatively small portion of the record-breaking total of 2,175,613 deaths in the United States during 1992. Furthermore, only during infancy do childhood death rates exceed or even compare with those of the population as a whole. After the hazards of infancy, children are relatively healthy individuals whose encounters with death are far more rare than those of older persons in our society. Thus, children 5 to 9 years of age had the lowest death rate of all age groups in our society in 1992, followed immediately by the death rate for children 1 to 4 years of age.

Nevertheless, a total of more than 45,000 deaths in childhood during a single year is certainly substantial. And surely the death of any one child will be an occasion of intense pain and grief for those who love that child.

Causes of Death During Childhood

Table 1.3 provides data for numbers of deaths and death rates according to the 10 leading causes of death for all races and both sexes in the United States in 1992, according to three age groups: infants, children between the ages of 1 to 4 years, and children between the ages of 5 to 14 years. (Note that this last age grouping differs from that given in Table 1.2). It is useful to examine these data in some detail with special attention to causes of death that are associated with developmental problems.

Infants.   The 10 leading causes of death among infants remained basically stable in the United States during 1991 and 1992. Among these, the first four leading causes of death in infancy—congenital anomalies, sudden infant death syndrome (SIDS), disorders relating to short gestation and unspecified low birthweight, and respiratory distress syndrome—are the most significant since they lead to more than one half (53%) of all infant deaths.

More generally, in terms of both absolute numbers and death rates, the major causes of death during infancy in the United States are of three basic types: (a) genetic anomalies inherent in the infant's very origins, (b) SIDS, and (c) and problems associated with the child's development before or at the time of birth. Clearly, developmental issues play a major role in a large portion of infant deaths.

TABLE 1.3 Deaths and Death Rates (per 100,000 Members in the Population Group) for the 10 Leading Causes of Death in Childhood, All Races, Both Sexes: United States, 1992

Rank	Infants			1–4 Years of age			5–14 Years of age		
	Cause of death	No.	Rate	Cause of death	No.	Rate	Cause of death	No.	Rate
—	All causes	34,628	851.9	All causes	6,764	43.6	All causes	8,193	22.5
1	Congenital anomalies	7,449	183.2	Accidents and adverse effects	2,467	15.9	Accidents and adverse effects	3,388	9.3
2	Sudden infant death syndrome	4,891	120.3	Congenital anomalies	856	5.5	Malignant neoplasms	1,105	3.0
3	Disorders related to short gestation and unspecified low birthweight	4,035	99.3	Malignant neoplasms	479	3.1	Homicide and legal intervention	587	1.6
4	Respiratory distress syndrome	2,063	50.8	Homicide and legal intervention	430	2.8	Congenital anomalies	448	1.2
5	Newborn affected by maternal complications of pregnancy	1,461	35.9	Diseases of heart	286	1.8	Suicide	314	0.9
6	Newborn affected by complications of placenta, cord, and membranes	993	24.4	Pneumonia and influenza	188	1.2	Diseases of heart	284	0.8

Rank	Cause	No.	Rate	Cause	No.	Rate	Cause	No.	Rate
7	Infections specific to the perinatal period	901	22.2	Human immuno-deficiency virus infection	161	1.0	Human immuno-deficiency virus infection	104	0.3
8	Accidents and adverse effects	819	20.1	Certain conditions originating in the perinatal period	113	0.7	Pneumonia and influenza	104	0.3
9	Intrauterine hypoxia and birth asphyxia	613	15.1	Septicemia	77	0.5	Chronic obstructive pulmonary diseases and allied conditions	100	0.3
10	Pneumonia and influenza	600	14.8	Anemias	65	0.4	Benign neoplasms, carcinoma in situ, and neoplasms of uncertain behavior and unspecified nature	97	0.3
—	All other causes	10,803	265.8	All other causes	1,642	10.6	All other causes	1,662	4.6

Source: Kochanek & Hudson, 1994.

The prominence of SIDS—the leading cause of death among infants from 1 month to 1 year of age—is ironic and challenging because the underlying cause of SIDS deaths is unknown. This is true despite the fact that the syndrome or pattern of events that SIDS represents can be identified with some precision by a thorough postmortem and circumstantial examination (Corr, Fuller, Barnickol, & Corr, 1991; DeFrain, Ernst, Jakub, & Taylor, 1991). Many knowledgeable researchers suspect that SIDS may have much to do with developmental problems during or before the 1st year of life because SIDS is rare after the 1st year of life.

Infections and accidents also cause several infant deaths, but those factors represent only a small portion of overall deaths during infancy.

Children 1 to 4 Years of Age. Table 1.3 also offers data for numbers of deaths and death rates listed according to the 10 leading causes of death for children between 1 to 4 years of age. As children move from infancy into toddlerhood, they typically become more mobile and more independent of their parents and other caretakers. It is also customary for toddlers to venture outside the family home more frequently, often under the supervision of an adult or older child. As a result, the pattern of the leading causes of death among children 1 to 4 years of age differs somewhat from that of infants.

Clearly, it is the first two causes of death that are by far the most significant for 1- to 4-year-old children. "Accidents and adverse effects" account for almost 37% of all deaths of children in this age group. Such deaths arise mostly from motor vehicle accidents as well as from drowning, burning, ingesting harmful substances, choking, misadventures with firearms, and falling. Taken together, accidental deaths and those caused by congenital anomalies lead to more than 49% of all deaths in this age group. These two causes combine both the increased risks experienced by members of this group of children as they become more mobile and more independent, along with the lingering effects of developmental problems, which have their origin in the child's genetic makeup.

Other leading causes of death for this cohort of children have similar characteristics: so-called natural causes of death like cancer (malignant neoplasms), heart disease, pneumonia, and influenza appear alongside homicide and HIV infection. Both homicide and HIV infection represent a kind of witting or unwitting violence inflicted on the child because HIV infection is typically acquired by young children from an infected mother before, at, or shortly after the child's birth across the placental barrier, in the birth canal, or through breast feeding.

Children 5 to 14 Years of Age.   Also included in Table 1.3 are data for numbers of deaths and death rates listed according to the 10 leading causes of death for children between 5 to 14 years of age. Again, the leading cause of death—accidents and adverse effects—is by far the most critical. Accidents—in or near motor vehicles, on playgrounds, or in activities like cycling—cause more than 41% of all deaths among school-age children.

Among other leading causes of death for children between 5 to 14 years of age, cancer and homicide, congenital anomalies and heart disease, and HIV infection and pneumonia/influenza all remain significant. New to the list are suicide, chronic obstructive pulmonary diseases, and various types of neoplastic disease. In part, this foreshadows adolescence when accidents, homicide, and suicide are the three leading causes of death in our society.

Two Notable Variables in the Death of Children: Race and Gender

The realities of death during childhood are not the same for all children. There are many distinguishing variables, of which race and gender are among the most notable.

Race.   Some differences in numbers of deaths and death rates for white and Black children have been mentioned earlier. Tables 1.4 to 1.6 provide more detailed information on these subjects, listed according to the 10 leading causes of death for each of three age groups during childhood. Because the total number of these deaths for white children is almost always much larger (usually around twice) those for Black children, the rank order of causes of death for white children in Tables 1.4 to 1.6 is typically close to that given earlier in Table 1.3 for both races together. (Note, however, that infant mortality rates in Table 1.4 are given in terms of 100,000 live births; this is slightly different from death rates given for infants in Table 1.3 and all other tables in this chapter, which are computed per 100,000 members in the population group.) Nevertheless, Tables 1.4 to 1.6 reveal significant differences between the races in all three age groups during childhood.

TABLE 1.4   Deaths and Death Rates (per 100,000 Live Births) for the
10 Leading Causes of Infant Death, by Race: United States, 1992

	White infants			Black infants		
Rank	Cause of death	No.	Rate	Cause of death	No.	Rate
—	All causes	22,164	692.3	All causes	11,348	1,684.6
1	Congenital anomalies	5,666	177.0	Disorders related to short gestation and unspecified low birthweight	2,025	300.6
2	Sudden infant death syndrome	3,239	101.2	Congenital anomalies	1,477	219.3
3	Disorders related to short gestation and unspecified low birthweight	1,926	60.2	Sudden infant death syndrome	1,471	218.4
4	Respiratory distress syndrome	1,321	41.3	Respiratory distress syndrome	705	104.7
5	Newborn affected by maternal complications of pregnancy	963	30.1	Newborn affected by maternal complications of pregnancy	466	69.2
6	Newborn affected by complications of placenta, cord, and membranes	659	20.6	Infections specific to the perinatal period	306	45.4
7	Infections specific to the perinatal period	573	17.9	Newborn affected by complications of placenta, cord, and membranes	298	44.2
8	Accidents and adverse effects	533	16.6	Accidents and adverse effects	251	37.3
9	Intrauterine hypoxia and birth asphyxia	404	12.6	Pneumonia and influenza	216	32.1
10	Pneumonia and influenza	357	11.2	Intrauterine hypoxia and birth asphyxia	185	27.5
—	All other causes	6,523	203.7	All other causes	3,948	586.1

Source: Kochanek & Hudson, 1994.

TABLE 1.5 Deaths and Death Rates (per 100,000 Members in the Population Group) for the 10 Leading Causes of Death, 1–4 Years of Age, by Race: United States, 1992

Rank	White children Cause of death	No.	Rate	Black children Cause of death	No.	Rate
—	All causes	4,685	38.1	All causes	1,799	73.2
1	Accidents and adverse effects	1,794	14.6	Accidents and adverse effects	574	23.2
2	Congenital anomalies	613	5.0	Congenital anomalies	208	8.5
3	Malignant neoplasms	388	3.0	Homicide and legal intervention	185	7.5
4	Homicide and legal intervention	224	1.8	Human immuno-deficiency virus infection	100	4.1
5	Diseases of heart	179	1.5	Diseases of heart	95	3.9
6	Pneumonia and influenza	116	0.9	Malignant neoplasms	62	2.5
7	Certain conditions originating in the perinatal period	64	0.5	Pneumonia and influenza	56	2.3
8	Human immuno-deficiency virus infection	60	0.5	Certain conditions originating in the perinatal period	43	1.7
9	Septicemia	53	0.4	Anemias	40	1.6
10	Benign neoplasms, carcinoma in situ, and neoplasms of uncertain behavior and unspecified nature	51	0.4	Chronic obstructive pulmonary diseases and allied conditions	28	1.1
—	All other causes	1,143	9.3	All other causes	408	16.6

Source: Kochanek & Hudson, 1994.

TABLE 1.6   Deaths and Death Rates (per 100,000 Members in the Population
Group) for the 10 Leading Causes of Death, 5–14 Years of Age,
by Race: United States, 1992

Rank	Cause of death	No.	Rate	Cause of death	No.	Rate
		White children			Black children	
—	All causes	5,989	20.6	All causes	1,876	33.7
1	Accidents and adverse effects	2,501	8.6	Accidents and adverse effects	738	13.3
2	Malignant neoplasms	904	3.1	Homicide and legal intervention	260	4.7
3	Congenital anomalies	343	1.2	Malignant neoplasms	159	2.9
4	Homicide and legal intervention	295	1.0	Congenital anomalies	91	1.6
5	Suicide	271	0.9	Diseases of heart	82	1.5
6	Diseases of heart	188	0.6	Chronic obstructive pulmonary diseases and allied conditions	47	0.8
7	Benign neoplasms, carcinoma in situ, and neoplasms of uncertain behavior and unspecified nature	82	0.3	Human immuno-deficiency virus infection	47	0.8
8	Pneumonia and influenza	80	0.3	Suicide	34	0.6
9	Human immuno-deficiency virus infection	55	0.2	Anemias	33	0.6
10	Chronic obstructive pulmonary diseases and allied conditions	50	0.2	Pneumonia and influenza	19	[a]
—	All other causes	1,220	4.2	All other causes	366	6.6

Source: Kochanek & Hudson, 1994.
[a]Figure does not meet standard of reliability or precision (estimate is based on fewer than 20 deaths in numerator or denominator).

Among *infants,* problems with disorders related to short gestation and low birthweight are evident both in the ranking of this category as the principal cause of death for Black infants (vs. its ranking as the third leading cause of death for white infants), and in the fact that more Black infants died from this cause in 1992 (2,025) than did white infants (1,926). This is likely to reflect several contributing factors, such as a higher incidence of early pregnancy, inadequate prenatal care, and premature birth among Blacks than whites.

Other leading causes of death among white and Black infants are relatively similar in identity and rank ordering, with only slight variations. However, as noted earlier, overall numbers of Black infant deaths are much higher proportionally (more than one third of all infant deaths) than would be expected from the relative share of Blacks in the total population. And it is a sad fact that death rates for Black infants are (as noted earlier) approximately $2\frac{1}{2}$ times those for white infants.

For *children between 1 to 4 years of age,* variances between white and Black children are a bit less dramatic than those for infants, but still substantial. Disadvantages for Black children are again evident in comparing death rates of 38.1 for white children to 73.2 for Black children as well as in the relatively higher rankings of homicide and HIV infection as leading causes of death for Black children versus white children in this age group.

Among *children between 5 to 14 years of age,* the patterns are again different for white and Black children. Not surprisingly, accidents are the leading cause of death in both columns in Table 1.6. But cancer and congenital anomalies precede homicide in rank order as causes of death for these white children, whereas homicide leads the other two causes for Black children. One notable disadvantage for white children in this age group is seen in the relatively high ranking of suicide as the fifth leading cause of death for white children, whereas it is only the eighth leading cause of death for Black children. However, for Black children in this age group HIV infection is seventh in the list, whereas it is only ninth for white children.

Gender. Tables 1.7 and 1.8 provide data that differentiate numbers of deaths and death rates by gender for children of all races in the United States in 1992 according to the 10 leading causes of death in each case. Table 1.7 gives data for male and female children between 1 to 4 years of age; Table 1.8 offers data for male and female children between 5 to 14 years of age. In both of these age groups, the leading causes of death are similar, although some differences in rank order are evident, espe-

TABLE 1.7   Deaths and Death Rates (per 100,000 Members in the Population
Group) for the 10 Leading Causes of Death, 1–4 Years of Age,
All Races, by Gender: United States, 1992

	Male children			Female children		
Rank	Cause of death	No.	Rate	Cause of death	No.	Rate
—	All causes	3,809	48.0	All causes	2,955	39.0
1	Accidents and adverse effects	1,513	19.1	Accidents and adverse effects	954	12.6
2	Congenital anomalies	460	5.8	Congenital anomalies	396	5.2
3	Malignant neoplasms	248	3.1	Malignant neoplasms	231	3.0
4	Homicide and legal intervention	242	3.0	Homicide and legal intervention	188	2.5
5	Diseases of heart	151	1.9	Diseases of heart	135	1.8
6	Pneumonia and influenza	95	1.2	Pneumonia and influenza	93	1.2
7	Human immuno-deficiency virus infection	88	1.1	Human immuno-deficiency virus infection	73	1.0
8	Certain conditions originating in the perinatal period	62	0.8	Certain conditions originating in the perinatal period	51	0.7
9	Anemias	39	0.5	Septicemia	44	0.6
10	Chronic obstructive pulmonary diseases and allied conditions	35	0.4	Chronic obstructive pulmonary diseases and allied conditions	28	0.4
—	All other causes	876	11.0	All other causes	762	10.1

Source: Kochanek & Hudson, 1994.

cially in 5- to 14-year-olds. For both of the age groups in these two tables, a higher number of deaths for male versus female children can be
noted in every causal category.

As a result of this last fact, in comparing the leading causes of death
for these two age groups by both race and gender, it is the male children (vs. the females) who are closest to the patterns indicated in Table
1.3 for all races, even though white male children continue to differ
rather obviously from Black male children.

TABLE 1.8 **Deaths and Death Rates (per 100,000 Members in the Population Group) for the 10 Leading Causes of Death, 5–14 Years of Age, All Races, by Gender: United States, 1992**

Rank	Male children — Cause of death	No.	Rate	Female children — Cause of death	No.	Rate
—	All causes	5,080	27.2	All causes	3,113	17.5
1	Accidents and adverse effects	2,280	12.2	Accidents and adverse effects	1,108	6.2
2	Malignant neoplasms	637	3.4	Malignant neoplasms	468	2.6
3	Homicide and legal intervention	375	2.0	Homicide and legal intervention	212	1.2
4	Congenital anomalies	238	1.3	Congenital anomalies	210	1.2
5	Suicide	232	1.2	Diseases of heart	124	0.7
6	Diseases of heart	160	0.9	Suicide	82	0.5
7	Human immuno-deficiency virus infection	67	0.4	Pneumonia and influenza	50	0.3
8	Chronic obstructive pulmonary diseases and allied conditions	55	0.3	Benign neoplasms, carcinoma in situ, and neoplasms of uncertain behavior and unspecified nature	46	0.3
9	Pneumonia and influenza	54	0.3	Chronic obstructive pulmonary diseases and allied conditions	45	0.3
10	Benign neoplasms, carcinoma in situ, and neoplasms of uncertain behavior and unspecified nature	51	0.3	Human immuno-deficiency virus infection	37	0.2
—	All other causes	931	5.0	All other causes	731	4.1

Source: Kochanek & Hudson, 1994.

ENCOUNTERS WITH BEREAVEMENT
DURING CHILDHOOD

No reliable data are presently available concerning the frequency or nature of encounters with bereavement during childhood. The death of a significant other can be an important bereavement experience for a child. However, such encounters vary greatly in terms of the types of death and loss that are experienced, the identities of the children who have such experiences, and their impact. Many encounters with bereavement may have particular meaning for a child, and may seriously affect his or her subsequent developmental work.

The four examples that follow illustrate possible impacts of encounters with bereavement on developmental tasks during the four eras of childhood previously identified, that is, on the developmental work of infants, toddlers, preschool children, and school-age children. These examples describe the death of a mother, a father, a sibling, a grandparent, and a pet. In terms of causes of death, these examples include a homicide, a suicide, an instance of SIDS, a natural or illness-related death, and an accidental death.

In real life, each death has its own distinguishing features and implications. Each response to bereavement may also be distinctive both in the coping strategies that are employed, and in the nature and availability of the support that is available to the bereaved child. All of these variables may differ from the examples that follow. Thus, these examples merely suggest what might happen as a result of a nonnormative, death-related encounter; they do not predict or insist on any specific set of developmental consequences that inevitably arise from any particular encounter with death.

An Infant

Tamika was just 10 months old when her mother, Althea, was killed in what at first appeared to be a random, drive-by shooting. It had been a hot, sweltering day in the small southern town where Tamika and her mother lived with her grandmother and other members of her extended family. When evening came, some family members and friends gathered to sit on the front porch just to talk and snatch a few moments of rest.

Suddenly—or so it seemed to those present—a car came round the corner, gunshots rang out, and people jumped for cover. They reemerged shortly to find one man slightly wounded and Tamika's mother, Althea, dead on the front steps. Nothing like this had happened before on this street, although there had been some recent incidents of violence in the larger neighborhood, and people had been worried that gang tensions were beginning to appear in town.

Nevertheless, a careful investigation led police to charge Tamika's father, Leroy, with the murder of her mother. Leroy and Althea had had a brief, tempestuous affair that led to Tamika's conception. When Althea announced that she was pregnant, Leroy promptly left town.

Recently, Leroy had moved back to town with a new wife, and Althea had seized the opportunity, with the help of a public aid lawyer, to sue him for child support. She did this, as Althea said, "to get my baby what she deserves and to teach that Leroy a mighty lesson." As the evidence later showed, Leroy was infuriated by Althea's action; his hot temper led to the violent response that resulted in Althea's death.

After her mother's death, Tamika spent several years shifting between members of her mother's extended family and social services agencies. During this period, Tamika experienced a lack of consistency in the sensitivity and responsiveness offered by her caregivers. Her life was often disrupted just as she seemed to be settling into a new situation. Eventually, especially at the time of her father's trial and after he was sent to jail, Tamika learned most of the central facts about her conception and the death of her mother.

Throughout her childhood, Tamika exhibited anxiety and a sense of insecurity. She had a poor self-concept and low self-esteem when she came to school. Perhaps understandably, Tamika experienced difficulties in social relationships and found it difficult to form secure attachments, even with those who tried to reach out to her. In these ways, the death of her mother when she was an infant and the circumstances of that loss became central elements in Tamika's subsequent life and development.

A Toddler

By the time Marcie was $2\frac{1}{2}$ years old, her mother, Angie, had become accustomed to leaving her at home with her father when she went out to her job at the truck stop on the highway. Marcie's father, Bobby, had been sick off and on for a long time. After he was fired from his job at the plant, he had only worked irregularly at odd jobs. Much of the time, Bobby was depressed, although every once in a while he would seem to perk up, and for a few days or weeks life would change for the whole family. Bobby and Angie would joke and laugh, and they would take Marcie out for special treats.

On the night before Bobby took his life, Angie felt a bit uneasy about working a long overnight shift at the truck stop. Bobby had seemed more moody and erratic lately, and he was drinking more. But Angie had asked for time off to be with Bobby and Marcie on several occasions during the preceding few *weeks, and they were short of help at work. So Angie put Marcie to bed, said goodbye to Bobby as he stared blankly at the television, and went off to work.*

The next morning, Marcie woke early and wandered out to the kitchen with her favorite doll in one hand. When she could not find her father, Marcie went through the open door into the attached garage. Bobby was hanging from an exposed rafter, twisting silently. Marcie called out to him and pulled at his feet but got no response. She did not really understand what had happened, but Marcie knew something was wrong, so she went to the telephone and dialed the operator just as she had been told to do in an emergency.

After the police and all the other people came and cut Bobby's body down, and after Angie had come home to this shocking scene, Marcie and Angie just sat together and cried. Angie kept saying that she knew Bobby was sick and that he had tried to hurt himself once or twice before, but that she had never believed he would really do anything like this. Marcie wanted to say something to make her mother feel better, but she did not know what to say. Her relationship with her father had been uneven and unsatisfying. And it was difficult to put into words her awful feelings of responsibility, guilt, self-doubt, and confusion. Maybe somehow, she felt, Marcie had done something that made her daddy do this terrible thing.

But these were frightening thoughts, so Marcie just closed off this part of her life from Angie, and her mother never knew about these dark places inside her daughter. As a result, Marcie grew up with a sense of shame that she was really a "bad" girl, no matter how much her mother praised her, or how well she did at home and later at school. Marcie regressed in her development to some degree, constantly doubted her own abilities, and was easily swayed into doing things that she really did not want to do by strong-willed people around her. This persisted until well into adulthood when protracted problems in her life led her to a sensitive therapist who helped her to unravel some of the implications of these early childhood experiences.

A Preschool Child

Michael's little sister, Laura, died suddenly one night just 2 weeks before his fifth birthday. Michael was the youngest of three boys in the family. His parents had had two sons shortly after they were married. In their financial situation at the time, that seemed enough for them to manage.

But Michael's parents very much wanted to have more children. When their fortunes improved several years later, they tried again and were delighted when Michael was born. Everyone loved Michael as the new baby in the family, and his parents saw his birth as the start of what they half-jokingly called their "second family" in their new home in California.

Nevertheless, Michael's mother seemed to find it difficult to become preg-nant again and when she did, she experienced two miscarriages and a still-birth. So when Laura arrived after what seemed like a blissful pregnancy, the whole family was greatly relieved and almost delirious in their joy. It seemed too good to be true: a healthy baby, a happy mother, and a little girl at last! And Michael was now, finally, somebody's big brother after so many years of being the "little kid" in the family.

Laura had her own room in the big new house they now owned. It was dec-orated with all the special things that Michael's parents bought for their "little princess." Michael played with Laura almost every day and even helped care for her sometimes. So everyone felt that life was good one night in February when they put Laura down to bed for the evening.

In the middle of the night, however, Michael's mother woke with a strange sense of emptiness and an odd feeling that something was wrong. She realized she could hear no sounds over the intercom from Laura's room and that Laura had not cried for her usual middle-of-the-night feeding. In Laura's room, the baby was turned into the corner of her crib and eerily still.

The screams from Michael's mother woke everyone in the house. Michael was terrified, but everyone was too busy to talk to him or even to think of his needs. His father tried to resuscitate Laura, one brother called 911, and the other brother held his mother. Almost immediately, the house filled with strangers. It seemed to Michael that these strangers were hurting Laura, but he did not know what to do. Then they just carried Laura out of the house, and everyone sat looking at the floor in a stunned silence.

Later, Michael was told that Laura had died of "SIDS," but he didn't know what that meant. His parents had changed in ways that he could not understand. No one seemed to know what to say to Michael except to urge him to be a good boy, and go out and play. Nothing that he could say or do seemed to cheer his parents up, and they seemed unable to realize what he needed. The funeral was even more confusing. Afterward, Michael's father went back to work right away. His brothers went off to college and never seemed to come home. There was just Michael and his mother, who seemed to float around aimlessly, lost in her own thoughts and tears. No one arranged a party or any other way of celebrating Michael's fifth birthday.

Michael felt that he must have done something to bring about all these changes. What had he said to Laura those times when he got angry with her? Why had everyone turned into themselves and away from him? Would the ter-rible thing that happened to Laura happen to him, too? Who would take care of Michael in this terrible time? Michael's concerns and his feelings of re-sponsibility were a big burden for him to bear. Because he did not know what to do, he, too, withdrew into himself, and lost much of his former energy and spontaneity.

In the death of his sister, Michael lost not only a cherished younger sibling, but also the comforting presence of his parents and older brothers. Michael's sense of security in the family home was threatened, and, like many young children, he believed himself to be somehow responsible for the bad things that happened. Michael experienced secondary losses in what he imagined to be threats to his own safety similar to those that had befallen his sister (although SIDS is not, in fact, a threat to a child of Michael's age), and in the inability of others to fulfill his legitimate expectations concerning plans to celebrate the anniversary of his own birth. Most of all, Michael lost a sense of purpose or direction, a confidence that what he was and what he did could contribute to a good life for himself and for those close around him.

A School-Age Child

Tommy's Grandpa Dan died when Tommie was 8 years old. Grandpa and Grammie Marge were special people in Tommy's life. They lived nearby and were the only grandparents that Tommy had ever known. Because Tommy was their only grandchild and because he had been born after many years of marriage almost as a surprise to his two career-oriented parents, Grandpa Dan and Grammie Marge just "loved him to pieces," as they often said. They were interested in everything he did, took him with them to special activities or for sleep-over weekends at their home, and gave him presents of all sorts.

But one day, Tommy realized that Grandpa Dan seemed to be forgetting things all the time. He no longer seemed to know how to do all of the many things that he used to teach Tommy to do. Eventually, he forgot the name of the dog, Pepper, that he had given Tommy for his seventh birthday. Grammie Margie said Grandpa had Alzheimer's disease, but she didn't seem to have much time to explain what was happening or to play with Tommy because there was so much to do to take care of Grandpa.

When Grandpa Dan died of a heart attack, everyone said it was a blessing. But Tommy did not understand how that could be true. All he wanted was to have Grandpa back alive and for things to be the way they used to be.

Nearly a month later, when everyone was still sad, Tommy went for a walk with Pepper. It was after school near the park where Tommy and Grandpa often watched the older boys practice sports. As Tommy and Pepper walked along, Tommy thought about how Grandpa had explained each sport to him and showed him how to hold a bat or kick a football. Tommy was not really watching Pepper carefully as he dashed from one spot to another to sniff out everything that he turned up. So when Pepper ran into the street and was hit by the truck, it was the screech of brakes that broke into Tommy's musings.

Tommy could not believe what had happened. He had the leash in his hand, but Pepper was lying in the street next to the curb. His first thought was: "How will I ever explain this to Grandpa?" But then he realized that it was too late. There was no real explanation for what he had done. And there was no Grandpa anymore to listen so carefully and find a way to understand.

Why had these terrible things happened? Tommy knew he should have paid more attention to what Pepper was doing and taken better care of him. Maybe he should have done that for Grandpa, too? If he had only done his jobs better, maybe Grandpa and Pepper would not have died? Without the support of his grandparents and the companionship of his dog, Tommy felt a sense of inferiority and lack of competence. He lost confidence in himself and did not seem to know how to focus his energies in productive ways. In the aftermath of Grandpa Dan's death, Grammie Marge appeared to be worn out by her own grief. Then, when Pepper died also just a little while afterward, Tommy's parents tried to help him, but they just did not know what to do.

CONCLUSION

Children have important work to do as they face the many challenges of life. For some, problems arise in development that can threaten a child's life, and cause his or her death. For others, the death or loss of an important person or significant relationship can have a powerful impact on a child's subsequent development. Although not predictable in their specifics, it is inevitable that many children will be confronted by these nonnormative, death-related challenges. Such challenges are grounded in the human and personal contexts within which children live their lives.

To ignore or turn a blind eye to these challenges is to abandon children and put them at risk of much harsher futures than they need experience. It is essentially to leave children alone just when they need the assistance of others around them. As Katzenbach (1986, p. 322) has written, "children can adapt wonderfully to specific fears, like a pain, a sickness, or a death. It is the unknown which is truly terrifying for them. They have no fund of knowledge in how the world operates, and so they feel completely vulnerable."

That is the positive message of this book: Adults can bring experience, insight, skill, and caring presence to the aid of children who may feel vulnerable and alone in the terrifying face of the unknown. In some cases, skilled adults can eliminate or minimize challenges that confront children. In many cases, thoughtful adults can guide children and help them cope more effectively with the challenges that arise in their lives. In all cases, wise adults can offer support while children are addressing meaningful events in their lives.

To be available to children in these ways, it is essential for adults to be aware of the realities of nonnormative, death-related events in the lives of children and to appreciate the many ways in which coping with situational tasks arising from death and bereavement can interact with coping with normative developmental tasks.

2

The Development of Children's Understanding of Death

Mark W. Speece and Sandor B. Brent

The systematic study of children's understanding of death began in the 1930s with studies by Schilder and Wechsler (1934), Anthony (1939, 1940, 1972), and Nagy (1948).[1] However, it was not until after 1970 that interest in this area blossomed, with 28 studies in the 1970s, 57 in the 1980s, and 10 so far in the 1990s. Altogether there have been more than 100 studies of children's understanding of death published in the English language (Speece, 1994). Because more than one half of these were published during the last decade, many were not included in either of the two previous reviews of this area (Speece & Brent, 1984; Stambrook & Parker, 1987). This chapter highlights the major research findings on children's understanding of death and discusses some of the principal theoretical and methodological issues.

There has been surprisingly slow progress in this area, despite the number of studies it has generated. This slow progress appears to be the result of several factors: (a) confusion over the names for and definitions of the various components of the concept of death that have been studied; (b) lack of reliable and valid standardized measures for these components[2]; (c) widespread lack of methodological sophistication; (d) the fact that almost one third of the studies, including some of the better ones, are only available as dissertations; (e) the fact that much of the research merely attempts to replicate or refute earlier studies rather than break new ground; (f) an overreliance on, and often a simplistic use of, a single theoretical perspective on cognitive development—the

Piagetian perspective; (g) the fact that the development of the concept of death has not been considered a worthwhile area of investigation by many mainstream investigators or funding sources; and (h) the focus on the bioscientific aspects of the concept of death, which, at times, has translated into a bias against religious views of an afterlife.

This literature has aptly been characterized as consisting of a "confusing array of results" (Stambrook & Parker, 1987). Consequently, comparisons between studies are often difficult. Despite these difficulties, however, there has been some progress. This chapter reviews the key components of the concept of death, discusses the definition and validity of the presumed mature adult concept, and, finally, reviews the major variables that have been studied in relation to the development of the concept. First, however, we shall look at the methodologies used to measure children's understanding of death.

METHODS OF STUDY

Although a variety of methods has been used to explore a child's understanding of death, the principal one has been the interview. However, the nature and content of the interview has varied from study to study.

Other methods, usually used in conjunction with interviews, have included (a) written essays (Bolduc, 1972; Childers & Wimmer, 1971; Nagy, 1948; Wainwright, 1987; Wenestam, 1984; Wenestam & Wass, 1987); (b) drawings (Childers & Wimmer, 1971; Gorman, 1983; Lonetto, 1980; Nagy, 1948; Wainwright, 1987; Wenestam, 1984; Wenestam & Wass, 1987); (c) play activities (Hansen, 1973; Hurst, 1980; Rochlin, 1967; Vianello & Marin, 1989; Wass, Dinklage, Gordon, Russo, Sparks, & Tatum, 1983a, 1983b; Weininger, 1979); (d) a child's story about death (McBride, 1987; Menig-Peterson & McCabe, 1978; Pitcher & Prelinger, 1963; Wass & Scott, 1978); (e) questionnaires (Gorman, 1983; Hui, Chan, & Chan, 1989; Zweig, 1977); (f) reactions to stories depicting attraction and repulsion to death (Orbach, Feshbach, Carlson, & Ellenberg, 1984; Orbach, Feshbach, Carlson, Glaubman, & Gross, 1983; Orbach, Rosenheim, & Hary, 1987); (g) definitions of the word "dead" (Anthony, 1972; Gorman, 1983; McWhirter, Young, & Majury, 1983); (h) descriptions of death-related pictures (Black, 1979; Schilder & Wechsler, 1934); (i) multiple-choice responses to hypothetical death situations (Bolduc, 1972); (j) ratings of death-related exemplars (Demmin, 1986); (k) Q-sorts of death-related statements (Fink, 1976); (l) group interviews (Guy, 1993); (m) thematic apperception tests (Hagey, 1991; Tallmer, Formanek, & Tallmer, 1974); (n) sentence completions (Hagey, 1991); and (o) sequencing of ordered death-related pictures (Hornblum, 1978).

The primary focus of this chapter is studies that used the interview. With that in mind, we can turn to a discussion of the concept of death.

THE CONCEPT OF DEATH

It is now generally accepted that the concept of death is not a single, unidimensional concept but is, rather, made up of several relatively distinct subconcepts. We have referred to these as components (Speece & Brent, 1984). In this section we discuss how each component has been defined by various investigators. Because much of the research has focused on the biological and scientific aspects of the death of the physical body, we know considerably less about other important aspects, such as beliefs in spiritual continuation after death, and the meaning and significance of death for children of various ages (Klatt, 1991).

Since the late 1970s most investigators have assumed that the concept of death comprises several logically distinct components. However, investigators have varied considerably in the exact number of components they have recognized and how they have defined them. Speece and Brent (1984) identified four components that account for the bulk of research: universality, irreversibility, nonfunctionality, and causality. More than 90 studies involve at least one of these.

Each is reviewed subsequently, focusing on its definition and operationalization, the various terms used to refer to it, and how children understand that component before they have achieved a mature understanding. This focus on the definition and operationalization of these components is an important first step toward a much-needed standardization of these key aspects of the concept of death.

Universality

Universality refers to the understanding that all living things must *eventually* die. Other words used to refer to aspects of this component include "inevitability," "death as personal," "awareness of personal death," "personal applicability of death," "personal mortality," "the necessity of death," and "unpredictability." These various terms reflect the fact that researchers have focused on three closely related dimensions of universality: all inclusiveness, inevitability, and unpredictability.

All Inclusiveness.   Most research on universality has focused on this aspect of universality, namely, on whether the child understands that everyone will eventually die and on identifying which individuals the child believes to be exempt from dying.

Inevitability.   The term *inevitability* has most often, but not always, been used interchangeably with universality (Cotton & Range, 1990). However, the two are not identical. Although, logically, if death is universal it must ultimately be inevitable, the converse is not necessarily true—death could be inevitable for some but not all living beings, and, therefore, not be universal. Miller (1988), one of the few investigators to have made this distinction, investigated both universality and inevitability. She defined the former as the understanding that "death will occur . . . to all living beings without limit or exception" (p. xxvi), and the latter as the understanding that "the necessity of death cannot be prevented nor eluded by strategy or dexterity" (p. xxvi)—that is, that death cannot ultimately be avoided.

The study of children's understanding of the inevitability of death has also sometimes been combined with that of their understanding of both universality and causality (Candy-Gibbs, Sharp, & Petrun, 1985; Goodman, 1990; Smith, 1992; Swain, 1979). However, the relationship between these three aspects is more subtle than is usually acknowledged. Universality focuses on the question of *who* is included in the set of *individuals who must die,* whereas causality emphasizes the set of *events or conditions* that might possibly cause an individual's death. Inevitability, in contrast, involves an integration of the two, namely, the fact that, although particular individuals can sometimes avoid particular causes of death (e.g., polio or car accidents), no individual can ultimately avoid some cause of death.

On the basis of this analysis, we recommend that in the future when investigators are interested in identifying the set of individuals (or living beings) children believe to be subject to death, they use the term *universality.* And when they are interested in the set of circumstances that children believe might cause or result in death, they use the term *causality.* Finally, we strongly recommend that the term *inevitability* be reserved for the notion that death itself is *ultimately unavoidable* for *all* living things *regardless of its specific causes.*

Unpredictability.   A third aspect of universality that has been investigated in some studies is the understanding that although everyone must die, the exact *timing* of an individual's death is in general unpredictable (Swain, 1979). Inevitability has to do with the fact that death is unavoidable, whereas unpredictability has to do with the notion that, with a few exceptions (e.g., suicide), in any particular case the time of an individual's death cannot be known in advance—in principal, anyone might possibly die at any time regardless of his or her age, or circumstances.

Questions Used for Universality. The most common type of question used to probe children's understanding of universality asks about universality in general (e.g., "Will everybody die someday?"). Others, however, ask about personal mortality (e.g., "Will you die someday?") or whether various classes of people (or animals) die (e.g., "Do children ever die?"). In addition, some investigators have asked specifically about the timing of death (e.g., "When do people die?" or "When will you die?"). Finally, as noted earlier, some questions concern the preventability (inevitability) of death (e.g., "Can we stop a person from dying?" or "Is there something I can do so that I won't ever die?").

Before Universality In general, younger children are more likely than older children to indicate that death is not universal. Exceptions have included the child himself or herself; children, in general; the child's immediate family; teachers; and even the investigators. Younger children are also more likely than older children to think that death is avoidable if you are clever or lucky (Nagy, 1948) and to indicate that death only occurs in the remote future (Candy-Gibbs, Sharp, & Petrun, 1985; Derry, 1979; Lee, 1987; Swain, 1979).

Schilder and Wechsler (1934) found that children attribute the possibility of death to *all* other people before they extend it to themselves. Most subsequent research, however, has not supported this finding (for an exception, see Lonetto, 1980). These later studies have suggested the opposite: that most children understand their own personal mortality *before* they understand that *all* other people die (Derry, 1979; Devereux, 1984; Hornblum, 1978; Jay, Green, Johnson, Caldwell, & Nitschke, 1987; Peck, 1966; Robinson, 1977; Speece & Brent, 1992; Steiner, 1965). In addition, these later studies have found that when children exclude themselves they almost always exclude other individuals as well. Thus, the data, in general, do not support the notion that for most children their personal mortality is the last aspect of universality they understand.

When younger children (or adults) project their own deaths into the remote future, most of the time their prediction will be accurate. The key issue here, however, is not whether death is likely to occur at all but whether it is possible for death to occur at any time.

Irreversibility

Irreversibility refers to the understanding that once the physical body dies, it cannot be made alive again. In offering this definition, we have specifically left open the question of some sort of noncorporeal continuation after death of the body—concepts such as reincarnation, resurrection, and so forth. We have also found it useful to distinguish the irreversibility of death of the physical body from the question of whether *any* kind of life functions continue after death. We refer to the latter as nonfunctionality. Both of these aspects are discussed subsequently. We believe that much of the disagreement among investigators in the way children's concepts of death have been conceptualized and investigated is a result of the fact that many investigators have failed to make these distinctions.

Irreversibility has been used to refer to both *process irreversibility*—that is, the fact that the processes that mark the transition from the alive to the dead state are irreversible processes (e.g., decomposition)—and *state irreversibility*—that is, the fact that the state of being dead, once it has been achieved, is a permanent state. Other words used to refer to aspects of this component include "irrevocability," "permanence," "death as immutable," and "finality."

In some research reports, however, the referent of these terms, including irreversibility, is ambiguous. For example, Childers and Wimmer (1971) used "death as irrevocable" to refer to what appears to be both irreversibility and nonfunctionality. Although they provide their interview questions, the questions used to measure irrevocability were not specified. Irreversibility has also sometimes been used to refer to a combination of components. For example, Swain (1979) combined what we have defined as irreversibility with both nonfunctionality and beliefs in an afterlife.

Questions Used for Irreversibility.   Several types of questions have been used to investigate children's understanding of irreversibility. The most common asks about irreversibility in general (e.g., "Can a dead person become alive again?"). Others, however, include nonspecific questions (e.g., "What happens after you die?"); questions that ask whether the deaths of specific individuals or animals can be reversed (e.g., "Can you come back to life after you die?"); questions that focus on the efficacy of various specific methods of reversing death (e.g., "If I gave some medicine to a dead person, could he become alive again?"); leading questions (e.g., How do you make a dead thing come back to life?"); and questions that focus on the permanence of death (e.g., "How long will my friend's parent stay dead?").

Before Irreversibility. Younger children are more likely than older children to view death as temporary and reversible. Some young children see death as similar to sleep (from which you will wake up) or like a trip (from which you will return). Children who think death can be reversed believe that it can happen spontaneously (Nagy, 1948), after eating or drinking (Beauchamp, 1974; Hansen, 1973), through wishful thinking (Hansen, 1973), by praying (Weininger, 1979), and as the result of magical or medical intervention (Speece & Brent, 1992).

The finding that children think death can be reversed as the result of medical intervention, taken in conjunction with the fact that some adults believe that cardiopulmonary resuscitation (CPR) can sometimes reverse death (Brent & Speece, 1993), raises an important theoretical and methodological issue. We discuss this issue later when we examine the validity of the presumed mature adult concept of death.

Nonfunctionality

Nonfunctionality refers to the understanding that once a living thing dies *all* of the typical life-defining capabilities of the living physical body (e.g., walking, eating, hearing, seeing, thinking, and learning) cease. Once again, specifying that nonfunctionality refers to the person's physical body distinguishes this aspect of the concept of death from the issue of whether some noncorporeal aspect of a person, such as the spirit, is capable of any life-like functions (e.g., loving, helping) after death.

Various investigators have used "cessation of bodily functions," "dysfunctionality," "insensitivity," "immobility," "finality," and even "irreversibility" (usually defined as a combination of nonfunctionality and irreversibility) to refer to aspects of this component.

Although "cessation of bodily functions" has been the most common description, we prefer nonfunctionality (Speece & Brent, 1984) because it identifies more clearly and concisely the key issue for this component (i.e., loss of function). Although "finality" is the second most common reference (Smilansky, 1987), it is less satisfactory because it has sometimes been used to refer to irreversibility by itself (Blum, 1976), sometimes nonfunctionality by itself (Smilansky, 1987), sometimes a combination of irreversibility and nonfunctionality (Gorman, 1983), and sometimes a combination of irreversibility, nonfunctionality, and the view that at death all existence ends, and there is no noncorporeal continuation (Hagey, 1991).

Questions Used for Nonfunctionality.   Several types of questions have been used to investigate children's understanding of nonfunctionality. Although the most common asked about specific abilities (e.g., "Can a dead person still hear?"), there is wide variability in both the number and range of abilities investigated. Other types include questions that were nonspecific (e.g., "What happens after death?"), questions dealing with general functionality (e.g., "Is there anything a dead person can do?"), and questions that focus on the difference between the states of being dead and being alive (e.g., "Are people different after they die?").

Before Nonfunctionality.   Younger children are more likely than older ones to think that the dead continue to be able to perform various functions (Hoffman & Strauss, 1985; Kane, 1979). Kane distinguished between those functions that are external and readily observable to the child (like eating and speaking), and those that are internal and, therefore, have to be inferred (like dreaming and knowing). She found that at any given age more children understand the cessation of external functions than of internal functions.

Causality

Unlike universality, irreversibility, and nonfunctionality, there is no consensus on the mature adult's understanding of this component. For example, some investigators have defined a mature understanding of causality as the ability to describe the abstract and generalized causes of death (e.g., old age or illness) (Koocher, 1973; Robinson, 1977). Others, however, have emphasized the understanding that death ultimately results from internal rather than external causes (Karpas, 1986; Wass et al., 1983b), the understanding that death results from both internal and external causes (Kane, 1979), the understanding of "realistic" causes (e.g., old age, illness, or accidents) as opposed to "unrealistic" causes (e.g., bad behavior or wishing someone died) (Devereux, 1984), or merely naming old age as a cause along with at least one other realistic cause (Smilansky, 1987). Collectively, these approaches suggest that the mature understanding of causality involves an abstract and realistic understanding of the external and internal events that might possibly cause an individual's death. This understanding is "abstract" in the sense that the causes specified are not restricted to particular individuals or events, but are classes of causes that are applicable to living things in general. It is "realistic" in the sense that the causes specified are generally accepted by mature adults as valid causes of death.

Only rarely was this component confounded with other components. As discussed earlier, investigators who used Swain's (1979) coding for inevitability combined causality with inevitability.

Questions Used for Causality. Among the several types of questions used to investigate children's understanding of causality, the most common has been the general question (e.g., "Why do people die?"). Others, however, asked for the causes of death of specific individuals (e.g., "How can you die?") or whether specific hypothetical causes could actually result in death (e.g., "Can people die because they were bad?").

Before Causality. In general, younger children are more likely than older children to provide unrealistic causes (e.g., bad behavior causes death) or specific concrete causes (e.g., guns or poison) (Devereux, 1984; Koocher, 1973; Robinson, 1977); to focus on external causes (e.g., violence and accidents) rather than internal causes (e.g., illness or old age) (Kane, 1979; Karpas, 1986); and to lack an understanding of the fact that death ultimately results from a failure of one or more internal bodily organs or systems (Candy-Gibbs, Sharp, & Petrun, 1985).

Noncorporeal Continuation

Although the bulk of the research has focused on the four components reviewed previously, our own research has now led us to recognize the importance of a fifth component, which we refer to as noncorporeal continuation. Noncorporeal continuation refers to the notion that some form of personal continuation exists after the death of the physical body (e.g., reincarnation in a new body or ascension of the soul to heaven without the body). This aspect has been referred to by others as "beliefs in an afterlife." The importance of this component is derived from both theoretical and methodological considerations.

Unlike the other components, noncorporeal continuation has seldom been identified as a separate component in the research literature (notable exceptions include Anthony & Bhana, 1988; Black, 1979; Blum, 1976). However, some investigators have referred to various aspects of noncorporeal continuation indirectly either by mentioning it in passing, illustrating it in the sample responses they provide for other components, or by including it as subordinate part of the coding system for irreversibility or nonfunctionality (Hagey, 1991; Swain, 1979). In these coding systems, responses of this type generally are considered as indicative of less mature understanding of irreversibility or nonfunctionality rather than of an independent aspect of the concept of death.

The failure of most investigators to identify noncorporeal continuation as a separate component in their analysis of children's responses appears to be primarily a result of the emphasis (often bias) in the child development literature on the bioscientific (naturalistic) aspects of children's conceptual development in general and children's concepts of death in particular. However, our own research (Brent & Speece, 1993) clearly indicates that not only children but many well-educated mature adults as well include such possibilities in their conceptualizations of death. Clearly, the mature understanding of noncorporeal continuation needs to be further investigated and articulated.

Because adults have a variety of different views of noncorporeal continuation, including the view that there is no continuation, our description of the mature adult understanding of this component will necessarily have to include several alternative views, all of which are developmentally equally as mature.

Questions Used for Noncorporeal Continuation. The question that has most often elicited noncorporeal continuation was an open-ended question (e.g., "What happens after death?"). Questions of this type were typically asked as a part of the investigation of irreversibility or nonfunctionality.

Before Noncorporeal Continuation. Children's early views (and, for that matter, their later views also) on the issue of spiritual continuation remain to be specified. Even some young children mention things like heaven. However, how their concept of heaven compares with that of older children and adults is presently unknown.

We have attempted here to define five components of the concept of death. The development of a generally accepted set of definitions and terminology for these components will be an important step forward in how the concept of death is conceptualized and investigated.

Other Components

Although we have focused on the five principal components of the concept of death, others that have been investigated include (a) death animism—understanding that animate, but not inanimate, things die (Berzonsky, 1987; Candy-Gibbs, Sharp, & Petrun, 1985; Derry, 1979;

Eskow, 1980; Gorman, 1983; Hornblum, 1978; Hurst, 1980; Jay et al., 1987; Lee, 1987; Montalbano, 1990; Robinson, 1977; Safier, 1964; Smeets, 1974; Steiner, 1965); (b) disposition—knowledge of what happens to the physical body after death including such things as funerals, burial, and cremation; (c) decomposition—understanding the process of organic decomposition (Atwood, 1984; Engel, 1981; Hansen, 1973); (d) attitudes toward death (Engel, 1981; Fink, 1976; Gartley & Bernasconi, 1967; McIntire, Angle, & Struempler, 1972; Montalbano, 1990; Orbach et al., 1984; Orbach et al., 1983; Orbach, Rosenheim, & Hary, 1987; Wenestam, 1984; Wenestam & Wass, 1987); and (e) themes of death in children's stories (Menig-Peterson & McCabe, 1978; Pitcher & Prelinger, 1963).

THE MATURE UNDERSTANDING OF DEATH

Studies of the development of children's understanding of death typically compare the children's understanding against a presumed mature adult understanding of death. The mature adult understanding is assumed to be the end-state toward which the process of conceptual development is directed. Therefore, it is important to establish the validity of the presumed mature adult understanding.

The presumed mature understanding of each component has been assumed to be its simple definition. The consensus among investigators regarding the presumed mature adult understanding of universality, irreversibility, and nonfunctionality suggests the validity of the presumed understanding for these components. However, the validity of the mature adult understanding of death has rarely been empirically validated. In this section we draw on our own research involving older children and adults (Brent & Speece, 1993; Brent, Speece, Lin, Dong, & Yang, in press) to discuss the validity of the presumed mature adult's understanding of each component.

Universality

The presumed mature adult understanding of universality is that all living things eventually die. Our own research suggests that this definition is an accurate representation of the concepts of older children and adults.

Irreversibility and Nonfunctionality

Elsewhere, we suggest that the simple definitions of these components do not adequately reflect the complexity of how many older children and adults conceptualize death (Brent & Speece, 1993; Brent et al., in press). This complexity was indicated by two types of responses: those that discuss the possibility of medical reversal of death and those that discuss noncorporeal continuation.

Medical Reversibility Responses.   The issue of medical reversibility first came to our attention in a study of children's understanding of death (Speece & Brent, 1992). When we asked about irreversibility, a few children referred to accounts of a dead person being brought back to life in a hospital as special exceptions to the general irreversibility of death. These children tended to be older, and their responses were qualitatively different from those of younger children who sometimes expressed an unrealistic notion that physicians could make all dead people alive again by relatively simple means (e.g., by giving them a pill).

Supposed reversals of death are common in news accounts of contemporary society, and many adults appear to accept their authenticity (Moody, 1975). Therefore, in a later study (Brent & Speece, 1993), we were not surprised to find that some adults believe that death can sometimes be reversed through medical intervention (e.g., CPR performed on a drowning victim who is thought to be clinically dead). The more complex concept of some of these adults has resulted in part from the fact that advances in medical technology during the past 30 years have radically altered our understanding of where to locate the boundary between "alive" and "dead" (Brent & Speece, 1993). More recently, we have found similar notions of medical reversibility in a cross-cultural study of U.S. and Chinese children's concepts of death (Brent et al., in press).

Thus, both anecdotal reports and our own research suggest that many children and adults are aware of instances where a supposedly "dead" person was subsequently successfully resuscitated, and that some people believe that these instances are bona fide exceptions to the general irreversibility of death. Others, however, view these cases as mistaken attributions of death—that the "dead" person only appeared to be dead. Still others remain uncertain about whether those instances really represent reversible death. It is important to note that even those children and adults who considered successful resuscitations as examples of reversible death typically emphasized the exceptional nature of those reversals by mentioning things like the availability of the appropriate medical intervention and the time elapsed since death. By doing so, they demonstrated that they did not reject the ultimate irreversibility of death.

Surprisingly, few previous investigators have considered this issue. In most cases, medical reversibility responses were coded as an immature (but not necessarily the most immature) type of response (Gorman, 1983; Ramsey, 1986; Robinson, 1977; Wainwright, 1987; Walco, 1984; Weber & Fournier, 1985; Weininger, 1979). Only Kalmbach (1979) scored medical reversibility as a mature response.

By contrast, Derry (1979) sought to avoid scoring medical reversibility responses at all by using a question that was worded specifically to "avoid potential confusion that might result from the child's awareness of the existence of extraordinary medical interventions" (p. 34). Derry's approach was to insert the word "usually" into the following question: "When someone is dead do they usually stay dead?"

We recommend that, at a minimum, future investigators explicitly describe how they plan to code responses that suggest that medical intervention can, in some instances, reverse death. Our own work suggests that at least some of these medical reversibility responses should be considered indicative of a more complex understanding of death.

Noncorporeal Continuation Responses.   We first became interested in the issue of noncorporeal continuation when we attempted to validate the presumed adult concept of irreversibility and nonfunctionality (Brent & Speece, 1993). In that study, we found that some adults gave responses that suggested the possibility of some sort of noncorporeal personal continuation after death. This occurred despite the fact that we specifically asked about the death of the physical body. These results demonstrated that at least some adults had non-naturalistic understandings of death alongside of their naturalistic (bioscientific) understandings.

A subsequent, closer examination of the research literature then revealed that noncorporeal continuation responses were more common than we had previously realized, and that previous investigators had chosen to deal with them in a variety of ways. For example, Swain (1979) scored afterlife responses as a 4 on a 5-point scale, on which the most mature response (scored a 5) was the understanding that death was the total, complete, and irreversible end of all life.

However, some investigators did score noncorporeal continuation responses as mature. For example, Blum (1976) scored "religious exceptions" to the irreversibility of death (e.g., Jesus' resurrection) as one type of mature concept. Similarly, Montalbano (1990) scored beliefs in an afterlife or reincarnation as equivalent to understanding that death is the total and complete end, and Seide (1983) scored the belief that some functioning continued in an afterlife as a mature response.

The existence of noncorporeal continuation responses raises both theoretical and methodological issues (Fetsch, 1984; Hagey, 1991) that will need to be addressed in future investigations. The mature adult concepts of irreversibility and nonfunctionality are more complex than is presumed by their simple definitions, which do not address the non-naturalistic aspects of death. Thus, even research that intends to focus specifically on the bioscientific aspects of death should be prepared for the fact that some children give noncorporeal continuation responses and should, therefore, consider in advance how such responses will be scored. Finally, as we suggested earlier, the development of the conceptualization of noncorporeal continuation should be studied as a separate component in its own right. The appropriate methodology for exploring children's understandings about nonnaturalistic aspects of death, as separate from their understandings of the irreversibility and nonfunctionality of physical death, remains an interesting challenge.

Causality

As we noted earlier, there is as yet no consensus among investigators as to the mature understanding of causality. However, on the basis of our review of the literature we propose that the mature adult understanding involves both an abstract and realistic recognition of the various general causes of death (e.g., illness or accidents) and the understanding that death ultimately results from the failure of one or more specific internal bodily systems or organs (e.g., circulation, kidneys, or brain).

Noncorporeal Continuation

Because research on noncorporeal continuation is so sparse, there is as yet no consensus on what would be considered a mature adult understanding of this component. Our own research suggests that mature adults represent this component in a variety of ways including reincarnation, heaven, and the notion that there is no spiritual continuation. We also assume that any of these representations could be considered correct and that the maturity of the individual's underlying conceptualization will show up in its degree of conceptual complexity. For example, just mentioning heaven would not automatically be considered a mature understanding of this component.

EXPLANATORY VARIABLES

Several independent variables have been examined in an attempt to understand how children's concepts of death develop including age, cognitive development, intelligence, gender, socioeconomic status, religion, ethnicity, nationality, death-related experiences, and health status. Each is discussed.

Age

Age is the most common variable examined in relation to children's concepts of death. Age by itself explains nothing, however. It is rather a convenient general, omnibus index of a wide range of loosely correlated biological and environmental variables.

Collectively, the studies that investigated the effects of age suggest (by a ratio of about 5:1) a significant relationship between children's age and their concepts of death. Older children's concepts are, in general, more realistic and abstract ("adult-like") than those of younger children.

Nevertheless, the specific age at which children achieved a presumed adult understanding of the key components has varied between 4 to 12 years or older (Speece & Brent, 1984). Despite this wide variability, however, most studies have found that by 7 years of age most children understand each of the key bioscientific components—universality, irreversibility, nonfunctionality, and causality.

Cognitive Development

It has been generally assumed that children's concepts of death develop in accordance with Piaget's general theory of cognitive development. Most of the support for this assumption has been the discovery of age differences combined with a simplistic application of Piagetian theory. Twenty studies have independently measured both level of cognitive development and concepts of death. Of these, 12 reported a significant and positive relationship (Cotton & Range, 1990; Demmin, 1986; Goodman, 1990; Gorman, 1983; Hornblum, 1978; Koocher, 1973; Krasnow, 1993; Mahon, 1992; Reilly, Hasazi, & Bond, 1983; Walco, 1982, 1984; Weber, 1981); three reported mixed results (Devereux, 1984; Kalmbach, 1979; White, Elsom, & Prawat, 1978); and five failed to find a relationship (Hagey, 1991; McBride, 1987; Sisson, 1987; Smith, 1992; Townley & Thornburg, 1980).

Because age and cognitive development are confounded, and because age has been shown to be positively related to children's concepts of death, a more accurate measure of the relationship between cognitive development and concepts of death requires controlling for the effects of age. Partialing out the effects of age allows for an examination of the unique contribution of cognitive development over and above the contribution of age. Of the five studies that controlled for age, two found that the significant effect for cognitive development still remained (Cotton & Range, 1990; Krasnow, 1993), whereas three found that cognitive development was no longer significant (Gorman, 1983; Hornblum, 1978; Walco, 1984).

Even where a statistically significant relationship has been found, the achievement of a specific Piagetian level of cognitive development—generally concrete operations—does not appear to be a necessary condition for understanding irreversibility, nonfunctionality, or universality, as demonstrated by the fact that in some studies a large proportion of preoperational children also understood a particular component (Hornblum, 1978; Kalmbach, 1979; Reilly, Hasazi, & Bond, 1983). Therefore, a higher level of cognitive development appears to be only helpful and contributory rather than necessary as predicted by a strict application of stage theory.

Limitations of Piagetian Theory. In this area of research, there has been an overreliance on Piaget's theory of the development of formal cognitive structures. Although many aspects of Piaget's general theory have been supported, his notion of stages of development has been called into question (Flavell, 1985; Gellman & Baillargeon, 1983). In addition, several investigators have suggested that the process of concept development in general is more complex, extends over a longer period of the life span, and results in more varied and individualized outcomes than is described or implied in a classical Piagetian-grounded approach (Carey, 1985; Flavell, 1985; Gellman & Baillargeon, 1983; Labouvie-Vief & Hakim-Larsen, 1989). The results of our own research with U.S. adults (Brent & Speece, 1993) and with U.S. and Chinese children (Brent et al., in press) are consistent with this view. We found that older children and adults possess more complex concepts of death, involving both naturalistic (scientific) and nonnaturalistic considerations, than would be predicted from the simple definitions of irreversibility and nonfunctionality. The concepts of many older children and adults can best be described as conditional, probabilistic, and "fuzzy" (Kosko & Sartoru, 1993). The conventional (naturalistic) understanding of death that develops during early and middle childhood becomes merely the stable core for the development of a more complex but "fuzzier" concept during late childhood and adulthood. This concept continues to be enriched and elaborated on by the child's gradual integration into this conceptual sphere of both nonnaturalistic aspects of death and the ambiguity of the modern conceptualization of the relationship between "alive" and "dead."

Intelligence

In general, there appears to be a significant positive relationship between measures of intelligence and children's concepts of death (Anthony, 1972; Clunies-Ross & Lansdown, 1988; Eskow, 1980; Gorman, 1983; Hornblum, 1978; Jenkins & Cavanaugh, 1985; Lansdown & Benjamin, 1985; Orbach, Gross, Glaubman, & Berman, 1985, 1986; Peck, 1966; Smilansky, 1987). A few studies, however, have found either mixed results (Derry, 1979; Karpas, 1986; McWhirter, Young, & Majury, 1983), or no relationship (Devereux, 1984; Miller, 1988).

Most of this research was based on mental age or subscale scores rather than on IQ. Because intelligence and age are confounded in these cases, a more accurate measure of the relationship between intelligence and concepts of death requires controlling for the effects of age. Only two studies examined the unique contribution of intelligence over and above the contribution of age. Gorman (1983) found that when age was partialed out statistically there were few remaining significant intelligence effects, whereas Hornblum (1978) found that doing so eliminated all intelligence effects.

Gender

After age, gender was the most commonly studied variable with 33 studies. Its "popularity" had more to do with its ease of collection than any a priori expectations of differences in how boys and girls conceptualized death. Gender does not seem to be an important factor because only two studies reported gender differences. Hargrove (1979) found that boys were more likely than girls to describe death as an irreversible biological process. Hui, Chan, and Chan (1980), in a study of Chinese children, found that girls were more likely than boys to indicate a belief in an afterlife.

None of the remaining studies found a relationship between children's gender and their understanding of death (Beauchamp, 1974; Black, 1979; Blum, 1976; Bolduc, 1972; Brun, 1981; Carlson, Asarnow, & Orbach, 1987; Derry, 1979; Devereux, 1984; Eskow, 1980; Florian,

1985; Florian & Kravetz, 1985; Hornblum, 1978; Jay et al., 1987; Jenkins & Cavanaugh, 1985; Karpas, 1986; Koocher, 1973; Krasnow, 1993; Lebovits, 1980; Lee, 1987; McWhirter, Young, & Majury, 1983; Miller, 1988; Moseley, 1974; Ramsey, 1986; Schonfeld & Kappelman, 1990; Seide, 1983; Sisson, 1987; Swain, 1979; Townley & Thornburg, 1980; Walco, 1982; Wass et al., 1983b; Wass, Guenther, & Towry, 1979; Wass & Towry, 1980; Zweig, 1977).[3]

Ethnicity Within the United States

Most of the studies of ethnicity and children's concepts of death have involved U.S. children. Eight studies have examined the effect of ethnicity by comparing white, Black, and Hispanic children (Hagey, 1991; Hargrove, 1979; Jay et al., 1987; Koocher, 1973; Mahon, 1992; Robinson, 1977; Schonfeld & Kappelman, 1990; Wass & Towry, 1980). Results suggest that ethnicity is not an important variable in determining children's concepts of death.

Nationality

Studies have compared children from the United States and Brazil (Wass, Guenther, & Towry, 1979), the United States and China (Brent et al., in press), the United States and Israel (Schonfeld & Smilansky, 1989), the United States and Jordan (Ramsey, 1986), the United States and Sweden (Wass, Guenther, & Towry, 1979), and Canada and Sweden (Gorman, 1983). For example, Schonfeld and Smilansky found that Israeli children had significantly more mature understandings of total death concept, irreversibility, and nonfunctionality than did U.S. children. There were no differences, however, for causality or universality.

The fact that all six studies reported at least some differences between cultures highlights the value of cross-cultural research in this area. However, no general conclusions can be made at this time, primarily because the studies involved different cultural comparisons and examined different components of the concept of death.

Religion

Twenty-three studies have examined the effects of religion, primarily along two dimensions: religious affiliation (Catholic, Jewish, etc.); and religiosity (the importance of one's religious beliefs, usually measured in terms of church or temple attendance). For U.S. samples, regardless of how religion was operationalized, most investigators found no significant differences that could be attributed to religion (Devereux, 1984; Engel, 1981; Gorman, 1983; Hagey, 1991; Jenkins & Cavanaugh, 1985; Kalmbach, 1979; Karpas, 1986; Miller, 1988; Seide, 1983; Sisson, 1987; Swain, 1979; Townley & Thornburg, 1980; Wass & Scott, 1978). The six that did report a significant effect (Blum, 1976; Candy-Gibbs, Sharp, & Petrun, 1985; Fink, 1976; Hargrove, 1979; Krasnow, 1993; McIntire, Angle, & Struempler, 1972) primarily involved differences in beliefs in an afterlife or with the broader philosophical meanings of death rather than with the bioscientific aspects of death. An exception to this general trend was the study by Candy-Gibbs, Sharp, and Petrun (1985), who found that Baptist children were more likely than Unitarian children to understand personal mortality, inevitability, and unpredictability, but less likely to understand natural causation.

Studies of the effects of religion using non-U.S. children, in contrast, have found a greater impact of religion (Florian & Kravetz, 1985; Hui, Chan, & Chan, 1989; Ramsey, 1986). For example, Florian and Kravetz, in a study of Israeli children, reported differences between groups of Jewish, Christian, Muslim, and Druze children in their understanding of irreversibility, causality, universality, and nonfunctionality. Similarly, Hui, Chan, and Chan found differences in the afterlife beliefs of Chinese children who attended different schools (Catholic, Protestant, and "other").

Socioeconomic Status

In general, socioeconomic status does not appear to be a major contributor to children's concepts of death. Most studies found no significant relationship (Beauchamp, 1974; Derry, 1979; Engel, 1981; Gorman, 1983; Hagey, 1991; Jenkins & Cavanaugh, 1985; Miller, 1988; Montalbano, 1990; Sisson, 1987; Swain, 1979; Wass et al., 1983a). However, three studies did report a significant effect (Hurst, 1980; Mahon, 1992; McIntire, Angle, & Struempler, 1972).

Death-Related Experiences

Although the effects of death-related experiences on children's concepts of death have been a focus of several studies, differences in their definitions of death-related experiences make comparisons difficult. For example, death-related experience has been defined as the death of an immediate family member (Bolduc, 1972), the deaths of pets or a nonfamily member (Cotton & Range, 1990), funeral attendance or discussions about death (Gorman, 1983), having a sibling with a life-threatening illness (Mahon, 1992), or merely living in a more violent area of Belfast (McWhirter, Young, & Majury, 1983).

Krasnow (1993) developed one of the more comprehensive measures of death-related experience. This included the number of deaths reported by the child, the number of deaths reported by the parent, the emotional value of each death, the child's reaction to the death, the number of euphemistic expressions of death used by parents, the number of parent-child discussions of death, the thoroughness of the parent's discussions of death, and the number of opportunities for making naturalistic observations of death (e.g., attendance at funerals).

Ignoring for the moment these differences in the definition of death experiences, 20 investigators reported a significant relationship between at least some aspects of death-related experience and at least some aspects of the concept of death (Bolduc, 1972; Cotton & Range, 1990; Derry, 1979; Engel, 1981; Hargrove, 1979; Hurst, 1980; Jay et al., 1987; Kane, 1979; Krasnow, 1993; Lebovits, 1980; McWhirter, Young, & Majury, 1983; Miller, 1988; Moseley, 1974; Normand & Mishara, 1992; Portz, 1965; Ramsey, 1986; Reilly, Hasazi, & Bond, 1983; Sisson, 1987; Smilansky, 1987; Weber & Fournier, 1985). However, 14 others have not found such a relationship (Demmin, 1986; Devereux, 1984; Gorman, 1983; Hagey, 1991; Jenkins & Cavanaugh, 1985; Kalmbach, 1979; Karpas, 1986; Mahon, 1992; McBride, 1987; McIntire, Angle, & Struempler, 1972; Peck, 1966; Seide, 1983; Tallmer, Formanek, & Tallmer, 1974; Zweig, 1977).

Although most of the 20 studies that did report a significant relationship found that more experienced children were more likely to have mature concepts of death, four found the opposite relationship (Cotton & Range, 1990; Miller, 1988; Ramsey, 1986; Smilansky, 1987).

In summary, the number of studies that reported a relationship between children's death-related experience and their concepts of death suggests the importance of these experiences for the development of that concept. However, the fact that we cannot as yet specify the exact nature of the relationship nor account for the large number of studies that failed to find a relationship highlights the need for further research.

Health Status

The potential effects of children's experience of illness has also been investigated. Bluebond-Langner (1978) was among the first to suggest that children who have experienced a life-threatening illness may have a more mature concept of death than healthy children of the same age.

Six studies have examined these effects, but the results are equivocal. Fetsch (1984) and Goodman (1990) found a significant relationship; Jay and colleagues (1987) found mixed results; and Clunies-Ross and Lansdown (1988), Hagey (1991), and Walco (1984) found no relationship. The issue is further complicated by the fact that both Fetsch and Goodman reported a positive relationship, whereas Jay found a negative relationship.

Both Jay (1987) and Walco (1984) also measured the degree of illness for children with a diagnosis of cancer—relative risk of dying, staging of illness, duration of illness, and number of hospitalizations—but none of these measures were significantly related to children's concepts of death.

CONCLUSION

Variability among investigators as to how the various components of the concept of death are selected, defined, measured, and scored is primarily responsible for the confusing nature of this empirical literature as a whole. However, despite the confusing nature of many of the results and the many issues that remain unresolved, there are still several general conclusions that can be drawn from this review.

1. The concept of death is best viewed as composed of several relatively distinct components. Most of the research on children's concepts of death has focused on four of these: universality, irreversibility, nonfunctionality, and causality. We proposed a fifth: noncorporeal continuation.

2. Although there is considerable interstudy variability regarding the age at which children understand each component, most studies suggest that by 7 years of age most children have a mature understanding of all four key components.

3. With increasing age, children's understanding of the bioscientific aspects of death becomes more like the presumed mature adult concept. However, the adult concept of death itself, as a developmental endpoint by which children's concepts of death are measured, needs further specification and validation. The simple definitions of the components generally used in this research do not adequately reflect the richness, complexity, and diversity of the ways in which many older children and adults actually conceptualize death.

4. Although the development of the concept of death demonstrates the general features of cognitive development (e.g., increasing abstractness), Piagetian stage-theory, with its emphasis on the development of formal scientific structures, needs to be modified by and supplemented with alternative theoretical approaches. Our own research suggests that the notion of "fuzzy" concepts and logic may be one such useful alternative.

5. Although ethnicity, gender, religion, and socioeconomic status have been found to be relatively unimportant factors in how children conceptualize the bioscientific aspects of death, cross-cultural differences, death-related experiences, intelligence, and having a life-threatening illness probably do affect their concepts of death. These latter variables all seem worthy of further study.

NOTES

1. Anthony (1940) is no longer in print; her data were included in Anthony (1972). Nagy's study was conducted in 1935 but not published in English until 1948.
2. Smilansky (1981, 1987; Smilansky & Weissman, 1978) developed an instrument for measuring children's concepts of human and animal death, and provided its validity and reliability. Subsequently, other investigators (Cotton & Range, 1990; Florian, 1985; Florian & Kravetz, 1985; Lazar & Torney-Purta, 1991; Orbach et al., 1985, Orbach, Gross, Glaubman, & Berman, 1986; Orbach, Talmon, Kedem, & Har-Even, 1987; Schonfeld & Kappelman, 1990; Schonfeld & Smilansky, 1989) have used the instrument. This represents an important step forward.
3. Five of these studies did, in fact, report minor gender differences, but overall gender had little effect on the development of the concept of death (Engel, 1981; Ramsey, 1986; Sisson, 1987; Wass, Guenther, & Towry, 1979; Wass & Towry, 1980).

3

Children, HIV Infection, and AIDS

Barbara Oberhofer Dane

The main message emanating from the international AIDS conference in Japan during August 1994 was sobering: The fight against this world-wide epidemic will have to be waged for a long time, without the help of a magic-bullet cure or preventive vaccine. The struggle to find cures and vaccines is lagging. The one genuine breakthrough of the previous year was the discovery that the drug azidothymidine (also called zidovudine), when administered to an infected woman during pregnancy, can often block transmission of the virus to the fetus. Otherwise, scientists reported only slow and incremental gains in treatment and in development of a vaccine ("The unyielding AIDS epidemic," 1994).

The battle against HIV infection and AIDS has altered the shape of our communities, resulting in the death of children, adults, and families. The plight of children diagnosed as positive for HIV and those left orphaned by the AIDS epidemic presents some of the most difficult needs of all. It exposes both the strengths and the inadequacies of our present health, educational, and social service systems in their efforts to meet the needs of children and families affected by this disease.

This chapter discusses children confronting their own HIV infection or AIDS as well as those who are not infected but orphaned by the death of their parents—particularly the death of a mother—in this second decade of AIDS. Drawing from the literature on grief, bereavement, and trauma, issues of stigma, shame, secrecy, fear of disclosure, and multiple loss are applied to the experience of infected and bereaved children. Case studies illustrate the range of practice issues and interventions. Policy implications to meet the complex challenges presented by these children are described.

OVERVIEW

The Centers for Disease Control and Prevention (CDC) in reviewing the 15 leading causes of death in the United States for 1989, noted the sharp increase—33% from the previous year—in deaths related to HIV infection. The CDC (1992, p. 142) commented: "The recognition of a disease and its emergence as a leading cause of death within the same decade is without precedent."

Nearly three quarters of HIV-related adult deaths have occurred among men and women aged 25 to 44—the prime reproductive years. Most AIDS cases have been reported among men, because of the epidemic's early and devastating spread among gay men in the United States. Over the more than 13 years of the AIDS epidemic, there has been a steady increase in both the number and percentage of women with HIV infection and AIDS. Women now account for 14% of all reported AIDS cases in the United States. Heterosexual transmission has recently become the most frequently reported mode of acquisition of HIV infection in women (CDC, 1994). This trend is expected to continue.

As of June 1993, approximately 4,710 children, including a small number of adolescents, have been reported to the CDC as having AIDS (Levine, 1993). An untold additional number of children, perhaps 2 or 3 times more, are infected with HIV. They will eventually get AIDS.

It is not generally appreciated that AIDS is only one of the severer manifestations of infection with HIV. Children infected with HIV may fall anywhere on a spectrum from being completely asymptomatic through suffering growth and developmental retardation to having a multisystems disease involving blood, skin, brain, heart, kidneys, and other organs.

At present, pediatric infections—other than those acquired previously through HIV-contaminated blood products—stem largely from mothers who themselves are intravenous drug users or whose partners either abuse drugs or are bisexual. If the virus continues to spread through these groups, there inevitably will be more heterosexual infections and more transmissions to infants, both within and outside the drug using and bisexual sectors. Denenberg (1995) has stated that the mothers' HIV status is inextricably linked to their babies' status. Because all children acquire their mothers' antibodies during pregnancy, all HIV positive newborns prove that their mothers are also HIV positive. Close to 80% of these children do not acquire the virus and will "revert" to HIV-negative over the next 10 to 18 months as they naturally lose maternal antibodies, suggesting that 20% of babies born to infected mothers will contract the disease.

Other modes of transmission of infection to children are sexual abuse, drug abuse, and sexual intercourse. With the expanding availability of antiretroviral agents to treat AIDS and the development of procedures to control serious secondary infections, children are living longer, and the disease has become a more chronic illness. Until a cure is found, the outlook for all of these children is almost certain—death.

The hidden impact of AIDS is beginning to have its effects on two groups of children who are uninfected with the virus. The first group is the uninfected children who are siblings of a brother or sister with AIDS or HIV infection. These may be older brothers and sisters, born before their mother contracted HIV, or younger children who escaped maternal-fetal transmission.

The second and largest but almost invisible group includes uninfected children whose mother or father or both parents, another adult relative, or a person unrelated by birth or marriage who has come to be considered family either had died of AIDS, or is living with AIDS or serious HIV disease. This latter group of children can rightly be called "orphans." Through the end of 1992, approximately 4,800 children are estimated to have been orphaned by HIV/AIDS in New York City (Levine, 1993). Unless the course of the epidemic changes dramatically, by the year 2000 the cumulative number in this metropolitan area alone will include 15,000 who were orphaned as children.

How families react to life-threatening illnesses, death, drug use, sexuality, and poverty is influenced by cultural background. Ethnicity, race, religion, political and philosophical beliefs, and sexual mores all play a role in how families cope with living with HIV/AIDS, how they mourn, and whether they do or do not develop custody plans for surviving children. At least 80% of these youngsters come from poor communities of color, which have already been devastated by society's neglect.

Typically, some children live in communities that are bereft of services, from supermarkets to mental health clinics, from safe playgrounds to adequate educational institutions. It takes little imagination to visualize the havoc these physical conditions constantly wreak on personality development, self-image, and sense of personal control as well as the subjective, more generalized discomfort of residents (Dane & Miller, 1992).

HIV infection and AIDS, with their stigma, physical and psychological devastations, and economic demands, pose yet another catastrophe for people of color. Family members struggle with the unique social stresses associated with this disease, including public fear and ignorance regarding the nature and transmission of HIV, discrimination, isolation, social ostracism, stigma, and fear of physical and mental disability. Many families have a history of drug dependence or exposure to drug users, and there is generally more than one member in the family who is either infected or ill. In addition, all too frequently, families lack the support of the communities that traditionally have rallied around the care and support of children facing life-threatening illnesses (Pizzo, 1990).

Nevertheless, even children from "troubled" homes may have had one or more extended family members or other supportive adults who acted as surrogate parents. And some youngsters' lives will have been relatively "normal" before the HIV-related illness and death in the family (Dudley, 1993).

Children from families with HIV/AIDS are not the only children in our country who need our care and attention. They are both like and different from other children who face a family or community crisis. What sets these children apart and generates a special concern is a particular combination of vulnerabilities. All children whose families are torn apart by violence, homelessness, or other social ills are profoundly affected by these crises. But those children whose families endure HIV and AIDS as well as these other deprivations are doubly affected.

CLINICAL ISSUES COMPLICATED BY AIDS

Children who live in a family with HIV/AIDS undergo a particularly wounding experience that encompasses stigma, shame, secrecy, fear of disclosure, multiple loss, and survivor's guilt. When death is accompanied by isolation, and is followed by instability and insecurity, the bereavement process is more difficult. This is combined with the child's (in)ability to understand the impact of the diagnosis and to live with the illness and death. Setting the stage for intervention requires a thoughtful understanding of some important issues that children experience in different ways as family members are affected by HIV/AIDS. To understand such barriers to successful grief and mourning as stigma and shame, secrecy and fear of disclosure, multiple loss, and survivor's guilt, one must understand a family's cultural heritage, which is a major determinant of attitudes toward pain, illness, and death.

Stigma and Shame

Social stigma is a barrier to successful mourning. Few children who live alongside and survive a death from AIDS emerge without some sense of stigma. Although they experience intense, painful feelings surrounding the death, most children in treatment have not shared their reactions with anyone before being referred to the clinician (Dane & Miller, 1992). Although some families and children are open about the diagnosis, most families keep it a well-guarded secret. The need to guard this secret is an immense burden for these children, their siblings, and other family members. In view of society's response to AIDS, it is often necessary to maintain the secret to protect the child and family.

The stigma associated with HIV/AIDS is a significant factor influencing coping in different phases of the illness and death (Schneider, 1984), and results in increased social stress related to issues of disclosure for children (Sinclair, 1989) and their families (Cates, Graham, Boeglin, & Tielker, 1990). Fears about the potential ramifications of disclosure lead persons with HIV and AIDS, along with their families, to become increasingly isolated and cut off from social support networks and other important resources. The cumulative effect of fear on surviving family members has been avoidance, shame, and guilt. These attitudes are communicated to children either explicitly or implicitly. Doka (1989) referred to AIDS as a "disenfranchising death" because of the fear and panic it generates. This can result in isolated survivors who do all their grieving alone.

Goffman (1963) described stigma as the spoiling of identity. In the case of bereaved children, this new, damaged, and devalued self is further handicapped by perceptions of difference from the rest of society, failure to meet its standards, and inferiority.

The consequences of stigmatization are usually unconscious. The spoiling of one's identity and the internalization of stigma change the way in which the bereaved person approaches and deals with others.

Children who survive any death feel uncertainty and shame. Not only do they experience resistance against feeling grief and despair, but the cause of death is unmentionable. The media positions HIV and AIDS as striking primarily "undesirable" members of society: minorities, drug addicts, and homosexuals. Children who fiercely guard their anonymity feel humiliated by a parent's AIDS diagnosis. In school, children tease one another about parents and AIDS to provoke fights; even school staff can be guilty of prejudices.

Community attitudes also contribute to the humiliation a child may feel. As a parent's illness progresses, his or her condition becomes recognizable by friends and neighbors. On occasion, children become ashamed to walk outside with the parent who is ill. Frequently with the end stage of AIDS comes a complete loss of body fat and muscle, which can be frightening for a child. A parent may lose his or her ability to cook, help with homework, even toilet one's self. Consequently, children may need to perform tasks, such as helping their parent to the bathroom, cooking, and even helping them bathe. In addition, parents sometimes lose their cognitive abilities and no longer recognize their loved ones. This is a traumatic period when children need an enormous amount of support and reassurance (McKelvy, 1995).

Frequently, children dread returning to school after the funeral or other rituals, wishing to avoid the questions posed or likely to be posed by their peers. Questions about death from AIDS may be extremely frightening because of the stigma complicated by the extant certainties and contradictions. Conversely, children may be avoided or subjected to anger or humor bordering on ridicule from their peers.

Secrecy and Disclosure

Alienation and isolation, resulting from stigma, influence the course of grieving. When they become protracted, the behavioral responses may lead to lifelong difficulties in interpersonal behavior. The double-edged sword of a parent's death and the stigma associated with HIV and AIDS results in the widespread experience of a conspiracy of silence. The difficulty in returning to a normal life after parental death, and the fear of other tragedies, such as the death of a second parent or another family member, are issues that confront inner-city, disenfranchised children. Loneliness and sadness after a parent's death from AIDS are often the emotional aftermath of a frightening and overwhelming experience (Dane & Miller, 1992).

Although many families with HIV/AIDS are strong and supportive in the most adverse of circumstances, some parents become overwhelmed by the dual demands of coping with both the illness and the response of their children. Action, rather than language, is more often employed to resolve conflict, and children may bear the brunt of adult anger (McKelvy, 1995).

Particularly important for children is the ability of both the diagnosed parent and the identified caretaker to talk about critical issues and maintain a stable environment (Raphael, 1982). Parents who have abused drugs frequently employ denial as a primary mechanism of defense (Shernoff, 1995). Denial can permeate the psyche, protecting the individual from unpleasant realities, such as HIV—"if it is not discussed it does not exist." These parents are unavailable for conversations that would help to minimize the impact of their diagnosis on their children.

Parents with a history of drug abuse (who may have been inconsistent in attending to their children) feel guilty that they have not, and with AIDS cannot, perform minimal parental tasks. As a result, they compensate with a final act of protection: they "shield" their children from information concerning their diagnosis. The problem is further complicated when parents who feel impelled to be "extra nice" to ease the guilt created by their diagnosis become too permissive, thus depriving children of limits and increasing the potential for the child to get into trouble (McKelvy, 1995).

Children are often aware of a parent's diagnosis before it is explicitly revealed to them, sometimes as a result of education in the schools, the media, and living in communities devastated by deaths from AIDS. A clinician needs to explore the rationale for the parent's efforts to protect the child and acknowledge that although protection is a primary responsibility, children who know a parent is sick have a right to understand the name and nature of the disease.

The idea of protecting a child can be sustained by parents' painful memories of their own experience of accepting and understanding their diagnosis. A parallel process with the parent is helpful to achieve an understanding and emotionally accepting view of the child's dilemma.

How the virus was transmitted to the parent can be a major factor in how a child understands the diagnosis of AIDS. Children who have or had drug-abusing parents can be particularly angry at their parents and have concern about transmission especially when parents are addicts or homosexuals. Although children worry about their parents, they are also concerned about themselves. They need to be told they are safe from contagion. Friedland and colleagues (1990) stated that household contagion studies have found no documented evidence of HIV transmission via casual contact.

Practitioners have stated that they observed some children "growing up overnight." Often adolescents "parent" their younger siblings and frequently they forego their own grief. Sometimes children go to extreme lengths in overprotecting their younger sisters and brothers in attempting to shield them from the insensitive remarks made by peers. One youngster related how she kept her brother home from school by saying he was sick. This was her way of protecting him from being singled out by other children in the class who referred to him as the "AIDS kid."

Clinicians working with parents to disclose to their children that they have HIV/AIDS need to assess where the parent is in the life course of the illness both physically and emotionally, knowing that this has a roller-coaster effect. However, parents who are HIV positive rarely show physical symptoms; they can be fully able to care for their families and live without medical complications for years. In such cases, a parent may choose not to inform a youngster. In families in which there are few healthy boundaries, parents sometimes tell children prematurely to manipulate their behavior.

Parents must be able to manage their own feelings about AIDS before telling their children of their illness or HIV status. Transmission needs to be explained in an age-appropriate manner so that children understand. Younger children tend to think of disease as a magical process, whereas latency-aged children are generally more aware of the negative connotations surrounding AIDS and are apt to feel shame about an HIV diagnosis in their home.

Because of the complex nature of living and dying from AIDS, parents should be given knowledge of local guardianship laws, HIV disclosure laws, survivors' benefits for children, hospice programs, schools, camps, funeral homes, and general AIDS services in their local community. The drafting of a custody plan is important for parents who have HIV infection or AIDS. In the formation of a custody plan, the father's rights need consideration. The child's wishes also need to be considered. When the plan is finalized, the child should be told as soon as possible. Knowledge of the plan is a relief and reassures children that their parent has taken steps, sanctioned a special individual, and answered the child's big question, "What will happen to me?" A child cannot tolerate the painful hiatus between relationships and must have a replacement before making an emotional move away from anticipating the impending death of the parent. It is ideal if the prospective guardian is already a valued and trusted person in the child's life (Wolfenstein, 1969) rather than the child becoming a ward of the state and placed in the foster care system. Trauma can be soothed, if children have an opportunity to work through the secret and this stage of the crisis, rather than turning against themselves and feeling depressed and burdened.

Multiple Loss

Many children and families have experienced the loss of multiple family members. This further compounds their trauma. We are just now beginning to confront the bleak realities of numerous family members dying of AIDS and a large community of mourners. Children, sexual partners and friends, parents and lovers of gay men, and health care professionals are all coping with multiple losses. The psychosocial implications are anguishing.

In our society, most young mothers suffering from AIDS, and their families, are poor and African-American or Hispanic American. Many of these mothers are experiencing their own illness as well as that of their infants. There are hundreds of cases of infants who, after their mother's death, are virtually abandoned and receive care from either hospital staff or the foster care system, having an impact on surviving older sisters and brothers who are placed in foster care. Children who do go home from the hospital often live with mothers and siblings who are dying or have lost a father to AIDS. This dynamic adds to the horror of coping with the illness and the anticipated death of one's child and sibling (Foster, 1988).

The pain and grief attached to the death of a child always remains. When it is unresolved, it can affect other siblings. The heavy emotional scars experienced by children whose parents, siblings, aunts, uncles, or friends have died from the disease are overwhelming. Biological children of foster parents who care for HIV-positive foster children are a hidden group of grievers and have received little attention in the literature (Kaplan, 1988). Most children cannot find words to express the grief and pain they are feeling. They expend a great deal of energy trying to keep their feelings buried because the environment, hardened with stigma, does not facilitate free expression. But suppressing emotions does not eliminate them. Rather, such emotions manifest themselves in many ways, for example in guilt, anger, tension, and uneasiness around other children. The numbing aroused by the disbelief and efforts to keep the secret limit their responsiveness (Dane & Miller, 1992). Biological children of foster parents experience the same fears, anxieties, and jealousies as siblings of birth parents. These feelings are compounded and multiplied when foster parents care for more than one HIV positive child.

Lindemann (1944, p. 143) stated that "one of the big obstacles to this [grief] work seems to be the fact that many patients try to avoid the intense distress connected with the grief experience and to avoid the expression of emotion necessary for it." Lindemann's subjects "required considerable persuasion to yield to the grief process before they were willing to accept the discomfort of bereavement." This process is difficult for survivors who have experienced bereavement overload through a series of AIDS deaths.

Hirsch and Enlow (1984) noted that "bereavement overload" occurs when an individual has not completed the mourning process for one person when another dies. Pervasive, unrelenting feelings of sorrow, loss, and abandonment are overwhelming. The magnitude of the loss must be validated before survivors experiencing multiple losses can think about their feelings of abandonment, fear, and anger.

This area of multiple loss has been greatly neglected in the lives of children living in the era of AIDS. It is common for survivors, especially those living in AIDS epicenters, to endure multiple bereavements arising from the deaths of persons from AIDS while, at the same time, some children are facing the possibility of their own death.

Survivor's Guilt

Guilt and shame are often reported by AIDS survivors (Christ & Wiener, 1985; Dane, 1989; Dane & Levine, 1994; Lomax & Sandler, 1988), and children are no exception. The concept of survivor guilt was first introduced into contemporary psychiatric literature by Niederland (1981), who described a severe and persevering guilt complex affecting survivors of the Holocaust. After a symptom-free interval, survivors developed symptoms, such as depression, anhedonia, anxiety, hyperamnesia, and psychosomatic conditions.

Niederland (1981) believed that these symptoms were identifications with loved ones who did not survive and ascribed to them a deep and pervasive sense of guilt. He further believed that the survivors' prior ambivalent attitudes toward, for example, a deceased parent, and the rage a youngster experienced toward the parent, were important factors and should be recognized in the treatment of survivors. Chodoff (1985) emphasized that survivors need to suffer and memorialize their generation. Danieli (1985) proposed that guilt is an unconscious attempt to deny or undo the experience of passive helplessness that many AIDS survivors undergo.

Children who grow up in an environment of continuous or even intermittent stress are likely to worry about their existence. They may assume that that world is not a safe place and that parents are unreliable. When parents die, these children may believe they will be left alone to cope.

Psychic trauma occurs when an individual is exposed to an overwhelming event, like parental death from AIDS, where the child feels helpless in the face of intolerable danger, anxiety, or instinctual arousal, thus prolonging grief and mourning. When a parent dies of AIDS, the process of loss starts long before the death. For many children, being orphaned results in a move from home to home, leaving siblings, school, and friends. This can cause mental suffering and in some situations irreversible psychological dysfunction (Dane & Levine, 1994).

Although trauma and grief are profoundly different human experiences, a single event can precipitate both responses. Although trauma is a direct injury, the stressful situation of being orphaned by AIDS creates indirect injuries. Eth and Pynoos (1985b) have found that traumatic anxiety is a priority concern, compromising the ego's ability to attend to the fantasies of the lost object that are an integral part of grief work. To offset his or her traumatic helplessness, the child must consider, if only in fantasy, alternative actions that could have prevented the parent's death. Developmental considerations are important determinants of this cognitive effort, and subsequent developmental maturity may bring about revisions.

Survivor guilt may represent a conflict over the proper assignment of human accountability. Heightened feelings of guilt arise when there has been a distortion of communication, denial, evasion, or closed discussion about the parent's death. Initially, the child may wish to avoid the discussion, but this provides only a temporary relief. Hostile wishes, fantasies, misconduct, and other specific behaviors before the parent's death can exacerbate the guilt and self-blame. The parent's death from AIDS may be viewed as the fulfillment of angry wishes, and conscious fantasies to offset the death and save the parent are likely (Dane & Levine, 1994). Gardner (1979) suggested that guilt "can also be a manifestation of the child's attempt to gain a sense of control over a situation that is clearly beyond his control" (p. 278). In their attempt to understand events related to AIDS, children may often assume responsibility for events over which they have no control.

On the basis of interviews with mental health practitioners in a variety of practice settings, Dane and Miller (1992) compared the emotions experienced by many of the children orphaned by AIDS with those of youngsters who witness parental homicide, rape, or suicidal behavior. Horowitz and Kaltreider (1980) reported that all of these children have an enormously intense perceptual, affective, and physiological experience. Two major examples of persistent physiological changes are the high frequency of sleep disturbances, including night terrors and somnambulism, and startle reactions to specific perceptual reminders. Experimental evidence indicates that, in adults, unwelcome intrusive imagery and autonomic physiological reactions can persist after a disturbing event. This response is not uncommon in children whose parent dies of AIDS (Dane & Levine, 1994).

Although the special vulnerability of these youngsters should be emphasized, none should be considered ill, disturbed, or exceptional. Such a stigma is likely to hinder children in their efforts to cope and build a new positive identity for themselves. Many orphaned children face these enormous stresses with courage and resiliency; they recover from parental loss and anticipate the future with enthusiasm and vitality. Forming new relationships, starting new families, exerting energy in school, and forming play and peer groups are ways of rebuilding their lives after their parent's death.

CHILDREN LIVING WITH HIV OR AIDS

The great needs of families and children offer the mental health clinician the opportunity to demonstrate a caring and committed response to clients who face immense burdens living with AIDS. Children with HIV/AIDS suffer from a wide range of medical problems, from the deadly to the common. Approximately 50% get *Pneumocystis carinii* pneumonia, the leading indicator disease for the diagnosis of AIDS. They also suffer from an increase in the frequency and number of common bacterial and viral infections (Karthas & Chanock, 1990). By the time they become symptomatic, 50% have neurological problems, such as walking problems, poor school performance, seizures, retardation, and cerebral palsy. As the disease progresses, 80% to 90% demonstrate neurological impairment (Hutman, 1990). Current research estimates that about 50% of children who get AIDS will become symptomatic within 1 year and 25% of these children die during this year (Diamond, 1989; Hutman, 1990).

The following case illustrates both clinical issues and the difficulties encountered by children and families as they attempt to contend with the uncertainties posed by HIV infection. This letter is taken from *Be a Friend: Children Who Live With HIV Speak* (Wiener, Best, & Pizzo, 1994, p. 24).

LIVING WITH KNOWING YOU CAN DIE

Everyone knows that you can die from HIV, but no one knows when. Also, no one knows how difficult this is to live with unless you actually have HIV yourself or you love someone with HIV. Living with HIV and knowing that you can die from it is scary. Knowing that you can die is very frightening. I think it is hardest in this order:
    Not knowing when this will happen.
    Not knowing where it will happen. (I would rather die at home.)

Worrying about my family. For example, will my mother and father ever stop crying? (I don't want them to cry but always remember me riding my pony and being happy.)

What will happen to my stuff and my room? (Casey will probably get most of it, but making a museum would not be such a bad idea.)

Thinking about what my friends will think.

Thinking about dying is hard, but it is good to do because you think about it anyway. Most people don't want to talk about this because it makes them sad, but once you do, you can talk about it more easily the next time. Then you can go on LIVING!

—Beth, age 12*

This letter captures in a moving way some basic issues, questions, and worries that children ask, speculate about, and reflect on as they live with HIV/AIDS. They imagine what HIV might look like, creating fierce monsters as well as having fantasies about becoming friends with the monster and fighting the illness together.

For some children with HIV, the virus is not a main concern. Instead, they worry about what will happen if they tell people they have HIV. Will they still have friends. Children who are symptomatic must cope with frequent visits to a physician, needle sticks, daily medications, and the "roller-coaster" syndrome of feeling good and periods of feeling ill. Wanting to be normal is an underlying cry that emerges in the therapeutic process. As illustrated in this letter, all children want to be remembered and worry about how their families will cope when they are dead. They think about an afterlife, depending on their religious beliefs, and seem less frightened of dying. Their fears are the separation and loss of family, siblings, and friends. Some children see their death as a reuniting with a parent(s) who has died from AIDS.

The needs of an HIV-infected child are extensive, requiring services from many sources. Caring for a child with HIV may require considerable involvement with the medical community, special attention to hygienic conditions in the home, dealing with the reactions of neighbors, relatives, school officials, and service providers, and coping with the terminal nature of the child's illness. The social, economic, and psychological difficulties that this chronic illness precipitates make it difficult for the biological parent(s) to care for these children and may result in contact with the public child welfare system (Anderson, 1986).

A difficult task for the clinician is preparing a parent, significant other, or foster parent for the death of a child. Discussing fear of death, drafting a will, and establishing future child care arrangements if the parent is also HIV infected or ill are all essential. After a worker has proved his or her commitment to the family, trust builds and members become more willing to share some of the other, more difficult burdens of living with AIDS.

Helping parents anticipate questions raised by a child with HIV or AIDS and his or her siblings minimizes the strain of the family secret. When a child knows his or her diagnosis, but is told "not to tell" anyone outside the family, children have the burden of protecting the secret. The burden can have a profound impact on the child, resulting in withdrawal from friends and social activities to avoid the need to cover up or lie. Isolation from peers leaves the youngster particularly vulnerable when he or she becomes ill.

Children's questions should be answered fully and honestly when the child initiates questions and expresses a need to know the answers. Initial caution is recommended in labeling the illness as AIDS because the disease carries such a stigma.

Rothbart-Mayer has stressed the difference between family privacy and stigma (Schaefer & Lyons, 1993). Family privacy is information that does not need to leave the family. Rothbart-Mayer stated that the real issue is self-protection and protection of your child. You must decide when it is important for someone to know and then ask, "If you tell this person, how will it help? Do you think the person will still be your friend?"

A holistic approach should be considered, as one cannot treat a child without treating the family. As difficult as it can be to engage the child's parent or parents, it can be even more difficult to engage siblings, grandparents, and significant others. Lewert (1988) observed that, although a strong relationship with the child's primary caretaker is most important, it does not ensure access to other family members.

CHILDREN LIVING WITH HIV OR AIDS IN A SIGNIFICANT OTHER

Communication about HIV/AIDS and the anticipatory death is sometimes managed as a family secret within and outside the family. If a child is not told the truth, this often results in a decrease in communication and increased feelings of isolation and burden.

Clinicians treating children who know of their parent's HIV/AIDS diagnosis should explore several questions with family members to ascertain the family's communications patterns. How did the children find out? Was it an accident or on purpose? What were their reactions? In particular, the clinician should discover who the children have identified as their support in the family. If there is no one, the therapist should encourage the family to choose a person for the child to talk with about HIV/AIDS. Parents need to be explicit. Is there a rule in the family about talking with outsiders about HIV or AIDS? If not, why not? How the virus was transmitted to the parent can be a major factor, especially if the parents were addicts or homosexual (McKelvy, 1995).

When there are multiple HIV-infected family members, a noninfected child is in danger of feeling excluded from the special bond that exists between family members who have the same diagnosis and who experience similar symptoms and treatments. A strong attachment and a bond of secrecy has been suggested in preliminary research on the relationship between infected mothers and infected children (Andrews, Williams, & Neil, 1993). At the same time, pressure may be placed on non-infected children "to be a good child and help out" (Weiner, Fair, & Garcia, 1995). Healthy siblings may assume the caregiver role. The uninfected child may feel guilty for not having the illness and worry that he or she caused the illness. Many children question why they too are not infected and may erroneously conclude that they are invulnerable to HIV/AIDS. Jealousy and sibling rivalry can also emerge when the infected child becomes the center of attention.

Survivor guilt is common and often continues after the parent has died. For example, one youngster reported: "My mother was in the hospital for a long time. I asked my aunt to visit her, but she always said, 'your mother will be home soon.' She never got better, and I [an 11-year-old girl] sometimes wish it was me who died."

Similarly, a Hispanic boy felt guilty because of his mother's death. He told his therapist that he did not treat his mother well, and that if he would have stayed up with her during the night when she was sick, she would not have died. "I felt I did not keep my promise to her," he said. This child may feel guilty for not being able to protect the deceased parent from illness and death or guilty for experiencing relief that the parent has died.

Implied in the notion "it's my fault" is the concept of control. The youngsters in the preceding examples harbor the delusion that they caused their parents' deaths, and presumably they have the ability to bring the parent back to life.

Therapists can help children who are struggling with guilt that may not only interfere with natural mourning processes but may also contribute to undesirable consequences. For example, one youngster whose father was diagnosed with AIDS reported going on a stealing spree in the midtown area of New York. This reflected efforts to reduce his guilt through antisocial behavior; apparently, he was hoping to get caught and punished. In another example, during a group therapy session a boy was talking about his mother and said, "She got what she deserved. She should never have used drugs. She should have known better."

The family, particularly the HIV-infected parent or the responsible caregivers, such as aunts and grandmothers, may perceive that the child is presenting unusual problems. However, these perceptions may be distorted by pain and suffering experienced by other family members. Zayas and Romano (1994) pointed out that one extreme of acting-out behavior may be anger that leads to violence and criminal activities. Swift and immediate intervention is certainly needed for the potentially self-destructive, acting-out youngster. How children cope with the emotional, physical, and environmental demands of the illness and death is dependent on family circumstances before the crisis as well as their developmental stage, level of cognition, and verbal skills.

The progression of HIV infection inevitably results in a realignment of responsibilities within the home. The child may be given more chores and responsibilities because of role realignments, which can either be understood as "being special" or be perceived as a punishment. The superchild like Paula is a good example of this compensatory reaction. As the oldest of four siblings, she goes to school, coparents her brothers and sister, and provides both the caretaking and emotional support for her mother. Although the superchild becomes overengaged in a care-providing role, other children may feel stressed and not be able to do all the things they previously did. For example, they may experience an inability to concentrate in school. To avoid intense feelings, some children like Anna, a 12-year-old, begin staying out of the house for extended periods during the day as a coping response to contain their pain and bring them closer to uninfected people.

LIVING IN THE AFTERMATH AS AN ORPHAN OF A PARENT'S DEATH

All children orphaned by the HIV/AIDS epidemic share a specific set of concerns related to the death of a parent, but they are by no means a homogeneous group. Because of their vulnerability, children who lose a family member to AIDS face unique issues as they grieve. Often they have watched their families disintegrate before their eyes. They struggle to make sense of a senseless situation and to feel in control, even as they confront circumstances over which they ultimately have no control. In addition to parental loss, many experience multiple deaths of a sibling, aunt, uncle, close relative, friend, or significant other. Many orphans of the HIV/AIDS epidemic have little or no predictability and safety in their lives. Parental death must be placed within a web of other losses resulting from divorce or separation, drug addiction, imprisonment, or mental illness as well as a community plagued by poverty, violence, drugs, and unstable housing. Sometimes the result is that mourning has a low priority.

Although there is no agreement among studies regarding the ages at which children are most at risk for long-term negative consequences from the death of a parent, early childhood appears to be a period of special vulnerability. Whatever the age, it is important to determine what the youngster understands about death and to help him or her distinguish reality from fantasy.

At any age, youngsters may not want to talk about their parent's death right away. Children deal with death in a piecemeal fashion, sometimes giving the appearance of disinterest. This is appropriate. Adults should be prepared to answer their questions about the death of their parent, whenever they ask, even if the questions appear at seemingly inappropriate times.

Learning to remember and finding a way to maintain a connection to the deceased that is consistent with the child's cognitive development and family dynamics are aspects of a constructive accommodation process (Silverman, Nickman, & Worden, 1992). The case of Charlie is an example of how a child was helped to express his fears and go on living in the face of the loss (Dane, 1993).

Charlie, a 10-year-old, African-American child, had been brought to the Family Service Center by his Aunt Ellen, who complained about his withdrawal, his crying when he thought no one was paying attention to him, and his manifesting clinging behavior. The aunt described Charlie as a different person since his mother died 2 months ago. As the worker accompanied Charlie to the office, he was impressed with how sad the youngster seemed.

Mr. Jones, the social worker, encouraged Charlie to tell him how things were going, but the youngster responded with stoic silence. The worker respected this silence, but periodically made comments informing Charlie that he thought he seemed sad, that the worker knew his teachers were complaining about his behavior at school, and that his aunt was concerned about him. It was not until the worker commented that he thought this was connected to Charlie's mother's death, that he noticed the first overt reaction. Two tears ran down Charlie's cheek as he turned to face the worker for the first time.

Charlie slowly told the worker that he was now living with his aunt. In the past, going to his aunt's house was great fun. Living with his mother in the nearby housing project allowed him to play with his friends, but his aunt always made it a special occasion when he went there. He talked about his last birthday, his 10th, when his mother took seven of his friends to his aunt's, and they had a great time playing and eating, and he got a lot of presents.

Based on the information the worker had received from Charlie's aunt, he commented that it was close to his 10th birthday when his mother became ill. Charlie agreed, saying that she had lost a lot of weight, but immediately after his birthday party she went to the hospital for the first time. He had to live with his aunt while his mother was hospitalized. Charlie was not happy because he worried about his mother. He was in school when his mother went to the hospital the second time. The school social worker called him out of class and told him that his aunt had called and would pick him up after school. When she did, Charlie could tell that something was wrong. He knew that she had been crying, which was something that she never did. She hugged him close and slowly told him that his mother was sick. He told the worker that it all started when she had a "trans - - -." The worker asked if he meant "transfusion." Charlie said yes, that was what it was, and she got some bad blood then. He went on to say that his aunt mentioned that no one could say whether his mother would live, but she assured him that his mother wanted him to live with her, and that she would take care of him because she loved him dearly.

With help from the worker, Charlie talked about his mother's death and how cold her body was in the open casket. He remembered that lots of people came to the funeral, and he also talked about how difficult it was to move his things to his aunt's house shortly after. The worker empathized with Charlie and told him that it was difficult to have a parent whom he loves die. He said that children always feel sad and frequently ask many questions about what will happen to them. He then asked Charlie what worried him the most.

With tears running down his cheeks, Charlie said that he was worried about two things. At night he would wake up seeing his mother who appeared to be skinny and hardly able to talk. He would hear her whispering to him "I love you," and he would get scared. His second worry was that his aunt might die and that he would be all alone. He knew that she was not sick, but she was all he had now, and he did not know who would care for him or what he would do if she died also. The worker commented that other kids have similar worries. Charlie recalled that the mother of two of his friends at school died from AIDS. Afterward, they had gone to live with their aunt, but she had died last week. Tom and Jimmy had to leave school and move to Brooklyn to live with another aunt.

The worker confirmed how difficult it is to be alone. He told Charlie that many children have these same worries when there is a death in the family, and suggested that he and Charlie could talk together over the next few months about this and other worries that he might experience. Charlie agreed that it would be helpful to do so, because although he loved his aunt and she talked to him all the time, he had not been able to tell her what really worried him.

PRACTICE AND POLICY IMPLICATIONS

Living with a diagnosis of HIV and then living in the aftermath of the death of a parent, brother, sister, or extended family member from AIDS is one of the most emotionally stressful events a child can experience. Coping effectively with such losses and with the child's grief responses is important to avoid several emotional, behavioral, cognitive, social, and physical problems that can emerge and invariably lead to dysfunction. Integration and assimilation of the pending loss and the finality of death is a slow process because it involves making sense of what is happening and what has already happened. For many children, loss has become all too common in their lives. The challenges facing clinicians, program managers, and policy makers are enormous in responding to the needs of this grieving population. Immediate and timely interventions can mitigate some of the negative, lifelong responses to this overwhelming trauma.

Families living with HIV and in the aftermath of a death from AIDS, are often reluctant to turn to traditional community mental health sources for counseling. Secrecy, shame, and stigma are powerful in themselves, let alone when coupled with financial troubles, housing difficulties, and institutionalized racism. Some states have confidentiality laws, but even when these are strong they do not resolve all the issues of confidentiality that affect people with HIV infection. Conflicts still exist between the benefits of disclosure and the potential for stigma and discrimination.

The issues of confidentiality that surround HIV/AIDS are more complex than any law can ever address. Among people with longstanding distrust of the health care system, the law alone may not overcome a reluctance to be tested, seek care, or make provisions for their dependent children. To serve clients facing conflicts like these, mental health clinicians must work toward sensitive, realistic policies that acknowledge the complex individual, familial, and social issues that accompany a diagnosis of HIV infection. Judicial education and activism are essential in the courts where racism, classism, cultural ignorance, and insensitivity exists. Legal services programs should be expanded to ensure that all who need assistance with custody planning have access to representation or to information that they can use to represent themselves. Dissemination of legal information for parents and guardians is essential to be informed of one's rights and options.

Immediate and timely professional interventions with children diagnosed HIV positive and those mourning the deaths of parents from AIDS can mitigate some of the negative, lifelong responses to this overwhelming trauma. Systematic and culturally sensitive efforts to reach out to children and families are essential components of a comprehensive mental health program. To engage children in treatment after the death of a parent, we must reach out during the parent's illness and work with the entire family including extended family members. Helping children to retain an inner image of the person who has died can permit them to maintain a good self-image and develop appropriate attachments in the future.

Support from foster parents and school personnel can combat the isolation and stigma experienced by these children. Providing monies for programs and research can provide an optimal model for treatment and alert practitioners to innovative ways of responding to the complex challenges presented in working with children who are diagnosed with HIV, and those who are living with or mourning the death of a loved one from AIDS.

4

Suicide and Life-Threatening Behavior in Childhood

Lillian M. Range

This chapter examines suicide and life-threatening behavior in childhood. Topics considered include epidemiological data on attempted and completed suicide in childhood; how children go about attempting or completing suicide; family and personal variables that are important in these behaviors; and instruments for measuring child suicidality. The chapter closes with recommendations for preventing child suicide and life-threatening behavior.

EPIDEMIOLOGICAL EVIDENCE ON CHILDREN'S ATTEMPTED AND COMPLETED SUICIDE

Do children attempt and commit suicide? Tragically, the answer is yes, children *do* take their own lives. In 1993 in the United States, there were 310 suicidal deaths in this age group (NCHS, 1994). Though death by suicide occurs less often among youngsters than among adolescents or adults, suicide is nevertheless the fifth leading cause of death in 1- to 14-year-olds, after accidents, cancer, homicide, and heart disease, respectively. These statistics are even more alarming in view of the fact that suicide is highly stigmatized, so that many experts believe that it is often underreported (Public Health Service, 1987), though some disagree (Kleck, 1988).

In addition, children attempt suicide at a much higher rate than they actually complete it. Among randomly selected, nonpsychiatric 6- to 12-year-old children, 3% had attempted suicide (Pfeffer, Zuckerman,

Plutchik, & Mizruchi, 1984). Among children in this same age group who were referred to psychiatric clinics, 10% to 40% had attempted suicide (Asarnow, 1992; Kosky, 1983; Pfeffer, Conte, Plutchik, & Jerrett, 1980). Among children admitted to inpatient facilities, from 17.5% (Myers, Burke, & McCauley, 1985) to as many as 78.5% had attempted suicide (Pfeffer, Solomon, Plutchik, Mizruchi, & Weiner, 1982). Further, children who have previously attempted suicide are at higher risk than nonattempters of actually completing suicide later in their lives (Shafii, Steitz-Lenarsky, Derrick, Beckner, & Whittinghill, 1988). Children's suicide attempts are often life-threatening, sometimes fatal, and more common than actual completions.

Gender differences in suicide attempts in children are unclear. Most studies report more suicide attempts among girls (Bettes & Walker, 1986; Kienhorst, Wolters, Diekstra, & Otte, 1987), though some disagree (Pfeffer et al., 1982). Actual deaths are more common among boys. In 1993, well over 80% of suicide deaths were boys, and most were white (NCHS, 1994). Suicide attempts, whether in girls or boys, are a serious problem and often portend future tragedy.

Children not only commit and attempt suicide, they also think about it. Among normal school children aged 6 to 12, about 12% report suicidal thoughts (Pfeffer, Plutchik, Mizruchi, & Lipkins, 1986). Among psychiatric outpatient children, about 25% (Pfeffer et al., 1986) to as many as 60% (Myers et al., 1991) report suicidal thoughts; and among psychiatric inpatient children, about 72% to 79% report such thoughts (Pfeffer et al., 1986). Between 16% and 30% of clinically referred children who thought about suicide actually attempted it (Kovacs, Goldston, & Gatsonis, 1993). Rates differ according to the intervals under consideration, and the diagnostic, age, and gender composition of the samples. Suicidal thoughts can take root in childhood and serve as the basis for future suicide ideas and attempts (Kovacs, Goldston, & Gatsonis, 1993). Thus, suicidal ideas in childhood persist into later life and have potentially fatal consequences.

HOW CHILDREN ATTEMPT AND COMMIT SUICIDE

Children attempt and commit suicide in a variety of ways. One way is with a gun. In the United States, more people kill themselves by using guns than by all other methods combined; most cases involve handguns rather than other types of guns (Kellermann et al., 1992). From 1933 to 1982, the rate of suicide involving guns increased 139%, whereas the rate of suicide involving all other methods only increased 32% (Boyd & Moscicki, 1986). Guns are the most frequent cause of suicidal death.

Guns are also an important part of suicidal ideas and plans. When they think about suicide, children think about using guns. Using a gun is the most frequent suicide method thought of in children under age 11 (Asarnow & Guthrie, 1989). Thus, guns are a major aspect of suicidal ideation as well as an essential feature of completed suicide.

As opposed to suicide completions, suicide attempts are most often drug overdoses (Kienhorst et al., 1987; Kovacs et al., 1993), the most typical being the overdose of household pain reliever (Garfinkel, Froese, & Hood, 1982). Overdoses usually occur in the home (Kienhorst et al., 1987). Thus, though guns are the most likely cause of suicidal death, drug overdoses are the most likely method of suicide attempts.

Other ways of attempting and committing suicide include jumping in front of ongoing traffic (Kosky, 1983) and hanging, the latter of which is more likely among children younger than 13.5 years compared with an older group (Garfinkel, Froese, & Hood, 1982). Older children use a greater variety, more accessible, and more lethal methods of suicide than younger children (Asarnow & Guthrie, 1989). Basically, children use the same methods of attempting and completing suicide as adults.

FAMILY VARIABLES IN CHILD SUICIDE AND SUICIDE ATTEMPTS

Why do children commit suicide? One of the first places to look is the family. Among severely disturbed inpatients, the child's perception of the family environment is the strongest predictor of suicidality (Asarnow, Carlson, & Guthrie, 1987), more important than depression, hopelessness, or coping strategies. Family variables associated with child suicidality include discord, sexual abuse, physical abuse and neglect, stress, suicidal contagion, and other family problems.

What are the families of suicidal children like? One prominent characteristic is *family discord,* which may be even more pronounced than in adult suicide because of the child's dependence on the family (Pfeffer et al., 1986). These families lack cohesion and have excessive conflict (Asarnow, 1992) including physical fights (Kellermann et al., 1992). Both parent and child perceive this conflict to be severe (Campbell, Milling, Laughlin, & Bush, 1993). Further, this conflict is chronic

(Kosky, Silburn, & Zubrick, 1990) and frequently witnessed by the child (van der Kolk, Perry, & Herman, 1991). When the child is suicidal, then, he or she perceives the family as having pervasive, severe conflict.

Also, these families are *emotionally unsupportive* (Asarnow, 1992; Asarnow & Carlson, 1988). They discourage openness and direct expression of feelings, and instead encourage the child's dependence, indecision, and unassertiveness (Meneese & Yutrzenka, 1990). They are disorganized in general (Campbell et al., 1993), and they lack achievement orientation (Campbell ct al., 1993). So, the suicidal child perceives much disharmony, and little or no emotional support, from his or her family.

In addition, families of suicidal children are more *depressed* than are those of nonsuicidal children (Friedman et al., 1984). When the parents are depressed, they have profound impairments in four areas of parental functioning: emotional involvement, communication, affection, and hostility (Weissman, 1979). The result of this impairment for the child is global and profound. These children feel hopeless. They wish to rescue the suffering parent and, paradoxically, to compete with that parent for the sick role in the family system. They often appear to act out the parent's suicidal wishes. They identify with the parent and often develop a hopeless-helpless view of themselves. They develop a suicidal style of life, particularly in response to stress (Friedman et al., 1984). The parents' depression probably contributes to their inability to provide for their children emotionally.

Further, these families have *pathological family members,* more so than families of nonsuicidal children. They have comparatively more psychopathology, in general; more suicidal behaviors; and more licit and illicit drug and alcohol use (Kellermann et al., 1992). The family's overall pathology and drug use are warning signs that the child may respond with suicide thoughts, attempts, and completion.

Finally, families of suicidal children are often characterized by *sexual and physical abuse,* which are highly significant predictors of suicide attempts (van der Kolk, Perry, & Herman, 1991), even in children as young as 2.5 to 5 years (Rosenthal & Rosenthal, 1984). Adolescents who were sexually abused as children are more likely to attempt and commit suicide than adolescents who were not abused as children (de Wilde, Kienhorst, Diekstra, & Wolters, 1992). Childhood sexual abuse, then, is associated with childhood, adolescent, and adult suicide and suicide attempts.

Who perpetrated the abuse may or may not make a difference in terms of later suicidality, but the type of abuse and when it occurs does make a difference. In one study, sexual abuse before the age of 12 by peers was just as associated with adult suicidality as abuse by adults

(Peters & Range, 1995). In another study, the child's adjustment was worse if the abuse was perpetrated by the father than if by another person (Adams-Tucker, 1982). Thus, the research on who perpetuates the abuse is inconclusive. However, regardless of the perpetrator, if the child's abuse involved touching, rather than other types of exploitation, the victim as an adult is more suicidal, feels less able to cope, and feels less responsibility to his or her family compared with nontouched controls (Peters & Range, 1995). Further, when the abuse happens may also make a difference in later suicidality. In one study, the earlier the abuse occurred, the greater was the likelihood of later suicide (van der Kolk, Perry, & Herman, 1991). In terms of suicidality, the type of abuse and when it occurred may be more important than who perpetrates it.

How the abuse is reported can make a difficult situation even worse. Children are often disbelieved or even blamed, and families sometimes split apart. In one study, 4% of child abuse victims attempted suicide between 3 and 33 months following substantiation of the abuse (Goodwin, 1981). So, though the circumstances surrounding the abuse make a difference, sexual abuse often has suicidal ramifications for the child.

Physical abuse and neglect is also more common among children who attempt and commit suicide than children who do not (Malinosky-Rummell & Hansen, 1993). Having been physically abused as a child is more common among suicidal than among depressed adolescents (de Wilde et al., 1992), though the research on this topic is scarcer than on sexual abuse. In one study, physical and emotional neglect was associated with self-destructive behaviors, but not suicide attempts (van der Kolk, Perry, & Herman, 1991). A problem with this research is that much of it combines physical and sexual abuse, so that it is impossible to determine which type of abuse (sexual, physical, or multiple) is most highly associated with suicidality. Nevertheless, the few studies that separate types of abuse suggest that physical abuse is related to self-injurious and suicidal behaviors (Malinosky-Rummell & Hansen, 1993). The type and duration of the physical abuse undoubtedly makes a difference in later suicidality.

Family stress is also associated with suicidality in children. This stress includes the child's separation from the parents (de Wilde et al., 1992), the parents' separation (van der Kolk, Perry, & Herman, 1991) and divorce (de Wilde et al., 1992), parental unemployment (de Wilde et al., 1992), family relocation (de Wilde et al., 1992), the child running away from home (Rotheram-Borus, 1993), changes in the family (Kienhorst et al., 1987), and total problematic life events (de Wilde et al., 1992). In addition to a great deal of internal conflict, then, families with suicidal children also have a great deal of external stress as well.

Suicidal contagion is another aspect of family functioning that may influence a child to be suicidal. Suicidal contagion is the phenomenon of one suicide happening and then being followed by others. Suicidal contagion is a type of behavioral contagion: One person commits suicide, and then a person who learns the news also commits suicide. Some evidence indicates that contagion happens after a suicide (Gould & Shaffer, 1986; Phillips & Carstensen, 1986), particularly for teens, and particularly after celebrity suicides (Stack, 1987). However, other evidence has failed to replicate earlier results (Phillips & Paight, 1987), or qualified earlier results in finding suicidal contagion in some locations but not others (Gould, Shaffer, & Kleinman, 1988). Thus, the evidence is mixed on whether or not suicidal contagion occurs.

That teens would be more vulnerable than adults to contagion after the suicide of a peer is not surprising in view of their greater responsiveness to peer influence (Costanzo, 1970). But what about children? Are they, too, vulnerable to suicidal contagion? In one study, 28% of suicide-attempting children had a family member who attempted suicide also, about one half of the time within 2 years of the child's attempt (Kienhorst et al., 1987). These results are evidence of suicidal contagion in children.

Other indirect evidence also suggests that suicidal contagion is a factor in childhood suicide. In a study of suicidal adults, the percentage of family members threatening, attempting, or committing suicide was 36% (Murphy & Wetzel, 1982). In a study of adolescents, a child's exposure to the attempted suicide of a parent was associated with increased suicidality as an adolescent (Friedman et al., 1984). Thus, children appear to be vulnerable to contagion after the suicide of someone in their family; in contrast, adolescents appear to be vulnerable to contagion following a suicide of a peer.

Overall, families of suicidal children suffer from a failure of generativity and a lack of self-differentiation (Pfeffer, 1981). These parents regress to states in which they indulge themselves as if they were children. They lack generational boundaries, have severely conflicted relationships with their spouses, project their own feelings onto the child, develop symbiotic parent-child relationships, and have an inflexible family system. They force the child into the special role of providing gratification to the parent, being an omnipotent protector for the distressed parent, and accepting the displaced parental hostility (Pfeffer, 1981).

Thus, the picture of the suicidal child's family is bleak. They fight extensively, fail to support the child, are seriously depressed, have other forms of psychopathology, and abuse the child. The parents are under a lot of stress and may be suicidal themselves. It is no wonder the child is suicidal.

PERSONAL VARIABLES IN CHILD SUICIDE AND SUICIDE ATTEMPTS

In addition to family variables, there are personal variables associated with a child being suicidal. These variables are (a) mood disorders, especially depression; (b) cognitive deficits including hopelessness, problem-solving weakness, preoccupation with death, and unique attitudes toward life and death; (c) negative life events; and (d) other psychopathology.

Mood disorders are common among suicidal children. *Depression* is consistently associated with suicidality in children, adolescents, and adults. Suicidal children are more depressed than nonsuicidal children (Kosky, Silburn, & Zubrick, 1990; Marciano & Kazdin, 1994) and may actually kill themselves. In one recent longitudinal study, 4.4% of children originally diagnosed with major depression committed suicide within 10 years (Rao, Weissman, Martin, & Hammond, 1993). Most suicide attempts occur during an episode of depression (Kovacs, Goldston, & Gatsonis, 1993). However, though depression and suicidal ideation may overlap, they are distinguishable. Some children are depressed only, some are suicidal only, and some are both depressed and suicidal.

One reason for the overlap between depression and suicidality is that both contain features of *hopelessness*. Among adults, hopelessness relates more highly to suicidal intent than does depression. Among children, the relationship is less consistent. Among inpatient children, hopelessness has been more strongly associated with suicidal ideation and attempts than depression in some studies (Asarnow & Guthrie, 1989; Kazdin, French, Unis, Esveldt-Dawson, & Sherick, 1983), but not in others (Marciano & Kazdin, 1994). Hopelessness, particularly in conjunction with depression, can be a warning sign of suicidality in children.

Anger or aggression is another aspect of the mood of some suicidal children. In fact, some suicidal children show intense depression, whereas others exhibit relatively less depression but show highly intense aggression (Pfeffer, Plutchik, & Mizruchi, 1983). Two types of suicidal children have been delineated (Pfeffer, Plutchik, & Mizruchi, 1983). One type is a child with relatively stable ego functioning, including good reality testing, who decompensates and becomes overtly depressed only under the influence of extreme environmental stressors. The other type is the child who has distinct ego deficits and is prone to identify with parental suicidality. The latter type is subject to a variety of symptoms including rage episodes and serious assaultive tendencies. Suicidal children, then, are intensely depressed, intensely angry, or both.

Notably, among children with a history of major depression or other affective disorders, the presence of *conduct* or *substance-use disorders* increased the risk of a suicide attempt approximately threefold. In contrast, conduct or substance-use disorder unaccompanied by affective disorder did not appreciably alter the odds of a suicide attempt (Kovacs, Goldston, & Gatsonis, 1993). Alcohol or drugs combined with depression are a dangerous combination for child suicide.

Another personal aspect of suicidal children is their *cognitive deficits.* Though their intelligence is equal to that of nonsuicidal children, their problem-solving skills are weaker. Further, they are preoccupied with death, and they are less attracted to life, more attracted to death, and less repulsed by death than nonsuicidal children.

Poor problem solving is one aspect of the cognitive deficits of suicidal children. When asked to respond to scenarios about life and death, suicidal children are able to generate fewer alternatives than normal or chronically ill children. This weakness is not there when they are given other dilemmas, however (Orbach, Rosenheim, & Hary, 1987). Furthermore, the solutions they do generate contain fewer active coping strategies (Asarnow, Carlson, & Guthrie, 1987) and less flexibility (Levenson & Neuringer, 1971) than nonsuicidal children. These problem-solving deficits hold true even when suicidal children are compared with nonsuicidal but psychiatrically disturbed children (Rotheram-Borus, Trautman, Dopkins, & Shrout, 1990). Thus, suicidal children are weak at generating solutions to life and death problems, and may be able to think of no solution to their problems other than suicide.

Cognitively, suicidal children are also preoccupied with death. They think of death repetitively and in detail (Pfeffer, 1990). Compared with nonsuicidal children, they worry more about family members and themselves dying, and they dream more of experiencing the death of others and being killed themselves (Pfeffer, 1990). However, they are no different from nonsuicidal children in their understanding of the irreversibility, finality, or unpleasantness of death (Pfeffer, 1990), although they may regress under pressure to a mistaken understanding that death is reversible or temporary (Pfeffer, 1985). Thus, though they are developmentally at the same stage as their peers in their understanding of death, they think of death more often.

These cognitive deficits of suicidal children also include their attitudes toward life and death. Orbach and his colleagues (Orbach, Feshbach, Carlson, & Ellenberg, 1984; Orbach, Feshbach, Carlson, Glaubman, & Gross, 1983) have described four such attitudes (see Table 4.1). The suicidal child's attraction and repulsion to life and death are different from the attitudes of nonsuicidal children. Suicidal children have moderate attraction to life, high repulsion by life, high attraction to death, and moderate or low repulsion by death. In contrast, normal children have high attraction to life, low repulsion by life, low attraction to death, and high repulsion by death. Thus, compared with their nonsuicidal peers, suicidal children are more attracted to death and see fewer solutions other than suicide to life's problems. These attitudes may contribute to their willingness and likelihood of making suicide attempts.

Suicidal adolescents report more *negative life events* in their childhood than depressed adolescents (de Wilde et al., 1992). For boys, experiencing a loss is a particularly devastating, negative life event and increases the odds of suicide attempts (Kosky, Silburn, & Zubrick, 1990). Attraction to death fluctuates with negative life events (Orbach, Rosenheim, & Hary, 1987), so that as negative events worsen, death comes to seem increasingly attractive, and the suicidal child sees fewer alternatives other than suicide as a solution to problems.

Other psychopathology is also present in suicidal children (Pfeffer et al., 1986). Suicide attempts almost never occur when a youngster is free of psychiatric illness (Kovacs, Goldston, & Gatsonis, 1993). Suicidal children may lack psychological investment in their bodies: three quarters of them in one study showed no pain or crying when injured (Rosenthal & Rosenthal, 1984). Suicidal children have high levels of anxiety, sleep disorders, irritability, and abnormal sensitivity (Kosky, Silburn, & Zubrick, 1990). They often have school problems (Kienhorst et al.,

TABLE 4.1 Attraction and Repulsion to Life and Death

Concept	Definition
Attraction to life	Degree that life has been satisfying, pleasant
Repulsion by life	Degree that life has had mental or physical suffering
Attraction to death	Cultural or religions beliefs, distorted perceptions, and fantasies about death
Repulsion by death	Degree that realistic perceptions and idiosyncratic fears of death cause fear and anxiety

1987). Further, the process that preceded the child being suicidal was prolonged and deeply rooted rather than being a mere attention-seeking manipulation or impulsive acting out (Orbach, Rosenheim, & Hary, 1987). There are a cluster of psychopathologies associated with a child being suicidal.

Thus, the picture of the suicidal child is bleak. The child is depressed, hopeless, anxious, and irritable, and may have recently lost a loved one. He or she is cognitively inflexible and poor at solving problems. He or she often thinks about death, and, unlike other children, views death as an attractive escape from life's problems. He or she has experienced a lot of negative life events, and many psychological problems.

MEASURING CHILD SUICIDALITY

How does one measure suicidality in children? Basically, the answer is the same way as one measures suicidality among adults: Ask them. Many questionnaires for measuring suicidality among adults exist; those for children are fewer in number.

One short (only four questions) self-report instrument that measures suicide directly is the Suicidal Behaviors Questionnaire (SBQ; Linehan, 1981), which has been adapted for children. The original SBQ was 45 self-report items that were asked of adults during a structured interview. A shortened version was introduced by Cole (1988), who used factor analysis to select 4 items from the original 45. In the children's version, the wording is slightly simplified to make it at the third grade reading level. The questions are: "Have you ever thought about or tried to kill yourself?" (rated 0 to 5), "How many times have you thought about killing yourself?" (rated 0 to 4), "Have you ever told someone that you were going to kill yourself?" (rated 0 to 2), and "Do you think that you might kill yourself someday?" (rated 0 to 4).

The adult version of the four-item SBQ is reliable over 2 weeks (0.95), and moderately internally consistent ($\alpha = 0.80$). Evidence of validity is its significant correlation (Cotton, Peters, & Range, 1995) with the Scale for Suicide Ideation (Beck, Kovacs, & Weissman, 1979), a commonly used, well-validated suicide assessment inventory. The child's version is also internally consistent ($\alpha = 0.84$; Payne & Range, 1994), but no other research on the reliability and validity of the children's version of the SBQ has been done. Because the SBQ is brief, reliable, valid, easy to administer and score, and direct, it is a reasonable tool for screening children who might be suicidal.

A longer, more comprehensive suicide assessment instrument for children is the Suicide Assessment Battery (SAB; Kazdin, 1985), which consists of as many as 40 questions (e.g., "Have you ever felt that your family would be better off without you or that you would be better off dead?") regarding suicidal thoughts, intentions, and actions. These questions are asked of children, their parents, and interviewers/assessors. Answers about suicidal ideation are scored on a 7-point scale (1 = not at all to 7 = very extreme). Other questions are answered in a multiple-choice format. For example, for a question about continuing to live, children answer (a) "I want to keep on living very much," (b) "I'm not sure if I want to keep on living," or (c) "I don't want to live at all."

Derived from the Schedule for Affective Disorders and Schizophrenia for School-Age Children (K-SADS; see later), the SAB can differentiate inpatient child suicide ideators from attempters, and both suicide groups from other child inpatients (Marciano & Kazdin, 1994). In addition to its thoroughness, another advantage is that it obtains information from parents and interviewers, as well as the child, about his or her suicidality.

A less-known measure of factors related to suicidality in children is the Life and Death Attitudes Scale (LDAS) (Orbach et al., 1983), a semiprojective technique consisting of four brief fairy tales. In each story, the main character is presented with a life/death dilemma that represents either attraction to life, attraction to death, repulsion by life, or repulsion by death. For example, attraction to life is a story of a wooden doll who considers becoming a real child, and attraction to death is the story of an old horse who considers becoming a statue. After hearing the story, the child responds either verbally or by gestures to a question about how the main character should resolve the dilemma. The child's response is a measure of the degree to which he or she is inclined toward that attitude. The attitudes are measured on a Likert scale (1 = not better off at all, to 7 = much better off).

It is impossible to ascertain internal consistency of the Fairy Tales because each attitude is measured by a single question and response. However, test-retest reliability is significant for all four attitudes in normal and suicidal children, and significant for the repulsion by death attitude in chronically ill children (Orbach et al., 1984). Validity of the Fairy Tales is supported by the four attitudes being able to significantly differentiate normal, suicidal, and chronically ill children (Orbach et al., 1983, 1984). Also, repulsion by death is associated with increased suicidal ideation in normal children (Cotton & Range, 1993). Thus, the Fairy Tales have acceptable reliability and validity, and are an attractive alternative to standard Likert measures because the stories are short, interesting, and novel. Also, they are not as obvious or direct as are the other questionnaires described here, and for this reason may be less threatening. Further, the testing procedure is semiprojective, which eliminates the child reading and responding via paper and pencil, and may also reduce self-report bias.

In addition to these instruments, which measure suicide directly, there are instruments that may be viewed as indirect measures of suicide because they measure related features. One such instrument is the Hopelessness Scale for Children (HSC; Kazdin et al., 1983). Modeled after the adult Hopelessness Scale, the HSC consists of 17 true-false statements, and is readable on a first- or second-grade level (Kazdin, Rodgers, & Colbus, 1986). An example of an item is "All I can see ahead of me are bad things not good things."

The HSC is moderately internally consistent when used with children. For example, coefficient αs and Spearman-Brown split-half reliabilities (SB) are moderate to strong (αs = 0.75, 0.97; SBs = 0.70, 0.96; Kazdin et al., 1983; Kazdin, Rodgers, & Colbus, 1986). Also, item-total correlations are significant for 15 or 16 of the 17 items (Kazdin et al., 1983; Kazdin, Rodgers, & Colbus, 1986). In addition, the HSC is moderately consistent over time, with test-retest reliability over 6 weeks being 0.52 (Kazdin, Rodgers, & Colbus, 1986). It is also valid. For example, factor analysis yields two factors, one focusing on future expectations and giving up, the other on overall happiness as well as future expectations (Kazdin, Rodgers, & Colbus, 1986). These factors account for 78% and 22% of the variance. Other evidence of validity is its significant positive correlation with depression (Kazdin, Rodgers, & Colbus, 1986), social behavior (Kazdin, Rodgers, & Colbus, 1986), and self-esteem (Kazdin et al., 1983), and its negative correlation with Good Events on the Children's Attributional Style Questionnaire (Spirito, Williams, Stark, & Hart, 1988). Further evidence of validity with adolescents is that suicide attempters scored higher (more hopeless) than did nonsuicide attempting outpatients and nonclinical groups (Spirito et al., 1988). Overall, then, the HSC is a reliable and valid instrument for measuring one component of childhood suicidality, hopelessness.

Another related measure is the Child Depression Inventory (CDI; Kovacs, 1981), which is 27 sets of three statements about behavioral, cognitive, and affective symptoms of depression (e.g., "I feel like crying everyday," "I feel like crying many days," "I feel like crying once in a while"). The child chooses the statement most descriptive of him or her over the past 2 weeks. Worded for the 8- to 13-year-old, the CDI has moderate to high internal consistency and good test-retest reliability over 1 week, which rapidly deteriorates over more time for inpatients but which remains strong for nonclinical outpatients (Saylor, Finch, Spirito, & Bennett, 1984). It is a valid (Saylor et al., 1984) and widely used measure of another aspect of childhood suicidality, depression.

Another related measure is K-SADS (Puig-Antich & Ryan, 1986), which is a structured interview by a mental health professional that yields a measure of the presence, absence, and severity of symptoms of depression. The K-SADS has good test-retest reliability (Apter, Orvaschel, Laseg, Moses, & Tyano, 1989) and sufficient internal consistency (Ambrosini, Metz, Prabucki, & Lee, 1989). It is a highly reliable, broad-spectrum diagnostic tool and is widely used with children.

All these measures assess suicidality or related measures in children, and all are sound instruments. Most are self-report, and most are intuitively obvious, the exception to both generalizations being the Fairy Tales test. However, though they are empirically strong, they all have the same disadvantage as do adult instruments that measure suicide. That is, these suicide measures can only estimate risk; they are unable to predict accurately which specific children will actually commit suicide.

PREVENTING CHILD SUICIDE AND LIFE-THREATENING BEHAVIOR

One aspect of prevention is *psychological intervention,* which should begin as soon as the child's suicidality is noted, and should be tailored to fit the child's age, developmental level, and individuality. Hospitalization may be necessary, depending on the child's immediate likelihood of self-harm. Medication may be helpful in lifting depressed mood. Children who have affective or bipolar disorder or schizophrenia should be identified and treated for suicidality (Blumenthal & Kupfer, 1988). A crisis resolution framework for intervention is needed, and a variety of resources inside and outside the family should be used.

Assigning a social worker to the suicide attempter seen in the emergency room has some benefits with adolescents (Deykin, Hsieh, Neela, & McNamarra, 1986), and may be helpful for suicidal children and their families as well. In one study, the support, exploration of potential services available, and assistance in keeping follow-up appointments were related to the teen being twice as likely as controls to comply with medical recommendations. However, the teens who were assigned the social worker were no less likely than controls to be admitted for a later suicide attempt (Deykin et al., 1986). These results may apply to children as well, so that assigning a social worker to a suicidal child's entire family would seem to be an appropriate step.

Note, psychological intervention for suicidal children must entail treatment for the entire family. Oftentimes, the child's progress toward individuation threatens the emotional stability of the parents or provokes depression in the symbiotic parent. One consequence of intervention, then, is that as the child gets better, family members undermine his or her progress by strengthening their efforts to retain the albeit shaky, family stability. Therefore, therapy for the entire family is essential, one goal of which is to provide psychological support to the parents and encourage them to deal with their parental conflicts as separate issues from the conflicts of the child (Pfeffer, 1981). Another goal is to help them provide a flexible though clearly defined structure within the family, and to facilitate their open expression of feelings within a supportive environment.

Therapy is also needed to help the child develop stress management skills. One recommendation is to encourage the child's developing cognitive mediational strategies to regulate his or her affective and behavioral responses. Another recommendation is for the child to receive training in coping skills (Asarnow, Carlson, & Guthrie, 1987), especially in view of his or her deficits in this arena. As part of this training, building the child's ability to brainstorm a variety of solutions other than suicide to his or her problems is recommended.

For adults and adolescents, "No Suicide" or "No Harm" agreements are a standard aspect of crisis intervention (Fremouw, Perczel, & Ellis, 1990). For children, however, such agreements get mixed reactions from experts. One survey of licensed professionals showed that "No Suicide" agreements were viewed as highly appropriate for adults and adolescents, but were slightly inappropriate with children, although a weakness in this survey was the assumption of adult wording in the contract (Davidson & Wagner, 1994). So, a "No Hurting Yourself" agreement, written in language that the child can understand, might be beneficial with some children.

Another aspect of prevention is *screening*. Because of the relatively high incidence of suicidality among psychiatric outpatients, all children who are evaluated psychiatrically should be assessed for suicidal behavior. The SBQ is ideal for screening because of its brevity and ease of scoring. In some research projects, for example, children's answers were evaluated as they took a battery of tests, so that intervention could be made immediately if they were suicidal (Cotton & Range, 1993).

Screening could involve mental health professionals, who should be aware of risk factors for childhood suicide. A list of warning signs is pro-

TABLE 4.2   Suicide Warning Signs

Global
    Specific plan   History of drug or alcohol abuse
    History of suicide attempts   Talk of suicide

Mood (affect)
    Feeling powerless   Panic attacks
    Depression   Unexplained mood change

Behavior
    Withdrawal/isolation   Recent loss
    Making final arrangements   Unexplained behavior change
    Drop in grades   Drop in activities
    Conduct disorder   Alcohol/drug use
    Change in eating or sleeping habits
    Outbursts of unusual/reckless behavior

Cognitions
    Rigid thinking   Preoccupation with death
    Feeling hopeless about future   Attraction to death
    Poor coping skills   Hopelessness

Family
    Excessive conflict   No emotional support of child
    Drug or alcohol abuse   Symbiotic relationship
    Depression   Other psychopathology
    Other stresses   Domestic violence
    Suicidal

vided in Table 4.2 to aid in this awareness. Parents or guardians must be notified if the child is suicidal.

Further, when evaluating adults, professionals should be aware that their children may be at risk for suicide. For example, the children of parents who suffer from chronic depression are a high-risk group. Early intervention for them might help to diminish their likelihood of attempting suicide (Friedman et al., 1984).

Screening is essential in the schools and could be in the form of suicide prevention training modules. A helpful resource for such modules is Poland's *Suicide Intervention in the Schools* (1989). Although suicide-attempting adolescents exhibit a negative reaction to them (Shaffer et al., 1990), school-based suicide prevention modules have several important functions and are often recommended (Ramsay, Cooke, & Lang, 1990). One function is administrative. Suicide prevention programs encourage schools to develop clearly defined, written procedures in which the roles of various school personnel are explicitly stated (Ross, 1985). They coordinate the school's suicide prevention programs with state and community agencies. They help school personnel, who often feel ambivalent and ill equipped to deal with this difficult problem (Ramsay, Cooke, & Lang, 1990). This administrative function is important because school personnel, like others, are often unsure about what to do when someone is suicidal and may be unaware of resources available to them.

School-based suicide prevention modules also serve an important educative function. They teach all school personnel that they can be the gatekeepers and detect suicidal students. They review warning signs and remind school personnel that talk about suicide does *not* provoke students to become suicidal. Because the gatekeeper role is difficult and stressful, they provide much-needed encouragement, reminders, and refresher in-service sessions. Also, they provide direct information concerning suicide risk in age-appropriate language, and discuss how the child can cope with alcoholic or affective-disordered parents (Blumenthal & Kupfer, 1988).

School-based suicide prevention programs also serve an important clinical function. They illustrate the help available to the suicidal youth, and encourage him or her to take advantage of it (Poland, 1989). They foster in school personnel an understanding of, and empathy with, the suicidal child and an improved ability to identify and respond to him or her (Ross, 1985). This clinical function is important to the potentially suicidal child.

The benefits of school-based prevention programs extend beyond suicidal children. They also help nonsuicidal students know what to do when they receive a suicidal communication from a peer. In fact, these nonsuicidal peers may be the group that is most amenable to suicide prevention programs (Range, 1993). Peers are often the first place a suicidal student turns for help, and can make a big difference in the outcome of a suicidal thought or plan.

One important aspect of peer training is teaching students that they *must* tell others when they hear of a suicidal communication. Often they find themselves in a sticky ethical dilemma: They are torn between breaking a confidence versus informing others and possibly preventing a suicide. Mental health professionals are trained in confidentiality and know that suicide is a time to break it, but students are often unclear about what to do in this situation. Thus, the clinical functions of a suicidal program extend from the suicidal child to the nonsuicidal peer.

A third aspect of prevention is to *detoxify the environment* (Blumenthal & Kupfer, 1988) by limiting access to lethal methods. Families should never keep a gun in the home. Owning a gun (Lester, 1988) and having a gun in the home (Kellermann et al., 1992) are strongly associated with an increased risk of suicide for women and men, regardless of age group. Keeping a loaded gun, or keeping more than one gun, or keeping the gun in an unlocked place are even riskier than just keeping a gun (Kellermann et al., 1992). Other potentially lethal methods of self-destruction should also be removed, particularly drugs and alcohol. Children who live in homes where they have access to lethal methods of self-destruction are at more risk for suicide than children who live in homes where there are no such methods. The message is obvious: Children and guns, drugs, or alcohol are a dangerous mix.

A fourth aspect of prevention is to *deromanticize suicide reports* because children may be vulnerable to suicidal contagion. Realistically, it would be virtually impossible to keep a suicide quiet in a community. Even if it were not in the newspaper, for example, children could learn of it through word of mouth. Therefore, one suggestion that might forestall children developing a romantic view of the suicide is to paint a realistic picture of the suicidal person and the suicidal death. Though it is natural to speak only well of the dead, truthfully portraying suicide as a deviant act by someone with a mental disturbance may discourage its imitation (Shaffer, Garland, Gould, Fisher, & Trautman, 1988).

A second publicity suggestion that could ameliorate the contagion effects of the suicide is to publicize children getting psychological help. Such positive publicity could be in the form of promoting family therapy, so that the child knows about respected adults, children, and families seeking and receiving help. Another form of positive publicity could be in the form of testimonials given by young people, particularly those who are popular or celebrities, or who have gone through difficult times and chosen positive methods of dealing with their problems. This publicity should include information about local resources available to suicidal youth.

Professionals and parents should *avoid euphemisms about death.* When a child experiences the death of a loved one, providing euphemisms about death may lead to internal conflict and misunderstanding (Cotton & Range, 1990). At such a time the child might develop the tragically mistaken idea that suicide (e.g., "going to heaven to be with God") is a viable alternative to life's problems. Direct, unambiguous language about death is usually best for the child.

Finally, adults who are working with children should *promote an open and frank discussion of death.* Children are often interested in but unfamiliar with the topic of death, even when they have some direct experience with it (Cotton & Range, 1990). An open discussion removes the mystery, answers questions, and helps children come to terms with this aspect of life.

CONCLUSION

Suicide is a serious problem throughout the life span, but in childhood seems particularly tragic because of the time lost, paths unexplored, opportunities unexamined, life untasted. Understanding the scope of the problem, the family and personal factors involved, the methods available to assess suicidality, and key elements in prevention may assist in identifying those children who are at risk and tailoring prevention efforts to lessen that risk.

5

The Cruel Paradox: Children Who Are Living with Life-Threatening Illnesses

Kenneth J. Doka

Even to address the issue of children who are coping with life-threatening illnesses is to bespeak a cruel paradox. One likes to think of childhood as a time that is healthy and free of concerns, such as illness, disease, or death. Yet the fact is that children do suffer from a range of life-threatening illnesses. Some, like cystic fibrosis or muscular dystrophy, are essentially diseases of childhood. That is, children are born with these diseases (although sometimes the disease only manifests itself at a later point) and struggle with them throughout childhood. Other diseases, such as cancer, can affect children as well as adults, although often in different forms. Still others, like HIV/AIDS, are diseases children may be born with or acquire during the course of childhood.

This chapter explores the cruel paradox of children who are living with life-threatening illnesses, considering ways that such children cope with life-threatening illnesses. The chapter begins by providing a general model of coping with life-threatening illness, one that views life-threatening illness as a series of phases. In each of these phases, individuals have to cope with a unique set of tasks. Second, the chapter explores particular issues that arise as children struggle with life-threatening illnesses. Finally, the chapter considers other children, siblings, and peers, who are affected by that struggle and who are also touched by the cruel paradox.

THE EXPERIENCE OF LIFE-THREATENING ILLNESS: A PHASE AND TASK MODEL

Before discussing the particular responses of children and families to life-threatening illnesses, it seems important to provide a model overviewing the experience of life-threatening illness. Building on the work of Weisman (1980) and Pattison (1969, 1978), Doka (1993) suggested that the experience of life-threatening illness can best be viewed as a series of phases, each with its own unique issues or tasks (see Figure 5.1). These phases include the following:

• *Prediagnosis phase.* The prediagnosis phase is the period from the point at which an illness is first suspected through the time when medical help is actually sought. For example, a child may notice increased tiredness and bruises, but may hesitate to tell his or her parents. When the parents are informed, there may be a period before they solicit medical help. This period is often instructive to review retrospectively because it usually shows the family's fears, levels of knowledge, and coping patterns.

Often the prediagnostic phase can be a source of significant guilt. For example, in a study of parental grief, Miles and Demi (1984) identified six types of guilt that bereaved parents may experience when a child dies. With only minor adaptations, these categories are equally

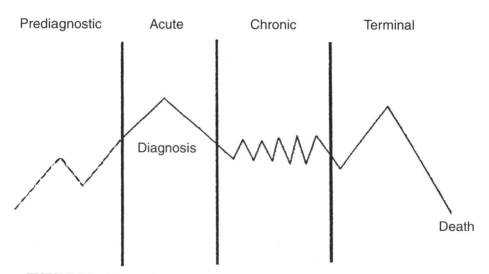

FIGURE 5.1   Phases of life-threatening illness, with the peaks representing points of higher anxiety. (Courtesy of K. Doka, PhD.)

valid for parents of a child who is coping with a life-threatening illness. They include the following:

Causation guilt: "Isn't it my fault that this is happening to my child?"; "Didn't I fail to protect my child from what is happening?"

Illness-related guilt: "Haven't I failed or been deficient during my child's illness?"

Role guilt: "Isn't it the case that I am failing to live up to society's or my own expectations in my role as a parent?"

Moral guilt: "Isn't this punishment or retribution for some moral violation on my part?"

Survivor guilt: "Isn't it monstrous that my child should be experiencing this awful illness rather than me?"

Grief guilt: "Shouldn't I be feeling guilty for how I acted or felt when the disease first appeared or when my child was diagnosed?"

The child may also experience some of these forms of guilt or at least guilt which is similar in notable ways.

It is critical to reflect on the prediagnostic phase with family members because they are often able to provide insight into any feelings of guilt or other feelings, such as anger, that ill children or their family members may be experiencing. For example, in one case the child's mother felt a high level of guilt and anger toward her husband because he had discounted their son's complaints of pain in his legs as "growing pains." The child was later diagnosed with osteogenic sarcoma. In many cases, however, physicians are able to reassure the family that they acted in a responsible and caring manner during the prediagnostic phase. Nevertheless, by exploring this period retrospectively, caregivers can learn much about the ways in which children and other family members may be responding to a child's illness.

• *Diagnostic or acute phase.* This phase, which may occur over a period of time, perhaps weeks, is centered on the crisis of diagnosis. Many families report that this period is extremely stressful and traumatic, second only to death itself. To many families, the diagnosis marked the point of demarcation between two different lifestyles. Before this point, they had often looked at the future and lived their lives in a carefree and optimistic way; after the diagnosis, the future may be considered much more forbidding and uncertain. Often the basis of family life is held hostage by the child's illness. Any planning, even for the short term, may be contingent on the ill child's health and pressing needs for diagnostic investigation or cure-oriented interventions (Gyulay, 1978). However, because the period of the diagnostic phase is a time-bound crisis, social support is generally available. Typically, family and friends do rally during this period and often can provide essential physical and emotional assistance.

- *Chronic phase.* This phase is characterized by ongoing treatments and therapies. During this time, children and families struggle to live with the problems of ongoing illness. In the chronic phase of a life-threatening illness, children and families find themselves coping with both the symptoms of the illness and the effects of treatment, even as they struggle with continuing issues common to all human development and family life. In fact, the twin aspects of the illness experience—symptoms and side effects—usually become the two critical issues in the chronic phase.

Adherence to a treatment regimen is especially difficult for children and their families. Often a child may not understand or accept the necessity for adherence, particularly if his or her own knowledge or understanding of the disease is limited. In addition, children can be present oriented, focused on immediate rewards rather than future benefits. Although adherence remains an issue for most families, Burton (1974) has identified two particularly problematic patterns that may emerge. In dysfunctional families, there was often poor and erratic regulation. In some families, there was a repressive, perfectionistic over-control that followed the treatment regimen to the letter, often impairing the child's present quality of life. As the child ages, he or she may find it increasingly difficult to mesh the demands of the treatment regimen with the ongoing activities of life, such as school.

Burton (1974) found that children often responded to heavy treatment regimens with regressive and dependent behaviors, aggressive nonadherence, and impaired self-esteem. Adherence may be facilitated if children are informed about the disease and treatment, given some control in planning the regimen, and helped to adapt the regimen into the ongoing activities of the child (Doka, 1993).

In addition, throughout the chronic phase the ability of the ill child and family to cope with the continuing demands of family life may be compromised. For example, Burr (1985) found that the division of labor within the family often needs to be restructured. There may be financial effects as well. Burr (1985) found that in one half of her cases one family member, frequently the mother, left work because of increased caregiving responsibilities.

Sometimes, children and families feel that social support from others, so evident in the crisis of diagnosis, is less available during the chronic phase. In fact, families of the ill child may feel increasingly isolated because the demands of the illness may constrain opportunities to socialize. In addition, other family members and friends may find it uncomfortable to interact with the family of the ill child.

- *Terminal phase.* In this phase, the goal of treatment frequently turns to palliation—the minimization of sources of distress and the maximization of present quality in living—as the child and family prepare for death. However, families may have a difficult time accepting that care is now palliative in orientation. There may be reluctance to issue "do not resuscitate" orders or even to accept hospice care because both acknowledge the impending loss of a child (Armstrong-Dailey & Goltzer, 1993; Corr & Corr, 1985; Doka, 1993).

- *Recovery phase.* Not every illness during childhood, even those that are life threatening, results in death. Nevertheless, even when recovery is achieved, children may experience ongoing physical, psychological, social, and spiritual residues of their encounter with illness. Central issues in the recovery phase typically involve learning to live with the consequences of an illness that is no longer life threatening or with the continued presence of a potential threat to life (Koocher & O'Malley, 1981).

Normally each person's experience or illness is individual. Some individuals experience an illness that is quickly diagnosed and successfully treated with surgery, radiation, or chemotherapy. Others may such succumb to a terminal phase. Still others recover, often after long, extensive, and demanding treatments.

THE VALUE OF A TASK-BASED PERSPECTIVE

The value of the task-based perspective that is at the heart of the model of life-threatening illness described in the previous section is that it encourages recognition that at each phase of illness, children and their families have to cope with different issues. This is because in each phase, unique physical, psychological, social, and spiritual issues are raised.

In recent years, task-oriented models have proved to be helpful approaches to exploring ways in which individuals cope with life-threatening illnesses, death, and bereavement (Corr, 1992a; Corr & Doka, 1994; Doka, 1993; Worden, 1991). The essence of task-based models is that individuals have to cope with specific tasks as they strive to manage crises in their lives.

Unlike earlier stage-based models, task-based models acknowledge individuality and autonomy (Corr, 1993b). In this way, such models place emphasis not on the needy patient but on the (potentially) active, living human being (child or adult family member) who is coping with the challenges of a life-threatening or terminal illness.

As they address the challenges arising from the illness, specific children and their families may find it easier or more difficult to cope with some tasks, whereas others struggle more or less effectively with other tasks. Particular individuals may cope with the same task in their own distinctive ways. Affirming autonomy also means that children and families may choose the time that they select to cope with these tasks.

Tasks that are most often encountered during the acute, chronic, and terminal phases of a life-threatening illness are delineated in Table 5.1. In addition, one could retrospectively understand the ways in which children and families cope with the tasks of the prediagnostic phase, such as the following:

1. Recognizing possible danger or risk
2. Coping with anxiety and uncertainty
3. Developing and following through on a health-seeking strategy that may provide useful clues to their coping strategies

Tasks evident during the recovery phase typically include the following:

1. Dealing with the physical, psychological, social, spiritual, and financial aftereffects of illness
2. Coping with fears and anxieties about reoccurrence
3. Examining life and lifestyle issues and reconstructing one's life
4. Redefining relationships with caregivers

COPING WITH LIFE-THREATENING ILLNESSES AS A CHILD

As a general rule, a child's struggle with life-threatening illness is both similar to and different from that of an adult. Like an adult, a child must cope with all the physical, psychological, social, and spiritual ef-

TABLE 5.1 Tasks in Life-Threatening Illness

General	Acute phase	Chronic phase	Terminal phase
Responding to the physical fact of disease	Understanding the disease	Managing symptoms and side effects	Dealing with symptoms, discomfort, pain, and incapacitation
Taking steps to cope with the reality of disease	Maximizing health and lifestyle Maximizing one's coping strengths and limiting weaknesses Developing strategies to deal with the issues created by the disease	Carrying out health regimens Preventing and managing health crisis Managing stress and examining coping Maximizing social support and minimizing isolation Normalizing life in the face of the disease Dealing with financial concerns	Managing health procedures and institutional stress Managing stress and examining coping Dealing effectively with caregivers Preparing for death and saying goodbye
Preserving self-concept and relationships with others in the face of disease	Exploring the effect of the diagnosis on a sense of self and others	Preserving self-concept Redefining relationships with others throughout the course of the disease	Preserving self-concept Preserving appropriate relationships with family and friends
Dealing with affective and existential/spiritual issues created or reactivated by the disease	Ventilating feelings and fears Incorporating the present reality of diagnosis into one's sense of past and future	Ventilating feelings and fears Finding meaning in suffering, chronicity, uncertainty, and decline	Ventilating feelings and fears Finding meaning in life and death

fects that an encounter with life-threatening illness brings. Similarly, children, at each phase of illness, must cope with the same tasks as any other person.

Yet there are two significant differences. The first involves *information and communication;* the second concerns *developmental issues related to childhood.*

Information and Communication

The right of an adult to be given truthful and accurate information about his or her condition is reasonably well established, at least in the United States and many other developed countries. However, parents and other adults may not choose to communicate information about an illness with a child. This is often understandable. Parents may adopt a protective stance, fearing if the child knows too much about the illness, it may depress or dishearten the child. In his account of his son's fatal bout with cancer, Gunther (1949) expressed this thought well:

> Any discouragement would have been a crushing blow. All he had now was his will to live. We had to keep that up at any cost. The cord of life was wearing very thin and if we took any hope away it would be bound to snap. (p. 159)

For many years, Gunther's perspective expressed the predominant viewpoint in this field. In this "protective" approach, death was thought to be the ultimate anxiety. Children were viewed as needing to be protected from the knowledge of death as long as possible, even if that meant evading a child's request for information.

Nevertheless, research has shown that these attempts to protect children from illness and death are often futile (Bluebond-Langner, 1978; Doka, 1982). First, in various ways children can acquire a tremendous degree of medical sophistication. Especially by middle childhood, they have often studied diseases, perhaps had experiences with the illnesses of others, and have certainly obtained information about disease from the media.

Second, children often have external cues concerning their own health situation. They can sense the anxieties and concerns around them. They know that some conversations cease when they enter a room. They witness friends and relatives visiting from distant places. One boy with leukemia told me he learned of the seriousness of his illness when he casually mentioned to his mother than he would like to be a firefighter one day. His mother hugged him tightly, fearfully telling him he would. The 10-year-old boy wryly remarked, "I never knew she cared so much about firemen." If they are in a hospital or outpatient clinic, children can often guess what types of patients are treated in such a setting.

Third, often their peers are effective sources of information for children. Bluebond-Langner's (1978) research indicated that children in hospital wards shared considerable information about disease, treatments, and even death.

Finally, children respond to their own internal cues. They know they are in pain; they can sense when they are weaker and sicker. It is not surprising that studies have indicated that children with life-threatening illnesses were well aware of their condition even when parents or other caregivers consciously sought to withhold information (Bluebond-Langner, 1978; Waechter, 1971). Bluebond-Langner (1978) found that at various phases in a serious or life-threatening illness children typically processed considerable information that changed their self-concepts. For example, at the diagnostic phase, such children usually acknowledged that they had a serious illness and that acknowledgment generally was then incorporated as a part of the child's own identity. Similarly, throughout the chronic phase, children interact with other ill peers, learning about drugs and their side effects, experiencing varying procedures, and often undergoing remissions and relapses. Throughout this phase, the self-concept of these children changes from "I am seriously ill and will get better" to "I am always ill and will get better," and eventually to "I am always ill and will never get better." In the terminal phase, children with a life-threatening disease characteristically understand that people die of this disease. Consequently, such children define themselves as dying.

Keeping information from a child is not only futile; it may also be harmful. Misguided protectionism of this sort can inhibit the child from seeking support, cut off or convolute interactions with others, create additional anxiety, impair trust, and complicate a child's response to the crisis (Bluebond-Langner, 1978; Waechter, 1971, 1984).

In deciding how to communicate or share information about the illness with a child, three questions are primary: What does a child need to know?; What does a child want to know?; and What can a child understand?

What Does a Child Need to Know?   If the child is going to have a sense of participation and control in the illness, he or she will need to know what is wrong and what is likely to occur. Naturally, this may be achieved differently at different ages and with different children. For example, a young child who is diagnosed as positive for HIV infection

(the precondition for the development of AIDS) may need to know that
he or she has a blood disease that requires him or her to take medicine
and special care. An older child may need more explicit information
about abstaining from or taking precautions in sexual activity or sharing needles in intravenous drug use.

One also needs to time information to the specific phase of the illness. At the time of diagnosis, for example, a child may not necessarily
need to know all the potential long-term implications of the disease, but
he or she should understand its immediate and short-term effects.

Also, a child needs to know "what can be done?" Explaining the actions that can be taken to treat the illness and its side effects can restore
a sense of control during what may be a frightening time. In this, it is
important to be honest. Blindly assuring a child that everything will be
all right may not be realistic and may make the child distrustful later.
Honest and hopeful responses, such as "we are doing all we can," are
both truthful and reassuring.

What Does a Child Want to Know?   In addition to what a child needs
to know, caregivers have to be sensitive to what a child wants to know.
It is important to recognize that a child's questions are good indicators of what the child is ready to hear. Adults, though, should clarify
a child's questions. "Am I going to die" can be a request for information, reassurance, or both. Talking about the question as well as the
answer, rather than simply and quickly responding, is the best way to
understand the child's concerns and keep open lines of communication.

Caregivers also need to listen for any underlying sensitivities. Many
questions may be subtly asking, "Am I to blame?" Children, especially
younger children, may exhibit magical thinking, not always clearly distinguishing between causes and effects. In addition, guilt is a common
response to any crisis. Children may feel that their own thoughts or behaviors may have brought the illness on themselves or others.

> *In one case, a 5-year-old girl with leukemia began to tell me a story of her
> mother's dog who was run over by a car. Some careless person, she related, had
> left the gate open. Surely that person would be punished, she commented—in
> way that was both an observation and a question. As we discussed this, she
> revealed that she was that careless person. Her illness, she reasoned, was God's
> way of punishing her. Only through sensitive responses to the underlying ques-
> tions concerning blame and guilt could this child find the reassurance she
> needed.*

What Can a Child Understand? All children do not understand things in the same way. As children grow and develop, they differ in their vocabulary, sense of cause and effect, presence or absence of magical thinking, and ability to understand abstract thoughts. Their life experiences may also differ. It is easier to explain an illness to someone who has had experience with illness, even the illness of another person, than to a person whose experience is more limited.

There may also be other considerations that can affect understanding. Children who have developmental disabilities may find it more difficult to understand illness than do children without such disabilities. In addition, other considerations may play a role. For example, the tremendous fear generated by HIV infection and AIDS can inhibit understanding. This fear may affect communication in other ways. For example, one child with sickle cell anemia, when told he had a blood disease, immediately assumed it was AIDS, given the widespread community concern about AIDS and the fact that it, too, is a disease often associated with the blood.

Developmental Issues Related to Childhood

The second important difference between children and adults in coping with life-threatening illnesses has to do with developmental issues related to childhood. A child's entire experience of illness will be greatly affected by his or her developmental level. At each point in development, a child's own developmental level will influence both how the child responds to illness and how the experience with illness may affect subsequent development.

In infancy, intermittent periods of separation, the changing environments of hospitals, outpatient clinics, and home, and painful and incomprehensible medical procedures may impair both the child's bonding and his or her development of trust. As the child continues to age, physical constraints caused by the disease or its treatment, and also by parental overprotectiveness, may inhibit a child's development of autonomy. In addition, parental attempts to set limits, so critical in toddlerhood and later eras in childhood development, may be inhibited by concern for the illness. Parents may become inconsistent in their discipline—at some times acting in lenient ways and at other times being more restrictive—based on an assessment of the child's physical condition. This can inhibit a child's exploration of his or her environment as well as recognition on the child's part of appropriate limits. At any age in a child's life, but especially in his or her early years, parents may have considerable anxiety about the long-term effects of illness.

As a child turns from the preschool years of early childhood to the school years of middle childhood, a life-threatening illness may present new challenges. Most significantly, children in middle childhood will need to manage their illnesses within the school environment. This may be problematic for several reasons. First, intermittent outbreaks of disease and side effects of treatment may impair academic performance. Second, the treatment regimen may be difficult to manage within the school environment. Third, schools unwittingly thrust ill children into interactions with healthy peers. In some cases, this may be positive, reinforcing a sense of normalcy for the child. In other cases, such confrontations may create difficulties. Interactions with other children may accentuate the ill child's sense of differentness. Or peers may share troubling information about the disease with an ill child.

Decisions about school are often critical to a child's sense of well-being. School administrators may suggest that the ill child be placed in special education classes. In some cases, this may be appropriate as the child may be disoriented or unable to concentrate because of the treatments that he or she has received, and may need to be absent a considerable time. At their best, special education classes can provide an individualized instructional program suited to the particular child. Yet, there may be considerable disadvantages as well. Placement in special education classes may reinforce any sense of stigma that the child has about the illness and may thereby impair self-esteem. In addition, special treatment may further isolate the child from the support that he or she could have received from peers and classmates in the regular school setting.

During this stage of development, the key developmental tasks of mastery and independence may be complicated by the illness. Here, too, the overprotectiveness of parents and the physical constraints of the illness can impair the search for mastery.

Yet this quest for maturity can also be effectively employed in coping with the illness. By extending to the child an active role in adhering to a treatment regimen and by giving the child a measure of control in treatment decisions, a sense of mastery can be developed and the child's effective coping with the illness strengthened.

Youngsters in childhood often possess two other notable strengths. First, they are usually able to accept the help of supportive adults, something they may be more reluctant to do in adolescence. Second, often they can also draw strength and comfort from their philosophical or religious beliefs.

Although there are a variety of counseling approaches and techniques that can be useful with children (Adams & Deveau, 1993), caregivers need to be sensitive to two overriding concerns. First, they will need to encourage, facilitate, and empower effective communication between parents and their ill child. Second, they should carefully attempt to nurture a sense of autonomy in the child, allowing the child as much control as the child can handle. Such approaches help the child to function as an active partner in the treatment of the illness rather than as a passive recipient of actions initiated and implemented wholly by others.

Naturally, caregivers have to consider a variety of variables in planning interventions for and with a child and his or her family. The developmental level of the child has already been stressed. Children, like adults but perhaps even more dramatically, develop continually—cognitively, behaviorally, psychologically, socially, and spiritually. Effective intervention needs to consider the child's level of development. In addition, each disease and treatment creates its own specific issues. Psychological and social variables, such as family structure, religious and cultural beliefs, and traditions, social class, informal and formal support, will all affect the child's and family's responses to both the illness and possible death.

DISEASE-RELATED VARIABLES

One of the critical variables in coping with life-threatening illnesses during childhood is the nature of the disease with which the child is coping. For a variety of reasons, each disease creates distinct issues for a child. Some diseases, such as muscular dystrophy, are characterized by a long process of inexorable decline. Others, such as leukemia or HIV infection, involve uncertain periods of remission and relapse, or a roller-coaster experience of opportunistic infection and treatment. Some diseases are clearly fatal; others are life threatening. Treatments for different diseases may differ from mild to extremely intrusive regimens. Finally, the way the disease is understood by others is also likely to affect the child's sense of stigma or the perceived nature and availability of support.

HIV infection in children provides an illustration of the unique issues that arise in any illness. Pediatric AIDS shares many problems that are typically of other chronic childhood diseases. Like cystic fibrosis, it is a life-threatening illness with no present cure but increasingly effective treatments that have, for many children, extended both the quantity and the quality of the lives of children with this disease. Similarly,

HIV infection and AIDS share several management issues with other chronic childhood diseases.

Pediatric AIDS also poses several distinctive concerns (see chapter 3 in this book) (Boyd-Franklin, Steiner, & Boland, 1995; Dane & Levine, 1994; Dane & Miller, 1992; Levine, 1993). For example, the mother of an infected child, and perhaps the father, are likely to be HIV infected as well. This may limit support that is available to the child. In addition, many of the families experiencing HIV infection are likely to be poor, persons of color, with histories of multiple problems, such as intravenous drug use. As a result, many HIV-infected children will be placed in the child welfare system or find themselves cared for by foster parents because their families of origin may be unable or unwilling to care for them. The disease itself is also highly stigmatizing.

Furthermore, many HIV-infected children will have varied developmental and neurological impairments. A positive HIV status, even followed by seroreversion, is highly predictive of subsequent developmental delays and learning disabilities. Physicians will need to screen, monitor, and evaluate any possible impairments in such children. Finally, the disease is characterized by an uncertain medical trajectory. A positive HIV status may revert to HIV-negative status when maternal antibodies are shed. Even then, some studies indicate that later reversion to HIV-positive status is possible, or that symptoms of immunodeficiency may appear even in the absence of positive HIV status. It is also not possible to forecast when symptoms evidencing immunodeficiency are likely to present themselves because this varies widely among HIV-infected children. In addition, survival varies considerably in HIV-infected children. In summary, each disease creates distinct issues not only for medical care but for psychosocial care as well.

THE WORLD OF THE ILL CHILD

Children will respond to life-threatening illnesses in a variety of ways, as do adults and all other human beings. They may deny the illness or react with several other responses including anger, guilt, sadness, regressive and dependent behaviors, mastery and control behaviors, and acting-out and resisting behaviors (Doka, 1993). These responses may be organized in several ways.

Gullo and Plimpton (1985) divided children coping with life-threatening illnesses into six categories, each of which describes a strategic response to the threat of death.

1. *Death acceptors* confront their illness and possible death, accepting its reality and marshaling their resources (in a paraphrase of Saint Francis's prayer) to change and maximize functioning when they can and to accept with some serenity what they cannot change.
2. *Death deniers* cope with illness by denying its reality in the early phase of the illness and its gravity in the later phases. Even in the terminal phase, they may insist that they will survive.
3. *Death submitters* collapse in the face of the menace of life-threatening illness and possible death. Feeling helpless and doomed, they put up no fight.
4. *Death facilitators* cope in ways that often seem counterproductive. They may fail to follow their regimen and treatment, and they engage in risky behaviors that seem to invite death.
5. *Death transcenders* focus on other issues and all but ignore life-threatening illness or possible death. Early in the illness, they may focus on completing essential goals; later in the illness, they concentrate on religious, spiritual, and philosophical concerns.
6. *Death defiers* fiercely fight the illness. Often, these children exhibit much rage and anger.

In addition, both families and ill children may experience considerable distress. One study of children with cystic fibrosis found that 59% of their sample may be characterized as mildly to severely disturbed (Cytryn, Moore, & Robinson, 1973). Similarly, Hobbs, Perrin, and Irays (1985) found higher rates of stress and abuse in families of chronically ill children.

SIBLINGS AND PEERS OF THE ILL CHILD

It is critical to realize that an ill child is not the only individual (child or adult) affected by a life-threatening illness. The lives of siblings and peers are also impacted. Bluebond-Langner (1989, 1991) and others (Adams & Deveau, 1987) have studied the effects of a life-threatening, chronic illness of a child on siblings. Bluebond-Langner described such siblings as living in homes of chronic sorrow. By this, she meant that the homes of these children were characterized by constant sadness and depression. Often, the parents were primarily or exclusively focused on the illness of the sick child. The normal, developmental problems of healthy siblings were often trivialized, and their own plans were made contingent on the health of the ill child. Consequently, siblings in these situations often experienced a deep sense of isolation and disruption, even as they frequently confronted anxieties about their own health.

In addition, when a family has a child with a life-threatening illness, siblings often have to cope with many other emotions. The bond between siblings is unique (see chapter 8); siblings are close kin. There is often a greater sense of equality among siblings than in other close familial but more linear relationships that children may experience, such as those involving grandparents or parents. Siblings are often woven into one's own identity as "big brother" or "kid sister." And siblings often share similar experiences and perceptions. Consequently, the life-threatening illness of a sibling is likely to generate strong responses in his or her brothers or sisters. In her studies of bereaved siblings, Rosen (1986) found especially intense reactions in relationships that were close or distant. However, although siblings may struggle with these problems and conflicted emotions, their own parents may be too absorbed in the crisis to offer significant support.

Caregivers can assist in several ways. First, they can be available to siblings, listening, validating their emotions and concerns, and assisting them as they evaluate their own coping with their sibling's illness. Second, they can sensitize parents to the ongoing needs of the ill child's siblings. When parents are unable to meet these needs, caregivers may be able to suggest alternative strategies or resources (Coleman & Coleman, 1984).

Not only are siblings affected. Friends, peers, and classmates may be struggling with anxiety and feelings. Teachers, counselors, and other school personnel can play a significant role in such circumstances. They can provide opportunities for sharing information, and exploring feelings and concerns. They can assist peers in finding ways to show support, perhaps by sending cards, letters, or videos. They can help to empower the healthy children's parents to be sources of support to the ill child, and his or her parents. And they may be able to provide counseling for students who are affected in particular ways by the crisis experienced by their classmate. This may not only include the ill child's close friends but also those with any significant attachment, even a negative one, as well as children, perhaps even less connected, who seem more vulnerable.

CONCLUSION

Life-threatening illness is a cruel paradox in childhood. Just when a child's potentialities should be expanding, he or she is threatened. Just when a child should be embracing life, he or she is struggling to maintain it, live with a life-threatening condition, or cope with dying. The paradox touches not only the ill child, but also parents, siblings, other children, and adults whose lives in intersect with that child. Caregivers often can do little to resolve that paradox, but they can make it more understandable and perhaps then more bearable.

II

Bereavement

The chapters in this section describe encounters with bereavement during childhood. These encounters involve death-related losses that are most likely to occur during the era of childhood in our society, factors that influence bereavement in childhood, grief reactions that are typical of children, and efforts by children to cope with loss and grief.

In chapter 6, John Baker and Mary Anne Sedney provide an overview of these subjects by exploring children's reactions to loss, their capacity for grief and mourning, distinctive features of children's grief reactions, a brief review of the most important research on childhood bereavement, developmental issues that influence ways in which children react to loss, and family dynamics that might affect a child's bereavement experiences. Perhaps the most distinctive feature of this chapter is the helpful theoretical framework that it offers to differentiate between early, middle, and late tasks in childhood grieving.

After that introduction, chapters 7 to 11 explore five distinct types of bereavement experiences that are most likely to be encountered by children in our society. In chapter 7, Beverly Hatter examines children's responses to the death of a parent. In chapter 8, S. D. Stahlman discusses sibling bereavement during childhood. In chapter 9, Tamina Toray and Kevin Ann Oltjenbruns explore issues related to the death of a friend during childhood. In chapter 10, Carolyn Butler and Laurel Lagoni draw attention to the often-neglected subject of children and pet loss, illustrating the impact of such a loss on children and showing how children can be involved when the death of a pet can be anticipated. Finally, in chapter 11 Kathleen Nader reviews in careful detail the implications of children's exposure to traumatic experiences, whether those experiences occur in the home or in the community, and whether they involve single incident trauma, or multiple and ongoing traumas. This chapter gives special attention to the interaction between trauma and grief, and to special features of interventions that are appropriate for children who have experienced traumatic bereavement.

Each of these discussions is sensitive to the importance of a child's relationship(s) with the deceased person or lost object, ways in which the loss occurred and concurrent circumstances in the child's life, the significant features of the bereavement experiences that follow these various types of death or loss, and the nature of the support that may or may not be available for bereaved children. Each chapter in this part also gives special attention to the specific features of the bereavement experience under consideration and to ways in which interested persons can help children to cope effectively with their losses. In addition, the chapters in this section offer suggestions for future research that can enhance our understanding of these and other bereavement experiences during childhood. The sensitivity displayed by these chapters in their explorations of the many and varied dimensions of bereavement during childhood is grounded in a critical review of empirical research and relevant professional literature as well as the authors' own direct work with grieving children.

6

How Bereaved Children Cope with Loss: An Overview

John E. Baker and Mary Anne Sedney

This chapter provides an overview of children's reactions to bereavement. It does so by exploring the following topics: children's reactions to loss; their capacity for grief and mourning; distinctive features of children's grieving; research on bereaved children; developmental issues; children's reactions to bereavement at different stages of their development; early, middle, and late tasks for bereaved children; and family dynamics.

CHILDREN'S REACTIONS TO LOSS

To understand a child's reactions to bereavement and loss, the first question to ask is: *What* has the child lost? Any child's reactions will depend very much on who the person or significant object that died or was lost was for that child, and what relationship(s) that person or object had to the child (Furman, 1974). Several types of important losses in the lives of children can be distinguished.

One type of loss is *the loss of a personally meaningful relationship.* By definition there must be some personal investment in the relationship or a child will not experience a loss. Children may show little reaction to the death of a distant relative or the death of a schoolmate who was a stranger to them. By contrast, they are likely to react in important ways to the death of a person whose company they enjoyed, who gave something to them materially or emotionally, or with whom they identified in some way. Such an individual could be a parent, a grandparent, a sibling, a close friend, a pet, or some other important figure in the child's life.

A second but overlapping type of loss for children is *the loss of an attachment figure.* An attachment relationship is one type of personal relationship, but it is a particularly intense and all-encompassing relationship. Accordingly, the reaction to the loss of an attachment figure goes beyond that of a personally meaningful relationship. An attachment figure is a person who nurtures a child physically and emotionally, someone who attends to the needs of the child, who serves as a source of protection and security, and who also serves as a figure with whom the child can identify (Bowlby, 1982). Parents usually are significant attachment figures, but grandparents and other regular caretakers can also become attachment figures for a child. It is because parents are attachment figures that the death of a parent must be seen as an especially severe loss for a child, one that will lead to different and more longstanding consequences for the child, and his or her development (Furman, 1984; see chapter 7 in this book).

Secondary losses are a third type of loss that also may overlap with the other types. This category of loss refers to aspects of life that are lost as a result of another loss, that is, losses that are secondary to or dependent on the primary loss of a parent or other important individual or object. Secondary losses include all the ways in which life changes after a death, such as moving to a new home, changing to a new school, changes in the routine of mealtimes and child care, and so forth. Although these are referred to as "secondary losses," they are not insignificant or unimportant. On the contrary, these changes are experienced as powerful losses by a child, and they are an additional source of stress that strongly affects children's reactions after a death.

A child's reaction to loss will depend, therefore, on which of these aspects of loss are present—the loss of a relationship, an attachment figure, or other important aspects of life.

CHILDREN'S CAPACITY FOR GRIEF AND MOURNING

A great deal has been written, especially in the psychoanalytic literature, on the topic of the child's "capacity to mourn" (Miller, 1971). The central question is whether children have the inner capacity to acknowledge the loss of a significant relationship and to cope with it effectively, or whether, instead, they need to deny the loss and replace it with internal fantasies that compensate for the loss they cannot admit or acknowledge.

Wolfenstein (1966) argued that children are unable to mourn a loss until they have gone through a period of "trial mourning" in adolescence, a process that is a normal aspect of adolescent development. Before adolescence, Wolfenstein maintained that children lack the "ego strength" that is needed to tolerate the sadness and despair that is a normal part of mourning, and that is required to give up voluntarily their internal attachment to the person they loved and needed.

A contrasting viewpoint is put forth by Robert Furman (1964a) and Erna Furman (1974). In the Furmans' view, children are able to mourn the death of a parent, but they need specific types of emotional support from adults to do so. That is, bereaved children need help in understanding why the person died, together with extra affection, reassurance, and comforting to tolerate the painful feelings of loss. With this kind of adult assistance, however, the Furmans maintained that children can, indeed, mourn the death of a loved one.

Bowlby (1980) identified important environmental factors that affect a child's ability to cope effectively with a death. He pointed out that children often are not given accurate information about the death, so they lack the information they need to grieve appropriately. In addition, children are especially dependent on the support of family members after a death. If this support is not available, they usually have nowhere else to turn. By contrast, adults can seek out information about a death on their own, and they also typically have a larger network of individuals to whom they can turn for support. These are aspects of children's psychosocial environment that affect their grief reactions and do not stem from their own developmental limitations as children.

Bowlby (1980) went on to identify four factors that facilitate a child's ability to mourn. In his view, children will be able to mourn if they (a) have a secure relationship to their parents before the death, (b) receive prompt and accurate information about the death, (c) are allowed to participate in the social rituals that follow the death, and (d) have the comforting presence of a parent or a parent-substitute in the days and months after the death.

WHAT IS DISTINCTIVE ABOUT CHILDREN'S GRIEF REACTIONS?

Rather than debating whether or not children can mourn, however, it is more useful to identify ways in which children's grief reactions are distinctive, and thus different from the reactions seen in adults. There are several ways in which children's grief reactions are distinctive.

First, children's grief reactions appear to be longer in duration than those of adults. Children's reactions often appear to be less intense during the period just after the death, but they tend to "work" on their psychological tasks of grieving in a gradual way. This tends to extend the process of grieving and mourning over a longer period for children than is usually found in adults.

Second, children need consistently available adult parenting figures to process a loss and tolerate the painful feelings that the loss stirs up in them (Furman, 1974).

Third, children under 11 years of age have more limited cognitive means with which to understand the nature of the person's death and the implications of the death.

Fourth, children have different ways of coping with loss than those usually found in adults. For example, children are more likely to distract themselves, cling to familiar activities or routines for comfort, deny the loss for periods, and use fantasy to cope with the suddenness of the loss (Sekaer, 1987).

Fifth, when a child's parent has died, the child's grief reactions will be affected by his or her strong developmental need to identify with the parent who has died. This need to identify with attributes of the deceased parent generally causes a child to hold onto those attributes in a way that is seen less often in adult mourning, because adults are more likely to separate or detach themselves from the characteristics of the person who died.

Sixth, a child's identity is more deeply affected by a loss in childhood because self-development is still in process.

Seventh, the processes of grieving and mourning become intertwined with developmental processes in children, such that it can be difficult to determine when grieving ends and normal development resumes.

RESEARCH ON BEREAVED CHILDREN

Although much has been learned about bereavement from clinical observations, there have been relatively few systematic research studies of bereaved children. Clinical samples have been described by writers, such as Arthur and Kemme (1964) and Furman (1974). However, these groups might not be representative of the general population of bereaved children, many of whom are not referred for psychotherapy or psychoanalysis.

Van Eerdewegh, Bieri, Parrilla, and Clayton (1982) reported on a study of 105 children drawn from a community sample of bereaved parents. They used a structured interview to question bereaved parents about their children's behaviors, symptoms, and adjustment. Results indicated that bereaved children displayed more sadness, more signs of mild depression, and a significant impairment in their school performance, when compared with nonbereaved children from an unselected community sample. There was not a high degree of behavior problems in the bereaved children, but they did show more bed-wetting and more temper tantrums than controls. There was no greater incidence of severe depression in the bereaved children, however. The authors concluded from their data that most children showed an immediate reaction to parental loss that was usually mild and short-lived.

In a later analysis of the same data, Van Eerdewegh, Clayton, and Van Eerdewegh (1985) looked at age and gender differences in their sample. They found that younger children (12 years of age and younger) displayed more bed-wetting, loss of interest in activities, and temper tantrums than older children, whereas the older children showed more sleep disturbance. Gender differences were also observed, in that bereaved girls showed a higher incidence of mild depression, more bed-wetting, and more sleep problems than boys.

Elizur and Kaffman (1982) conducted a study of a group of 25 Israeli children whose fathers were killed in wartime. Though their sample was smaller, they were able to follow these children over a longer period, extending to $3\frac{1}{2}$ years after the death of the father. These investigators found high rates of emotional and behavioral problems in bereaved children, according to parent report. For example, crying spells were common in most children (86%) when they were rated 6 months after the parent's death; by the 42-month point, these had decreased but were still observed in almost one half of the children (43%).

The most common behavioral problems reported by Elizur and Kaffman (1982) were overdependence on the surviving parent, separation difficulties, negative and defiant behavior, and restlessness, which were observed in roughly one half of the children at 6 months. Although these behaviors had decreased somewhat 3 years later, they were still common. The authors concluded that more than two thirds of the children reacted with severe psychological problems and impairment in functioning at some point during the study period. It should be noted that these authors did not use a control group, so it is not possible to estimate how elevated these levels of behavioral problems are compared with normal samples of children.

Weller, Weller, Fristad, and Bowes (1991) studied 38 bereaved children (5 to 12 years of age) to measure the frequency of depressive symptoms. Unlike earlier studies, they used child as well as parent interviews to get information about symptoms and emotions. Children were interviewed within 12 weeks of the death of the parent, so it was their initial grief reactions that were being measured in this study. The authors found that, according to *Diagnostic and Statistic Manual* (3rd ed., rev.) (DSM III-R) criteria, 37% of the children were experiencing a major depressive episode at the time of the interview. This is a much higher percentage than was found in the large, community study noted earlier (Van Eerdewegh et al., 1982) and indicates much greater cause for concern about the emotional status of bereaved children.

The authors of the more recent study (Weller et al., 1991) also found significant differences between parent and child reports of depressive symptoms. Although only 8% of the children were rated as depressed by their parent, 26% of the children's own self-reports indicated depression, and 37% of the children were rated as depressed by *either* parent or child report. Thus, the use of self-report data from the children was crucial to identifying depressive symptoms in these children.

Silverman and Worden (1992a) studied 125 children who were examined 4 months after the death of one of their parents. Using a different set of instruments than those employed in earlier studies, Silverman and Worden found a lesser degree of disturbance in these children than had been reported previously (by Weller et al., 1991). Silverman and Worden (1992a) used a self-report depression scale for the children, and a behavioral checklist for the parent report, in addition to scores from child and parent interviews. In this sample of children 6 to 17 years of age, they found that 38% reported crying frequently, 30% had difficulty sleeping, and 19% reported having difficulty concentrating in school. Psychosomatic symptoms were common in these children including 74% who reported having had frequent headaches since the death. Overall, Silverman and Worden identified 21 children (17% of their sample) who appeared especially distressed, based on overall elevations in the frequency of problem behaviors. This is much lower than the 37% of children that appeared depressed in the earlier study (Weller et al., 1991), although the figures are not strictly comparable.

Silverman and Worden (1992a) also reported some interesting data about the children's attempts to maintain an emotional connection with the parent who had died, which they developed in a later article (Silverman, Nickman, & Worden, 1992). According to the children's self-report, 57% of the children would "speak" to the deceased parent in some way, 55% dreamed of the parent who had died, and 81% felt the parent was watching them. The authors concluded that children's attachment to thoughts and memories of a dead parent may be a sign of positive adaptation rather than a sign of pathology. Despite the children's frequent thoughts about the parent however, only one half (54%) of the children said that they talked to one of their friends about the deceased parent. This indicates that these children tended to be fairly protective of themselves and their emotions when they were with other children.

In short, the research to date provides a provocative but incomplete picture of children's bereavement reactions. Many issues remain to be investigated including developmental differences in children's bereavement reactions.

DEVELOPMENTAL ISSUES

The age and developmental status of a child will strongly influence the ways in which that child reacts to a loss. Most of the literature on children and death has focused on the cognitive development of children and how their intellectual understanding of the facts of death affects their reactions. However, there are other aspects of development that also are important. Besides cognitive understanding, a child's degree of separation-individuation, along with the developmental maturity of the child's ego defenses and ego functions, will influence his or her psychological reactions to bereavement.

Developmental changes in children's concepts of death have been studied by Nagy (1948) and Koocher (1974); more recent reviews of this area have been provided by Lonetto (1980), Wass (1984a), and Kastenbaum (1992). Also see important work by Speece and Brent (1984; and chapter 2 in this book). Children's concepts have been characterized according to three primary developmental periods: preschool children, school-age or latency children, and preadolescents and adolescents.

Until approximately 6 or 7 years of age, it is thought that children are typically unable to comprehend the finality and irreversibility of death. Adults are often surprised that children of this age seemingly "forget" that they were told the dead person would not ever be coming back. Even after being given a full and age-appropriate explanation of death, these children will still ask at some future date, "So when is Daddy coming back?" At best, children of this age are able to hold in their memories the words and concepts they were told by adults, which act in conflict with their more natural concepts and beliefs—that people they love cannot simply cease to exist.

Between approximately 6 and 9 years of age, most children appear to have acquired a concept of the irreversibility of death, even though they may harbor unrealistic fantasies about the dead person's return. Against this, these children are usually still not convinced that death is a universal and inevitable event. Children's thoughts at this age revolve around different ways in which death can be avoided, ways that may be realistic at times or that may also be superstitious and fantastic. Although they may be able to verbalize the concept that all people die sooner or later, they focus on ways in which they themselves could delay, forestall, or prevent the occurrence of death.

After about 10 years of age, however, children come to understand that death is universal and inevitable as well as irreversible. As Kastenbaum (1992, p. 105) stated, children come to the realization that "there is no escape, no matter how clever or fast we are." Although adolescents may become preoccupied with different aspects of death as they continue to mature emotionally (Gordon, 1986; Noppe & Noppe, 1991), their conceptual understanding remains equivalent to that found in most adults.

In addition, Koocher (1973) has demonstrated that each child's individual level of cognitive development is a more important influence on the child's death-related concepts than his or her chronological age alone.

There are other important facets of child development that affect a child's reactions to death. A second facet is the degree to which the child has developed a separate, well-individuated sense of self. Although the classic separation-individuation process occurs within the first 3 years of life (Mahler, Pine, & Bergmann, 1975), psychological individuation continues throughout the remainder of childhood and adolescence. Younger children experience themselves as less differentiated from their parents, and are strongly dependent on parents for emotional support and reassurance. Older children have achieved a greater degree of independence, and feel more able to take care of and protect themselves from outside dangers. They are less likely to turn to parents for support, but more likely to feel safe in their own ability to protect themselves from death-related fears and fantasies.

A third aspect of child development has to do with the types of psychological defensive and coping strategies that are used at different phases of psychological development. Younger children tend to use more primitive defenses, such as denial and projection, which distort their perceptions of reality to a significant degree. School-age children and adolescents are more likely to use defenses, such as intellectualization and isolation of affect; these defenses allow older children to split their emotions off from their thoughts and repress the more unpleasant affects. Adolescents may be able to use more mature defenses, such as suppression and sublimation, that are often seen in healthy adults as well. Vaillant (1977) provided a helpful review of defense mechanisms and their developmental aspects.

BEREAVEMENT REACTIONS AT DIFFERENT STAGES OF DEVELOPMENT

Most of the information we have on age differences in children's bereavement reactions comes from clinical observations. There have been some findings from research studies of bereaved children (Elizur & Kaffman, 1982; Van Eerdewegh et al., 1982), but no systematic studies of developmental differences in grief responses have yet been carried out. Raphael (1983) and Wass (1984b) have provided the most comprehensive discussions of age differences in grief reactions.

Preschool children up to 5 years of age most often show manifestations of anxiety or of aggressive behavior. Separation anxiety is usually prominent, with the child clinging and protesting whenever he or she must separate from the parent. Sleep disturbances, such as nightmares and night terrors, are also common in preschool children. Anxieties are heightened by the tendency of young children to see death as a result of aggression or murder, and, therefore, to feel especially vulnerable to attack after a death.

Temper tantrums and other aggressive behavior are also frequently seen in young bereaved children. Children may become "wild" and uncontrolled in their play, requiring frequent calming or limit setting by an adult. Temper tantrums may occur at any time when a child is frustrated or feels disappointed about not getting something that he or she wanted. Temper tantrums are often seen at times of separation, however, so that clinging and tantrums can both occur at the same time.

Regression in behavior and in bodily functions is also commonly seen in young bereaved children. Periodic loss of bowel and bladder control may reflect a wish to regress to a younger age, and "babyish" behavior can also be observed in these children. Regressive behavior is often an attempt to elicit more comfort and protection from parents or caregivers, which can calm some of the deep anxieties that are felt by these children.

School-age children between 6 and 10 years of age may appear to deny that a death has occurred, and maintain an appearance of emotional control and life going on as usual (Raphael, 1983). This does not necessarily mean that a child has denied the fact that someone died, although he or she may deny the emotional significance of the death.

The control shown by children of this age appears to reflect their attempts to appear grown-up to others; fear of feeling helpless and vulnerable; and wish to appear normal in the eyes of their peers, who may perceive them as being different or defective as a result of the death. The need to inhibit normal expressions of sadness and fear can be strong in children of this age and older. Genuine expressions of emotion are only seen occasionally and only when the child is feeling especially safe and protected, usually with a parent figure.

Assuming the role of a caretaker is another pattern that starts to appear in this age group. This involves inhibiting a child's personal emotions and concentrating on helping others—usually younger siblings, although this can include the surviving parent as well. As Raphael (1983) has noted, by this age children have a more realistic notion of death and are aware that the surviving parent could also die and leave them alone. This can lead to an attentive and solicitous attitude toward the surviving parent.

Excessive guilt is also a common feature of children's responses in this age range. With the development of a more mature conscience during the Oedipal years of ages 4 to 6, school-age children may harbor thoughts and fantasies of things they could have done to help or even save the life of the person who died. Becoming preoccupied with personal failings and possible mistakes also reflects the increased intellectual range of children at this age.

Phobic and hypochondriacal behavior may also be seen in older children in this age group. A greater awareness and understanding of bodily functioning can lead to fears that every new or unpleasant sensation in the body could be a sign of a potentially fatal illness.

Adolescents, and to some extent preadolescents, show some of the same trends described earlier, along with some new patterns of response as well (Corr & Balk, 1996). Emotional reactions are often kept private at this age, in an attempt to appear normal, especially to peers. Although school-age children may confide in their parents at special times of comfort, adolescents are less likely to seek out such moments or to accept an offer of condolence when it is given. The influence of the peer group is especially important from the preadolescent years onward. The strong psychological need to "fit in," and not to be "different" or abnormal in any way, leads bereaved adolescents to be especially cautious about everything they say or do when they are feeling vulnerable.

Adolescents are more likely than younger children either to become depressed and withdrawn after a death, or to try to escape from their emotions through acting-out behavior. A depressed adolescent may control the outward signs of despair out of fear of worrying others, yet feel lonely and abandoned internally. There may also be a withdrawal from customary activities, however, or from well-established friendships that are now avoided by the adolescent.

Acting-out behavior, such as running away, delinquent behavior, promiscuity, excessive drug use, and risk taking of various kinds, can be attempts on the part of adolescents to escape from feelings of sadness and vulnerability. Taking risks with drugs or with reckless driving can induce feelings of power and grandiosity, which offset feelings of depression and abandonment.

An intellectual struggle over the meaning and implication of death is also seen in some adolescents (Fleming & Adolph, 1986). Being preoccupied with the "unfairness" of death, or making judgments about the appropriateness of how other people react to the death, are ways for adolescents to exert intellectual control over an emotionally uncontrollable event. Similarly, a guilty preoccupation with one's own mistakes, such as having been insensitive to the needs or feelings of the person who died, can serve a similar function for bereaved adolescents.

Finally, some adolescents attempt to arrest or inhibit their normal feelings of grief and sadness, and take on a caregiver role in their family after a death. This role brings them immediate gratification in the form of appreciation from others for their helpfulness and also serves to deny their inner feelings about the loss. It may also reflect an awareness, which may be more or less accurate, that their family system cannot offer them support at the moment, and that they are helping the family by denying their own needs and putting others ahead of themselves.

PSYCHOLOGICAL TASKS FOR BEREAVED CHILDREN

Psychological coping with or accommodation to loss is a process that occurs over time, as the bereaved person gradually comes to accept the loss. In the past, this process has often been described in terms of a set series of stages or phases (Bowlby, 1980). Currently, it is more commonly conceptualized as a series of tasks to carry out over time (Baker, Sedney, & Gross, 1992; Fox, 1985; Furman, 1984; Worden, 1991).

A task-based model focuses in a positive way on what the bereaved must do, emotionally, cognitively, and behaviorally to cope with the loss and move on (Corr & Doka, 1994). Task-based models are usually sequential, with each task building on earlier tasks. Although time is important to mourning, a simple passage of time is not sufficient to grieve successfully. Only by accomplishing these tasks can mourning proceed in constructive ways.

Furman's (1984) model is representative of task-based models. Working from within a framework of seeing children in a clinical setting, Furman conceptualized the first task for bereaved children as understanding and coming to terms with the reality of the death, the second task as mourning, and the third task as resuming and continuing with life. Fox's (1985) work was in a community intervention program for children and she conceptualized the tasks more broadly: (a) understanding, (b) grieving, (c) commemorating, and (d) going on with living and loving. Within her second task (grieving), Fox incorporated the four tasks described by Worden (1991) on the basis of his work with adults: (a) accepting the reality of the loss, (b) working through to the pain of grief, (c) adjusting to an environment in which the person who has died is missing, and (d) emotionally relocating the deceased and moving on with life.

Building on these earlier models as well as a recognition of developmental differences between children's and adults' grieving, Baker, Sedney, and Gross (1992) developed a model that was more detailed than its predecessors and that focused specifically on children. According to this model, psychological tasks that children face in mourning the loss of a loved one can be separated into early tasks, middle-phase tasks, and late tasks.

Early Tasks

Children cannot begin to grieve until they know that someone has died and feel that they themselves are safe. Thus, the initial tasks facing bereaved children involve (a) *understanding* that someone has died and the implications of this fact; and (b) *self-protection* of themselves, their bodies, and their families.

Understanding.   Children's understanding of death progresses from thinking of it only in concrete terms to understanding it abstractly as part of an inevitable and permanent process (Nagy, 1948; Speece & Brent, 1984). Children's associated emotional needs to deny the reality of death frequently coincide with adults' needs to protect their children from the pain of acknowledging its finality.

Well-meaning relatives' descriptions of death as "she's in heaven now" or "he's watching you from heaven now" also reinforce young children's tendency to think of death as a mere change in place of residence. To many children, this means that the deceased person could return from heaven if she or he desired to do so. Children may also worry about the misdeeds that a dead parent may be observing from heaven, or just fervently hope for a quick visit on a special occasion.

In light of children's tendency to misunderstand death, it is particularly important that they be given accurate information in terms they can understand. Ideally, they will have received this information about death in general before they are faced with the specific death of someone close to them. This general information can be a base on which to build in explaining a particular death. Despite many adults' tendency to emphasize the spiritual ("she's happy in heaven now") over the physical ("his body stopped working") aspects of death, children need to know about the physical aspects of death to understand their loss.

When children are bereaved, their cognitive needs go beyond understanding what death is in general to understanding the details of this particular death. In age-appropriate terms, they need to know "the story" of this death (Sedney, Baker, & Gross, 1994): how the person died, why he or she died, and when the death occurred. One girl was seen in therapy when she was 6 years old, 3 years after her teenage brother was shot to death. She was unable to concentrate in school, remaining preoccupied with him and images of things mysteriously going "up." When asked about her brother, she spoke vehemently: "I don't know *how* he died, or *when* he died, or *why* he died!" She could not begin to grieve the loss, for her family had protected her from knowing the basic details of his tragic death. Without this information, she had not yet accomplished the earliest task in her grieving.

Self-Protection. Grieving involves taking emotional risks for children and adults; the grieving person is immersed in raw and painful emotions. This risk taking is only possible once the person feels safe, secure, and protected. Thus, a second early task is self-protection of the child's body, psyche, and family.

Issues of protection are particularly important for children when it is a parent who died, or when a death occurred under traumatic or violent circumstances. Faced with the death of a parent, one of a child's first concerns is, "Who will take care of me now?" This concern is real and needs to be addressed in concrete terms including where the child will live, who will provide meals, who will care for the child when he or she is ill, and so forth. The child's need to feel safe and secure often contrasts with the disruptions in family functioning that can accompany the death of a central family member. These disruptions can delay the child's readiness to move on to middle-phase tasks.

When a death occurred under traumatic or violent circumstances, it is more difficult for a surviving child to feel safe. Because of self-protective concerns, trauma takes precedence and, until the trauma is resolved, the child will be unable to work on other tasks of grieving. The child's fears after a loss may be based in fantasy or reality. In either case, these fears must be addressed before grieving can continue. Addressing the fears will require parental reassurance but may also require psychotherapy in some cases. In extreme cases, such as war or frequent violence, progress in grieving is limited until physical and psychological security can be reestablished.

The issues of protection that concern a child include emotional safety. Needs for emotional safety may be evidenced by children's avoidance of reminders of the death, unwillingness to talk about it, or even denial. Because children's emotional safety frequently is based in the well-being of their parents, they may address self-protective tasks by taking care of their bereaved parents or a surviving parent. One 7-year-old boy whose little sister died moved into a new caretaker role with his mother, helping her up the stairs when necessary and gently comforting her. A 7-year-old girl whose little brother died turned into a near-constant performer and jokester in an attempt to rouse her mother from her grief into a brief smile.

Middle-Phase Tasks

Once children truly understand their loss and feel reasonably safe and secure, they are ready to face the difficult middle-phase tasks associated with mourning their loss. These middle-phase tasks are (a) emotional acceptance of the loss, (b) reevaluating the relationship to the deceased, and (c) bearing the emotional pain that accompanies this loss.

Emotional Acceptance. The first of these tasks, emotional acceptance of the loss, requires a child to move beyond an intellectual understanding that the person is dead, to a deeper *emotional* realization of all that is lost. When children can let go of some of their self-protective defenses, they can allow themselves to react emotionally to the death and to think through all of the implications of the person's death: that they will never see the person again, will never share the pleasures or the comfort of the person's presence, and that their life has been changed unalterably and can never be the same as it was before. This is the full acknowledgment that the person has been irretrievably lost and cannot be replaced.

Reevaluation of the Relationship.   Central to middle-phase tasks is a focus on the relationship with the deceased. Emphasis on the relationship is necessary for the child to come to grips with what has been lost. In the course of this middle-phase task, a child will review a range of memories of the relationship, both positive and negative. Any unresolved emotional issues concerning the deceased are likely to surface at this time.

Reevaluating the relationship is sure to evoke ambivalent feelings. At the very least, this beloved person died and abandoned the child. At the same time, there is often a tendency to idealize the deceased, erasing memories of any negative qualities or interactions. To the extent that children have a limited capacity for tolerating ambivalent feelings, they may have trouble reevaluating the relationship. The fact that one can have both loving and angry or hateful feelings toward someone who is now dead can be difficult for children, especially younger children, to accept.

Some children work through some of the relationship issues with transitional objects and imaginary parents or friends. Such behavioral methods are particularly useful for young children who are more likely to play out than talk about their concerns. One girl wanted to take a piece of her birthday cake to the cemetery for her dead brother. Another little boy had an imaginary friend with the same name as his dead brother and took toys to the cemetery so he could play with the dead brother. One could interpret these behaviors in pathological terms, suggesting that these children were denying the reality of their losses. An alternative interpretation (which we prefer) is that these are ways these children found to remain connected with their deceased siblings and to process the death in a developmentally appropriate way.

The centrality of memories and connections in this view of the grief process stands in contrast with the traditional psychoanalytic view that mourning is about detachment from the lost object (Freud, 1974). In her study of bereaved preschool children, Furman (1974) emphasized the importance of loosening ties with the deceased. Yet in studying a community sample, Silverman and Worden (1992a) found that bereaved children commonly engaged in a variety of behaviors that allowed them to feel connected with their dead parent in an adaptive way (Silverman, Nickman, & Worden, 1992).

Bearing the Pain.   There is no escaping the fact that a central task of grieving is simply to bear the pain—not to avoid it, not to deny it, but to feel it. Supports are critical, but, ultimately, the bereaved child has to be able to tolerate painful feelings. Children usually approach this difficult task slowly, tentatively, and intermittently. As noted earlier, their immature defenses are not strong enough to allow them to cope with sustained emotional pain. So, they experience the pain in small, bearable doses. The result is a more prolonged mourning process than one might witness in an adult. To an observer, a bereaved child may appear deeply distressed for a time and then, later the same day, deeply involved in normal play activities as if nothing is wrong.

Late Tasks

For children, grieving processes gradually merge into developmental processes, as they move on, forever changed by the loss. Once middle-phase tasks have been accomplished, so that the reality of the loss is fully acknowledged and conflictual feelings toward the deceased have been experienced and resolved, the child integrates these experiences into his or her emerging identity and network of relationships.

There are five tasks during the late phase. The child needs to (a) form a new sense of personal identity which incorporates the experience of the loss and some identifications with the deceased person, but is not limited to them; (b) invest in new emotional relationships without an excessive fear of loss and without a constant need to compare the new person to the dead person; (c) consolidate and maintain a durable internal relationship to the dead person that will survive over time; (d) return wholeheartedly to age-appropriate developmental tasks and activities; and (e) cope with the periodic resurgence of pain that often occurs at points of developmental transition or on specific "anniversaries."

Forming a New Sense of Personal Identity.   The normally difficult task of identity development is complicated by bereavement, particularly when the person who died is a parent or sibling. As development proceeds, bereaved children may be handicapped in their choices of identifications. Some children may channel their loyalty or guilt into an overly close identification with the person who died, so that they seem to be picking up the other person's interrupted life course. For example, the previously disinterested athlete may strive to carry on the athletic legacy of a sibling who died, or the "good kid" of an alcoholic parent may begin to drink heavily after the parent's death. Other children may choose a counteridentification, designed to avoid any similarity to the one who died; families can play an important role in helping to create and maintain these counteridentifications. For example, a young boy developed behavior problems in school after his younger sister, described by him and his parents as an "angel," died.

Investing in New Relationships. Children may avoid new relationships for fear of suffering another loss or because issues with the deceased remain unresolved. Alternatively, a child may appear to try new relationships, but they fail because the new person cannot live up to the idealized image of the dead person. These new relationships need to be entered into freely, with only minor distortions from the past.

Because children are likely to take a long time to work through early and middle-phase tasks, they may not be ready for new relationships as soon as their parents are. It may be that the child did not feel safe enough to move into the middle-phase tasks while the parent was immersed in grief; however, as the parent begins to feel good enough to resume life, the child will begin to feel safe enough to begin to mourn. Thus, a child's parent may be ready to remarry after the death of a spouse or to have another baby after the death of a child, long before his or her surviving child is ready to accept these new relationships. The tension accompanying these generational mismatches in timing can be considerable.

Constructing a Durable Internal Relationship. As discussed earlier, the result of grief need not be an emotional detachment but, rather, can be a new kind of attachment. Ideally, a child will be able to find a way to remember the person who died, forming a new relationship with that individual that recognizes his or her absence while incorporating some part of the deceased person into the network of inner relationships that forms the self. For many children, the beloved becomes a new kind of inner presence that sustains and comforts them, even while they are able to develop new relationships with other people.

Returning to Developmental Tasks. In childhood, mourning processes become intertwined with developmental processes, so that it is difficult to determine where one begins and the other leaves off. Some of the tasks of grieving, such as forming a new sense of personal identity, incorporate normal developmental tasks, in this case identity formation. Profound loss interrupts development, and it is only after addressing the aforementioned tasks of grieving that children can return to their age-appropriate developmental tasks. However, even after completing the tasks of grieving, a child will face the remaining developmental tasks as a changed person, typically within a changed family context.

Coping with Periodic Resurgence of Pain.   There is no real end point of grief, because there will always be events, dates, situations, and people that can reevoke memories and their attendant pain. Anniversary reactions (Plotkin, 1983) are resurgences of grief around the anniversary of the death or at other times of year (e.g., holidays, birthdays, Mother's or Father's Day, etc.) that evoke memories of the deceased. Children, especially those who have had a parent die, are also vulnerable to a type of anniversary reaction evoked by developmental transitions throughout life. Normal joyful transitions, such as graduation, marriage, or birth of a child, can become sad occasions years after a death, as a "child" mourns the absence of the parent who would have celebrated them. For example, a 16-year-old girl, whose father died 4 years previously, wept when she won a scholarship award; she knew he would have been proud of her. As she wept, this girl said, "for my whole life my father will never be with me again."

Although these resurgences of painful affect in an otherwise well-functioning person are difficult, they can also be considered as opportunities to reexperience the loss with new developmental capabilities. For example, the 16-year-old girl mentioned previously was recognizing, in a way she could not have done before, the profundity and permanence of her loss. Similarly, a young woman who remourns her own deceased mother when her first child is born may be stimulated to find ways to know her mother as another adult who bore and raised children; she now has the opportunity to explore her relationship with her own mother from a vantage point she could not have had previously.

FAMILY DYNAMICS

A child's psyche is affected not only by the loss of an important love object but also by any other changes that may be occurring in the family after a death. It is often difficult to tease out a child's reactions to loss from reactions to the changed family situation. Therefore, in this section, we expand on the types of changes that are often seen in families after the death of a family member and how these changes might affect a child, in turn (Walsh & McGoldrick, 1991b).

The family system is deeply affected when a member of the immediate family dies. First, family life often changes dramatically after a death. If a parent has died, surviving children often need to adjust to a different financial situation, and the family may need to move to a new house. To the children, this means losing the house or apartment they have grown attached to, and losing some of the small luxuries and special outings they came to expect when the parent was alive. If a primary caretaker goes back to work after the death of a parent or sibling, a child loses his or her sense of family routine as well as some of the attention he or she may have received before the death. These changes in family life will often be experienced by a child as major losses in their own right; inevitably, these secondary losses will compound the child's emotional reactions to the loss of a love object.

Communication patterns within the family also can be seriously disrupted after the death of a family member (Silverman & Silverman, 1979). Each person may be trying to contain his or her personal emotional reactions to the loss and will often restrain expressions of emotion. The effect is to reduce the amount of emotional communication in the family, even though the child may observe isolated expressions of emotion at times, such as a parent's crying or an unexpected period of anger or irritability.

A child's responses are strongly affected by the information he or she is given about the death. However, family members often avoid any mention of the person who died or the circumstances of the death. This can be puzzling to the child, who may want to talk about the death but feels an unspoken prohibition against such conversation. It also strengthens the effect of the child's own personalized interpretations of the events surrounding the person's death, which may be inaccurate but cannot be corrected by accurate information from outside sources (Baker, Sedney, & Gross, 1992).

Parents often tend to become strongly protective of their children after another family member has died, whether it is a parental death or the death of a sibling. Certainly a death increases the anxieties of all family members, parents and children alike, and surviving parents often react to their fears of loss by redoubling their efforts to watch and protect their children. In the short term, this can be reassuring to the children, who feel protected and cared for during a time of great anxiety. Over the long term, however, parental overprotectiveness can reinforce a child's anxiety by giving special attention to any potential threats or fears in the child's life.

Overprotective parental behavior can also give the unconscious message that the surviving children are, indeed, unsafe and need to be carefully watched if they are to remain safe. Also, in the long term, overprotectiveness discourages the normal development of independence and self-sufficiency, which are crucial to a healthy adolescent developmental experience (Baker, in press). Thus, an untimely loss in a family can interfere with normal family developmental tasks, such as supporting children in their eventual emancipation from the family.

Another frequent change in bereaved families is that parents find it much more difficult to be firm in setting limits on their children's behavior. Partly, they are exhausted by their own personal feelings of grief and lack the energy to be as firm and consistent as they were before the death. However, parents may also sympathize with their children's loss and feel that any harshness or punishment would place too much of a burden on them. Although children may enjoy this newfound lenience at first, the absence of parental control can itself be anxiety provoking (Baker, in press). Behavioral problems may reflect a child's anxiety about no one being in control and can serve as a plea to the parents to reassert a normal degree of control over their children's behavior.

Surviving children will also be affected by other changes in a parent's behavior after a loss. When a parent becomes depressed or emotionally disabled, this has definite effects on his or her children. Parents often become emotionally unavailable for periods because of their own feelings of grief. Children quickly notice their unavailability, and often feel sad and lonely as a result. If parents are at times emotionally irritable or unpredictable, this will increase children's feelings of anxiety as well because they will feel unable to predict their parents' desires or reactions. Parental depression can also lead children to behave in an "exemplary" manner to "take care" of their parents by putting less of a burden on them. In contrast, some children behave in aggressive or intrusive ways which are designed to stir the parents out of their withdrawal and reengage them with the child.

Another important point is that the death of a family member leads to an imbalance in the interlocking family role relationships that existed before the death (Walsh & McGoldrick, 1991b). Each family must cope with this imbalance in some way, trying to restore the previous balance either by replacing the figure in some way or rearranging the role relationships in a new way. When a child in a family dies, another child may jump at the opportunity to fill the deceased child's role and reap the benefits that are imagined to come from attaining that role. Parents, too, may encourage another child to "replace" a lost child, but this is ultimately an impossible arrangement that will founder on the child's own individual needs, which are unlike those of the deceased child (Cain & Cain, 1964).

When a parent has died, the surviving parent will necessarily struggle to fill the roles of both mother and father, which is an extremely difficult and taxing task. A child may also be encouraged to fulfill a parental role, such as a preadolescent boy taking on many of the duties of his deceased father after his death. Although this can be gratifying at first as the child feels important taking on that role, sooner or later it will interfere with the child's own needs to develop as an individual, build healthy peer relationships, and separate from the family. These family pressures can have an enormous impact on a child after a death in the family because the child must choose between being loyal to his or her parents or becoming separate.

CONCLUSION

In this chapter we have reviewed several issues that are pertinent to children's reactions to bereavement. In particular, we have discussed the question of children's capacity to grieve, developmental differences and distinctive features in children's grief reactions, psychological tasks for bereaved children, and family dynamics in bereaved families.

One question that remains is how damaging bereavement is for a child. Even if children are capable of grieving in an age-appropriate way, do they emerge from grief intact and whole, or are they irreparably damaged by the loss? The answer will depend on who the person is that died and on how the loss occurred. In terms of parental death, some researchers describe children's grief reactions as moderate and time limited, whereas others find problematic long-term effects lasting several years at least. Clearly, there is room for additional research in this area, both on this particular topic and other topics, such as developmental changes in children's grief reactions. In any case, we can conclude that children are exceedingly *vulnerable* after a death, and that they require special attention, support, and education to help them cope successfully with loss.

7

Children and the Death of a Parent or Grandparent

Beverly S. Hatter

> Childhood is the kingdom where nobody dies.
> —Edna St. Vincent Millay, *Collected Poems* (1956, p. 286)

Until recently, it was difficult, if not almost impossible, in the United States to publish a storybook for children that tells the story of a child whose mother or father has died. Publishers typically rejected such a terrifying theme (two exceptions are Cleaver & Cleaver, 1970; Whitehead, 1971). Today, although there are a few excellent books available for children with realistic yet hopeful themes about survival in the face of parental loss (Blume, 1981; Krementz, 1981; Little, 1984; Powell, 1990; Rylant, 1992), the impact of the death of a parent on children remains a topic worthy of further examination—for adults and children.

What has been and continues to be our resistance to helping children explore the death of a parent when 1.5 million children in the United States live in a single-parent family because of death (U.S. Bureau of the Census, 1993)? The enormity of the loss that a child experiences when a parent dies, both in the sense of present, day-to-day losses and potentially compounding future losses, often fills us, as adults with dread. How do we assist children to integrate the primary and secondary losses that are associated with parental death? How do we help them learn to go on with healthy living and loving?

This chapter examines the impact of parental death on children. It considers four major variables that influence that experience, unique aspects of this type of childhood bereavement, and typical responses of children when a parent dies. Attention is also given to the death of a grandparent or other parental figure in a child's life.

IMPACT OF THE DEATH OF A PARENT: RISKS AND COMPLEXITIES

> Sorrow makes us all children again.
> —Ralph Waldo Emerson (1970, p. 165)

We know that with each new loss that occurs, there can be a reawakening of past losses. Perhaps bereaved children awaken in adults the specter of their own childhood losses. Beyond our own fears and assumptions, there are several existing studies (Berlinsky & Biller, 1982; Furman, 1974; Silverman & Worden, 1992a) that explore the risks faced by children experiencing parent death.

What are the risks socially, psychologically, intellectually, behaviorally, and physically for children who experience the death of a parent? Are children at risk for dysfunction in later life? Berlinsky and Biller (1982) conducted an extensive review of research related to the impact of parent death. They concluded that nearly all the studies noted differences in areas of functioning between bereaved and non-bereaved subjects both early on and years later when the children reached adulthood. Functional areas of difference included "emotional disturbance, sex-role and related behavior, delinquency and criminal activity, and cognitive, academic and creative performance" (Berlinsky & Biller, 1982, p. 126). Berlinsky and Biller (1982) further noted that "most of the empirical research has been consistent in showing parentally bereaved children to be more submissive, dependent and introverted, and less aggressive than children from other family backgrounds" (p. 126). They drew the following conclusion:

> The analysis of the literature has thus demonstrated that parental bereavement may be a significant event in a child's life, one that will result in the individual's behaving in ways that he/she would not if the family were not disrupted in this fashion. The relationship between parental bereavement and subsequent behavior is complex, however. It is not the simple fact of a death having occurred, but rather the variables associated with the loss of the parent as well as characteristics specific to the child, that will predict the child's subsequent adjustment and development. (p. 127)

Other experts in the field of grief and bereavement have discussed the risks posed to the bereaved child if appropriate support is not available. For example, Rando (1984, p. 155) wrote: "All the available evidence suggests that not to assist the bereaved child in actively confronting the death is to predispose him to significant pathology and life-long problems."

Silverman and Worden (1992a), citing the work of several authors (Berlinsky & Biller, 1982; Brown, Harris, & Bifulco, 1986; Elizur & Kaffman, 1983) who suggested that the death itself may not be sufficient to place a child at risk, added that "the way the surviving parent responds to the child, the availability of social support, and subsequent life circumstances make a difference in whether a child develops problems" (p. 93). A complex set of interrelating factors determines whether or not a child copes effectively with parental death.

The major variables that influence the course of the grief process for children can be divided into the following four primary categories:

* Unique characteristics of the child
* Meaning and power of the relationship that existed with the deceased
* Unique circumstances of the death
* Nature and availability of support received from the child's environment.

UNIQUE CHARACTERISTICS OF THE CHILD

Child's Age and Developmental Level

The age of the child, together with his or her cognitive and emotional developmental levels, profoundly influences grief responses. Assuming that most children before 7 years of age are unable to comprehend the irreversible, inevitable, and universal truths of death, they are already at a severe disadvantage in their efforts to make sense of the event and process its meaning. Nevertheless, all children engage in efforts to understand and make meaning out of significant events in their lives—often in piecemeal fashion and with renewed exertions at each new developmental juncture. When a child is capable of assimilating new understandings, these will be integrated cognitively and emotionally, if the necessary supports are in place in the child's environment.

For our purposes, we will assume that children do grieve, regardless of age, at their own level. In infants or children younger than 2 years old, this grieving is thought to take the form of sensing the absence of the deceased parent or significant other, sometimes expressed in irritability, crying, calling out for, or searching for the missing person. It is generally accepted that the younger a child is, the more likely there are to be adverse effects. There are many opinions in the literature as to other especially vulnerable developmental phases. For example, Worden (1991), citing material from Polombo (1978) about children who have lost parents, observed that

> Children between the ages of five and seven years are a particularly vulnerable group. They have developed cognitively enough to understand some of the permanent ramifications of death but they have very little coping capacity; that is, their ego skills and social skills are insufficiently developed to enable them to defend themselves. (p. 125)

In later childhood, from 8 to 12 years of age, more independence has been forged, yet children in this group are at risk of hiding behind this newfound and fragile facade of independence, and failing to find opportunities to share their grief (Rando, 1984). It would appear that each developmental phase has its own unique set of inherent risks and opportunities. Much like the comparison of differing death circumstances, each age and developmental phase has its set of pitfalls that deserve special attention.

Child's Personality

Children's personality predispositions, coping styles, and past and present mental health status will affect the way they will grieve. For example, a more sensitive or fearful child may be overwhelmed by the enormity of the loss of a parent. Among those aspects of personality that are most likely to affect grief responses, Rando (1984) identified "self-esteem, conscious and unconscious conflicts, emotions, beliefs, attitudes, values, desires, needs, strengths" (p. 46). Likewise, a child's predeath coping styles will almost always come into play. To enter into this arena, a good question to ask is, "How would the child have coped before his or her father died?" In this way, helpers can begin to understand and interpret each child's unique responses. Dramatic differences in behavior after the death can be red flags, indicating unmet grief needs (Wolfelt, 1993).

Child's Loss History

Children's experiences both with death-related and non–death-related losses affect the ways in which they will be able to cope with parent loss. The death of a parent is generally recognized as one of the most stressful events that can happen in a child's life. If there have been multiple losses, even young children can suffer bereavement overload or the inability to cope effectively with one loss before another occurs. The impact of multiple stressors in a child's young life can lead to disorganization and fragmentation of coping abilities (Webb, 1991a, 1993b). Thorough assessment of each child's loss history is necessary to understand the nature and meaning of these losses to the particular child.

The Loss Inventory for Kids (Wolfelt, 1983; reprinted from Babensee & Pequette, 1982) is one instrument that helps to measure the impact of cumulative loss on children. It does this by asking a child to list loss events in his or her life, assigning an "impact" score to each loss (ranging from 10 for the death of a parent to 3 for an argument with a friend), multiplying each impact score by a time factor (5 for 0 to 6 months; 3 for 6 months to 1 year; and 1 for 1 to 4 years), and adding up a composite score. Keep in mind that although there is a numerical score attached to assessing or measuring the impact of parental death and other losses, each child will experience death and loss in relationship to his or her own complex and interwoven set of circumstances. Thus, the most important aspect of this inventory may be the process of working with the child to help to achieve a mutual understanding of his or her losses and responses.

Child's Background

The world around a child will play a large part in how the death of a parent and its impact will be defined. Thus, young children are dependent on their families to assist them in giving meaning to events as well as to guide them concerning beliefs, behaviors, and emotional reactions regarded by the family as appropriate responses to these occurrences (Raphael, 1982). It is necessary to observe each child's response to the death of a parent in his or her family's social, cultural, ethnic, religious, and philosophical context.

As a child leaves home for school, other adults and peers will help define his or her reality. Thus, Webb (1993b) observed that "it is helpful to know not only what the child has been taught, but also what he/she has 'caught' with regard to the religious/cultural practices of the child's family" (p. 41). Family, peers, and community communicate to children in many ways about beliefs and attitudes concerning the meaning of life, death, and afterlife. This informal learning, together with the associations that each child idiosyncratically ascribes to the death, will play an important role in shaping a child's responses.

MEANING AND POWER OF RELATIONSHIP
WITH THE DECEASED

A parent plays such a central role in a child's life that some researchers have found it difficult not to describe all parent death as traumatic (Altschul, 1988). The degree of attachment is related to the feeling of how much is lost and the strength of the child/parent bond, together with the type and number of roles that the parent played in the child's life (Rando, 1984; Raphael, 1982). The amount of time the child spent with the parent in day-to-day events, as well as the quality of the time spent together govern the nature of the relationship between parent and child. Young children often define their time in terms of parental contact: who wakes them, feeds them, and puts them to bed. A child may ask, "Who will read me my bedtime story now?" The strength of the attachment, the sense of security created by and in their relationship, and the degree of dependency that the child feels all affect responses to the death of a parent. At some point in his or her grief process, each child will come to recognize what has been lost in terms of the unique and irreplaceable aspects of this relationship.

If the relationship between the child and parent is ambivalent or conflicted, or if the child and parent have been separated or estranged, a child may be confused about the true nature of the relationship that has been lost. Consequently, a bereaved child may need help to identify and clarify the unique relationship with the deceased parent. Often, it may be necessary to differentiate a child's perception of that relationship from the way it has been or is viewed by his or her family members. The extent to which the family can allow a child to express his or her unique loss in these potentially conflictual situations will strongly influence the child's healthy grief process.

SPECIFIC CIRCUMSTANCES OF THE DEATH

The specific circumstances of the death also influence a child's grief reactions. The way in which a child is told of the death and the support received in the ensuing days and months can often help to ameliorate complicating events. Like adults, children struggle with comprehending a loss when the death is sudden or unexpected, and when it leaves no time for good-byes. In these instances, children have been observed to be working and reworking their last contact or conversation with the deceased parent. Often this reworking includes things that they wish they had said or done. Guilt at anger that was expressed, and self-blame at thoughts or wishes held, can surface with any type of death.

In cases of prolonged illness, the family's resources are likely to become exhausted. Children struggle with the erratic course of illness, especially in situations when time after time a parent has rallied after coming close to death. When the death finally occurs, it may not seem possible that it has actually happened after all the close calls. Relief may be felt when a long illness is finally over. And that can then lead to feelings of guilt or other unhelpful reactions.

If the death involves unexpected causes, like suicide, murder, violent death, disaster, accidents related to alcohol or drug use, or other stigmatizing elements, children will experience a more complicated mourning process. When a child witnesses any of these events, the initial emphasis must be placed on the traumatic responses. If the death is perceived as preventable, the duration and severity of grief and mourning will be further compounded. Rescue fantasies and magical thinking may dominate.

Unusual circumstances, like the death occurring on or near a birthday, holiday, or other special occasion may color that season or time for the child.

NATURE AND AVAILABILITY OF SUPPORT

Most children do not have at their disposal skills to ask for help in ways to which adults who are under great stress can respond. Similarly, most parents who are coping with the death of a spouse do not have the coping reserves to be able to handle their children's needs in addition to all the other superimposed demands of grief. In situations of such intense stress, children's needs are often overlooked or minimized. For example, when a parent dies, a child is frequently sent to stay with neighbors or relatives in the initial time of the crisis. Or if children remain at home, they often feel no control about the invasion of well-meaning adults. Behaviors that spell out a need for help, such as crying, withdrawing, regressing, or acting out are frequently misinterpreted as willful misbehavior. Children who behave in these ways after a significant death are commonly further isolated or punished. Not surprisingly, their sense of confusion, isolation, and anguish grows.

The amount and quality of support available to a child over the months and years after the death of a parent may be the most significant factor in determining the consequences that will be experienced. Accordingly, it is of critical importance to provide parental substitutes and solace to bereaved children (Volkan & Zintl, 1993). Significant adults in a child's life can provide occasions to ask questions about the circumstances of the death, to learn more about the deceased parent, and to reflect on memories of shared experiences. All of these give a bereaved child valuable opportunities to work and rework basic tasks of mourning (Baker, Sedney, & Gross, 1992). The degree to which the social and familial system can provide this sort of support is critical. Acceptance and support by peers is important to children. A sense of shame, of feeling "different," may be expressed by children who have no peers who have experienced a death in their family.

UNIQUE ASPECTS OF PARENTAL DEATH FOR CHILDREN

Young children are dependent on their caretakers, usually their parents, for their very lives and for satisfaction of their basic needs. In the early months and years of a child's life, an extraordinarily strong process of bonding is at work, shaping the relationship between parent and child (Raphael, 1982). The baby's need for, or attachment to, the parent is "just as much an inborn biological entity as having a left arm or a left leg" (Parkes quoted by Myers, 1986, p. 32).

As a child grows, and becomes less dependent on his or her parents for survival, attachment to the parent decreases or changes in its character, just as the parent's attachment to the child gradually alters as the child moves into adulthood. Parent death during these early years of strong attachment and high levels of dependency threatens the child at deep levels. Basic survival needs may be met by another, but the unique qualities of the parental bond can never be replaced. The more positive and more frequent the contact has been with the deceased parent, the more acutely a young child will be aware of the parent's absence (Norris-Shortle, Young, & Williams, 1993).

Perhaps no other loss affects so many aspects of a child's life as the death of a parent. If our parents are the cornerstones of our family structure, a child whose parent dies loses at least half of his or her sources of emotional support and love, physical and psychosocial assistance, and opportunities for learning. For adults, themes of abandonment and vulnerability are stirred within us when we explore our perceptions of what a young child's experience of parental death must be like. We may believe that no one will love us as much, know us as well, or accept us as completely as our parents. Who will teach us to play baseball, cook, or solve a math problem? How will we know our family history, and who will remember what we were like when we were a baby? The pervasiveness of the loss both in its day-to-day changes and the absence that is compounded over the years is enormous.

Long-term implications of the death of a parent arise because children must grow up with the loss. When a parent is not there for all the events he or she would never have missed otherwise, such as a birthday, holiday, or graduation, the reality of the death sharpens for the child (Rando, 1984). As understanding matures, a child must take the loss into account in his or her reckoning with each developmental task. As one looks back on the event of parental death and its consequences, one can see that although the death itself was a source of major stress for a child, "in addition, its impact pervaded most aspects of the child's life. It reached to the inner workings of the child's meaning-making system and to the way his or her world was structured" (Silverman & Worden, 1992a, p. 102).

Trust, self-concept, and self-esteem are directly affected by the death of a parent. The child's family life will never be the same again. The child can no longer regard his or her parents as omnipotent. Trust in the surviving parent or other adults in their roles as protector is diminished. The child may also be fearful for the safety of the remaining parent. If one parent can die, is it not possible that the other could die, too? Anxiety and worry about family safety is frequently expressed through drawings, stories, and verbal sharing.

Bereaved children are often willing to discuss with empathetic adults their difficulties in sharing with peers about the death of a parent and their ongoing struggles with grief. For most children, some stigma is attached to living in a family in which a parent has died. Because there are many children today who live in single-parent homes, the impact of this stigma may be minimized. Nevertheless, in support groups with peers who have experienced parent death, children frequently share their shame and secrecy.

Much of the research that has been completed on the effects of parental death on children, according to Berlinsky and Biller (1982), has not considered whether the child lost his mother or his father. Of the studies done that pay attention to the gender of the parent who died, almost all relate to paternal death, probably because it occurs more frequently (but see Edelman, 1994). In summarizing their research on variables unique to parent death, Berlinsky and Biller (1982) concluded the following:

> Family and situational variables related to the death of a parent are associated with subsequent behaviors observed in the child. . . . One of the best-supported outcomes concerns children's reactions to different

forms of parent loss. Children of divorced parents have shown a pattern of acting-out and of undercontrolled behavior, while bereaved children tend to be more constricted and socially acceptable in their actions. . . . A great deal of research has focused specifically on paternal bereavement, which has been associated with emotional disturbance, personality variables, sex-role and related interpersonal functioning, cognitive functioning and delinquent behavior. Except in one study on genius, father absence due to death has been related to deficits or problems in these areas. Death of the mother, which has been less frequently studied, possibly because it occurs less often, has been linked only with emotional disturbance. This research does not necessarily indicate differences in the effects of maternal and paternal bereavement, but does seem to show that death of either parent may make a difference in children's subsequent behavior. (p. 105)

Differences in children's grief responses that were noted in studies between children who had experienced the death of a father and those whose mother had died are described by Silverman and Worden (1992a):

With one or two exceptions, the mothers seemed to be the parents who dealt with the affective life of the family and upon whom the stability of daily routines was dependent. . . . When a father was left in charge, the children were less likely to talk with him about their feelings or their dreams, and they experienced many more changes in their daily lives. . . . The parents' ability to assume a new role and to adapt to a single-parent household became an important factor in the children's overall adaptation to change. (p. 102)

The gender of the bereaved child is also a factor in his or her grief responses. Silverman and Worden (1992a) found differences between girls and boys in terms of how comfortable they are in expressing their feelings related to the social reinforcement they receive:

The study looked not only at gender-specific roles to which these children and their parents have been or are being socialized, but at how these children were learning the roles of bereaved child and of a child with only one parent. (p. 102)

The death of a parent brings many secondary losses, which may initially be more distressing to a young child than the absence of the deceased parent. The surviving parent, in his or her distress may be unavailable emotionally to the grieving child, so that in effect both parents are lost to the child survivor. The basic care, security, and nurturing needs of the child may not be met at a time when those needs are greatest.

Many other changes for the bereaved child are likely to follow in the days and months to come. The roles performed by the deceased parent will be fulfilled or taken up in new and different ways. Children often cite increased responsibilities and higher expectations placed on them soon after the death of a parent. Some children attempt to take care of their surviving parent. In part, in these ways they may be seeking to guard themselves and their families from further harm by working extra hard at being "good." Children who adopt this course may be attempting to gain some measure of control over their disrupted lives by bargaining away their childhood. Often, these superachieving children are held up as models of behavior to their peers or siblings. Their unmet grief needs seldom come to the attention of their caregivers.

Other secondary losses may include moving, leaving school, a neighborhood, or friends; having reduced financial resources; losing time with the surviving parent because of increased work demands; and missing a sense of family as it had previously been known. One child expressed this by saying, "I miss us." Another child talked about how hard school had become because "I can't think so well." A third child described family changes in the following way: "I miss having fun. We never laugh anymore."

Children also become aware of the amount of time they may be left in child care or with baby-sitters when their parent resumes socializing or dating. Fears about replacement of the beloved deceased parent, loss of the surviving parent to a new relationship, the implications of remarriage, or further changes may be present as the child attempts to make sense out of the bereavement experience, and a new and different family system.

In their study on children and parental death, Silverman and Worden described the children as "dealing not only with the death of a person, but with the death of a way of life" (1992a, p. 102). The child is living in a family in which many of its dreams have died along with the parent. The surviving parent mourns the end of the parenting partnership. "It wasn't supposed to happen this way," or "I never bargained for this" are statements that can be frequently heard in widowed support groups. Children also mourn the loss of these family dreams.

Many of the losses and feelings expressed by children who are coping with parent death are also heard from children whose grandparent, step-parent, or other relative has filled many of the parental roles. In situations where children are being reared by their grandparents or other surrogate parents, the special qualities of the relationship and frequency of contact with these "other" parents will determine the nature of the loss for each child.

GRANDPARENT DEATH

The death of a parent may affect nearly every aspect of a young child's life. There are other family deaths that bring fewer changes and less interruption of care, for which a child will also grieve. Often a child's first experience of family loss is with the death of a grandparent. Such a death may be the first time a child has seen his or her parents cry openly, the first funeral ever attended, in short, the child's first experience with death. Crenshaw (1991) noted that "the degree of loss experienced by children will vary with the quality of the attachment to the grandparent and sometimes is quite profound" (p. 90). Grandparents may well be important figures in a child's life as sources of unconditional love and caregiving. Alternatively, in our transient culture, a child may have had little opportunity to spend time with grandparents beyond an occasional telephone contact or holiday visit relationship. In the latter circumstances, a child may experience little personal loss on the death of a grandparent, but will nonetheless be affected by the grief responses of his or her parent(s) (Rando, 1988). Webb (1993d) described the responses of children to grandparent death as both an individual or personal experience, based on the quality of the relationship lost, and as a part of the larger experience of the family system, based on other family members' reactions and interactions.

Children sometimes express confusion about the expectations that are placed on them by adults in response to grandparent death. A child may feel that he or she is expected to grieve in ways that differ from his or her individual responses, particularly if there is little personal loss involved. That is why Rando (1988), in discussing adult loss of a parent, suggested that

> the death of your parent, unless that parent was an integral part of your own family of spouse and children, most probably will not be viewed by them in either the same fashion or with the same importance as it is for you. . . . Although your parent may have been the most influential person in your life, and for years was the closest person to you, an essential part of your existence, that parent may have been no more than a peripheral figure to the others who are so close to you now. (pp. 149–150)

Grandparent death may bring a whole host of confusing thoughts and feelings for children. Just what is death, anyway? What happens to people when they die? Where do you go when you're dead? Questions, thoughts, and feelings like this may lead to anxiety about the safety of other family members, particularly parents. Fears about one's own safety and death, in general, may arise. If a child is permitted to ask questions, express deep feelings, and obtain appropriate support, the death experience can be a time of great learning and preparation for the inevitable losses that will occur throughout the life cycle.

CHILDREN'S RESPONSES TO THE DEATH OF A PARENT OR OTHER PARENTAL FIGURE

We can obtain assistance in understanding children's responses to the death of a parent or other parental figure from general literature on grief and mourning (Osterweis, Solomon, & Green, 1984; Rando, 1984; Raphael, 1983), as well as from other accounts of bereavement in childhood (Baker, Sedney, & Gross, 1992; Fleming, 1985). But the death of a parent during childhood is a unique and overwhelming event. Not surprisingly, a death of this sort will create critical physical and psychosocial survival issues for children, and each child is likely to respond in manageable increments over a long period (Rando, 1988).

In the case of young children, it may be months before there is an observable response. For example, one 4-year-old girl displayed little emotion on learning of her beloved father's sudden death. She participated in the memorial rituals and quietly observed the adults around her shedding tears and attending to the business of grieving. It was not until her birthday 5 months later that she shed her first tears. Apparently, she had been holding hidden within her the fantasy that her father would come back for her birthday celebration. After all, her special birthday wish had been for his return. As the day closed and her mother was rocking her to sleep, her father had still not come. She began to cry, and her grief was inconsolable. With each additional passing day and each special event, the reality of her father's absence was reinforced.

This little girl demonstrated common coping responses in young children that are especially characteristic in the aftermath of parental death. An inability to understand the permanence of death and the many changes that had occurred in her family, had left her coping in the only ways at her disposal, denial and magical thinking. A need for some sense of control or power in a changing and frightening world was evident. Perhaps, as she comes to feel safer and more supported, she can begin to mourn her loss and its many implications. It probably was only with the dawning of understanding of "no return" that the loss began to be real for her, along with its attendant sorrow.

Caring adults may feel unsure about how to help children who are experiencing parent death when the children display no observable grief reaction. It is important that adults do not label these children as callous when they are temporarily unable to grieve in the face of so pervasive a loss. In most situations, children who have opportunities to explore and the emotional support to question their experiences will demonstrate outward manifestations of their internal processes. In any event, internal working and reworking is almost always occurring, and children need to be given time and assistance to cope with their losses and grief reactions in their own ways.

If a deceased parent had been an integral part of the child's day-to-day life, it may be especially important for a bereaved child to envision where that parent is now. This can create opportunities for much age-appropriate discussion about death, discussion that helps the child to develop an account of death that integrates the loss within a framework of meaning. Often this process involves much repetition of the death circumstances for the young child, leaving the parent confused about whether the child is receiving the right information or if the information is being presented correctly. Even older children will have many questions and inconsistencies in their stories, which may be confusing to them. Repetition of the facts as they are known in relationship to the circumstances of the death can be a valuable tool in helping children incorporate their losses into ongoing living.

Children are concrete in their grief processes. It must be assumed that a bereaved child is listening to the discussions of the death that are occurring in his or her environment, even though he or she may appear to be playing or otherwise engaged. Care needs to be taken with the terms and expressions that are used as well as the content of any information that may be inappropriate or confusing. One mother told the story of her 6-year-old son, who was continually making a great racket with his drums and cymbals. When his behavior was explored, he volunteered, "I'm making enough noise to raise the dead. Do you think Daddy will hear?"

Although adults cannot control the expressions that children may pick up in their world, we can explore, encourage, and support the sorting through of all the new and confusing information about death. And we can try to assist children in their attempts to assert some control within their environment.

In our family grief support center, BRIDGES: A Center for Grieving Children, in Tacoma, Washington, we have frequently worked with children who are struggling with their idealized image of a deceased parent. The anger experienced as a result of the abandonment by the deceased is often directed at the surviving parent. Perhaps this is also a way for children to express fear about the possibility of further abandonment, or anxiety concerning unmet needs for security and routine.

Grief and anger may also be expressed in other ways, such as forgetfulness, daydreaming, procrastinating, and losing things (Furman, 1984; Jewett, 1982; Webb, 1993b).

In the face of their own similar feelings, parents often report their frustration in coping with children's varied expressions of anger and insecurity. It is critical to view a child's grief responses at the loss of a parent in the context of the family system (Shapiro, 1994). We have observed families moving through phases of idealizing the deceased, feeling anger at abandonment, recognizing common needs across the age span, coping with diminished emotional resources and sorrow, and developing family customs aimed at preserving the memories and meaning of each member's unique relationship with the deceased spouse and parent. Great growth and change can come about for the family in these healing processes.

Children frequently engage in behavior that is aimed at feeling close to the deceased parent. They may choose Dad's favorite food for dinner or wear clothing particularly liked by the deceased parent. It may be difficult for the surviving parent to understand the intensity or rigidity of these behaviors. Occasionally, older children have talked about ways in which they thought they could bring back the parent through their behavior. This magical thinking may be demonstrated by a child's attempts to be very good. One little boy believed if his softball team won the tournament that his Dad would return to present his trophy.

Some children choose activities that the deceased especially enjoyed, which bring them a sense of partnership with the deceased parent. Others choose articles of clothing that were significant to the parent to keep, sleep with, or wear. Closeness or connection may be found by sitting in Dad's favorite chair, or choosing later in life to go into a career like the one pursued by the deceased parent. Children are often creative in seeking comfort or meaning to their parent's absence through their continuing connection to the deceased.

Parents may become distraught when they hear their child make statements like, "I want to go to be with Daddy." Unsure if this is an indication of some sort of suicidal tendency, parents may contact professionals to assess children who make such statements. Exploring with children their understandings of death can help to clarify the meaning of their communications. With young children, "dead" or "heaven" are often perceived as very much like being in a distant city. Helping a child to find constructive ways to express his or her great longing and need for the deceased parent is important.

In his book, *When Parents Die*, Edward Myers (1986) interviewed John Bowlby about the relationship between attachment and bereavement

after the death of a parent. Bowlby commented that "attachment relationships *persist*. The idea that this [attachment] is a very little matter,
and just disappears, is not true. It undergoes a metamorphosis as the
other generation gets older, but it doesn't disappear in any conceivable
sense" (p. 32).

The nature of the child's relationship with the deceased parent in
the process of converting it from one of active interaction to one of
imaginative metamorphosis is explored in research by Silverman, Nickman, and Worden (1992). They found that in the early months after the
death, children typically developed an inner construction of the dead
parent that assisted them in coping with their losses and with all of the
ensuing changes in their lives. This inner representation of the deceased parent is described as "colorful, dynamic, and interactive" (p.
495). Rather than encouraging the child to detach, the authors suggested that it is normal to maintain a connection with the deceased and
that over time the child will be forced to deal with the circumstances of
the death and what the parent would have been like. In this way, the
child recognizes "*what* is lost" (p. 496).

To maintain this connection the children were observed as employing the following five strategies (Silverman, Nickman, & Worden,
1992):

1. Making an effort to locate the deceased
2. Actually experiencing the deceased in some way
3. Reaching out to initiate a connection
4. Remembering
5. Keeping something that belonged to the deceased

These activities serve bereaved children in helping to understand the
meaning of death. In addition, they contribute to establishing a sense
of the meaning of the relationship with the deceased in the child's ongoing life.

WHAT HAVE WE LEARNED FROM THE CHILDREN?

"A child can live through *anything*, so long as he or she is told the truth
and is allowed to share with loved ones the natural feelings people have
when they are suffering" (LeShan, 1976, p. 3).

Repeatedly, children have indicated a need to be given correct, age-
appropriate information about the circumstances of the death of a parent. When opportunities are given for participation in funeral rites and

other rituals of memorialization, children are usually open to participation (Corr, 1991; Weller, Weller, Fristad, Cain, & Bowes, 1988). Most often, they use these opportunities in creative ways to process their grief (Silverman & Worden, 1992b). Openly sharing with other children who have had similar experiences is ordinarily a welcome way to question without fear the feelings, thoughts, and behaviors related to their grief processes. A child needs to feel safe enough in his or her environment to share strong reactions to loss openly. Often, expression of such reactions will be withheld until such safety is achieved. Children have frequently offered comments like, "it was too scary to think about before," or "I didn't want to make my Mom cry."

Play is an important part of coming to terms with the loss. Children need to be children, even when they are bereaved. Far too many children who have experienced the death of a parent carry emotional and physical responsibilities beyond their capacity to manage. Nevertheless, children are often creative in their processes of discovering ways to transform their relationships with a deceased parent into a caring and protective interaction through their thoughts, dreams, and visualizations. Thus, one child said, "even though I know I can never see Daddy again, I can be with him in my heart."

From my work with children who have experienced the death of a parent, I have learned a great deal about the purposefulness of mourning, the importance of processing one's grief through a variety of experiential avenues, and the meaning, value, and beauty of ritual in manifesting and integrating both internal and external processes. The durable, enduring, and indomitable qualities of the human condition and human connection are demonstrated repeatedly in the grief work of bereaved children.

CONCLUSION

This chapter has considered issues related to the death of a parent, grandparent, or other parental figure, together with the impact of such a death on children. It has been argued that such a death is a significant event in a child's life, one with unique and powerful features. The impact of parental death on a child is mediated by four principal variables: the unique characteristics of the child (his or her age and developmental level, personality, loss history, and sociocultural background); the meaning and power of the relationship with the deceased person; the distinctive circumstances of the death; and the nature and availability of support for the bereaved child. There is much that adults can do to help children who have experienced the death of a parent or other parental figure. In their efforts to help, adults are well advised to learn about children who have experienced this type of bereavement, and to learn from bereaved children about their needs and coping processes.

8

Children and the Death of a Sibling

S. D. Stahlman

It is estimated that eight million Americans experience the death of an immediate family member each year in the United States (U.S. Bureau of the Census, 1993). Death in the immediate family is not an uncommon occurrence. This chapter examines one particular type of familial death during childhood: the death of a sibling. Topics discussed include siblings and the sibling relationship; sibling responses to death during childhood; familial responses to the death of a child as the context for sibling bereavement; factors that influence sibling and familial responses; and implications for helping professionals.

SIBLINGS AND THE SIBLING RELATIONSHIP

The sibling relationship is one that begins in childhood but continues well beyond the childhood years. The nature of the sibling relationship is particularly significant because it is typically the longest and most enduring familial relationship—lasting some 60 or 70 years in most cases. Because siblings share a common family, culture, traditions, events, and memories, there is a familial and societal expectation that the tie between them will endure throughout the life span (Moss & Moss, 1986).

The common experiences shared by siblings create an emotional bond that extends well into adulthood in ways that have not been fully explored. The influences that siblings have on one another are often profound and overlooked. Siblings serve as role models to one another, provide a practice arena for interaction skills, and extend social support to one another. Social activities, such as birthdays, holidays, and anniversaries, leave an indelible imprint on the sibling relationship.

Approximately 80% of the population in the United States grows up with the presence of one or more siblings (Adams, 1972; Cicirelli, 1980). Empirical studies on the sibling relationship have focused primarily on the childhood sibling relationship, and have specifically related it to issues of rivalry, deprivation, or birth order (Adams, 1972; Kammeyer, 1967).

The significance of the sibling relationship is evidenced by the lifelong contacts that siblings have with one another over the life span. For example, Cicirelli (1982) found that only 3% of siblings had not seen their sibling within the last 2 years. Forty-one percent of adult siblings visit at least one sibling each month (Cicirelli, 1980). In a similar study, Rosenberg and Anspach (1973) reported that 68% saw a sibling weekly. Clearly, the sibling relationship that is established early in life has a lifelong impact during the course of the life cycle.

What happens when the development of this significant relationship is ended prematurely by death? Although the significance of the sibling relationship is dramatic, there have been few empirical studies that have examined the grieving response and the sequelae of events when a child experiences the death of a sibling. Perhaps for theoretical and practical considerations, the focal point of most empirical studies on familial relationships has been on the marital dyad or parent-child relationship. Similarly, childhood bereavement studies have usually focused either on the familial response to the death of a child, which is usually depicted in terms of the bereavement of one or both parents or on childhood bereavement arising from the death of a parent (Elizur & Kaffman, 1983; Kaffman & Elizur, 1979; Raphael, 1982; Van Eerdewegh, Bieri, Parilla, & Clayton, 1982; Van Eerdewegh, Clayton, & Van Eerdewegh, 1985).

Nevertheless, we know that a child experiences the death of a parent or sibling in approximately 5% of all families in the United States (Blinder, 1972). Also, a unique characteristic of the childhood sibling relationship is its sense of "universal ambivalence." This phrase means that child sibling relationships are characteristically intense. Siblings can often be identified by their loyalty, companionship, rivalry, love, jealousy, and hate. This mixture of sometimes inconsistent feelings often influences the grief responses and the mourning of surviving siblings. When a sibling dies, the surviving sibling, in addition to his or her own grief, may also feel guilt because of a belief that earlier hostile thoughts and actions are somehow responsible for the death.

SIBLING RESPONSES TO DEATH

Death ends only the life; it does not end the relationship. This seems especially applicable to the death of a childhood sibling. The death of a brother or sister during childhood is an untimely event whose unhealthy consequences may endure far beyond the last person to bid farewell at a graveside service. Cain, Fast, and Erickson (1964) described this traumatic event as adding newly warped lives to the one already tragically ended. Children are expected to survive their parents; when they do not do so, this strange turn of fate produces a disruption in the family unit, which is more deeply felt and has a more enduring legacy than that found in many individuals who experience other kinds of losses (Rosen & Cohen, 1981). The death of a childhood sibling has the potential to be a driving force that may lead to unhealthy response patterns.

At the same time, when circumstances are optimal, such a death may provide opportunities for growth and maturation. Through the death of a sibling, bereaved brothers and sisters learn at an early age difficult lessons about the preciousness of human life, the importance of close personal relationships, the vulnerability of such relationships and the individuals who share them, the multiple impacts of loss on themselves and other family members, and the significance of the legacy left to them by the sibling who died. In these ways, the effects of a brother or sister's death during childhood have immediate as well as long-term consequences for surviving siblings. In contemporary families, the death of a sibling may have special implications because a decrease in overall family size may leave the surviving sibling as the "only child" in the family.

One question of critical importance in understanding childhood sibling bereavement is the degree to which children are capable of experiencing grief and mourning in response to the death of a family member. A review of the literature suggests that children are capable of experiencing the full range of responses of adults, although their specific ways of addressing and expressing these responses may differ significantly from adults (see chapter 6). An adult's response to a significant death may be all-consuming. By contrast, children are less fixated on the loss; they may be laughing and playing one minute, while crying and needing comfort the next minute (Cook & Dworkin, 1992).

Adult reactions to the deaths of family members are well documented (Parkes, 1987; Parkes & Weiss, 1983). However, our knowledge of childhood bereavement is less well developed. This is particularly true in what is known about childhood bereavement as a result of the death of a sibling. Most of the literature on childhood bereavement focuses on the death of a parent (Van Eerdewegh, Clayton, & Van Eerdewegh, 1985; Weller, Weller, Fristad, & Bowes, 1991). The experience of having a child die is one of the most devastating losses that any family could experience.

Direct reactions, such as denial, fear of separation, sadness, anger, guilt, and anxiety, have been identified in children experiencing childhood bereavement (Hafen & Frandsen, 1983; Krell & Rabkin, 1979; Rosen & Cohen, 1981; Van Eerdewegh et al., 1982; Van Eerdewegh, Clayton, & Van Eerdewegh, 1985).

However, children's reactions to the death of a sibling can also be manifested in indirect behaviors, such as bed-wetting or problems related to school performance (Van Eerdewegh, Clayton, & Van Eerdewegh, 1985; Vida & Grizenko, 1989). Regressive behaviors, such as thumb-sucking and bed-wetting may be common among younger children. Furthermore, younger children may experience the fear of being separated from other family members, which results in clinging and other dependency behaviors. In addition to these regressive behaviors, anger is a frequent response to this type of loss and may be exhibited by temper tantrums, discipline problems, and negativism (Vida & Grizenko, 1989).

In addition to behavioral problems in children who have experienced the death of a sibling, physiological responses have also been identified. Thus, Koocher (1983) identified frequent nightmares, persistent insomnia, headaches, and loss of appetite in such children.

The devastating potential of sibling bereavement has been noted by many researchers (Binger et al., 1969; Cain, Fast, & Erickson, 1964; Hilgard, 1969; Kaplan, Grobstein, & Smith, 1976). Children's responses to such a death, both short term and long term, are influenced by a variety of factors relating to the sibling's death, such as the age of the surviving sibling, relationship to the deceased, size of family unit, familial responses to the death, family coping skills, and the presence and effectiveness of a support network.

The variable of age may have a significant effect on the surviving child's ability to cope with the sibling's death. For example, younger children will display behaviors that are more magical in their thinking and they may be limited in understanding the finality of the sibling's death (Gogan, Koocher, Foster, & O'Malley, 1977; Thunberg, 1977). By contrast, older children realize that death is universal; what lives, dies, and no magical thinking can change that fact.

As previously noted, a surviving sibling's response to the death of a brother or sister is to a large degree dependent on the response of the parents. Adults in the process of grieving can seek out details of the death directly from physicians, friends, and other family members. By contrast, parents typically decide what information is appropriate to share with surviving siblings. Such siblings are then almost entirely dependent on their parents as a source of reliable information surrounding the death of the deceased sibling.

Most children will have few sources of support to turn to if parents do not create an open and favorable environment necessary for facilitating a child's grief and mourning. Accordingly, interviews with surviving siblings report common feelings of isolation and loneliness, coupled with the view that no one understands their situation. Surviving siblings observe and recognize the all-consuming suffering of their parent's grief, which often leaves little emotional energy for responding to the needs of the siblings.

Children experiencing the death of a sibling may be inadvertently prohibited from expressing the full range of their grief reactions concerning the death of a sibling. Because the death of a child is such a traumatic family event, much of the attention from typical sources of support is given to the grieving parents. This may tend to reduce or minimize the importance of the child's grief (Rosen, 1986). In addition, surviving children themselves usually feel the need to be especially good so as to create no additional burden for their grieving parents. And children who experience the death of a brother or sister often take pains to engage in behaviors that will fulfill their need for safety and security—even at the cost of suppressing their own grief reactions to the death.

FAMILIAL RESPONSES TO THE DEATH OF A CHILD

The death of a child and its effects within the family are especially significant because these events involve parents burying their children rather than the more typical, "on-time" pattern of children burying their parents. In this context, the death of a child will simultaneously affect parents, siblings, and the entire family system. For this reason, it is important to consider the responses of a child to the death of a sibling within the context of the family's responses to the death.

From the moment of a child's death, families are left with a variety of decisions and opportunities that will forever change the family system and have a lifelong impact on the surviving family members. The death of a child creates an immediate crisis for the family as well as subsequent stresses that will have an impact on all family members (Binger,

1973; Cain, Fast, & Erickson, 1964; Cook & Dworkin, 1992; Gogan et al., 1977; Krell & Rabkin, 1979; Rosen, 1986; Rosen & Cohen, 1981; Sourkes, 1980).

Major decisions that must be made concerning surviving siblings include answers to a variety of questions. Who should tell the surviving siblings about the death? How much information should be shared about the specific details of the death itself? Should the surviving siblings be required or offered an opportunity to attend the funeral? What effects will there be in having surviving siblings view the lifeless body in a casket? If the death was a horrifying death involving disfiguring or dismemberment, should that information be shared? If so, who should share such information? These questions represent only the issues that need to be decided in the immediate hours and days after the death of a sibling.

As the weeks and months unfold, additional decisions must be made that affect the grief and bereavement of surviving siblings. Is it acceptable to continue to talk about the sibling's death? What will happen to the personal items of the deceased sibling? What keepsakes will be retained and what items will be displayed or discarded? Will pictures of the deceased sibling be displayed and, if so, where? If the deceased sibling had his or her own room, will it now be used by other family members or left untouched as a kind of shrine to the deceased? What discussions about the deceased sibling are permitted?

These questions represent immediate and short-term issues that must be addressed by surviving family members. Other questions, perhaps never voiced by family members, can only be answered as a process and function of time. These questions focus on the family void created by the death of the child. Who will fill this void? Is there an expectation that a surviving sibling will assume the characteristics of the deceased sibling? If so, will the surviving sibling "accept" these traits or characteristics? Will the family continue to talk openly about the death of the sibling, or will there be a "ghost sibling" always present in the family household? Who will assume the roles that were performed by the deceased sibling? Will the family ever be the same again?

The death of a childhood sibling may not always put surviving siblings at risk, but there are numerous opportunities for the parents to struggle or fail to assist surviving siblings in their healthy coping with bereavement. Parents are expected to maintain a marriage and explain the details of the death to relatives and friends. In addition, they may need to act as a buffer or source of support for their own parents in the grief of the grandparents. Responsibilities at work may continue to grow. And during all of this activity bereaved parents are expected to cope with their own grief in the midst of overwhelming stress.

Although the literature is silent on the situation of single parents who experience the death of a child, it is possible that additional difficulties may be experienced by single-parent families because the tasks associated with the bereavement are being managed by one person alone.

With so many personal issues and responsibilities falling on the shoulders of the parents, who will take time to address the surviving siblings' own feelings of loss and confusion surrounding the death of a brother or sister? Surviving siblings and their needs may not receive sufficient attention in the process of adaptation at a time in which a parent's emotional reserves are limited. This creates a situation in which children often are not given the attention that they need to assist in coping with the death of a brother or sister. The inability of parents to devote full attention to their surviving children, combined with a child's inability to cope with partially developed emotions and other grief reactions, may create an arena for unhealthy responses.

Hollingsworth and Pasnau (1977) have described a three-stage grieving process that is experienced by parents in the death of their child. The three stages are (a) shock, disbelief, and denial; (b) longing for the deceased; and (c) resolution. These three stages parallel similar, stage-based models of grieving identified by other authors (Parkes, 1987; Parkes & Weiss, 1983). The initial stage of shock is more pronounced in situations when the family had little or no knowledge of the impending death, thus eliminating the opportunity for anticipatory grief. Although this stage generally does not last more than a couple of days, it is characterized by avoidance of the reality that the death has occurred. "Oh no! it couldn't possibly true" seems to be almost a universal expression. When this stage of shock and disbelief lasts more than a few days, it may indicate that a problematic reaction is developing (Hollingsworth & Pasnau, 1977).

The second stage of parental response to the death of a child is characterized by periods of intense longing for the deceased child. The death of a child leaves constant reminders for survivors about what used to be. A favorite toy, a comment from a friend, and daily activities all serve as painful reminders of the deceased child. Special events, such as holidays and birthdays, often trigger intense feelings of longing and pining for the deceased child. This intense longing is also manifested by parents who report "seeing" or "feeling" the presence of the deceased. Paranormal auditory and visual experiences are reported to occur in as many as 50% of families that experience the death of a child (Hollingsworth & Pasnau, 1977).

Approximately 3 to 6 months after the death of a child, these feelings of longing usually begin to diminish in frequency and intensity. As that happens, parents begin to work toward integrating the child's death in their ongoing living. Although there still are periods of episodic sadness, brought on by birthdays or other special events, parents begin to regain interest in daily activities. Another characteristic of the third stage is the ability to discuss openly both happy and sad memories of the deceased child. Application of this stage model would suggest that over time the family is able to "get over" the death of a child.

An alternative model described by Davies (1988a) suggests that the nature of the "shared life space" is a predictor of the degree to which survivors will accomplish the tasks of grief. Drawing on the work of Parkes (1987), Davies (1988a, p. 340) defined "life space" as "those parts of the environment with which the self interacts and in relationship to which behavior is organized." Life space involves shared activities, feelings, and emotions with the deceased. Davies (1988a, p. 340) proposed that "the greater the shared life space, the greater is the potential for disruption and stress; the less the shared life space, the less is the potential for intense disruption during bereavement." In this view, siblings that have shared a significant life space may never "get over" the loss and grief, and an "empty space" may be ever present (McClowry, Davies, May, Kulenkamp, & Martinson, 1987). This interpretation of mourning does not view grief as something to "get over" but rather as an ongoing process that may have no final resolution.

Findings indicate that siblings who were closest to a deceased brother or sister had the most difficulty in coping with the death of that brother or sister (Davies, 1983, 1985, 1988a, 1988b). Similar findings have also been reported with adult sibling death (Stahlman, 1993). Further research is warranted that will examine the quality of the sibling relationship and the level of shared involvement related to the "empty space" model of grieving.

A family's immediate and long-term responses to the death of a child will be critical elements in setting the stage for both the short- and long-term effects of grief involving the deceased sibling (Arnold & Gemma, 1994). The surviving child will attempt to fit into the environment that has been created by the parents (Krell & Rabkin, 1979). If a positive environment has been created, then a satisfactory and growth-producing experience can be achieved. If parents, through their grief responses, create an environment of suspicion, silence, or guilt, then the family system may not return to a sense of balance experienced before the death of the child. We can characterize familial responses to the death of a child as "unhealthy" or counterproductive versus "healthy" or productive.

Unhealthy Familial Responses

Various response patterns have been identified that promote an unhealthy environment for surviving siblings, that is, that do not facilitate their grief work (Krell & Rabkin, 1979). One pattern that has been identified as unhealthy is known as the "conspiracy of guilt." In situations in which one or both parents believe that the death was preventable, guilt and blame may become the central issue that often may prohibit a healthy response to the sibling's death. Such situations are characterized by indirect communication, distortions, and evasive responses surrounding the details of the death event. The disabling guilt of each family member remains unspoken for fear that revealing one's feelings would lead to the exposure of the "responsible party." Guilt and shame lead to the suppression of the details of the sibling's death.

In extreme cases, a surviving sibling may not even be aware that a sibling existed. However, a more typical consequence is a "conspiracy of silence" when surviving siblings ask any questions about the death of their siblings. Such questions are usually ignored, or they lead to vague answers that leave surviving children wondering what lies behind the great mystery. Over time, a surviving sibling learns that something is mysterious and that seeking clarification is inappropriate within the family setting.

A second protective response pattern involves overprotectiveness of the surviving siblings. This response pattern is characterized by efforts to afford the surviving siblings a special status in the family. This special status often takes the form of shielding or overprotecting surviving siblings for fear that they also will experience events and situations that are life threatening. As a result, the sibling becomes bound in the context of a family that needs to control the forces of fate that have befallen it. Ritual and imagined dangers become the operating forces that lead parents to behave in ways that would not have occurred under previous conditions.

Surviving siblings in these situations are not given much freedom to explore life and discover new experiences for fear that some danger may befall them. On occasion, parents will begin to withdraw emotionally from surviving siblings in an unhealthy preparation for another impending loss (Krell & Rabkin, 1979). In these circumstances, the deceased sibling remains "alive" in an unhealthy way in the representation of the surviving siblings. The new status for the surviving sibling is overwhelming in the sense that he or she possesses his or her own identity and development in addition to the fantasized potential of the deceased sibling.

A third unhealthy familial response to the death of a child occurs when parents engage in efforts to provide a substitute for the deceased child (Cain & Cain, 1964). Depending on the child-bearing age of the mother, a literal substitution may be made through reproduction. However, more commonly a replacement is made by selecting a surviving sibling who is designated to assume the roles of the deceased sibling. In addition to his or her own normative developmental processes, the surviving sibling then also consciously or unconsciously takes on the roles and expectations of the deceased sibling. Attempts at resurrecting the child are usually found in parents who have encountered some early traumatic experiences in their families of origin (Krell & Rabkin, 1979).

Healthy Familial Responses

All families struggle with the difficulties of grieving the death of a child, but all families do not present symptoms of unhealthy patterns. Open communication patterns will ease the difficulties that confront a family that is coping with the death of a child (Arnold & Gemma, 1994). If parents are comfortable with their own grief, able to convey their own feelings of sadness, and can express fond memories of the deceased child, then their actions convey the message that it is acceptable to talk about the death. When details of the death event are communicated to the surviving sibling in age-appropriate language, an environment for a healthy response has been created. Encouraging, but never forcing, the surviving sibling to be involved in familial and societal rituals of mourning, and attending the funeral are often first steps in creating a healthy response (Corr, 1991).

Healthy familial responses to the death of a child also include providing social support to surviving siblings or assisting such siblings to obtain suitable support outside the immediate family. Research has repeatedly demonstrated that support systems can facilitate coping with loss and grief (Klass, 1988; Parkes, 1987; Parkes & Weiss, 1983; Vachon & Stylianos, 1988; Zisook & DeVaul, 1985). In terms of families that had experienced the death of a child, Davies (1988b) found that social support gained by having an emphasis on social, cultural, recreational, and religious events served a protective function for children who had experienced the death of a sibling. Grieving is an individualized, often lonely experience. The ability to reconnect and resume life's daily activities can be facilitated by sharing one's experiences with those who will take the time to listen. If a healthy family environment has been created, then family members may be able to support one another in important ways.

Other social support networks may also exist for the family unit and specifically for the surviving siblings. For example, the extended family and other relatives may serve as significant sources of social support for surviving siblings. However, extended family members often find it difficult to offer the support needed in light of their own grief processes.

A family's spiritual belief system may also function as a form of social support to assist grieving and mourning in surviving siblings. Previous studies have indicated that one of the roles of religion is to provide support to fellow believers in times of crisis (Canda, 1988; Canda & Phaobtong, 1992; Lowenberg, 1988). The presence of a belief system may serve as a means of providing an explanation for a tragic event or a framework within which the death can be found to have meaning. Davies (1988b) compared families that experienced the death of a child to nonbereaved families. She found that families that are more cohesive and active, and that place a greater emphasis on religious aspects of living, have children who display fewer behavior problems up to 3 years after the death of a child.

Another mechanism of social support may be provided by the professional community, such as physicians, nurses, social workers, psychologists, and members of the clergy. Although the professional community can provide and facilitate the mobilization of a support system, every family that experiences the death of a child is not necessarily at risk. Further exploration and research are needed to determine which children could benefit from the services offered by the professional community in facilitating healthy outcomes of bereavement.

FACTORS THAT INFLUENCE SIBLING AND FAMILIAL RESPONSES

Central to an understanding of the processes of grieving and mourning in children who experience the death of a brother or sister are a host of variables that affect the degree to which the outcome is positive or negative. Davies (1995) identified and categorized these variables as they relate to individual, situations, and environmental factors. Similarly, Webb (1993b) identified individual factors, factors related to the death, and family, social, and religious/cultural factors.

Individual factors include the age and gender of the surviving child. The ability of a child to understand some of the components of the death experience has been documented at around 6 or 7 years of age (Donders, 1993; see chapter 2 in this book). Children have some understanding that death is final, irreversible, and inevitable around this age (Reilly, Hasazi, & Bond, 1983; Speece & Brent, 1984). Studies that have examined this aspect of the bereavement outcome present inconclusive findings. For example, Blinder (1972) found that the effect of the sibling death on surviving siblings is influenced by both age and gender, which influence the intensity of the relationship. Similarly, McCown (1983, 1987) reported that younger children are more prone to difficulty after the death of their brother or sister. Betz (1987) recounted statistically significant differences in bereavement reactions based on age, with school-age children more likely to withhold the expression of feelings. By contrast, Davies (1983) reported that age differences are not related to bereavement outcome in the death of a brother or sister. These mixed findings may be the result of the difficulty in establishing adequate control groups to isolate specific variables, combined with small sample sizes.

The limited number of studies that have examined gender and bereavement outcome of siblings indicate that gender is not a significant predictor of bereavement outcome in experiencing the death of a brother or sister (Davies, 1983; McCown, 1983). Additional research in determining the effect of age and gender is warranted.

Davies (1995) has identified situational variables as those that are associated with the duration of the disease or illness. Studies that have examined this aspect of sibling bereavement are limited. Spinetta (1981), in a 3-year, longitudinal study, found that siblings experience the crisis situation with the same intensity as the sibling who has been diagnosed with a terminal condition. This finding suggests that the intensity and duration of the illness can affect subsequent bereavement responses. Similar studies report that the duration of the illness has an effect on the outcome of bereavement in the death of a brother or sister (Payne, Goff, & Paulson, 1980; Schwab, Chalmers, Conroy, Ferris, & Markush, 1965).

Families that experience the death as a sudden loss with little or no warning typically display responses that are rather pronounced, resulting in protective maneuvers, such as withdrawal, denial, and fantasy (Blinder, 1972). Manifestations of guilt are more intense in such circumstances, and there is more willingness to place blame on others for the cause of death. When an extended illness or terminal condition is experienced, parents and other family members have an opportunity to engage in anticipatory grieving (Goldstone & Gamble, 1969; Parkes, 1987). However, when sudden death occurs, surviving family members are faced with higher levels of stress for which the family has had no preparation. In addition, sudden and unexpected death often implies that the death could have been prevented, thus increasing the likelihood of a blaming response within the family. Additional research is needed that examines sibling responses from the time of diagnosis through the duration of the illness and subsequent bereavement responses to the death of the sibling.

Environmental factors that may contribute to the bereavement outcome of children include quality of family relationships, parental characteristics, communication, and shared life space. As previously noted, the responses of the surviving siblings to the death of a brother or sister are related to the climate that is created by the parents. For example, Davies (1988b) noted a positive relationship between family environments characterized by high cohesion levels and behavior responses after the death of a brother or sister.

Parental characteristics and how these may influence the bereavement responses of surviving siblings have not been fully examined. However, Spinetta, McLaren, Fox, and Sparta (1981) reported that families who were consistent in values, lifestyles, and beliefs were best able to cope with the diagnosis and subsequent experiences of the death of a family member. Clearly, there is a need to examine further the quality of relationships in the family and how these relationships affect the grieving process.

IMPLICATIONS FOR HELPING PROFESSIONALS

In working with children who have experienced the death of a sibling, there are several factors to consider that are helpful in determining a positive outcome of bereavement. Professional helpers should take an inventory of the extent to which surviving siblings have been involved in grief-related rituals. Involvement in rituals, such as attending the funeral, provides an opportunity for the child to say "good-bye" to the deceased sibling. Often, parents want to "protect" their surviving siblings by having them stay with neighbors or friends. If the surviving siblings were not involved in normal grief-related rituals, they may need to be reconstructed in counseling or therapy (Cook & Dworkin, 1992).

It is also important to ascertain to what degree there may be any unanswered questions surrounding the details of the death of the deceased sibling. Even though a child may have been involved in anticipatory and postdeath activities, he or she still may have been given distorted or incomplete information. In most situations, the truth is less painful than the wildest imaginations of children (Bluebond-Langner, 1989). Consider the following example:

> Jeanne's sister was killed instantly in a car accident while returning home from a friend's house. Her third-grade classmates at school told Jeanne that they had heard that her sister's head was "cut off" when she was thrown through the car window. The casket was closed at the funeral, and Jeanne had no information to indicate that this in fact did not occur. Weeks after the funeral, she had continuing nightmares stemming from this rumor, which was embellished at each telling. She eventually shared this horror story with her therapist. The therapist was able to reassure Jeanne that her sister died of massive internal injuries and that her sister's head was not "cut off" as was rumored.

To be certain that a child has been informed about the details of the sibling's death, the following questions should be asked: Did the surviving sibling have a chance to ask questions about the death of his or her brother or sister? Were the questions answered in terms and language that the child could understand? Are there any remaining questions that need to be addressed? Although adults should not overwhelm the child with information, a child's questions can be used as a guide to determine what kind of information he or she is seeking.

In working with younger children who possess limited skills in the expression of thoughts and feelings, helping professionals should consider the use of nonverbal methods of communication, such as drawings. A child's drawings may convey important aspects of what he or she is thinking and feeling. When using drawings as a tool to facilitate a child's thoughts or feelings, it is advisable to be nondirective to allow the child to form his or her own frame of reference in the creation of the drawings (Cook & Dworkin, 1992). Helping professionals should use caution in assigning value judgments concerning the quality of the child's use of colors and content. Such judgments may influence the content and style of the child's drawing. Drawings that focus on the death event or family dynamics may be useful in helping the child to express thoughts or feelings about the death of a brother or sister. However, the results should be interpreted with caution and in the context of other available information provided by the child, parents, siblings, and other significant individuals who are familiar with the death of the sibling.

Children's literature can also be used to help younger children understand the concept of death and to provide vehicles to stimulate interactions with surviving children concerning the death of their sibling.

Children's books can provide an excellent source of information for understanding death. Some of the most widely read include *Charlotte's Web* (White, 1952), an intriguing story about the death of a spider; *The Tenth Good Thing About Barney* (Viorst, 1971), which describes the "good" characteristics of a child's pet cat who dies; and *My Grandpa Died Today* (Fassler, 1971), a tender account of the death of a child's grandfather.

Fleming and Balmer (1991) have also recommended the use of group intervention as a means of providing beneficial services to children who have experienced the death of a brother or sister. Bereavement support groups for children can provide a clear sense that others have experienced similar thoughts, emotions, and feelings, which can, in turn, be a source of support and comfort to surviving siblings (see chapter 15). In addition, groups for bereaved children can be a useful means of validating a child's experiences in the context of others who have had similar experiences. Nevertheless, this approach should be employed only when a thorough assessment of the individual child has been made, and it has been determined that a support group is likely to be a productive intervention.

CONCLUSION

The childhood sibling relationship is a bond that has the potential of lasting longer than any other familial relationship. Tragic events, such as a life-threatening illness or unexpected death, can prematurely sever this meaningful familial relationship. Surviving siblings are then left with an immense task of mourning the untimely death of a brother or sister.

The present state of our knowledge about bereavement responses of children who are experiencing the death of a sibling is not fully satisfactory. However, there is much that professional helpers and other adults can do to help surviving siblings cope effectively with loss and grief. Information, insights, and practical wisdom of the sorts described in this chapter are already available to assist in this work.

In particular, professional helpers can play a significant role in facilitating the grief of surviving siblings and their families by being attentive to both the sibling's and the family's responses to the child's death. Efforts should be made to ensure that accurate age-related information has been shared with the surviving siblings. In addition, research has clearly indicated the importance of identifying an appropriate support system for surviving family members—including the siblings. An effective social support system may include extended family, friends, or members of the professional helping community.

Experiencing the death of a brother or sister and coping with the ensuing bereavement will never be easy. Nevertheless, the empathetic presence of knowledgeable, skillful, and caring adults can do much to provide opportunities for growth as a child learns to live with the death of a sibling.

9

Children's Friendships and the Death of a Friend

Tamina Toray and Kevin Ann Oltjenbruns

In the past decade, there has been frequent reference to the child as the "forgotten mourner." Most often this has been in the context of the child who has lost a sibling. More and more emphasis, however, has been placed on developing an understanding of this significant childhood loss (Davies, 1988b; Gibbons, 1992; Leder, 1992; McCown & Davies, 1995). To date, there is a significant gap in the professional literature focusing on the death of a friend during childhood. One exception is work done by Pohlman (1984). Other authors, such as Park (1992) have studied the loss of a friend because of causes other than death. Sklar and Hartley (1990), who make the argument that we must address the needs of this "hidden population" of bereaved friends, focused on adolescents and adults, not children, and Oltjenbruns (1996) described various issues related to the death of a friend during adolescence.

This chapter provides a foundation for much-needed work in understanding a child's experience of losing a friend to death. We first explore the world of children's friendships to gain a better understanding of how they develop, their importance, how they differ from adult/child relations, the multifaceted nature of a friend's death, interventions appropriate to the family system and also a school-based setting.

CULTURE OF CHILDHOOD

Many developmental textbooks refer to the "culture of childhood." A significant part of that "culture" refers to the way in which children spend their time and to the friendship bonds that are developed with agemates. Before we can understand the impact that the death of a friend has on the surviving partner in a given relationship, we must understand the nature of the relationship and the multifaceted nature of the loss which results.

> We went home and when somebody said, "Where were you?" we said, "Out," and when somebody said, "What were you doing until this hour of the night?" we said, as always, "Nothing." . . .
> But about this doing nothing: we swung on swings. We went for walks. We lay on our backs in backyards and chewed grass. . . .
> We watched things: we watched people build houses, we watched men fix cars, we watched each other patch bicycle tires with rubber bands. . . .
> We sat in boxes; we sat under porches; we sat on roofs; we sat on limbs of trees.
> We stood on boards over excavations; we stood on tops of piles of leaves; we stood under rain dripping from the eaves; we stood up to our ears in snow.
> We looked at things like knives and immies and pig nuts and grasshoppers and clouds and dogs and people.
> We skipped and hopped and jumped. Not going anywhere—just skipping and hopping and jumping and galloping.
> We sang and whistled and hummed and screamed.
> What I mean, Jack, we did a lot of nothing. (Smith, 1957, pp. 70–71 & 97–98)

OVERVIEW OF CHILDREN'S RELATIONSHIPS

Children spend a lot of time doing such "nothing things" together. Their friendships represent a unique world filled with fantasy, play, and the learning of some of life's most important lessons. In this special world of equals, devoid of adult structure and rules, children come together to formulate their own reality. Most adults observing children interacting with their close friends can easily see these special bonds in action. Think back for a moment to your best friend in grade school. How difficult is it to recall him or her? Can you easily conjure up a moment from the past when the two of you were immersed in your special world? Most adults have little difficulty remembering such relationships.

Although we often think of the family as the most powerful and influential socializing agent in a child's life, peers, and, more specifically, friends also have substantial impacts. Children from a young age are greatly influenced by the experiences they have outside the realm of the family. Peer relations in most cultures provide informal contexts in which children are socialized. From a young age, children are exposed to an extensive network of learning via their peer relations. "Friendships are among the central ingredients of children's lives, from as early as age three—or, in some cases, even earlier—through adolescence" (Rubin, 1980, p. 3).

In the past decade, much attention has been paid to children's friendships (Asher & Coie, 1990; Berndt & Perry, 1986; Furman & Bierman, 1984; Park, Lay, & Ramsay, 1993; Parker & Asher, 1993). Findings from these studies suggest that peer interactions serve vital roles in many areas of the child's development including social skills (Hartup, 1986), moral understanding (Damon, 1977), and gender role development (Fine, 1980). Piaget (1965) and Sullivan (1953) pointed to the importance of early peer relations on a child's development, especially in the development of a sense of self.

Peer relations may play an even more significant role in today's society than in previous periods. As the numbers of working mothers and single-parent families increase, a child's involvement in organized peer groups also increases. Children now spend more time in settings such as day care and preschool, as well as after-school groups (Asher & Coie, 1990). Thus, on a daily basis, children's contact with similar-aged peers is increasing.

DEVELOPMENT OF CHILDREN'S FRIENDSHIPS

As with many facets of a child's life, the meaning and importance of children's peer relationships also follow a developmental unfolding. Though there is some disagreement on the exact timetable for changes in children's friendships, most authors agree that transformations in the quality of these relationships are greatly influenced by concurrent social, cognitive, and physical maturation in children. Each new step in the developmental process allows for new and different types of peer interaction.

The earliest peer interactions occur during the 1st year of life. Vandell and Mueller (1980) found that about 60% of American 6- to 12-month-olds have contact with other babies at least once a week. These early child-child interactions are for the most part nonreciprocated and isolated social interactions. However, these early social contacts gradually evolve into interactional patterns that are reciprocal and complex in nature (Berk, 1991). Park, Lay, and Ramsay (1993) found stability in preschool-aged friends over a 1-year period, as well as increased positive interactions, revealing a developmental trend in young children's friendships. Furman and Bierman (1984) found evidence of increased closeness and support in children during middle childhood compared with younger children.

Developmental changes in children's friendships have also been identified by Selman (1980, 1981) and Berndt (1983, 1986) who have written extensively about children's ability to understand and coordinate social relationships. Both authors have identified changes in the characteristics of children's friendships as a child develops. Preschool-aged children (3 to 5 years of age) tend to be egocentric in their thinking, and this egocentrism is reflected in their behavior with peers. In this stage, children are able to recognize thoughts and feelings within themselves and others, but are unable to distinguish their own feelings from those of others. An example of such behavior is a preschooler bringing a new toy to school and assuming that every child will like it as much as he or she does. Children at this stage are also unable to distinguish intentions of others. For instance, if another child accidentally takes his or her toy, the child will assume that was done on purpose and will have a difficult time understanding that there was no intention to do harm. Preschool-aged children often understand friendships in terms of concrete characteristics. A friend is someone they spend time with, someone whom they are physically close to, and someone with whom they share toys.

The elementary-aged child (6 to 12 years of age) is able to take a self-reflective or reciprocal perspective (Selman, 1981). Children at this age are able to understand that they themselves can be the object of another person's feelings or thoughts, a concept referred to as reciprocal trust (Berndt, 1983, 1986). Being helpful and trustworthy become important characteristics that define friendships during this stage. Friendship moves from being based primarily on physical factors, such as proximity and interest in sharing toys, to more of a psychological base, such as shared qualities and interests. Friends are people with whom one can share innermost feelings and thoughts.

IMPORTANCE OF CHILDREN'S FRIENDSHIPS

"Friendships are important children tell us, because of the pleasures and excitement of the joint play that happens with a friend; because of the companionship, the support, and the help they provide; and the affection that is felt in a friendship" (Dunn, 1993, p. 62).

Simple observation of children spending time with a friend will provide evidence of the functions friendships serve. Rubin (1980) described two ways in which children serve distinctive functions for one another: (a) by providing opportunities for the learning of social skills and (b) by furnishing a context for comparison of self to others.

Peer interactions allow children to learn techniques for establishing and managing social interactions and relationships including the ability to successfully communicate. These fundamental skills, learned within a peer context, may have significant impact on social relationships throughout an individual's life. Rubin (1980) suggested that although parents play a key role in the teaching of many social skills, they often make communication too easy for their children. For example, parents often "decode" a child's incomplete communications and move to satisfy them without expecting the child to complete his or her communication. In peer relations, children cannot engage in such incomplete communication. To get their needs met, they are forced to learn to relay their desires and needs more effectively. Thus, peers provide a different and important context for children to learn social skills. Such interactions may help to facilitate direct communication, something that may be lacking in adult-child interactions.

Erik Erikson (1963) described the psychosocial task of the school-aged (6 to 11 years of age) child as that of attempting to gain a sense of "industry." This sense of importance or productivity is accomplished by the child via his or her interactions with peers, and the comparison of self with those peers. "How fast can I run?"; "How smart am I?"; and "How tall or short am I?" all can be answered only in the context of comparison with peers. The information gained in such comparisons is used in the formation of a child's sense of and self-esteem. A negative resolution to this developmental stage may mean a sense of "inferiority" (Erikson, 1960) or a feeling of being "less than" one's peers in one or many arenas. Thus, there is a strong need for children to enter into the world of their peers for the purpose of comparing their skills and abilities with others. Adults can not provide such sources of comparison.

UNIQUE CONTRIBUTION OF CHILD–CHILD RELATONS

Most socialization theories tend to emphasize the importance of external agents, primarily adults on a child's social development. It is through these adult agents of socialization, primarily parents and teachers, that children's behaviors, thoughts, and actions are said to develop

(Youniss, 1980). However, there is another primary agent or influence in children's social development—friendships. Children's relations with each other differ from their relations with the adults in their world. Relationships with friends are voluntary, and provide a unique environment for children's social development.

Youniss (1980) examined the unique contribution of friends in a child's life by presenting what he described as the "Sullivan–Piaget thesis." His thesis draws together Sullivan's (1953) theory of children's friendships, and Piaget's (1965) work on children's cognitive understanding of social relationships. Youniss suggested that although parents and other adults are important agents in the social development of a child, peer relations, and particularly children's friendships, are a primary and vital force in their social development. "Through peers, and especially friends, children learn to become interpersonally sensitive, how to handle intimacy, and ways to achieve mutual understanding" (Youniss, 1980, p. 1).

Both Sullivan and Piaget posited that there are primary processes by which children acquire social meaning. The first such process is through another person. Children attempt to conform to and adopt another individual's standards of behavior; this person is often an adult or high-status peer. This type of externally motivated socialization leaves children with little power or ability to impact their own development according to this thesis.

A second way in which children find social meaning is based on a process in which they serve as coagents of their own socialization. It is within this more cooperative rather than conforming process that the children collaborate with an equal, a friend, to gain understanding and meaning in a social situation. In this type of cooperative interaction, children and others involved in the interaction are simultaneously both agents and recipients of instruction. Thus, in a spirit of cooperation, children learn from one another through an interactive medium which allows them to work out compromises between both parties.

In their interactions with adults, children's sense of reality and sense of worth is often based on the adult's criterion for approval. In their relationships with each other, children come to agreement on standards they should meet, and these standards are not imposed on them from outside forces. This is not to say that these mutually agreed-on standards are easily achieved! Children can set difficult standards for acceptance or approval; however, such standards are worked through bilaterally, in a child-to-child manner, creating a different dynamic than those dictated unilaterally by adults. Thus, friendships may allow for a mutuality and reciprocity unseen in adult-child socialization. In these social interactions children fully participate in the cocreation of their own socialization.

Sullivan (1953) viewed children's friendships as "a perfectly novel relationship with the person concerned; he becomes of practically equal importance in all fields of value. Nothing remotely like that has happened before" (Sullivan, 1953, p. 245). Because of this unique relationship, the loss of a friend during childhood means the loss of that "perfectly novel relationship" that will never again exist.

LOSSES RELATED TO DEATH OF A FRIEND

Children's friendships provide a rich world of social learning. What happens when this world is disrupted by the death of a friend? There is almost no empirical data available to describe this process. However, there is literature that relates to the loss of a childhood friend through one child moving to a different neighborhood. One such study was done by Park (1992) who studied young children's reactions after a best friend moved away. She found several common reactions to this type loss: sadness (76%), loneliness (71%), and anger (12%). Certainly these reactions are parallel to components of a normal grief response.

Lofland (1982) suggested seven ways in which we maintain a human bond and explained what is lost when that bond is broken by death or loss. The model presented here is an adaptation of those areas originally described by Lofland, together with an application of those areas to a child's loss of a friend through death developed by the authors of this chapter.

1. *Role partners.* In any loss of a significant relationship, there is a loss of someone who played an important role in our lives. Within that relationship, numerous functions were served to meet the needs of both parties. In the case of a child experiencing the death of a friend, the deceased child may have served several important roles and functions, such as classmate, neighborhood chum, teammate, comrade, playmate, and much more. Although role partners can be replaced in terms of their general function, they cannot be replaced in their unique and specific nature. Each individual plays out his or her functions in a friendship in a distinctive and individual manner. Each friendship represents

a unique union between two individuals, and the death of a friend represents a break in that special union.

When 9-year-old Maggie died in a car accident, her friend Shawna was devastated and had a difficult time coping in the months after the May death. The summer months loomed like an eternity; these two friends had been inseparable during daylight hours in previous years. Maggie and Shawna lived next door to one another. They swam together, biked together, shared picnic lunches in the neighborhood park. Shawna, in addition to experiencing many feelings typical of a grief response, cried "I just don't even know how to spend my time! We used to do everything together! I am scared—every day takes forever to end."

2. *Daily assistance.* Fulfillment of our daily tasks requires the help and support of individuals in our social world. In a child's friendship, such assistance may range from building a tree house to fixing a bike. A child's social network of friends provides a great deal of such assistance. The death of a friend represents a significant loss in such aid.

Ten-year-old chums, Kyle and Derek, were in Scouts together, went to church together, attended the same school, and engaged in joint activities on an almost daily basis. Kyle was the physically stronger of the two and was more than willing to help Derek with his paper route. When Kyle died, Derek gave the job up—both because it was a painful reminder of his friend but also because it was such a difficult task for him to do alone.

3. *Ties to others.* Children's peer relations allow them to feel linked to a network beyond that of a given individual friendship. Primary friendships often lead to secondary relationships or acquaintanceships that are linked to the initial friendship. For example, Gary and A.J. had been friends for years. When Gary joined the swim team, he met a number of other agemates who shared similar interests. Gary then introduced A.J. to Jerad. When Gary initiated the interactions, the three of them would engage in various activities. After Gary's death, A.J. found it difficult to maintain a comfortable relationship with Jerad; both had depended on Gary to facilitate their mutual interaction.

When the deceased friend (Gary) played a strong intermediary role in connecting secondary friendships (A.J. and Jerad), the loss of that primary friend is significant. Not only is the primary friendship bond severed at the time of the death, but the secondary friendship bonds may be weakened or broken when the decease friend is no longer available to provide linkages to others.

4. *Maintenance of sense of self.* Friends reflect back to us a unique view of the self; they often see dimensions of our self that we have difficulty acknowledging. For example, Cathy's sense of humor seemed to be much more apparent when she was with her friend Keri than when she was around other classmates. "I never thought of myself as very funny, but Keri always told me how much I made her laugh. When I was around Keri, it was really easy to think up funny things." Keri's death brought about a loss of that part of self—a sense of playfulness and a sense of humor—that Cathy had felt in the presence of her friend. "That aspect of self (or those multiple aspects) that was significantly and uniquely generated or sustained in interaction with the other is, quite literally, lost when the other is lost" (Lofland, 1982, p. 226).

Lofland also suggested that maintenance of self is not completely threatened by the death of a significant other because memory often allows an individual to represent that relationship internally. However, over time, memory may have numerous limitations.

5. *Buffer from life's hazards.* Close relationships with others provide children comfort and buffer them from unforeseen hazards of existence. Such hazards may include the illness or death of a family member or friend, divorce of parents, and fear of abandonment by loved ones. A close friendship provides a buffer comprised of a sense of security and solace. Friendships often provide much comfort in a world filled with daily hardships, or sudden and catastrophic events. The maintenance of this security resides largely in the ongoing support of an important friend. The death of such a friend results not only in a strong sense of grief, but also greatly diminishes a sense of personal safety, leaving a child feeling vulnerable and alone.

Toni's mother often treated her harshly—both verbally and physically. The only one Toni ever confided in was Leah who comforted her tears and reassured Toni that it was her mother who was bad, not Toni herself. When Leah died in an apartment building fire that claimed many lives, Toni had no one to whom to turn. She became increasingly withdrawn until a very caring teacher sought help for her. With much counseling support, Toni was finally able to come to terms with Leah's death and her mother's treatment of her.

6. *Maintenance of reality.* Every significant relationship individuals have with others serves to validate their reality, their existence. The daily interactions children have with their friends provide an active flow of validation through actions and words. The conversations children

have and the games they play, all reflect back to them an understanding of their current existence. On the death of a friend, this commonly shared social construction may dissolve leaving children, at least temporarily, unable to maintain their previous reality.

The grief process itself gives clues to the changing nature of the world around us. Often grieving individuals talk about feeling "out of touch with reality," as if separated from the rest of the world around them. Children's daily interactions with friends allow for a construction of reality that is vastly changed by the death of a friend.

7. *Maintenance of "possible futures."* This last connection to others refers to the role close relationships play in providing an influence on each other's future. To lose a friend to death is to lose a part of one's planned future. One may experience changed goals, diminishing an earlier level of comfort or pleasure concerning the future. In the case of a child experiencing the death of a friend there may be numerous "futures" lost.

"I don't have anyone to go to my new middle school when it opens next year. Nobody understands me like Jessie did. We talked a lot about what it was going to be like. We wanted our lockers to be next to each other. We had lots of plans. We were going to ride our bikes to school together. We wanted to get into the same computer class. Now Jessie is gone and none of this will come true." This refrain illustrates one arena of future loss experienced by the death of a close friend. Such a death confronts the child with a feeling of being deprived of a future possibility. The plans that the child had with that particular friend will never actualize.

Summary of the Application of Lofland's Model

In summary, Lofland (1982) has posited seven ties that bind individuals in close relationships and has suggested that there may be a connection between the breakage of those ties and the grief experience. We believe this framework is useful in understanding the responses of grieving children who have lost significant friendship ties in their lives. For school-age children, the loss of a friend often means the loss of an important member of the classroom community and even the entire school. Teachers and counselors can serve vital roles in offering support and providing information about death and facets of loss.

SCHOOL-BASED INTERVENTIONS

Several different intervention strategies have been explored by teachers and counselors as useful in relationship to the death of a friend during childhood. Many school systems are now including various death education units in their regular curricula so that there can be some discussion about loss, the dying process, and the resultant grief experience before a child dies. Complementary to these preparatory strategies are various intervention strategies that may be implemented following the death of a child.

- One intervention strategy involves having children "tell their story," that is, to tell others about the relationships they shared with the child who died, describe their feelings, and deal with questions of concern. Children should be encouraged to participate in this sharing process using many different modalities—writing a story or poem, drawing a picture, describing photographs or significant objects that symbolize a link to the child who has died.

  As children interact with others in their social system, there are multiple benefits. The children are able to acquire information about their friend's death. Often misconceptions are clarified or the children gather information that they may not have had previously. Clear information and honest communication help to create an atmosphere that allows children to deal with their feelings and concerns. Additionally, this interactive process of providing support and sharing information often serves to help children understand various facets of death, can validate children's feelings, and help normalize the grief experience for those involved (Fleming & Balmer, 1991).

- Bibliotherapy may be used effectively both to educate children about facets of the death experience as well as to throw light on various aspects of bereavement. Klingman (1985) explained that exposure to various stories and books may help children to "map feelings, achieve insight, develop new attitudes, and then to explore new ways of responding" (p. 450). One classic example of a book used to help children understand the death of a friend better is Doris Smith's (1973) *A Taste of Blackberries*. In this story, a young boy's best friend dies suddenly. Caring adults struggle to explain the meaning of death, encourage him to participate in the funeral, and reach out to support him in dealing with a variety of emotions.

- Art is also a powerful tool in helping to express feelings. Some children either do not have the words to describe their experiences or are hesitant to do so verbally with others. Multiple benefits may accrue from the use of art therapy. The act of engaging in a particular art activity may be cathartic to the child, and the end product may provide an impetus for discussion with others (Zambelli, Clark, Barile, & deJong, 1988).

- Fleming and Balmer (1991) advocate the use of a "question box," which allows children to ask questions anonymously about the death that they might not otherwise feel comfortable doing. Sometimes children feel that they should already know the answer and do not want to embarrass themselves. Alternatively, they may not feel that a question will be regarded as an appropriate one to ask. As answers and reactions are shared publicly, many will derive needed insight.

Role of the Teacher/Counselor

Many of the strategies described earlier are appropriate for either classroom use or for group counseling sessions. Regardless of the setting, it is crucial that the adults leading such activities be knowledgeable in the area of bereavement, have strong facilitation skills, and be comfortable in interacting with others about death, dying, and grief. Cullinan (1990) observed that "teachers' ability to handle death of self, their level of death anxiety, their perception of their role with students who have experienced loss, and their ability to feel comfortable in counseling grieving students were among the factors found to predict their perceived ability to help grieving students" (p. 147).

Cullinan (1990) discovered that teachers' own reactions to death situations can influence their classes' understanding of death. Teachers in the sample of this study taught kindergarten to grade 12; grade 7 was the mean. Approximately 90% of these teachers had had classroom experience with death. Cullinan's findings also indicated that many teachers felt unprepared to aid grieving students in that only 81% of her sample of teachers had had any preparation in death education themselves, whereas 93% felt that this was important. Eighty-seven percent noted that they did not feel comfortable counseling grieving students, yet 93% said that it is proper for a teacher to counsel a grieving student. Clearly, there is a discrepancy between educational preparation and comfort levels as related to the role teachers feel they should play in supporting their bereaved students.

The relationship between teacher and student is a special one. School counselors recognize the importance of a teacher's daily interactions with bereaved students, in addition to the more formal therapeutic support provided by the counseling staff (Arena, Hermann, & Hoffman, 1984). When there is a child experiencing a terminal illness, the teacher must be comfortable in offering support to both the dying child and to his or her classmates (Bertoia & Allan, 1988). School systems, then, should carefully plan ways to better prepare teaching personnel to interact with students dealing with multiple facets of a death experience. This task becomes all the more difficult when the teachers themselves are grieving the death of a child for whom they, too, cared.

FAMILY SUPPORT

Family members also play an important role after the death of a child's friend. Certainly, the strategies noted earlier (e.g., art activity, exposure to books, and honest communication) are just as appropriate in the family's efforts to comfort the grieving child. Although not focused directly on the death of a friend, many straightforward and helpful suggestions are found in Fitzgerald's (1992) book, *The Grieving Child: A Parent's Guide*. These include the following:

- How parents' can understand changes in children's behavior after the death of a loved one
- How to explain the reality of death to a child
- How to help a child to prepare for a loved one's impending death
- How to help a child deal with a variety of thoughts and feelings (e.g., fears, guilt, depression, anger, and guilt)
- How to plan a meaningful ritual to help recognize the death and the significance of the loss.

CONCLUSION

As important as friends are during childhood, little attention has been paid to bereavement outcomes that result when this relationship bond is severed by death. To understand how to give support, caring adults must first understand the multiplicity of losses that stem from the death of a friend. Lofland's model was adapted to provide this insight.

It is important that caregivers be attuned to developmental differences among children (Cook & Oltjenbruns, 1989). There are stage-specific characteristics that influence a bereaved child's understanding of the death itself as well as certain manifestations of grief. Further, life stage may also have an influence on the essence of "friendship" and thereby help to define the nature of the loss. Adults should realize the many intertwined roles that are lost when a child's friend dies. Such understanding can help adults avoid minimizing the loss with such statements as, "You can find other friends."

10

Children and Pet Loss

Carolyn L. Butler and Laurel S. Lagoni

During the last 30 years, a new area of interest called human–animal interactions or the human–animal bond has emerged as an important, interdisciplinary field of study. Researchers working in this field have learned a great deal about the relationships that develop between people and the animals who share their lives. A major thrust of this research has focused on the attachments children form with pets or "companion animals," as they are more commonly referred to in the literature. Overall, findings suggest that children who are highly attached to and involved with companion animals often benefit from their interactions with such animals. In fact, recent evidence indicates that certain types of relationships between companion animals and children can positively affect children's cognitive development (Kidd & Kidd, 1985), empathy, perceived competence (Melson, Sparks, & Peet, 1989), and social adjustment (Melson & Taylor, 1990).

Clearly, pet ownership has many beneficial aspects, yet there are difficult aspects too. For example, because of companion animals' relatively short life spans (e.g., dogs and cats have approximately one fifth the life span of humans), few pets outlive their owners. Some companion animals die from acute or chronic illnesses. Others are victims of accidents. Many pets die of old age or are euthanized because of unresolvable behavior problems or untreatable terminal illnesses. Thus, companion animal death is an inevitable part of pet ownership.

Portions of this chapter previously appeared in Lagoni, L., Butler, C., & Hetts, S. (1994). *The human–animal bond and grief.* Philadelphia: W. B. Saunders Company. Reprinted by permission.

Because of this fact, in recent years many professional helpers have begun to see the need for skilled interventions during pet loss. Some have created practice specialties in pet loss and grief, and have begun working in veterinary schools, in private therapy practices, and in conjunction with local humane societies. Through their efforts, they provide grief education and support to adults and children experiencing pet loss. Additionally, national organizations, such as The Delta Society, promote the study of the human–animal bond and provide resource information about pet loss. The Delta Society also publishes a national directory of pet loss counselors, a directory whose membership grows in size and scope annually.

When children are confronted with the death or loss of their pets, helpers (e.g., mental health professionals, teachers, child care providers, veterinarians, and other well-informed adults) play significant roles in facilitating their grief. These helpers are most effective when they base their assistance on understanding the significance of the human–animal bond, together with specific knowledge about helping during companion animal loss.

CHILDREN AND THE HUMAN–ANIMAL BOND

Children have had relationships with animals for thousands of years. Still, many contemporary relationships between children and their companion animals are deeper and more significant than in the past. This may result from the various pressures of modern, mobile society, which have changed children's traditional support systems and the nature of their familial relationships. For instance, today many children grow up with working, divorced, or single parents. Children may also live far away from grandparents and other members of their extended families. In addition, it is not uncommon for children to spend considerable amounts of time alone at home in self-care situations both before and after school.

Children in these situations, as well as those who are simply highly attached to their pets, may rely heavily on their companion animals for emotional and social support. Under these circumstances, pets often take on key roles in children's daily routines and rituals. For example, companion animals may be the ones who play and "watch television" with children, or who protect and comfort them when they are frightened or lonely. Companion animals may also provide children with consistent unconditional love and acceptance, and with increased feelings of self-worth when they successfully care for their pets' needs.

Many variables affect the attachments that form between children and companion animals. These include the amount of time spent with pets, the roles animals play in children's lives, and the knowledge children have of their pets' characteristics and needs. These variables affect the quality and intensity of children's attachments to their pets.

Time Spent with Pets

The desire to be close to or maintain proximity with an attachment figure is a measure of attachment often used to assess the strength of the human–animal bond (Cairns, 1966). This method of assessment can also be applied to attachments between animals and children (Bowlby, 1982). Thus, it may be deduced that children who spend much of their leisure time with their companion animals may be more attached to them. For example, children who are often home alone before or after school, or on weekends with only their pets for company may become more attached to their pets than children who have other sources of emotional and social support (see Figure 10.1). Melson (1988) found that the average amount of time spent with pets was positively correlated with children's reports of their emotional closeness to the animals.

FIGURE 10.1 Photograph of a young girl with a pet. Photograph by Betsy Wade.

Interest, Behaviors, and Emotions
Directed Toward Pets

Another measure of attachment is the degree to which the attachment figure can comfort and calm someone who is stressed (Ainsworth, 1979). For example, children who are home alone, ill, socially isolated, or in conflict with their parents or siblings, or whose families are in the midst of divorce, moving, or dealing with another family member's serious illness, may not receive the support and attention they need. Instead, they may turn to their pets as a source of comfort. Children who talk to their pets, and who consider them to be "special friends" whom they can talk to when they are upset, can be considered to be more attached to them than children who do not engage in these behaviors (Bryant, 1987).

Understanding of Pets' Needs

Attachments to animals are more likely to develop when people know how to communicate with them. Thus, mutual communication between people and animals is more likely to occur when humans are knowledgeable about animals. Children who have primary responsibility for their companion animals and who become familiar with their animals' habits, behaviors, and care requirements usually become very attached to them. A good example of attachments formed in this way are the relationships that children who belong to 4-H clubs form with the project animals they raise.

WHEN THE HUMAN–ANIMAL BOND IS BROKEN

Children who form strong attachments to their pets frequently describe their companion animals in terms most often used to characterize human relationships. These terms include "best friend," "brother or sister," and even "parent." It is understandable, then, that when the human–animal bond is broken by the death of a pet, a child's grief can be intense and even overwhelming.

The death of a companion animal may be, in fact, one of the most significant losses that people, adults and children alike, experience in their lives (Gage & Holcomb, 1991; Hart, Hart, & Mader, 1990). Through research and clinical experience, experts have gained a greater understanding of the true impact pet loss has on children. They have found, for example, that children feel much the same way when pets are given away as they do when pets die because both experiences generate similar kinds of stress and feelings of grief (Bryant, 1990).

Children experience pet loss in two primary ways. In the first, the animal's death is expected because of old age or a terminal illness, and is carried out through a planned, humane euthanasia. In the second, the loss is unexpected and may involve an accidental death, death resulting from an acute illness, or a situation in which animals either run away or need to be given away. Whether the death is expected or unexpected, children benefit from being involved before, during, and after the loss. When pet loss occurs and children are involved in the entire process, parents and helpers have many opportunities to teach children valuable life skills about grieving, while at the same time helping them say good-bye to special childhood companions.

HELPING CHILDREN WITH PET LOSS

In Western culture, people are probably more familiar with myths about loss and grief than with the facts. Therefore, most of society abides by the myths. Some of the most damaging myths about loss and grief involve children. For example, one myth says that children are resilient during times of crisis and loss. This myth adds that children do not grieve with the same intensity as adults. Another myth says that pet loss serves primarily as a "dress rehearsal" for the "real thing" and that pets' deaths are fairly trivial losses for children.

Societal beliefs dictate societal behaviors. Thus, the experience of childhood pet loss rarely gets the attention it deserves. For example, there are no customary, socially sanctioned rituals, like funerals or memorial services, through which children can mourn their pets' deaths. In addition, adults usually expect and may even demand that children recover rapidly from loss, often encouraging and sometimes even forcing the quick replacement of pets. When companion animals are injured or ill, children are commonly ignored during the medical crisis, left out of the decision-making process, and even lied to when the deaths of their pets actually occur. As grief education and support become more commonplace, however, new beliefs are dispelling these myths, proving that more sensitive and effective ways exist to deal with the experience of childhood pet loss.

Writers on children's development have long advised parents to prepare their children for loss by taking advantage of informal "teachable moments" involving death (Carson, 1984). At one time, suggested teachable moments included the discovery of lifeless birds or bugs in the yard, delivery of news regarding an elderly neighbor's heart attack, or the death of a family's pet. All of these situations were deemed unemotional enough to allow opportunities to talk with children about death under nonthreatening circumstances. The thought was that unemotional conversations about death would arm children with the basic knowledge necessary to help them cope when someone they really *did* love died.

Birds and bugs aside, the long-held belief that pet loss serves primarily as a "dress rehearsal" for the "real thing" has now fallen into disfavor, which is a big step in the right direction. It is now known that many children genuinely love their pets and are deeply affected by their deaths. Pet loss, then, does not present an opportunity for parents, helpers, and children to have unemotional discussions about death and grief. Rather, it presents an opportunity for adults to ensure that children are informed, educated, included, comforted, and reassured about death so they gain the confidence and skills necessary to face loss and cope with it effectively.

Adults may help children prepare for and cope with a pet's death in many ways. Parents and helpers can begin by providing children with basic grief education that is developmentally appropriate. In particular, parents and helpers can read books about pet loss together with children. Many veterinarians have books, pamphlets, and videotapes about children and pet loss available for parents to check out. A bibliography and resource list are included in Appendixes 10.1 and 10.2.

In addition to grief education, helpers should assess the unique needs of the family and the specific needs of the individual children (Table 10.1). When the loss that has occurred is the death of a companion animal, grief education should be paired with accurate and detailed information about what occurs when animals die. Three simple steps for parents and helpers to follow are to (a) be honest with children; (b) encourage children to be involved; and (c) avoid euphemisms about death.

Being Honest with Children

Parents and helpers should talk honestly with children about their pets' illnesses, injuries, treatments, and deaths. Unfortunately, it is not uncommon for parents and other adults to collude in a lie about what actually happened to a child's companion animal. Many parents and professional or paraprofessional helpers, like veterinarians, teachers, and care providers, feel it is kinder to tell children their pets ran away

TABLE 10.1   Assessing Children's Needs During Pet Loss[a]

Helpers can learn to assess which children may need extra support during their pets' deaths. How children deal with pet loss depends on several key factors. These factors include the following:

- Child's age and level of cognitive and emotional maturity
- Role the pet played in the child's life
- Other events currently occurring in the child's life (parental divorce, recent move, illness, etc.)
- Role the child played (if any) in the death of the pet
- Child's personal loss history
- Child's ability to cope with crisis
- Circumstances surrounding the pet's death
- Parent(s)' confidence in assisting children with loss and grief
- Quality and availability of other means of support

[a]If helpers determine that children are deficient, unskilled, or unsupported in several of these areas, additional assistance from professionals in the human service community may be appropriate. Human service professionals might include teachers, school counselors, social workers, family therapists, members of the clergy, and counselors or support group facilitators who specialize in pet loss.

or were given to new homes rather than to say their pets were accidentally killed (e.g., hit by a car or poisoned) or humanely euthanized.

These tactics are not used maliciously by parents and helpers. In fact, the opposite is often true. In times of crisis, many sensitive parents and helpers are simply inadequately prepared to discuss loss, death, and grief with children. Thus, they deceive themselves into believing they can spare their children pain by protecting them from painful experiences. This belief is unfounded. It soon becomes evident that children who are shielded from one kind of pain must eventually deal with another. For example, a child who is told her cat ran away must bear the pain of feeling rejected and abandoned by a pet whom she thought of as her best friend. Additionally, parents often tell the truth about what really happened to the pet months, and even years, later when they believe the child has "recovered from the loss." With the truth revealed, the child is then forced to deal with the breach of trust in the relationship with his or her parents and may ask, "If my parents lied to me about this, what else have they lied to me about?" When lies are exposed, children's abilities to trust, empathize, and grieve normally may be damaged.

Most parents who ask others to lie to their children are really asking for help and support. Many of them are concerned that their own strong emotions may frighten or confuse their children. A request for collusion with them in a lie signals a need for more information and guidance. In the long run, lies create more problems. When children are lied to or otherwise "protected" from experiences with death and from adults' expressions of grief, they are denied opportunities to learn how to master their feelings of loss. They are also denied the role models necessary to learn normal, healthy coping behaviors.

Encourage Involvement of Children

Many children are actively involved in their pets' daily health care. It is only fair to give them the option of also being involved in the circumstances surrounding their pets' deaths. Children of all ages can be included in decisions, euthanasias, and good-bye rituals and ceremonies for their pets. For instance, with adequate preparation, most children who are old enough to think and speak for themselves can choose whether or not to be present at euthanasia. They can also decide for themselves how to say good-bye to their pets, how to honor their pets' memories, and whether or not to view their pets' bodies after death.

All of these decisions and actions help to empower children during times of grief and to minimize regrets later. The key to exposing children to any of these potentially upsetting experiences is preparation. For example, if children want to be present at their pets' euthanasias, they need to be told clearly what will happen while they are in the room, what they will see, how their pets will look, feel, and behave, and what appropriate actions they can take after the pet is dead (e.g., petting, hugging, crying, or spending time with their pets' bodies). In this case, preparation means that parents and helpers structure the grief experience by giving children permission to think, feel, and behave in ways that are suitable for them. This approach does not include allowing children to behave in ways that would cause harm to themselves or others.

Parents and helpers can also suggest that children create "transitional" or "linking" objects as mementos of their pets. For example, before or just after the pet's death, children can clip a bit of their pet's fur to keep as a special reminder of their friend. They can also make an ink or clay print of their pet's paw, save the pet's collar or leash, or keep the "cremains" of the animal.

After death, parents and helpers can encourage children to organize and participate in memorial ceremonies for their pets. Memorials are effective ways to say good-bye and to draw closure to relationships. Examples of memorial ceremonies and rituals include funerals (where children may read poems, stories, or letters they have written about or to their pets), planting trees or flowers as visual tributes to pets, making scrapbooks of mementos and photographs of their pets, and making donations to animal-related service organizations in memory of their pets.

Avoid Using Euphemisms

Children, like adults, respond well to straightforward explanations and concrete words. Using words and phrases like "died," "dead," and "helped to die" may seem harsh, but they help children clearly understand and accept the reality of their pets' deaths. Remember, it is not what is said but how it is said that has the greatest impact on children.

Thus, when working with young pet owners, parents and helpers should avoid inaccurate terminology (euphemisms) like "put to sleep" and "went away." Because children are "put to sleep" every night, use of these words may cause them to fear that they may also die in their sleep. Children may also have negative responses to explanations like "Heidi got sick and died" or clichés like "Heidi is happy with the angels now." Because children get sick, the first phrase may mislead them to believe that all sicknesses end in death. In addition, because children see people crying and acting depressed when a pet dies, the cliché about Heidi's happiness may confuse them about how they should feel. It may also make them resent and dislike angels!

Helpers can also protect veterinarians from becoming animal executioners in children's eyes. Parents should be cautioned about using phrases, such as, "the vet made Heidi die." It should be clarified that disease, injury, or the euthanasia drug caused the pet's death and that the veterinarian helped to end the animal's suffering. Helpers should also let children know through their words and behaviors that everyone (especially the veterinarian) shares in their sadness.

COMPANION ANIMAL EUTHANASIA

The presence of pet owners, especially children, during companion animal euthanasia has traditionally been discouraged by veterinarians. Typically, euthanasias have been carried out in "sterile" environments with no one present, except the members of the veterinary staff. Contemporary veterinary medicine, however, is beginning to see euthanasia in a new light. More and more frequently, euthanasia is coming to be viewed, by veterinary professionals and companion animal owners alike, as both a privilege and a gift, one that can be lovingly bestowed on dying animals.

Many of the euthanasias performed by today's compassionate veterinarians are conducted like ceremonies, with the process itself treated with the respect and reverence it deserves. Helpers and parents who have experienced the profound effects of owner-present euthanasia are beginning to see it as a powerful grief intervention tool. These parents and helpers understand that well-planned euthanasias can be effective in facilitating healthy grief processes and creating positive grief outcomes for children, too. Research and clinical experience supports this as witnessing a peaceful death or viewing a loved one's body after death has been shown to provide grievers, young or old, with a sense of finality and allows their grieving processes to begin or continue (Fulton, 1988; Glick, Weiss, & Parkes, 1974).

The term *euthanasia* is derived from two Greek words—*eu,* meaning "good," and *thanatos,* meaning "death." These words qualify euthanasia as a "good death" (Fogle, 1981). Words, such as humane, painless, and loving, are also associated with euthanasia. Yet putting these positive attributes aside, euthanasia is still, in reality, the purposeful act of terminating a life. Because of this reality, no doubt can exist that the euthanasias of companion animals often impact the adults and children involved in intensely emotional ways.

With this in mind, during the last decade, progressive veterinarians, animal health technicians, and grief counselors from across the country have worked together to create and perfect euthanasia protocols that consider the comfort and well-being of both the pets and the pet owners. These teams of professionals have taken many variables into consideration including the attitudes of those involved in the euthanasia process, the physical surroundings and emotional ambience of the euthanasia site, and the combination of drugs and methods used to induce peaceful and painless deaths (Andrews et al., 1993). How to best prepare pet owners for their companion animals' deaths and how to best help them plan the circumstances surrounding the euthanasia procedure have also been studied (Lagoni & Butler, 1994; Lagoni, Butler, & Hetts, 1994). These protocols, as they apply to helping children, are briefly described in the following section.

Understanding the Euthanasia Procedure

To decide whether or not to be present at their companion animal's death, children need information about what the actual euthanasia procedure entails. This information can be provided to them by a veterinarian, an animal health technician, or a well-informed parent or helper. Once the process has been explained, helpers should demonstrate nonjudgmental support during children's decision-making processes (Table 10.2).

Although euthanasia procedures vary from one veterinarian to another, the basic procedure always involves the injection of a fast-acting, fatal drug into the animal's system. If performed correctly, euthanasia is almost always quick, painless, and peaceful. Before offering to children the option of presence at euthanasia, parents should consult with their veterinarian to ensure that he or she is prepared to support children through this process.

The following is an example of what helpers might say to inform and prepare children for their pet's euthanasia. The words used are probably most appropriate for school-aged children, but even older children benefit from simple language when they are in the midst of an emotional crisis. Altogether, this explanation would take about 10 minutes.

TABLE 10.2 Helping Pet Owners with Euthanasia Choices[a]

Once helpers realize that the time for a pet's euthanasia is near, it is beneficial to help parents and children do as much planning and preparing ahead of time as possible. The purpose of this list is to make helpers aware of the many choices pet owners have about their pets' deaths. Helpers can assist parents and children during euthanasia decision making by encouraging them to do the following:

- Ask the veterinarian to describe the methods and details of the euthanasia procedure.
- Decide whether or not to be present during their pet's euthanasia.
- Decide who else (if anyone) they would like to have present during the euthanasia. (If they wish to be alone during the procedure, they may still want to ask a friend or family member to accompany them to the appointment so they will have support before and afterward.)
- Plan the logistical details of the pet's euthanasia.
    —When should it take place?
    —Where should it take place?
    —How will they care for the pet's body?
    —What will they transport and bury the pet's body in if they take it with them?
- Consider a postmortem examination. Such examinations may be able to answer questions about the pet's illness or injury.
- Think about how they want to say good-bye and memorialize the pet.

---

[a]This sample list can be used to facilitate the euthanasia planning process. Ideally, it should be introduced to pet owners several days or weeks before their pets' deaths. Helpers should encourage pet owners to discuss with their veterinarians any procedures about which they are uncertain.

It should be emphasized that this information should not be delivered in a dry, continuous monologue. During the explanation, children (and adults) should be encouraged to cry, to interrupt with questions, and to express their thoughts, fears, and feelings openly.

"We know that Shaggy is very important to you. Therefore, we are committed to making this experience as meaningful and as positive for you as possible. To decide whether or not you want to be with Shaggy when he dies, you need accurate information about euthanasia. Would you like me to explain how we would help Shaggy die now?" With the child's permission, the helper continues.

"The first thing that would happen in preparation for Shaggy's euthanasia is to place an intravenous catheter in a vein, most likely in one of his rear legs. Veterinarians use catheters so the euthanasia drug can be given more easily. Shaggy would need to be taken back to a treatment area and have a small area of fur shaved on his leg. Catheters also allow veterinarians to do what they need to do without getting in your way while you hold Shaggy's head and front paws.

"After the catheter is placed, Shaggy will be brought back to you and you will be given some time to spend with him if you want it. Then, when all of us agree that it is time to proceed, we will begin the euthanasia process. The method used involves three shots. The first is a saline solution flush. This lets the veterinarian know that the catheter is working. The second is a barbiturate, usually thiopental, which will make Shaggy feel sleepy and relaxed. The third shot is the euthanasia solution, usually pentobarbital sodium. This injection will actually stop Shaggy's breathing, brain activity, and his heart, and ultimately cause his death. Many people are surprised that death occurs within a matter of seconds.

"You should also know that, although humane death by euthanasia is painless and peaceful, Shaggy may urinate, defecate, twitch, or even sigh a bit. He will not be aware of any of this, though, and he will not feel any pain. In addition, Shaggy's eyes may not close because it takes muscles to close your eyes and, once he's dead, his muscles won't work anymore. Do you have any questions about any of this?" If the child expresses understanding, the helper concludes with, "After Shaggy has died, you can hug him, say good-bye to him, and stay with his body for as long as possible."

Some circumstances call for modifications in owner-present euthanasia procedures. For example, sometimes the veins of old or ill cats cannot be catheterized. Also, many of the small "pocket pets," like guinea pigs, hamsters, mice, and rabbits, or nontraditional pets, like turtles, snakes, lizards, and birds, may not be euthanized in the manner described previously. In these cases, it is important for helpers to explain to children why a catheter cannot be used and to tell them that it may take you several tries before an acceptable vein can be found. Methods for euthanizing these pets while owners are present have not been standardized or perfected. Therefore, parents and helpers need to ensure that the veterinarian tells children about the particular euthanasia protocol to be used with these types of animals *before* the euthanasia occurs.

The American Animal Hospital Association offers a videotape portraying a version of owner-present euthanasia similar to the one described in this example. It is called "The Loss of Your Pet." Children, parents, and other helpers can view this videotape while they are at the veterinarian's office or they can check it out for viewing at home. Many pet owners who have toured and chosen an appropriate euthanasia site or viewed a videotape about euthanasia say they have found these visual representations helpful. Knowing what to expect helps calm their anxieties about being present at their companion animals' euthanasias.

Choosing a Euthanasia Site and Explaining Body Care Options

If children decide to be present at their companion animal's euthanasia, veterinarians can provide them and their families with a tour of possible euthanasia sites. For example, there may be a special private room designed for owner-present euthanasia at the veterinary clinic or an inviting outdoor area that would be suitable for a last good-bye. Home euthanasias are also desired by some families, and many veterinarians are happy to provide their clients with this service.

Just as important as deciding where to help a companion animal die is the decision about how to care for the animal's body after death has occurred. When it is possible to do so, most pet owners find it helpful to make this decision before their pet actually dies. This allows pet owners to explore their options as thoroughly as possible. Children often have strong opinions about body care for their pets. Thus, body care options should be explained in a direct, honest way so that, along with their parents, children can make the choice that is right for them.

When explaining body care to children, it is important that parents and helpers talk to them with sensitivity and enough detail so that they are able to understand what is happening to their pets' bodies. Helpers should keep children's cognitive abilities and developmental levels in mind as they select body care terminology. Drawing pictures and using appropriate "props" (caskets, urns, cremains, etc.) also helps to explain what will occur.

The following is an example of what helpers might say to inform children about the body care options for their pets. The words used are probably most appropriate for young children. The concepts can be more developed for those who are older. Altogether, this explanation would take about 10 minutes. It should be emphasized that this information should not be delivered in a dry, continuous monologue and that during the explanation children (and adults) should be encouraged to cry; to interrupt with questions; and to express their thoughts, fears, and feelings openly.

When talking to children about caring for animals' bodies after death, parents and helpers can say something, such as the following:

> When animals die, their bodies don't work anymore. They can't breathe, move about, eat, drink, or play. After a little while, they become stiff and cold, and can even start to smell. This happens naturally to anyone who dies. Because we still love our animals, though, we must take care of their dead bodies. There are several ways to handle a pet's body after death. I can explain them if you want me to.

Helpers might also think ahead about how they want to explain burial, cremation, disposal in a landfill, and rendering.

Burial.   To explain burial, parents and helpers can say something, such as the following:

> Burying means you dig a hole in the ground deep enough so other animals can't dig Shaggy's body up. Then you put Shaggy's body in it. Some people like to put their pet's body in a blanket, cardboard box, or a casket before burying it. A casket is a box that is made especially for burying animals in the ground. We have some pictures of caskets here at our office that I can show you if you like.
>
> You might want to put special toys or treats in the ground with Shaggy. Most people say another good-bye to their pets at the time of burial. I think this is a good idea.
>
> Once Shaggy's body has been placed into the hole, it is covered with dirt. Then, this special place where you have buried Shaggy is called a grave. After the grave has been filled with dirt, you can place something special on top of it, like a big rock, some flowers, or a marker with Shaggy's name on it. Pets can be buried at home [check the city code], in pet cemeteries, or other appropriate places. If the grave is close by, you can go and visit Shaggy's grave whenever you feel like talking to or remembering him. If you decide to bury Shaggy, it will be important to remember that pets don't feel anything when they are dead. They don't need to breathe and they don't need to eat. Once they're dead, they cannot come back to life.

Cremation.   To explain cremation, parents and helpers can say something, such as the following:

If Shaggy's body is cremated, it is put into a large oven that gets very, very hot. It is larger and hotter than the ovens people have in their houses. It is an oven that is made especially for cremating animals. The temperature in the oven gets so hot that it causes the animal's body to burn and to crumble down into small pieces. The heat from the oven causes the fur and all the other soft parts of the body to melt away or disappear. Then, all that remains are the bones. The bones are usually in very small pieces because the heat in the oven also causes them to crumble. These small bone pieces are called 'cremains.' The cremains usually look like a mixture of light-colored sand and small pebbles or rocks.

It might help you understand cremation if you think about a log in a fireplace. As the log gets hot in the fireplace, it gets smaller and smaller, leaving only ashes behind. You might also want to think about cremation as a form of recycling. During his life, Shaggy's body was in one form, but now that he is dead his body must go through a process that will change it into a different form. However you decide to think about cremation, the most important thing to remember is that animals don't feel anything after they're dead. Although we can feel a burn from things that are hot when we are alive, dead animals don't feel burns. They don't feel anything.

After cremation, some people like to keep the cremains of their pets in a jar, a box, or an urn. Others scatter them in a special place. If people don't want their pet's cremains returned to them, the crematory usually buries or scatters them.

Mass Burial in a Landfill. To explain mass burial, helpers can say something, such as the following:

> When people decide not to bury their animals themselves or to cremate them, the veterinarian often takes care of the animal's body for the owners. Veterinarians wish they had a good way of doing this burial, but most often their only choice is to take the animals' bodies to a place where many different kinds of animals are buried together. This place has a giant grave where animals and dirt are all mixed together, and it is usually located at the landfill.
>
> The landfill is also used to bury people's trash. However, if you decide on mass burial for Shaggy's body, it will not be in with trash. It will be in a separate section, and he will be buried with other animals only. Once Shaggy is buried with the other animals, you won't be able to visit his grave. But you can think about him whenever you like and remember the special times you shared together.

Rendering. If the companion animal who has died is a large animal, rendering is usually the most common and cost-effective body care option. To explain rendering, parents and helpers can say something, such as the following:

When large animals, like your horse Comet, die, it is difficult and expensive to bury or cremate them. Because of these difficulties, most people send their large animals, like horses, llamas, mules, cows, and goats, to places called "rendering plants." These businesses use animals' bodies for other good purposes. Many animal foods, fertilizers, and even some kitty litter is partially made from the remains of dead animals. Because animals can't use their bodies after they are dead, rendering is one way to reuse or recycle them.

Some people feel upset at the thought of having their animals rendered. Others believe that the spirit and personality of their pet was what made him or her special, not the body. Whatever you decide about rendering Comet's body, it's important to understand that, although rendering may be difficult to think about, it is an effective way to take care of his remains.

UNEXPECTED DEATH OR LOSS

The unexpected death or loss of a pet creates special circumstances for children and their helpers. Such situations must be handled with care. Unexpected deaths or losses are difficult because they are unforeseen; generally they occur with little warning, if any at all. Unexpected deaths result from acute illnesses (of which the cause may or may not be known) or from accidental events (e.g., hit by a car or poisoning). Unexpected losses also occur when animals run away, are lost, or are relinquished (because of moves, divorces, or a family member's allergies).

Difficulties associated with unexpected death or loss include (a) lack of time for anticipatory grief, a process that might otherwise have permitted children time to prepare themselves emotionally for the loss; (b) the need to make decisions about treatment, euthanasia, and body care quickly while in a state of distress; and (c) the lack of time to prepare a meaningful good-bye ritual. Children often express regret about not having opportunities to say good-bye to their pets and about being rushed through the process as the animal is dying.

Guilt is also commonly associated with unexpected death or loss. Guilt is the critic, the inner voice that judges thoughts, feelings, and actions. It generally stems from children's beliefs that they breached the "contracts" that they had made with their pets—contracts that focused on keeping the pet alive, safe, and healthy. When children or adults feel guilty about their losses, they repeatedly and painfully ask, "What if . . . ," or "If only I had. . . ." This point is particularly true if they were responsible for the death or were not present during the death to comfort or perhaps to save the animal.

Unexpected death or loss is often more difficult for children than a death that is expected because of the frequently ambiguous nature of

the event. In general, the more ambiguous the loss, the more complicated is the grief response, and the more difficult it is to mourn. Children who must cope with their animal being lost or given away may
express concerns about the animal's well-being, or may worry that the
animal feels they abandoned it. Additionally, children whose animals
are lost may not know when to stop searching for them. They may
also experience disruption in their attachments to new animals in the
future.

Parents and helpers can assist children with unexpected death or loss
in several ways. For example, if animals are present but will soon be
gone (because of death or relinquishment), helpers can assist children
by helping them consciously identify what they want to say or do for
their pets before the final separation occurs. This process helps to minimize any regrets the children may have later. This ending ritual may include helping children say final words, such as, "I'm sorry," or "I will
miss you forever." It may also include providing pets with special treats,
petting or holding the animals, or creating transitional objects (e.g.,
clipping a bit of fur or making a paw print).

When pets are finally gone, parents and helpers can assist children
by providing direction and structure to their grief processes. For example, helpers can encourage children to write letters to their pets, draw
pictures of them, talk to the spirits of their dead or lost pets, and create
funeral or memorial ceremonies. Most important, helpers should assist
children in finding their own solutions for coping with their losses.

When the time is right, parents and helpers can also use the unexpected death or loss experience to discuss how the children might deal
with unexpected losses that may occur in the future. After all, it is helpful to prepare for this type of loss by identifying in advance the wishes
of each family member should the "unexpected" tragically occur.

AFTER-DEATH CARE

After pets have died—whether by accident, natural causes, or euthanasia—several details call for attention. When children are involved, some
of these demands are more insistent than others. For example, if a companion animal has died suddenly without the child present, parents
and helpers can prepare children to view the pet's body. Not as immediate, but just as important, after a companion animal's death, parents
and helpers should contact other adults who are significant to the child
so they might provide additional support and perhaps even follow-up
with children either by telephone or with a written condolence.

Preparing Children to View Their
Pet's Body

Sometimes, children and other friends or family members who have
not been present at the death or euthanasia of a pet may want to view
the animal's body before it is buried or cremated. Grief experts agree
that seeing dead bodies can help both children and adults accept the
fact that death has occurred (Glick, Weiss, & Parkes, 1984; Rando,
1988). If a pet's body is going to be viewed *immediately after death,* children need to be prepared for what they will see and for what will be acceptable for them to do.

Here is an example of what parents and helpers might say to children to prepare them to view their pet's body. If the animal has been
dead for some time, the description would be sightly different. For example, the body would most likely have been preserved in a cooler and
would, therefore, be hard and cold to the touch.

> When you see Shaggy, his body may still be soft and warm, but it may
> be slightly soiled because of the natural release of his bowel and blad-
> der. Shaggy's eyes will not be closed, and his tongue may hang slightly
> from his mouth. Shaggy may be covered with a towel or blanket from
> the head down, but you may remove it if you want to see his entire
> body.

At this point, parents and helpers should provide children with a detailed, but not gory, description of the pet's body. Depending on the circumstances of the death, the body may have large areas that are shaved,
scraped, or bruised. Adults should also alert children about stitches,
bloody areas, or medical equipment. Most mental health professionals
agree that it is more damaging to forbid children from seeing their pets
one last time than to allow them to see their pet's body, even if it has
been damaged in some way. Children are imaginative, and, often, what
they can imagine is much worse than what actually occurs. Thus, experts suggest that parents and helpers paint an honest, nonjudgmental
portrait of what children could expect to see should they decide to view
their pet's body, and then let children make their own decisions based
on that information. Once these details have been provided, parents
and helpers should continue the preparation.

> It's alright for you to touch Shaggy, pet him, and even hold him if you
> want. There is also a brush and a scissors in the room if you want to
> groom him or clip some of his fur to take with you. I will be happy to go
> with you when you see him. Would you like me to do that, or would you
> prefer to go into the room alone?

If children ask helpers to accompany them, helpers should lead the way and make the first move toward touching, petting, and talking to the animal. This is a prime time for helpers to act as role models for children so they will have a better idea of what to do. After helpers have spent some time talking with and listening to children as they interact with their pet, they should ask again if the children would like some time alone. If the answer is yes, helpers (even parents) should leave the room and tell the children how soon they plan to return.

If children wish to view their pet's body, the body should be positioned so it will be pleasing to see. In other words, it should be curled slightly, with the head and limbs tucked into a "sleep-like" position. This is most easily accomplished by placing the body in an animal casket, an animal bed or basket, or a box that has preferably been padded with a towel, blanket, or pad. Positioning bodies is especially important if they are to be placed in a casket or other container for burial or transport at a later time. This is vitally important if the animal's body must be kept in a refrigerated room until other family members can view it or pick it up. If animals (particularly large dogs) are allowed to stiffen, placing them in a casket or even on the back seat of a car, is nearly impossible.

Finally, regarding viewing the body, all family members have unique responses to the deaths of family pets. Therefore, both parents and children should be offered opportunities to be alone with pets before and after death. These opportunities allow each person to say a private good-bye. Whether or not individual family members take advantage of opportunities to say good-bye, most individuals usually appreciate the offer.

Contacting Significant Adults

After pets die, it is wise for parents and helpers to contact other adults who play significant roles in their children's lives. These adults may be teachers, care providers, and adult friends or relatives. They should be asked to provide understanding and additional support to children during the grief process. They should also be encouraged to say their own good-byes to the pet and to demonstrate openly any feelings of grief they may have because of the companion animal's death.

Grief is isolating; it is usually easier to bear when adults whom children look up to demonstrate and talk to them about their own experiences with pet loss and grief. During these conversations, adults should encourage children to explore a wide range of emotions, focusing on more than just sadness. Adults should also be prepared for children to express anger and blame, and should not get defensive regarding children's comments.

Following-Up with Children

One way helpers (especially veterinarians) can follow up with children after the deaths of their pets is by specifically addressing them in the condolence cards they send. If helpers are trained mental health or veterinary professionals, they can also contact children directly by office visit or telephone to make sure their grieving is progressing normally. Children appreciate it when helpers contact them personally. In addition, direct contact keeps helpers from falling into the trap of getting their information about children's well-being from parents. Parents and children often have different views of the same experience. Children may also talk more openly to their helpers than to their own parents. During follow-up, helpers can be sure that both parents and children have plenty of reading material, as well as the names and telephone numbers of local support services at hand.

ADOPTING NEW PETS

One of the most common ways adults, particularly parents, attempt to soothe children who are distraught over the loss of their pets is to adopt new pets almost immediately. Sometimes this solution works. If families have anticipated their pets' deaths and talked about getting new ones, children may be able to bond fairly quickly with a new pet, while at the same time grieving the death of their former pet.

However, children who have not been prepared for the arrival of a new pet may resent the intrusion. Worse, they may feel that, if their old friend can be forgotten and replaced so quickly by a new one, they themselves could be forgotten and replaced quickly too. Replacement as a solution to the pain of grief is a risky practice. It usually does not work. Replacement interferes with bonding, complicates grief with feelings of guilt and disloyalty, and perpetuates damaging myths about how to cope with loss and grief.

All too often, children want to adopt new pets in an attempt to avoid or distract themselves from fully experiencing the sadness and loneliness of grief. Parents and helpers should be aware of some of the "red flags" or warning signs that arise when new pets are adopted for the wrong reasons. For instance, if children are motivated to adopt new pets as a way to circumvent the grieving process, they will often make comments, such as, "I want another golden retriever just like Shaggy," or "I'm going to get another white, female kitten and name her Muffin, the Second." These comments should alert parents and helpers to the possibility that children may be trying to "bring back their dead pets" in the form of a new companion animal. However, animals are as individual as people. They have different personalities, temperaments, habits, and needs. In most cases, even if it is the same gender, breed, and species, the new pet is nothing like the one who died.

Still, children and pets like and need each other. Thus, the eventual adoption of new pets should be encouraged by parents and helpers alike. One study revealed that parents who did not give children the option of adopting new pets after the deaths of their former pets unwittingly created "unresolved bereavements" for their children (Stewart, 1983). This study suggested that, in time, another animal's presence may lessen feelings of grief for children. In most cases, when children are ready for new pets they will ask for one, and, if the rest of the family agrees, the search for a new pet can begin.

APPENDIX 10.1
Suggested Reading List about Children and Pet Loss

Reading books to and with children, such as the following, about pet loss can create opportunities for discussions about death and grief:

Brown, M. W. (1990). *The dead bird*. New York: Harper & Row. (Original work published 1958)

Brackenridge, S. (1994). *Because of flowers and dancers*. Santa Barbara, CA: Veterinary Practice.

Buscaglia, L. (1982). *The fall of Freddie the leaf: A story for all ages*. Thorofare, NJ: Slack.

Carrick, C. (1981). *The accident*. New York: Clarion Books.

Cazet, D. (1987). *A fish in his pocket*. New York: Orchard Books.

Gipson, F. (1989). *Old yeller*. New York: Harper & Row. (Original work published 1956)

Grollman, E. A. (1990). *Talking about death: A dialogue between parents and children* (3rd ed.). Boston: Beacon.

Hamley, D. (1989). *Tigger and friends*. New York: Lothrop, Lee & Shepard.

Heegaard, M. (1988). *When someone very special dies: Children can learn to cope with grief*. Minneapolis: Woodland.

Heegaard, M. (1990). *Coping with death and grief*. Minneapolis: Lerner.

Hewett, J. (1987). *Rosalie*. New York: Lothrop, Lee, & Shepard Books.

Jewett, C. L. (1982). *Helping children cope with separation and loss*. Harvard: The Harvard Common Press.

Rogers, F. (1988). *When a pet dies*. New York: Putnam.

Sanford, D. (1987). *It must hurt a lot*. Portland: Multnomah.

Stein, S. B. (1984). *About dying: An open family book for parents and children together*. New York: Walker & Co.

Varley, S. (1984). *Badger's parting gifts*. New York: Lothrop, Lee, & Shepard.

Viorst, J. (1971). *The tenth good thing about Barney*. New York: Atheneum.

White, E. B. (1952). *Charlotte's web*. New York: Harper & Row.

Wilhelm, H. (1985). *I'll always love you*. New York: Crown.

Wright, B. R. (1991). *The cat next door*. New York: Holiday House Books.

APPENDIX 10.2
Suggested Resources for Helpers

It is beneficial for helpers to have available for use by both parents and children educational videotapes and handout materials such as the following:

Death of a Pet: Answers to Questions for Children and Animal Lovers of All Ages. Guideline Publications, P.O. Box 245, Stamford, NY 12167; tel. (800) 552-1076.

The Loss of Your Pet, Counseling Clients, and Understanding Pet Loss. The American Animal Hospital Association (AAHA). AAHA offers this videotape series on pet loss counseling designed for pet owner use and for veterinary staff training. It can be ordered, along with accompanying workbooks and brochures from AAHA's national headquarters at 12575 W. Bayaud Avenue, Lakewood, CO, 80228, or call AAHA's Member Service Center at (800) 252-2242.

Saying Good-bye: Activity Book. Santa Rosa, CA: Jim Boulden Publications, 1989. This coloring and activity book encourages children to explore their feelings about death. Copies can be ordered from Jim Boulden, P.O. Box 9358, Santa Rosa, CA 95405; tel. (707) 538-3797.

Will the Sadness Go Away? Cooperative Extension Service, Kansas State University, 1991. This videotape is appropriate for use by helping professionals, veterinarians, parents, 4-H leaders, teachers, and others who deal with the issue of pet loss. Available from the Instructional Media Center, 24 Umberger Hall, Kansas State University, Manhattan, KS 66506; tel. (913) 532-1159.

11

Children's Exposure to Traumatic Experiences

Kathleen Olympia Nader

This chapter examines children's encounters with violence and disaster. Traumatic deaths and losses are experienced by children both within their families and within the larger community. In either case, it is important to understand the distinctive features of traumatic death and loss as well as differences between children who are exposed to a single-incident trauma or multiple and ongoing traumas. On that basis, the central topics of the chapter are the interaction between trauma and grief, and the special features of interventions that are appropriate for children who have experienced traumatic bereavement.

CHARACTERISTICS OF TRAUMA IN THE LIVES OF CHILDREN

Traumatic Death and Loss

According to the DSM IV (American Psychiatric Association [APA], 1994), traumatic death occurs when (a) the circumstances of death have included experiencing, witnessing, or being confronted with actual or threatened death or serious injury or a threat to the child's or another's physical integrity (e.g., disaster, war, other violence, suicide, severe accident); and (b) the child's responses involve intense fear, helplessness, horror, or disorganized or agitated behavior. Children respond to these experiences, with or without a resulting death, with the full range of posttraumatic stress disorder (PTSD) symptoms: reexperiencing, numbing/avoidance, arousal, and altered functioning. Several factors may increase the risk or severity of traumatization (see Table 11.1; Pynoos & Nader, 1988). Although grief reactions occur independently of traumatic exposure, feeling continued responsibility toward or knowing one who died during the event may increase severity of traumatic reactions and result in traumatic bereavement (Nader, Pynoos, Fairbanks, & Frederick, 1990; Pynoos et al., 1987).

In addition to PTSD symptoms, traumatic exposure may result in adjustment reactions; symptoms of attention deficit disorder or hyperactive behaviors; conduct disturbances including increased aggression; affective disturbances including depression or panic; phobic behaviors; obsessive-compulsive behaviors; repetition of traumatic behaviors in-

TABLE 11.1   Risk Factors for Traumatic Reactions

Pretrauma Factors

Family psychopathology/ dysfunction	Individual psychopathology
Previous trauma or loss	Previous developmental or characterological difficulties

Trauma factors

Exposure	Lack of emotional distance
Life threat or threat of harm	Worry about the safety of a family member or significant other
Witnessing death, threat, or injury	Severe injury
Intense helplessness and sense of threat to self, physical integrity, or to another	Sense of personal damage
Familiarity with victim(s)	
Sense of abandonment	
Guilt or sense of responsibility	

Posttrauma factors

Loss of faith	Inability to discuss the trauma/emotions
In self	Overuse of avoidance
In adults/authority	Lack of support
In a supreme being	Sense of abandonment
Family response	
Discomfort with traumatic symptoms	
Overdependent parents	
Parents traumatized	
Lack of support	

cluding those of victim, perpetrator, rescuer, or witness; and somatic complaints (Nader, in press–b; Pynoos et al., 1987; Terr, 1979, 1981, 1983).

When these events remain unresolved, the long-term consequences of traumatic exposure may interfere with a child's ability to engage, over time, in productive behaviors and to function adequately socially, academically, professionally, and personally. These long-term effects may include personal traits (e.g., lack of confidence or inhibitions); disturbances to interpersonal functioning (e.g., loss of friends, irritability/bullying, or withdrawal); cognitive dysfunction (e.g., memory and concentration problems); disruptions to moral development (e.g., a sense that there is no reason to behave if you can be hurt or die anyway); mental health disturbances (e.g., chronic or complicated PTSD, conduct, major affective, personality, phobic, panic, dissociative, or obsessive-compulsive disorders); attempts at numbing the emotions (e.g., drug abuse, alcoholism, or overuse of medication); compulsive repetition of traumatic behaviors and sequences (e.g., promiscuity or prostitution after molest); attempts at self-punishment or warding off (e.g., self-mutilation); and somatic disorders or general ill health (e.g., headaches or immune deficiency) (Garbarino, Kostelny, & Dubrow, 1991; Herman, Perry, & van der Kolk, 1989; Nader, Blake, & Kriegler, 1994a; Nader & Fairbanks, 1994; Nader & Pynoos, 1993; Pynoos & Nader, 1988; Terr, 1991; van der Kolk & Saporta, 1991). In addition, there is a growing body of evidence that individuals who experience traumas are more likely to have children who experience traumas (Nader, 1994b).

The cycle of trauma as well as of violence may be perpetuated by the deeds of individuals whose traumatic reactions or traumatic grief remain unresolved. For example, since the liberation of Kuwait from Iraqi occupation, an increase in violent crime in Kuwait has been reported (Ibrahim, 1992; Nader & Fairbanks, 1994). Similarly, following the floods in the midwestern United States, domestic violence and child abuse have increased in Missouri (Kohly, 1994). Trauma or unresolved traumatic grief has been found in the psychological histories of some of the perpetrators of traumatic events. For example, a young man in his 20s was grieving the traumatic loss (as a teenager) of eight family members who died in the Jones Town massacre in Guiana. While on a waiting list for mental health services, he began shooting at passing airplanes. In February 1984, he opened fire on a crowded elementary school playground. Furthermore, in 1987 a woman whose father had earlier committed suicide and who had not found relief from traditional mental health intervention entered a fifth-grade classroom in Orange, California. She took the classroom hostage and dictated a suicide note. Next, she waved two guns at the children and in her agitation, fired one gun, nearly hitting a child. Finally, she shot herself in front of the children (Nader, in press–a). Also, a young man in his mid-20s had, as a child, been neglected by his parents and had witnessed the physical abuse of his mother by his step-father. His minor brushes with the law began before he was 15 years of age. In January 1989, the young man returned to his own elementary school in Stockton, California, and opened fire on children.

In view of the possible consequences of unresolved trauma and traumatic grief, it is essential to understand trauma, grief, and their interaction. This chapter discusses the effects of traumatic grief on the bereavement process and treatment of traumatic bereavement. The interaction of trauma and grief may affect grieving through (a) the intensification of symptoms common to both; (b) the complications of trauma and grief reexperiencing; (c) the hindrance or complication of aspects of normal bereavement, such as grief dream work, the relationship with the deceased, issues of identification, the processing of anger and rage; and (d) the interference with healing interactions resulting from a sense of posttraumatic estrangement or aloneness. Treatment of children following a traumatic loss must address the interaction of trauma and grief.

Multiple or Ongoing Trauma

Terr (1991) has provided a preliminary profile of children exposed to single-incident (type I) versus long-standing (type II) traumas (see Table 11.2). Many factors, however, may determine a child's reactions to an event(s)—for example, the nature of the event, phase of the event, and phase of child development (Nader, in press–a). Consequently, clearly determining an accurate profile for children exposed to ongoing versus single-incident experiences is complicated. Some traumas are endured essentially alone and others in a group. For example, in both the ongoing trauma of war and large-scale, single-incident traumas, many known and unknown individuals have shared and understand the experience with the child. Issues of shame or betrayal vary. The child who has undergone continual abuse or molest will likely react differently from a child who has gone through the repeated and ongoing horrors of war. In the former, the betrayal is often by someone known to the child (e.g., a family member or family friend). In the latter, the enemy is usually another nation or group, and any betrayal is less personal. Moreover, phase of development may influence the im-

TABLE 11.2 Single Incident Versus Long-standing Traumas

Both types of trauma include
Repeated, intrusive thoughts/images of the event
Repeated traumatic play or reenactment
Trauma-specific fears
Changed attitudes toward people, aspects of life, and the future

Type I	Type II
Marked by extreme fear and intense surprise	Prolonged and sickening anticipation
Meets the DSM IV criteria	Generates attempts to protect the psyche, such as massive denial,
Full, detailed, "etched-in" memories	dissociation, repression, self-anesthesia, self-hypnosis,
Retrospective reworkings, attribution of reasons, cognitive reappraisals, and turning points	identification toward the aggressor, or aggression toward the self
	Emotional consequences
Misperceptions and mistimings	Absence of feeling, sense of rage, or unremitting sadness

When a single psychological shock is combined with the death of a parent, consequent homelessness, handicap or disfigurement, or prolonged hospitalization and pain, the child may develop type II characteristics as well as the features of type I trauma.

Source: Adapted from information in Terr, 1991.

portance of a symptom or the degree to which a child experiences a symptom, such as disruptions to impulse control, sexual identity, or trust (e.g., trust in one's safety in the world; trust of the integrity, protection, or good will of others).

The phase of an ongoing event is an additional factor influencing children's reactions. For example, children in Kuwait in 1991 after the Gulf crisis was over, seemed to be in a different phase of their reactions than refugee children in Croatia in 1992 while the war continued. Children enduring ongoing war conditions, those suffering ongoing child abuse, and inner-city children enduring violence with no end in sight may of emotional and energic necessity ward off symptoms until "the war is over" (Nader, in press–a; Nader & Stuber, 1992).

The DSM IV Field Trials examined three groups of traumatized adults: victims of interpersonal violence (sexual or physical assault) starting before 14 years of age, victims of interpersonal violence starting after 14 years of age, and victims of natural disasters only (van der Kolk, Roth, Pelcovitz, & Mandel, 1992). A group of symptoms in addition to PTSD were found to occur most particularly when trauma begins at an early age, is prolonged, and is interpersonal in nature. The symptoms included chronic affect dysregulation, aggression against self and others, dissociative symptoms, somatization, and character changes. Clinical evidence exists that, in addition to repetitive interpersonal traumas, such as sexual or physical abuse, dual or multiple unrelated traumas, or one single trauma combined with previous loss, may result in the more complicated forms of traumatic response (Nader, in press–a).

Domestic Violence

Domestic violence is often an ongoing or repeated trauma. When it results in the death of a spouse or parent, it may precipitate a complicated traumatic bereavement. The incidence of family violence (including spousal *and* child abuse) is estimated at 4 million occurrences per year. Its occurrence may result in stigmatization or a sense of stigmatization of the victim(s). The experience may be seen as a sign of weakness or instability (Salasin & Rich, 1993), which may be one contributing factor to an underreporting of its occurrence.

In the same way that the child abuse cycle repeats itself through generations, it is many times more likely (up to 1,000%) that an abusing husband will either have been abused himself or have witnessed his own father abusing his mother in childhood, and that a woman who has witnessed family violence will be battered (Zeanah & Zeanah, 1989). The repetition of this pattern of abuse has been attributed to cultural acceptance of violence; identification with the parent's punitiveness, aggressive style, or violent pattern of parental interaction; imitation of or the learning of inadequate parenting styles; modeling by abusive men of inadequacy, dependency, anxiety, depression, and aggression; impairment of impulse control subsequent to traumatization; or the transmission of organizing themes of the parent-child relationship and their associated internal working models (Davies, 1991; Jaffe, Wolfe, Wilson, & Zak, 1986; van der Kolk & Saporta, 1991; Zeanah & Zeanah, 1989). Davies (1991) described a pattern by which the mother reinforces the son's identification with the aggressor by carrying aspects of her relationship with the father into her relationship with the son. In an attempt to defend against the memories and affects of the violence, the mother is unable to respond with empathy, appropriate explanations, and support to the child's reactive distress. Consequently, the child's reactive behavior escalates. For toddlers and young children, the characteristic behavior expressions of anxiety include provocative, aggressive acts, disturbed sleep, regressive behaviors, and clinging behavior. The mother may interpret the increased aggressive and other symptomatic behaviors to mean that the child is acting "just like his father." This may increase the mother's angry, negative, and withdrawing responses. The ongoing cycle may result in the failure of the attachment relationship.

The relationship between trauma and domestic violence is sometimes, in general, circular. Either one may result in the other. The traumatic effects of witnessing violence, including witnessing violence between parents, have long been documented (Nader, Pynoos, Fairbanks, Al-Ajeel, & Al-Asfour, 1993; Pynoos & Eth, 1986). Additionally, traumatic experiences have resulted in increased domestic violence. For example, Vietnam veterans with PTSD have a high incidence of marital discord and domestic violence (Harkness, 1993), and an increase in domestic violence and child abuse after some disasters, such as the flooding in the Midwest, has occurred.

Children who witness spousal abuse have been compared with abused children who have exhibited a variety of anxiety disorders (including PTSD), disturbances in affect, and impaired impulse control (Goodwin, 1985; Green, 1993). Children who witness spousal abuse often fall somewhere in between nonabused comparison children and abused children (or abused witnesses of domestic violence) in the levels of their symptomatology. They have been found to be similar to children who are abused in the degree of their behavior problems, subjective symptoms, and depression, and have exhibited lower levels of social skills than normal children (Jaffe et al., 1986; Sternberg et al., 1993). Studies are needed to determine any differences between children who witness severe violence versus those who witness milder forms of violence, and between those exposed to repeated incidents over time compared with single-incidents of spousal abuse. An 8-year-old girl who observed her father beating her mother to unconsciousness on two occasions exhibited symptoms of fear and anxiety, sexual identity problems, nightmares, repeated thoughts and images about the incidents, avoidance of emotions, both anger and protectiveness toward her victimized mother, avoidance of reminders of her father's violence (sometimes disavowal of the violence and a focus on his admired strength), irritability, sleep disturbance, and attention problems at school. Her drawings often included women or girls without hands or feet, and strong-looking, admired men. Sometimes the men had spike hands. Her rejection of her mother's helplessness was obvious in her actions and conversations. She greatly feared the death or permanent injury of her mother and became extremely anxious when the topic of her father's violence was raised. She preferred to avoid these discussions.

Following spousal abuse, the victim's fear, shame, guilt, anger, and other traumatic reactions to the violence as well as the sense of hurt and abandonment by spouse and external protectors (e.g., police or medical personnel) (Salasin & Rich, 1993) may result in parental emotional unavailability. The lack of support of children or the need for children to be unaffected by traumatic events can exacerbate the children's levels of trauma (Davies, 1991; Pynoos & Nader, 1990). Because the capacity to continue functioning and to overcome the trauma is affected by the strength and comforting role of internalized objects (Malmquist, 1986), the reduction in supportive behaviors in a situation of ongoing family violence may hinder the recovery process.

When the violence between parents results in the death of one or both parents (e.g., murder-suicide; murder-incarceration), both traumatic and grief reactions may be complicated (Malmquist, 1986; Pynoos & Eth, 1986). The very nature of spousal abuse may result in children's increased traumatic reactions, disturbances in identification with primary caretakers (and same-sex parent), increased likelihood of identification with the aggressor or victim, and a variety of symptomatic disturbances. Added to this are the interaction of trauma and grief reactions, secondary issues of loss (e.g., loss of income, home, or status; cruelty from other children who now see the child as different or want to ward off the possibility of a similar loss or victimization by rejecting the child), and the secondary issues of traumatic loss at the hands of a parent (e.g., the concern of others that the child will be like the deceased or perpetrating parent, and issues of loyalty).

INTERACTION OF TRAUMA AND GRIEF

Studies of children's traumatic responses have provided evidence of both an independence, and an interaction between trauma and grief reactions (Eth & Pynoos, 1985a; Nader et al., 1990; Pynoos et al., 1987). When a traumatic death occurs, the child must contend with the symptoms of trauma, grief, and the interaction between the two. The response to traumatic death is further complicated by the fact that catastrophic events can affect entire communities. Treatment for bereavement alone after a traumatic death may be ineffective and have harmful effects (Nader & Pynoos, 1993; Nader, in press–a).

When traumatic aspects of grief responses remain unattended, the result may be increased difficulties for individual, family, or community. Pathological grief is common for individuals after sudden unexpected death (Raphael, 1983). Traumatic grief may occur for those who are not directly exposed to the trauma as well as to the directly traumatized (Nader et al., 1993; Nader, in press–a). After a tornado that killed his brother, an unexposed surviving brother had repeated traumatic images of his brother's smashed body. Despite grief therapy, he began to express suicidal thoughts that were relieved only after his referral for trauma treatment. After catastrophes, dissension may exist between community groups. Families of the deceased may want many reminders to ensure the memory of their dead children in contrast to families of survivors who may want to protect their children from constant reminders of the trauma, which may intensify their reactions.

Intensification of Symptoms

Several symptoms have been reported for both bereavement and trauma. Inasmuch as bereavement studies generally have not adequately distinguished between traumatic loss and loss of a less catastrophic nature, some difficulty exists in sorting out the differences between the two (Nader, in press–a). Following DSM IV (APA, 1994) guidelines for bereavement and trauma, the two disorders share the following symptoms: feelings of sadness, repetitive thoughts, diminished interest in activities or pleasure, sleep disturbance, impaired concentration, anger/irritability, associated dreams or play, and somatic reactions. Numbing is more common in the beginning phases of bereavement and may be more persistent in some form for trauma. Anxiety, agitation, helplessness, emotional pain, loss of energy, and guilt are associated with both disorders. Moreover, the intensity of a traumatic experience, perhaps in combination with the biochemistry of traumatic response, may intensify the emotions and cognitions related to each moment or memory of the traumatic loss.

The overlap of trauma and grief-related symptoms may intensify the symptoms (Nader, in press–a). For example, trauma may add to the arousal symptoms of grief, hypervigilance, or exaggerated startle response. Anger may become traumatic rage. The intensity of the traumatic helplessness or of the offense to rightness may be a predictor of the intensity of the resulting rage. The intensity, multiple levels, and complicated nature of the anger/rage may result in impairment of impulse control, or, conversely, in inhibition of the expression of anger and may complicate recovery. Sleep disturbance is common to both traumatic and grief reactions (Richters & Martinez, 1991; Rosen, 1986). After traumatic events, children have described disturbed, restless sleep, nightmares, and early awakenings, and have had difficulties getting to sleep related to repetitive intrusive thoughts of the traumatic experience, thoughts of the deceased, or fear of the deceased or dreaming (of the deceased or of the trauma).

Increased fears after traumatic events (Famularo, Kinscherff, & Fenton, 1991) may be related to the deceased. Children who have already learned the permanence of death may become frightened of the possible return of the dead. For example, after the Stockton and south central Los Angeles school shootings, children were afraid that the angry dead would return and take them away (Busher, 1995; Pynoos & Nader, 1988).

For both trauma and grief, diminished interest in activities or a reduced ability to enjoy activities (APA, 1994; Pynoos & Nader, 1988) may be related to preoccupations, depressions, or disturbances in the ability to experience joy. After traumatic experiences, however, the reduction of activities may be related to avoidance of reminders of the event (e.g., people, things, places, or topics); emotions (e.g., any emotion or emotions associated with the event); or fear-producing stimuli (e.g., the location of previous activities or play items that remind one of the death). For both traumatized and grieving children, these complicated and intensified symptoms may disrupt normal development and interfere with learning and school performance (Dawes, Tredoux, & Feinstein, 1989; Jesse, Strickland, & Ladewig, 1992; Krupnick, 1984; Terr, 1983).

Reexperiencing

After traumatic events, children may repetitively reexperience aspects or significant moments of the trauma. These repetitions appear in the children's visual, auditory, or olfactory thoughts; dreams; play or activities; fears or experiences of recurrence; and reactions to reminders of the event.

After noncatastrophic loss, children may review specific moments with the deceased (e.g., during the ailment or injury, happier times, missed rituals, or moments regretted). They may yearn or search for the dead in the early stages of bereavement and, subsequently, may reminisce about the deceased (Raphael, 1983; Rosen, 1986). In normal bereavement, remembering the deceased is a part of the course of adaptation, reorganization, and recovery. It may engender pleasurable as well as sad thoughts and generate play that assists the child in working through, accepting, and redefining the relationship with the deceased (Raphael, 1983). In contrast to these thoughts, which are aimed at reprocessing regretted moments or at recapturing the relationship with the deceased, traumatic reexperiencing includes (often unwanted) intrusive distressing thoughts and images, dreams that recall fear or horror, intense psychological distress in response to symbols or reminders of the event, and reenactment or play of frightening or up-setting aspects of the event as well as those recalling better times (APA, 1994; Nader, in press–a; Pynoos & Nader, 1988). Traumatic memories may be sufficiently stressful that they can not be integrated without assistance (Horowitz, 1976). Play may often be unrewarding, dangerous, or distressing, or may provide only temporary relief (Nader & Pynoos, 1991; Terr, 1979).

Traumatic reexperiencing may interfere with the processes of grieving in several ways. Thoughts of the deceased are ongoing in the process of grief resolution. For example, reminiscing about the deceased, and longing for her or his return are normal components of the grieving process. Attempts at remembering the deceased may lead to traumatic recollections, such as thoughts of the manner in which the death occurred or thoughts of disfigurement. For example, every time Ronny thought of his friend Rick, he remembered his face, flattened by the large block wall that fell on him during the tornado.

Preoccupations with aspects of a traumatic event may prevent or delay grieving. These preoccupations include engrossment with specific episodes of the traumatic event (e.g., the moment of endangerment, call for help, or injury), concerns about the cause (e.g., determination of fault, perpetrator's reasons, or issues of guilt), personal impact of the manner of the death (e.g., proximity to threat, location of the death, or continued threat), threat from the angry spirit of the victimized dead (e.g., things going wrong because of the dead spirit or the spirit coming to take away the surviving child), threat from the perpetrator (e.g., for telling or testifying because of the child's anger toward him or her), concerns about being like the perpetrator or victim (e.g., being like father who kills the mother or being like the mother who was beaten repeatedly by the father) or imagined horrors (e.g., fears of torture or humiliation of self or others). For example, a Kuwaiti boy who had been out of the country during the Gulf Crisis had loved his uncle like a second father. Hearing of how his uncle had died during the war, the boy could only think of the horrible knife wound and profuse bleeding. He imagined in elaborate detail what it must have been like to be hiding and afraid, and then caught by the enemy soldiers. He obsessed over rumors about how the Iraqi soldiers had humiliated people, for example, by making them disrobe before killing them.

Traumatic reminders may elicit psychological or physiological distress (Armsworth & Holaday, 1993; Newman, 1976; Saylor, Swenson, & Powell, 1992). Items or events that symbolize the trauma may elicit both traumatic memories and memories of the person whose presence, interactions, and other qualities are lost to the bereaved. Both trauma and grief may result in somatic reactions and increased illness (Krupnick, 1984; Nader & Fairbanks, 1994; Raphael, 1983; van der Kolk & Saporta, 1991; Van Eerdewegh, Bieri, Parilla, & Clayton, 1982). Normal grief reminders, such as the empty chair or the time of day usually spent with the deceased, may, like repetitive thoughts of the deceased, serve as reminders of the traumatic nature of the loss and again throw the child into traumatic reprocessing or avoidance.

Complications of Response and Recovery

Traumatic aspects of the loss may hinder or complicate aspects of grief resolution, such as grief dream work, the child's continued relationship with the deceased, issues of identification, and the processing of anger. Specific symptoms of trauma may interfere with normal processes of bereavement. For example, avoidance of reminders may interfere with expressing sadness, reminiscing, and discussing/playing to work through the loss. Moreover, traumatic experiences may result in multiple losses including loss of a significant other killed in the event (e.g., friends, enemies, or family members); preexisting relationships (e.g., emotional loss of parents or others); one's own expected life course (e.g., related to traumatic changes in life circumstances, abilities, and characteristics); and previous aspects of the self (e.g., happiness, confidence, innocence, humor, or courage). These multiple losses may increase posttraumatic senses of helplessness and hopelessness (Nader, in press–a).

Grief dreams of the deceased as he or she was before the death, for example, may be of reunion or restoration of the previous relationship with the deceased, reassurance that the deceased is now okay, or reminiscences of times past. Traumatic dreams, conversely, incorporate aspects of the trauma, such as the action, witnessing, injury, sense of threat, or fear of loss (Bilu, 1989; Nader, in press-c; Terr, 1979). Resolution of specific traumatic issues may necessarily precede the dream work of bereavement. Traumatic preoccupations may disrupt grief work in dreams. For example, Angelica would begin to have a dream about the good times spent with her father before the robber shot and killed him. Just as she was beginning in the dream to enjoy being with her father, his face would become blank and staring, the way it had looked when she tried to call him back to consciousness after the robbery.

One consequence of a traumatic experience can be changes in the relationship to the deceased. For example, children or adolescents may feel an attachment or connectedness to the deceased without a prior re-

lationship. This may result from compassion for the deceased perpetrator (e.g., when the person has some reason to feel sorry about the
perpetrator's life circumstances, or in cases of the Stockholm syndrome
when the individual develops a dependent relationship with the perpetrator during the event); a sense of responsibility toward the deceased
(e.g., after hearing cries for help or feeling the need to revive the person); unresolved issues toward the deceased (e.g., previous harsh
words, or accidentally or purposely bothering or hurting the deceased
in the past); a sense that it should have been the child or adolescent
who died and not the deceased (e.g., a near miss, the other person was
younger, nicer, smarter, more lovable, or better); or the reactions of
others (e.g., someone saying the deceased was a lot like the child or
adolescent, or suggestions that it should have been the child or adolescent). As noted earlier, the intensity of a traumatic experience may intensify the emotions and cognitions related to each moment or
memory of the traumatic loss. Moreover, sympathy or attachment to the
deceased or the perpetrator may hinder the resolution of aspects of the
trauma (Nader, in press–b).

After the traumatic death of a significant other(s), issues of identification become complex. In moderation, identification with the deceased following nontraumatic death can be enriching, for example,
when adaptive internalizations of positive aspects of the personality or
interests of the deceased occur (Raphael, 1983). The tendency to idealize the dead may lend to overidentification or may interfere with processing anger toward the deceased (Krupnick, 1984; Nader, in press–b).

Taken to an extreme or after trauma, identifications can become
frightening, for example, when they imply adoption of symptoms,
death, or victimization, or result in peer rejection or criticism, attempts
to replace a deceased parent, sibling, or friend can compromise a
child's own identity development (Krupnick, 1984). Children and adolescents may search for ways in which they are like the victim (e.g., they
may identify with the victim after a suicide) (Nader, 1994a). When the
perpetrator or the victim of a traumatic event is a primary caretaker,
concerns about being like that individual may affect both child or adolescent and current caretakers (e.g., when the depressed father stabs
the mother and children).

Issues of identification may become apparent in the choice of friends
after trauma or traumatic death (e.g., when children gravitate toward
others who are traumatized or who have had difficult lives) (Stuber &
Nader, 1995). In addition to identification with a deceased relative or
friend, children and adolescents commonly identify with several roles

or individuals after traumatic events (e.g., with rescuer, victim, perpetrator, or witness). These identifications may result in difficulties or
even endangerment for the child (e.g., when the child as rescuer gets
into a fight to protect a friend, and is himself or herself injured)
(Nader, in press–b).

Some children fear identifying in any way with the deceased. Therefore, they may become afraid of taking on even the good characteristics
of the deceased, may be fearful of reaching the age when the person
died (and may develop a life script or expectation of doom for that age
or set of circumstances), may become extremely afraid if they develop
a physical characteristic (e.g., a mole or wart), a gesture (e.g., a characteristic laugh or hand signal), an injury (e.g., a broken arm), or a personality trait (e.g., warm kindness) that the person had when he or she
died.

Outrage after traumatic experience may be directed toward multiple
individuals for multiple reasons (Nader, in press–a)—for example, at
the perpetrator for doing harm, for not valuing the physical and emotional lives of the victims; at the victim(s) for being victimized, for en-
dangering themselves, not protecting themselves, and dying, thus
leaving the survivors behind; at adults for not protecting children; and
at the self for lack of self-protection, not helping someone else, and not
preventing harm. Anger at the deceased as well as the assailant, a sense
of the unfairness of the death, or the helplessness associated with both
trauma and grief may complicate resolution of factors associated with
decreased impulse control. Thus, relationships, identifications, self-
esteem, and other issues affecting development may be disrupted. The
lack of resolution or displacement of traumatic rage has resulted in
punishing behaviors toward undeserving others, acts of aggression, and
failed attempts to resolve grief.

Sense of Estrangement

Supportive behaviors by others have proved to be therapeutic both for
grief (Marris, 1991) and trauma resolution (Nader et al., 1990). The
sense of estrangement after traumatic events may interfere with these
healing interactions. For example, after a tornado, a girl who had been
held back by her friend from running away had watched the friend
lying breathless and bloody after being slammed under a table. Unable
to be angry at her friend, she displaced anger onto her mother. This in-
terfered with her ability to receive comfort and use her mother effectively to discuss her experience.

The child's or adolescent's response to the current or a previous trauma may interfere with the ability to receive comfort and support (e.g., when the child has lost a parent at an earlier age and fears depending on an adult again). Adolescents urgently insisting on independence or affected by peer pressure, and children with a damaged sense of trust (e.g., after ongoing abuse or molest) may also have difficulty accepting intervention, support, or comfort. Children may hide their own sorrow from others, thinking that other children are already over the disaster or the loss, or they should be asymptomatic after a certain period. For example, 14 months after a sniper attack, children felt they should now be okay.

Differences in exposure to the traumatic experience or recovery may result in a sense of separateness for family or community members who have experienced a traumatic event (Pynoos & Nader, 1989). For example, when an assassin entered a home and attempted to stab the father, the oldest son had tried to intervene. The younger son, in response to his big brother's instructions, had locked himself in his room; the mother had been away from the house. The father and the oldest son were badly traumatized by the incident. The injured father needed to recover physically as well as emotionally. The youngest son was worried about his father but untraumatized. The mother was contending with the injuries to her husband, the distress of her husband and oldest son, and the rift that developed between the two children. The oldest son began to resent his younger brother who he felt did not understand what they had been through and who seemed to respond superficially to the assault. Similarly, children and adolescents who had remained in Kuwait during the Gulf Crisis felt that those who had been out of the country did not understand what they went through and had not shared their attempts to save their country and country people (Nader et al., 1993).

When the death is subsequent to spousal abuse and relatives of the deceased become caretakers, difficulties may occur when the children need to express positive feelings toward the abusing parent or resolve issues of identification. Differences in personal timetables for recovery may have a similar effect (e.g., when some of the members of the family or community are traumatized and others are not). The latter may be ready to grieve for dead individuals, whereas others may need to engage in trauma recovery first or in addition to grieving. This difference may result in frustrations between the two groups rather than in supportive behaviors (Nader, 1994a; Nader & Pynoos, 1993).

SPECIALIZED TREATMENT OF
TRAUMATIC GRIEF

Interventions for traumatic grief require special attention to several posttrauma issues. These include interaction of symptoms of trauma and grief, and the nature of the trauma (as discussed earlier), the phase of response, and attention to the basic principles of traumatic grief recovery.

Phases of Response

The phases of trauma response include primary and secondary prevention, immediate and secondary first aid, initial interventions, and ongoing intervention programs (Nader, in press–a; Nader & Pynoos, 1993). Children may need family contact, restoration of order, or some time for initial recovery before they can give detailed descriptions of their experiences and reactions. Initially, rumors are common, and fear is contagious (Pynoos & Nader, 1989); consequently, arousal symptoms may be common to the traumatized and untraumatized within the first 2 to 3 weeks after a catastrophic incident. During initial first aid, interventions are aimed at comfort, reunion, restoration (e.g., physical restoration, restoration of safety, and a sense of safety), and giving accurate factual and age-appropriate information about the incident, the next step, and expectable reactions (Nader, in press–a).

Schools and communities are often prepared to provide assistance up to and including "Secondary First Aid." After severe catastrophic events affecting large groups, ongoing prevention efforts are well served by creating a comprehensive school intervention program that addresses all posttraumatic reactions including grief (Nader & Pynoos, 1993; Pynoos & Nader, 1988). A comprehensive program includes periodic groups for administrators, school personnel, and parents; individual treatment for identified adults and children; and small groups for grieving children and, if possible, for injured children. Coordination of helping groups and individuals is necessary for an effective overall effort and to prevent the formation of community subgroups working at cross purposes (see Nader & Pynoos, 1993). The following are descriptions of some of the initial and ongoing interventions for schools:

After the sniper attack in south central Los Angeles, a sampling of children from the entire school was completed at 1 and 14 months. One specialized clinical interview was conducted with specific identified children at each of those phases, and referrals were made to nearby agencies. Children who were afraid to return to the school were reintegrated into their classrooms, two brief grief groups were held to address the children's fears and concerns about the deceased, and teacher and parent consultations were conducted. Trauma clinicians provided screening, therapeutic diagnostic interviews, referrals, and crisis interventions to the children and parents for approximately 2 years.

A plane crash off Hawaii resulted in sudden, unexpected, tragic deaths and a sense of traumatic loss. No direct witnessing of the horror and no direct life threat to the peers of the third grader who died occurred, however. One extended parent meeting and one teacher meeting were conducted with suggestions to assist the children and parents in their recovery processes. Ongoing consultation was given to the teacher of the dead boy's class and administrators.

After a tornado, cooperative efforts between state, county, and local agencies (to provide personnel and specialized funding) and the efforts of the school district made possible a comprehensive intervention program. Consultation visits were made 1 week approximately every 2 months to train interviewers and clinicians, hold group and planning meetings, provide training and specialized interventions, and monitor the progress of children and adults. A trauma treatment team provided ongoing services for the children, teachers, parents, and school.

In 1991, a post-Gulf Crisis program in Kuwait was carried out in two segments: (a) in June, four psychologists from the Ministry of Health of Kuwait were trained in the methods of screening children for their postcrisis responses; and (b) in October through December, approximately 75 psychologists and social workers were trained to screen children systematically in the schools of Kuwait. An extensive translation process for screening instruments was undertaken. In June, a pilot sample of children was screened to collect preliminary information, and test the translated and adapted screening instrument. In November and December, a representative sample of more than 2,000 children was evaluated using two final versions of the screening instrument. In addition, during both the summer and fall, a group of clinicians underwent the first phase of training in the treatment of children with posttraumatic stress and grief reactions (Nader & Fairbanks, 1994; Nader & Pynoos, 1993). With an instance affecting an entire nation, many trainers were engaged in the ongoing training and recovery process.

Specialized Methods

Specific specialized methods of trauma treatment used by the former University of California at Los Angeles (UCLA) Trauma, Violence, and Sudden Bereavement Program have evolved out of the needs of traumatized children and communities (Nader, 1994a; Nader, in press–b; Nader & Pynoos, 1991; Pynoos & Eth, 1986; Pynoos & Nader 1989, 1993). The premises of treatment and intervention described subsequently include those that have been used primarily in the former UCLA program, together with additional premises and elaborations by this author. This method assumes a working knowledge of basic psychotherapeutic principles and techniques, and assumes the use of good skill, timing, and intuition in the implementation of these methods. The following is a summary of basic principles and understandings underlying this method of directive and interactive childhood trauma intervention (Nader, in press–b).

1. Observation of specific aspects of the traumatic situation is essential for effective intervention (e.g., the phases of response, cultural differences, phase of the traumatic event, and need of the adults in the community to recover from their own distress and traumatic reactions) (Nader, in press–b; Nader & Pynoos, 1993).

2. The clinician or his or her appointees act as advocate, and enlist the support of family, friends, and community for the child or adolescent to minimize secondary adversities and promote recovery (Nader, 1994a; Nader & Pynoos, 1993).

3. Cooperative efforts, at all phases of intervention, between clinicians and intervention teams is essential to prevent working at cross-purposes and to prevent divisiveness (Nader, in press–b; Nader & Pynoos, 1993).

4. Recognition of the interaction of trauma and grief reactions is essential to recovery and to the prevention of harmful reactions and behaviors by the bereaved. This interaction includes but is not limited to the understanding of trauma and grief reexperiencing, traumatic rage and helplessness, and intensification and complication of reactions (Eth & Pynoos, 1985b; Nader, in press–a, in press–b).

5. The goals of treatment include both repair of the injured aspects of the child and recognition of, recovery of, or reconnection with healthy aspects of the child, which may have been hidden by traumatic response and changes (Nader, in press–b).

6. The goals of effective individual intervention include the following: (a) to hear everything including the worst (Nader, 1994a; Pynoos & Nader, 1993); (b) to recognize initial distortions, omissions, spatial

misrepresentations, and desired actions and their emotional meaning for the child or adolescent (Johnson & Foley, 1984; Pynoos & Nader, 1989; Terr, 1979, 1991); (c) to acknowledge the intensity of traumatic moments and its impact on response (Nader, in press–b); (d) to recognize the multiple visual and perceptual experiences for a child during a traumatic event (Pynoos & Nader, 1989); (e) to discover the emotional meaning that becomes embedded in the details of the event (Nader & Pynoos, 1991; Pynoos & Nader, 1989, 1993); (f) to identify the results of trauma and posttrauma mental activity including assessments, interpretations, and desires or fantasies of action (Nader, 1994a; Nader & Pynoos, 1993; Pynoos & Eth, 1986; Pynoos & Nader, 1989, 1993); (g) to facilitate the child's or adolescent's facing emotional moments with the associated affect and to reenter the fantasy/moment with the child or adolescent resulting in release, reprocessing, and redefinition (Levy, 1935; Nader & Pynoos, 1991; Pynoos & Eth, 1986); and (h) to restore a healthy ego and return to a normal developmental path (Nader & Pynoos, 1991; Pynoos & Nader, 1993).

7. This method of treatment is directive while observing the child or adolescent's timing and need for closure (Nader, 1994a). The therapist takes an active role in addressing the impact of the traumatic experience (Nader, 1994a; Pynoos & Nader, 1988). Trauma recovery is often characterized by progress and periodic exacerbation of symptoms. Each child establishes his or her own rhythm(s) of review and focus on the issues of trauma and bereavement (Nader, 1994a). Specific symptoms may serve as methods of avoidance of a sense of helplessness or the reality of the event (e.g., guilt; Nader, in press–b). Achieving the proper closure at the end of each interview prevents leaving the child with renewed anxiety and an unnecessary avoidance of the therapeutic situation (Nader, 1994a; Pynoos & Eth, 1986).

8. Children may take one of several roles in their play and actions after traumatic events (e.g., victim, perpetrator, rescuer, or witness). The child may change role or identification over the course of treatment. Remaining in one of the roles without resolution may lead to changes in personality or life choices and to dangerous or troublesome behaviors (Nader, in press–a, in press–b).

9. Both boys and girls entertain anger (or rage) and strong wishes or fantasies of revenge during and after traumatic events. This method of treatment permits, facilitates, and works toward resolution of these issues for both genders (Nader, 1994a; Nader, in press–b; Nader & Pynoos, 1991, 1993).

CONCLUSION

Early bereavement may interfere with normal ego development and psychological growth; it greatly increases a child's susceptibility over time to school dysfunction, depression, and delinquency (Krupnick, 1984). The possible consequences of unresolved traumatic bereavement include a variety of disorders; personality and life changes; interferences with productive and successful living; and, in some cases, the perpetuation of violence and trauma. Treating traumatic grief requires understanding trauma, grief, and the interaction of the two. Although trauma work often precedes grief work, the two must occur in a child's or adolescent's own rhythm. Symptoms common to both trauma and grief may be intensified after traumatic events, symptoms are complicated by the interaction of the two responses, and recovery may be hindered by the interference of specific symptoms. Consequently, recuperation may be complicated, and adverse effects on development may be increased. Understanding the relevant principles of posttrauma intervention is essential to a child's or adolescent's recovery after traumatic death.

III

Interventions

Earlier chapters in this book frequently mention ways of helping children who are confronted with specific types of deaths or bereavement experiences. Chapters that follow in part III examine intervention modalities that are distinguished not by the kind of death-related encounter that has occurred in the life of a child but by the way in which assistance is offered.

This discussion of ways to help children who are coping with death and bereavement begins with an analysis of the families within which such children live and function. In chapter 12, Elliott Rosen argues for the importance of considering both the family context of a child's life and the resources that the family may be able to mobilize to help a child who is coping with death or bereavement. Showing how families can function as a healing resource for their bereaved children is simultaneously a way of empowering family systems and directing professional helpers to a valuable asset in their bereavement work.

In chapter 13, Margaret Metzgar and Barbara Zick describe ways to complement efforts undertaken in the home and by religious institutions through educational programs aimed at preparation before a traumatic event. While acknowledging and explaining sources of resistance that such programs have sometimes encountered, the authors emphasize the great value to be found in prior preparation as a way of helping children prepare themselves for encounters with loss, death, and bereavement before they actually occur. The heart of such programs is a proactive combination of education, communication, and validation. The work itself can be implemented through a host of simple and practical suggestions offered throughout this chapter.

Prior preparation is no longer possible once a traumatic event has occurred, but it is still not too late to undertake "postvention" or intervention after the fact with children in educational institutions. In chapter 14, that subject is explored in detail by Antoon Leenaars and Susanne Wenckstern. The authors set forth eight principles to guide postvention activities and seven elements that enter into the implementation of the postvention process. These principles and elements are then illustrated through two extended case examples.

Interventions that can supplement short-term postvention or that can be conducted independently, usually over an extended period, are represented here by separate discussions of support groups for bereaved children and individual treatment of the bereaved child. In chapter 15, Joan Bacon describes in detail the rationale behind bereavement support groups for children, their potential benefits, and issues to consider in establishing and running such groups. In chapter 16, Corinne Masur explains the role of a professional therapist in assisting children who are encountering difficulties in coping with death and bereavement. Both authors are sensitive to the value of carefully assessing each bereaved child to determine the services that will best serve his or her needs, and both identify indicators for professional referral. In addition, Bacon explores different types of support groups and different ways in which such groups may be used for bereaved children, whereas Masur articulates basic principles that guide individual intervention and practical methods of treating a child, either directly or through a parent or caretaker. In both of these chapters, the authors share numerous examples and concrete suggestions arising from extensive work in their respective fields.

12

The Family As Healing Resource

Elliott J. Rosen

This chapter presents both a rationale and a method for helping children cope with death and grief within the context of the family system. Concerned adults frequently recognize that a child is having difficulty in the aftermath of the death of a family member. After that recognition, they often look for appropriate resources to help that child. In some instances, a child might require or benefit from individual professional help to cope effectively with loss and bereavement. More often, families can play a prominent role in the helping process. However, this resource is too commonly overlooked.

Family therapists have long recognized that families seeking treatment for a troubled child may unwittingly be presenting merely the symptom bearer of larger family dysfunction (Minuchin, 1974). In fact, some argue that this concept is at the core of family systems thinking (Haley, 1976; Selvini Palazzoli, Boscolo, Cecchin, & Prata, 1974). Certainly, this concept may not always be the final clinical assessment. However, it is common enough to suggest that what troubles a child is often initially perceived by his or her parents to somehow be residing within the youngster. That is, the difficulty is seen as the child's problem, tangential to larger family dynamics.

This thinking is especially common in the aftermath of the death of a loved one. In such circumstances, a child's difficulty with resuming normal function or other manifestations of grieving are understandably a focus of great concern to parents and other family members. For professionals as well, the source of the child's emotional pain may be identified as revolving around the loss. Accordingly, it will be assumed that

223

the child's difficulties will be best treated by methods attuned to the child's intrapsychic makeup, cognitive status, and affective development.

Much of the literature on childhood bereavement bears out these points. Furman's pioneering study (1974) of children who experienced a parental death focused on traditional psychoanalytic treatment. Nearly 20 years later, Webb's *Helping Bereaved Children* (1993a) maintains much the same perspective, while presenting a wider variety of treatment options. Baker, Sedney, and Gross (1992) reflect the general therapeutic stance that treatment with children needs to focus on psychoanalytic principles of loss. Most commonly, literature on working with children who are grieving emphasizes developmental issues, guilt, the necessity for expression of feelings, and opportunities for "working through" the necessary emotions attendant to the grief process (Anthony, 1972; Furman, 1973; Grollman, 1967, 1995; Segal, 1984; Wolfelt, 1991a).

It has become fairly common to suggest group work as an important modality in treatment with children who have experienced the death of a family member. Broadening that lens, Munsch (1993) and Van Dexter (1986) examined the school and classroom setting as a venue for helping children cope with grief, the former presenting interventions in the aftermath of violent death and the latter suggesting excellent guidelines for treatment, both psychodynamic and psychoeducational. Similarly, Tait and Depta (1993) presented a play therapy model for working with grieving children based on Worden's (1982, 1991) four tasks of mourning.

Few experts would completely discount the importance of family as a vital healing resource. Nearly all understand the place of family dynamics in the child's adjustment. But few present a framework for thinking about ways in which families, themselves, might serve as a therapeutic force in a child's recovery from grieving. In fact, the family is the central stage on which the drama of our psychic life begins, and is ultimately shaped and nurtured. The centrality of family in the life of a child, although self-evident, may not be reflected in the ways in which many professionals seek to help children. Classical psychoanalytic methods of child treatment, for example, explicitly exclude parents and family from the treatment process. Even less traditional child-focused therapy usually considers family more as a helpful adjunct than an integral part of the process.

One danger presented by traditional, individual-focused methods of thinking about and treating children in the aftermath of a loved one's death is that of pathologizing a process that is inherently normal and necessary. "Treatment" implies the presence of a disease entity and thus the suggestion that a child needs "treatment" is tantamount to labeling that child as "sick." Although it has long been a concern in the family therapy field that children not be identified as being the family problem, it is an even greater concern that we not label a child who is grieving as one who is sick.

This concern does not mean that all of the excellent work done in the field of child bereavement be ignored. Indeed, regardless of our approach, it is vital that we have a firm understanding of the developmental stages through which children pass. Our knowledge of how children learn, how they express themselves, the ways in which they use symbolic play, and how they characteristically cope with loss are all essential to whatever approach we take to working with young people. Thus, it is important to remember that although this chapter emphasizes a nonpathologizing, normal, family process-based, task-oriented modality, none of this would be possible without a firm grasp of who children are and how they function.

However, to focus on children as resources unto themselves is shortsighted. It ignores the fundamental interpersonal dimension of grief and mourning. Although grief certainly does occur within the minds and hearts of children, it is also true that this same grief is played out in the lives of the families within which children find themselves (Pincus, 1974). Thus, Bowen (1976) demonstrated how powerfully a death impacts on the family system, Herz Brown (1988) examined the intergenerational impact of loss on the process of the family life cycle, Rando (1986) analyzed the nature of anticipatory grief and postulated a significant familial dimension to the process, and Rosen (1988a) suggested a strong correlation between pathological grief and the family's failure to help children heal from loss adequately.

THE FAMILY AS A SYSTEM

Few clinicians are unaware of the concept of family as a system. However, experience over many years in training and supervising mental health professionals and hospice personnel who work with families has revealed how little that concept impacts on choices guiding clinical interventions, particularly with children. For example, a colleague recently asked whether I would accept a young boy for treatment. The boy's mother had died some eight months before, and he was showing signs of distress, particularly in school. As I discussed the case with my colleague, she informed me that he had four younger siblings, each of whom was in treatment and being treated by a different therapist. Further discussion revealed that their father was also in psychotherapy treatment. I was being asked to become this family's sixth concurrent therapist! I strongly suggested to my colleague that perhaps she might be able to arrange at least a few sessions of family therapy consultation with the father and his five children together, but that I did not feel it would be wise to take on the treatment of the eldest sibling alone.

Some 5 months passed before I heard about this family again. The father called, on the advice of the colleague with whom I had originally spoken, although against the advice of two of his children's therapists. I worked together with them as a family for about 12 sessions with a strong focus on how frightened they were to speak with each other about their pain and how fearful the children were that their father would be unable to care for them. Labeling their feelings as normal and emphasizing to them how helpful it might be if they created opportunities to talk with each other about their mother and wife—and doing just that in the sessions—allowed for a shift in their heretofore depressed family affect.

What was also helpful was exploring with the family the circumstances around the mother's illness and death, and the father's revealing to his children information regarding his own mother's death when he was a child. In both, instances it became clear that the family's ethos was one of "silent suffering" and "keeping a stiff upper lip." Toward the end of our work together, I suggested to the father that he enter a group for single, bereaved parents where he would have the opportunity to speak with others in his situation.

In an earlier work (Rosen, 1990), two metaphors were proposed for understanding the family as a system: viewing the family as an intricate machine, consisting of a complex of reciprocally interactive parts; and considering the family as a human body in the process of compensating for injury. These are metaphors that strongly illustrate the interlocking, interdependent relationships of family life. In short, the impact of any psychosocial stressor on individual family members will be felt throughout the system; in the case of death, particularly, Bowen (1976) first described its impact as an "emotional shock wave." However, it is important to view this emotional shock wave not only as affecting the family as the clinician is likely to meet them for consultation but also as resounding across generational lines (Herz Brown, 1991; Rosen, 1991; Walsh & McGoldrick, 1991a). What this means, in practice, is that loss in previous generations is likely to play a powerful role in the present family's current coping and adaptation. Past losses of this sort need to be addressed as part of the treatment process (Imber-Black, 1993; Rosen, 1987, 1991).

A broadening of this multigenerational lens also allows an understanding of the family from a "multicontextual" perspective. This perspective demands that work with families consider the contexts of social class, race, gender, and especially ethnicity. In fact, for treatment to have a constructive impact, it must include an assessment of the family's social and financial status, the ways in which family roles have been determined by gender, and the part that the family's religious and ethnic values, beliefs, and rituals play in lives of its members (Rosen, 1988b; Rosen et al., 1991). Children do not exist in a vacuum, nor do families. We are likely to be more successful in helping a child who is coping with bereavement and grief in the degree to which we involve the largest circle of persons associated with that child.

TASKS FOR THE GRIEVING FAMILY

Worden (1982) first suggested a series of four tasks that constitute a healing process for persons who are grieving. In recent years, various task-based models of recovery from grief have been introduced, many of which use Worden's original and revised (Worden, 1991) work. Task-based approaches can be especially valuable in helping families set attainable goals, particularly when the "tasks" are presented as flexible and not time constrained (Corr & Doka, 1994). Such an approach frees the family from the popular notion that grief, as well as other psychological phenomena, progresses in strictly defined stages (Attig, 1991; Corr, 1992a).

Worden's four tasks reflect a psychological course of mourning that begins with an initial acceptance of the reality of death and culminates in a final cognitive and emotional integration of the loss with movement toward a future without the deceased. Walsh and McGoldrick (1988) initially adapted those four tasks to the larger family system, Rosen (1990) expanded that formulation with specific methods for family grief resolution, and Walsh and McGoldrick (1991b) revisited the concept, emphasizing the "overwhelming complexity of any family mourning process" (p. 10). Although it is common to think of tasks of grief as intrapsychic in nature (and most task-based theories reflect that notion), it is important to note that from a family systems perspective, grieving is also an interpersonal process (Shapiro, 1994). Thus, in encouraging the family's mobilization as a healing resource, a counselor might do best by delineating the system tasks and presenting them as a broader dimension of what transpires within the individual. Indeed, because children typically view their pain as distinctly private, this experience can point to entirely new directions for them and their families.

Let us now look at these four tasks and their specific applicability to children. The four tasks for grieving families are:

1. To share acknowledgment of the reality of death
2. To share experience of the pain of grief
3. To reorganize the family system
4. To redirect the family's relationships and goals (see Table 12.1)

The family able to perform these tasks is bridging a gap between life as it once was and life as it will be in the future. Ideally, families begin working on these tasks during the early stages of a family member's illness (Rando, 1986) and will continue to do so through the terminal period. Although none of these tasks can be fully realized until after the death, once accomplished, the survivors will be able to continue their lives in what will have become a new family system. Let us look at these four tasks and how they apply to children in the family.

TABLE 12.1 Tasks for the Grieving Family

Task (The family must . . .)	Emotionally	Behaviorally
Share acknowledgment of the reality of death	Accept finality of loss	Communicate openly Celebrate rites and rituals with full participation
Share the experience of the pain of grief	Accept a wide range of emotions	Share these feelings with each other Allow for individual differences
Reorganize the family system	Accept that the family can never be the same	Realign old relationships Delegate new role functions Cope with short-term disorganization
Reinvest and redirect its goals and relationships	Imagine a future without the deceased	Allow for four seasons Accept the need for flexibility

The Family's Shared Acknowledgment
of the Reality of Death

The process of grieving requires that the family as a whole acknowledge that loss is final and death irreversible. Denial of this reality, although common at various stages of the dying process and even afterward, may impede a family's recovery from loss. The family's shared acknowledgment of death is reflected in their communicating about the subject in clear, noneuphemistic terms. Language can be a powerful psychological tool. Families that avoid use of direct terminology may be sending signals that they have not fully integrated the reality of their loss. It is imperative that the entire family share in the acknowledgment of the reality of death, beginning as early in the process as possible. This process is frequently impeded by misguided concern for children. Most often, it is in families where children are deemed incapable of understanding loss or too vulnerable to manage it that the widest incidence of difficulty in adjustment is found.

This point does not mean that there need be a hard-and-fast rule for all families in all situations. All family members, for example, do not necessarily need to be informed of every fact immediately. In the earliest stages of an illness—for example, when a fatal diagnosis may still be uncertain—children might be spared specific information. Similarly, if a remission of the illness is likely, it might be appropriate to delay the bad news of the diagnosis. Despite these exceptions, a tendency exists in families to keep the truth from children on the grounds that their constitutions are "vulnerable," which is likely to do more harm than good.

Young children who are told "Granny has gone on a trip," or "God took Daddy up to heaven" may become needlessly confused. Not only do such children assume that death is reversible and anticipate the loved one's return, but for them knowledge of death is replaced with a sense of rejection and abandonment. Excluding children from rites, such as wakes and funerals, prevents the family from sharing the acknowledgment of their loss and blocks resolution of grief. New secrets create new tensions in the family system and prevent it from moving on to a different state of equilibrium.

The natural tendency to misrepresent the facts of loss and death to children and to use language that obfuscates hard realities is a function of adult anxiety with the subject. In a recent interview with a family where a young child had died a few years before from leukemia, the surviving siblings expressed their anger and resentment at having been kept from the reality of their brother's dying until literally the last hour of his life. As one sister poignantly stated, "If I'd only known, I could've had time to say good-bye to him." The parents in this family were able to admit that their difficulty in sharing information with the other children was actually less an attempt to protect the children and more a function of protecting themselves from the pain of having to talk openly about their dying child.

The cognitive ability to absorb the notion of death's irreversibility is probably not present in most children until around 8 or 9 years of age (Kastenbaum, 1967; see chapter 2 this volume), although our own clinical observation has been that a wide variation exists among children. A child's mythology of a loved one's return—particularly in times of trouble—or of fantasizing reunification with a deceased parent is often misinterpreted by adults as a sign of maladaption.

> *For example, the wife of Tom, a 34-year-old man, died in an accident. Some months later, he asked if he might bring his daughter along for one of his sessions. He was troubled that her talking about "wanting to be with Mommy" might reflect suicidal thoughts.*
>
> *The two sessions spent with Tom and 7-year-old Jenny, were poignant yet delightful. Jenny was a bubbly, intelligent, imaginative child who spoke freely about her mother. Although clearly bewildered by her mother's death and unable to absorb it fully, Jenny was most certainly not suicidal and did not seem depressed. She wondered aloud whether she would ever have "another" mommy and in nearly the same breath assured me that her mommy would be back. When I questioned her directly about whether Mommy would return, she told me that she "knew" she wouldn't—because everyone had told her that— but she gave me a conspiratorial look that indicated that we both knew she was not entirely convinced.*
>
> *What was most notable about these sessions was not Jenny's presentation but Tom's. As his daughter talked about Mommy, Tom winced noticeably. It was clear that listening to Jenny talk about her loss was nearly unbearable for Tom. When Tom and I met alone again, he told me that after the sessions together with Jenny, he realized that it was he who felt suicidal at times and wished to be with his dead wife. He understood that Jenny was merely verbalizing his forbidden thoughts and that his reluctance to allow her to talk a lot about her mother spared him the pain of having to face his loss. With this insight, Tom was able to strategize ways in which he could spend time talking with Jenny and help her without losing his own emotional balance.*

Children's fear of abandonment is set in motion with prospective loss and is exacerbated after death. Unwittingly, family members may fuel this concern by withdrawal, anger, shortness of temper, hypochondriasis, depression, and a host of other behaviors. A surviving parent, for example, may likely misinterpret a child's behavior as reflecting the pain of loss when it may more accurately reflect a reaction to the survivor's attitude.

Lois, whose husband had died of colon cancer 18 months earlier, called to request that I see her and her children, 10-year-old Robert and 12-year-old Andrea, for family therapy. Lois indicated that she was having a difficult time with the children ever since she had begun going out socially. Both were angry at her, and Andrea directly accused her of not having loved Daddy if she could go out with other men.

Treatment with this family was short term and effective in helping Lois to realize that she could not go about "living my own life" without considering that the children would likely react to this behavior with apprehension that she might abandon them. One particular exchange between Robert and Lois in a session so shocked her that it took weeks to recover from it.

Robert: Anyway, I don't want you to go away with that guy. You'll have sex with him.

Lois: [shocked] What makes you say that? I'm not having sex with . . . well, my private life is not your business. That's ridiculous. We're just going away to the beach for one weekend. And you know where we're going.

Robert: Yes you will, you'll have sex with him, and you'll get AIDS and die.

Lois: [beginning to cry] Where do you get such crazy ideas?

Lois was amazed to hear the depth to which Robert worried about whether she might die and leave him parentless. To this point, she had seen Robert and Andrea as "two selfish kids who don't care whether I'm alone for the rest of my life." Sessions with this family focused on the children's need to feel some reassurance that their mother would be a steady presence in their lives and on Lois's desire to begin a new social life. However, simply talking about these issues was not enough. It was also necessary to create concrete opportunities for mother and children to spend time together in ways that were productive and fostered the reassurance in them that their mother would not leave. Lois, too, needed reassurance from the children that she could pursue an independent social life without their feeling jeopardized. What had been absent in the family had been structured opportunities for deeper communication that all three had unconsciously avoided.

As mentioned earlier, how families use language to describe their experiences with death and loss is a powerful indicator of how they are able to help their children heal. A poignant personal memory is the plaintive cry of a friend's young daughter to her father after the untimely death of her mother: "but you promised we'd all go to heaven in the car some day." The number of books on talking to children about death is an indication of how serious this concern is for parents. A recent, cursory look in the "self-help" section of a local bookstore revealed several examples of books on how to talk with children about death and loss (e.g., Grollman, 1990; for guides to this literature see Corr, 1993a, 1995; Rudman, Gagne, & Bernstein, 1993).

No hard-and-fast rules dictate how to communicate with children on this subject. Instead, parents ought to be encouraged, when deemed appropriate, to use their instincts and the knowledge of their own children in deciding what to say. What commonly influences parents and other family members in these instances is their own uncertainty about how to talk about death. Despite the proliferation of violence and the banality of death all around us, we are a death-denying culture in many ways (Becker, 1973). From a family systems perspective, however, we want to focus on the context of death in the life of each particular family. Less important than the specific words used to discuss death, our encouragement to family members that they talk about their own feelings, experiences, and fears with children is paramount. What adults tend to do is "childspeak"—that is, they talk "at" children rather than with them.

One potent method for helping children's emotional healing is fostering in them a sense of empathy, which is best accomplished by open and honest sharing. Helping the family achieve a broader perspective on the importance of multigenerational loss potentiates the development of this empathy. When, for example, a parent is able to share personal experiences of loss with a child, openly expressing the pain of that loss, the child is given an accessible model for experiencing his or her own grief and confusion. In working with families facing life-threatening illness or death, encouraging their elders to talk about themselves is a most effective method for helping children cope. This kind of dialogue fosters the shared acknowledgment of the harsh reality of death as well as a sense of hope for personal survival.

The Family's Shared Experience of the Pain of Grief

For family therapists, the primary goal of nearly all treatment is helping the family to achieve an open system. For this state of openness to exist, two essential ingredients are necessary: (a) family members must feel the freedom to express themselves without fear of censure or disenfranchisement; and (b) the system must allow family members to leave and return freely, both physically and metaphorically. Let us look at this open system, within which the family can create an atmosphere that allows all family members, including children, to heal the wounds of grief.

Although not all people can be expected to express pain identically, it is not uncommon for families to demand uniform reactions from family members. Although loss may be mutual, the expression of emotions is likely to be widely variable. In an open family system, an acceptance of a wide range of emotions—disappointment, helplessness, guilt, relief, and anger—occurs. However, we frequently encounter situations in which children are labeled as emotionally troubled when their way of expressing themselves does not fit the expectations of the family. *Pseudomutuality* is a term used to describe the kind of facade created in families where everyone is expected to feel and behave according to an (often) unconscious family script. In such families, the individual expression of "deviant" emotions is forbidden.

A psychoanalyst colleague recently recounted an experience with a child who was referred for treatment after the death of a grandfather with whom the boy was extremely close. The child's parents, also both psychoanalysts, were disturbed by the boy's refusal to talk about his dead grandparent. Within a few sessions, it became clear that this child was adjusting well to the loss but refused to talk about it in a way that satisfied his parents that he was grieving "correctly." The child's therapist was wise enough to terminate the intervention quickly and advise the parents that they needed to create an atmosphere in which their son would feel comfortable grieving in his own way.

Our objective for children in working with families who are grieving should be to help the children to accept whatever emotions they feel and to manage those emotions in appropriate ways. For children, the pain of loss may take many forms. Among the most common reactions are anger and fear. Both can, and should, be managed within the family whenever possible. Encouraging the family in its role as a healing resource for grieving children is a natural extension of the family's shared experience of the pain of loss. Indeed, the capacity to accept loss is a core element of a healthy family system (Walsh & McGoldrick, 1991a). What is often difficult for families is the expectation that somehow children will achieve that which the adults themselves find nearly impossible: a complete resolution and healing from the pain of loss. Helping children to heal is helping them to understand that death is, indeed, a form of abandonment and that feeling angry is not abnormal. The fear that accompanies the enormity of death is a normal expression of the pain of grief and may never completely disappear.

The second important ingredient of the open family system is its capacity to manage family members' freedom to leave and return, both physically and metaphorically. This approach has particular relevance to children at various stages of the life cycle where feeling the freedom to leave and return is essential to the process of individuation. Death is a disruption of the family life cycle as well as the individual life cycle. In the circumstances of such disruption, staying and leaving become increasingly more powerful psychological tasks (Solomon & Hersch, 1979). The importance of understanding the family life cycle cannot be understated. Carter and McGoldrick's (1988) seminal work on this subject emphasizes the significant changes in family status that are required as families pass through predictable developmental stages. Life-threatening illness and death disrupt the family's ability to perform the tasks necessary to achieve appropriate shifts in family status (such as launching children, for example) and may have a profound impact on a child's potential for healing (Hoffman, 1988; Rosen, 1990, 1991).

At a recent hospice team meeting, a nurse recounted her upset with two teenagers in a family where the mother was actively dying. While making a home visit she encountered the two youngsters as they returned from school. As she reported, one of the two hollered, "hi Mom" from the hallway; the other completely ignored his mother; and both proceeded to grab something from the kitchen and leave the house. The nurse was disconcerted by this behavior and commented on how sad it was for the mother that her children seemed oblivious to her condition. The hospice social worker demurred, explaining that she knew this family well and that the children's behavior was not only acceptable to their mother but encouraged. Mother was determined that they continue to lead as normal lives as possible and was aware that this adolescent behavior was, indeed, appropriate.

For younger children as well, families need to be taught to allow grieving children the opportunity to come and go, physically and figuratively. The attention span of younger children is such that it is unrealistic to expect consistency, particularly in grief. One is often struck by how easily children shift from what seems the depths of pain and despair to the normal tasks and fun of childhood. Families that allow children to make these shifts comfortably are providing a healing atmosphere; parents and others often underestimate the capacity of children to manage their own emotions. This point leads naturally to a consideration of children's participation in the rites and rituals of death because the questions raised by many families relate to their concern that such participation might be harmful.

In an open system, the encouragement that all family members participate in some way in the rituals surrounding death (wakes, funerals, burials, etc.), is reasonable when individual choices are also respected (Corr, 1991). Children almost always take their lead from significant adults. When children are hesitant, for example, to attend a funeral or take part in some other ritual, they are often responding to a subtle message from an adult who doubts his or her own ability to manage the emotions that might be stirred up by the experience. If permitted the latitude to do so, children will usually find ways to move in and out psychologically (and even physically) so as to maintain a manageable equilibrium. At times, the well-meaning intentions of adults will interfere with this natural process. To foster the family's role as a healing resource, it is necessary, at times, to remind such adults that "benign neglect" is often the best medicine.

Reorganization of the Family System

Death is certainly the most disruptive event in our lives (Holmes & Rahe, 1967). In its aftermath, relationships within the family must undergo a major realignment. Because the fundamental equilibrium of family life is subject to the emotional shock wave discussed earlier, a realignment of relationships and reallocation of roles is nearly always in order (McGoldrick & Walsh, 1983). Because it is common for most organisms (and families are no exception) to adjust toward stasis, it is often difficult even to convince family members that changes need to be made. Particularly when the deceased has played a central role in the family's life, realignment and role reallocation are more vital, and usually more difficult (Vess, Moreland, & Schwebel, 1985).

For children, accepting that roles have to change is seldom easy. Accustomed to depending on a particular parent in certain circumstances, a child may either struggle to shift that dependence immediately to another available adult or find it impossible to imagine someone else filling those shoes. Families in which roles are rigidly fixed, such as those with traditional gender roles, often have great difficulty accomplishing the task of realignment. Not only do children find it difficult but adults are also frequently unable to make the necessary shifts (Vess, Moreland, & Schwebel, 1985). In fact, many children who display signs of psychological disturbance in the aftermath of one parent's death may be reacting as much to the loss of that parent's function in his or her life and the inability of the surviving parent to provide it, as to the actual loss of the deceased parent (Rosen, 1990).

This third family task can be seen clearly in one family following the death of the 40-year-old mother. Her surviving 41-year-old husband felt unable to meet the demands of caring for his children, 10 and 12 years of age. Managing his household, job, and grief proved daunting. Assuming another person's functional and emotional tasks is especially complicated for fathers in our culture, because most men are not skilled in maintaining open relationships, communicating feelings, and nurturing children. In this case, the father had initially called on his mother and sister to help him with the home and children, but soon found their presence in his life intrusive. This attempted realignment did not work and after employing a nanny to fill the role also failed to meet his expectations that things function smoothly in the home, he feared that no other options were available. He and the children were in serious conflict, and it was clear in our first meeting that his expectations of them were unreasonable. The children also unrealistically assumed that their father would automatically take on their mother's responsibilities. Work with this family primarily involved helping them to realign household chores more sensibly by pointing out to Dad what he could reasonably expect from his kids and by letting the children know what they now needed to do for themselves. The work also included exploring with father and children what Mom's loss meant to them, both emotionally and functionally, and helping them to understand what reorganizing the family would mean to all three. But most important was helping them understand that family life could no longer be what it was.

It is reasonable to expect that families will experience some breakdown in the system after a death. Even though this outcome will likely result in a period of "anarchy," that may not be entirely destructive. What it can create is an opportunity to abandon old patterns and adopt a new, more functional structure. For the family to achieve this goal, the likelihood exists that the children will be better able to adjust to current and future losses.

Ironically, a family's move toward reorganization can also be maladaptive, particularly when it involves the premature adoption of a replacement for the deceased. Because families naturally adapt toward stability rather than toward change, this action is an attempt to restore equilibrium. Although the replacement usually is a new person invited to join the family system, such as a boyfriend or girlfriend, in-law, or new spouse, it may also manifest itself in a physical move, the selling of a house or business, or a similar dramatic action. Rosen (1990) described a fascinating example of this phenomenon: a family—a young widow with four young daughters—who bought a dog a few days after the father's funeral and called the pet by the dead man's name! When, in a session with them, the therapist wondered aloud about the choice of name, none of the five seemed to make the connection between the deceased and the dog. Although the dog, despite his name, could not replace the father, the family was so anxious to fill the gap in their system that they looked to the dog to restore balance.

Redirection of the Family's Relationships and Goals

This final family task is more aptly characterized as a long-term process whose end is never fully achieved. Nor, in fact, need that be a family's goal. The observation of many practitioners who work with families facing death and life-threatening illness, as well as recent research (Wortman & Silver, 1989), reinforces the family systems' notion that rather than grief ever being fully resolved, a loss is best conceived as a constantly evolving dimension of the family across three generations. "Death ends a life, but it does not end a relationship," says Robert Anderson (1968, p. 5), in his powerful drama, *I Never Sang for My Father.* Significant relationships resound across generations, enriching the family and adding to the complexity of its communal psyche. For these relationships to have meaning and for the family to be the resource needed for healing, it is imperative that the system be as open as possible, particularly in terms of allowing children the latitude necessary for grieving.

Although the notion that mourning takes about a full year has become a generally accepted maxim in the field (Glick, Weiss, & Parkes, 1974; Parkes & Weiss, 1983), many a clinical error has been made in treating children who present with symptoms that are grief-related more than a year after a death. This observation does not indicate that children are never in need of individual psychotherapy or other intervention at that juncture, but it is vital that a careful assessment of family function also be made. That four seasons—of holidays, birthdays, and other events—need to pass for real healing to be felt is logical. The family reshaping internal relationships and reorganizing itself should, by the first anniversary of the death, be prepared to consider a new life without the physical presence of the deceased. However, in many families at least one family member will offer evidence that suggests to the insightful observer that the family is, in fact, not prepared for the next steps in its life. Frequently, that one family member is a child.

When the Kellys were told by their daughter's guidance counselor that they needed to get help for 10-year-old Meghan, they were not surprised because Meghan had been displaying some troubling behavior in the year since the death of her older sister, Mary. Sucking her thumb, frequently appearing to be in a daze, and spending a lot of time at a friend's home had concerned her parents, but neither felt comfortable with seeking professional help. Meghan's dad believed that she was still grieving; her mom said that Meghan's behavior was not atypical because she had a history of looking for attention in immature ways. Both parents claimed that they, themselves, were "moving on" after their elder daughter's death, and Mrs. Kelly had recently announced that she was pregnant.

I first informed the Kellys that I did not usually work with children individually, and I invited them to work together with me as a family for six sessions. At the end of that period, we would assess where we might go from there. My initial history taking revealed that Mrs. Kelly had suffered a loss similar to Meghan's: When she was 11 years old, her first cousin was drowned at a camp they attended together. Without any encouragement, she tearfully recounted the tragic story including her lifelong guilt that had she been with her cousin that day the accident would never have happened. Her husband, who was unaware of this history, gently remarked that as she spoke he was reminded of how she sounded in the weeks after Mary's death—that somehow she was responsible for her daughter's death and should have known how to save her. Further exploration with the couple—with Meghan present in the room—revealed that Mrs. Kelly was depressed and remained withdrawn from her husband and daughter. Both were having difficulty engaging her, and Meghan, without rancor, indicated that she really liked her friend's mom, who told her she could hang out at their house anytime.

The few remaining sessions with the Kellys were spent with the parents alone. I reassured them that they were going to be the most effective therapists for Meghan as soon as they could develop the necessary commonsense skills. What this process actually involved was a brief course of short-term, goal-directed couples treatment in which the Kellys could talk openly about their loss, its echo in their own families of origin, and the obstacles they felt to being more available to Meghan. It was also important to assure them that their impatience with "moving on" was natural but perhaps unrealistic. Not only was more time needed for healing to occur, but they would need to accept that a loss of this magnitude was never fully resolved.

How a family goes about this final task of healing has powerful repercussions for the child's future adjustment. This point is why, when we speak of the family as a healing resource, we need to reiterate that a child's grieving is neither a self-contained task, removed from the dynamics of family relationships, nor is it time bound, needing to happen within a circumscribed period. The opportunity for children to use a healthy family as a touchstone for healing across the developmental spectrum is a gift that families have the power to bestow.

AN EXTENDED CASE EXAMPLE: THE HOWELLS

Not too long ago I received a call from a 22-year-old woman, Allie Howell, who wanted to talk with me about her 11-year-old sister, Debbie. Her boss had suggested she call me because Allie was distressed that Debbie was constantly fighting with their father, crying a great deal, had lost weight, and was generally having a difficult time adjusting, some 9 months after their mother's death from Hodgkin's disease and complications from diabetes. We spoke for a while, and I suggested that she, her father, 19-year-old sister, Nan, and Debbie come in together for a consultation. Allie thought that was a great idea but doubted her father would be amenable. I wondered aloud whether she could persuade him to call me directly and arrange for the appointment rather than her taking on that responsibility. Her tone suggested to me that she found this idea unsettling, but, after some coaxing and strategizing as to how to convince Dad, she agreed.

James Howell did call me just a few days later, expressed surprise at his daughter's having contacted me but willingness to come in with the three girls, "if Allie thinks that would be a good idea." A week later I met with the family, and with few preliminaries, they began to tell me of the family's 5-year ordeal of caring for Marianne Howell. The two older daughters did nearly all the talking, with Debbie occasionally weeping or interrupting to "correct" some description of her interaction with Mom. James barely spoke, rather deferring to Allie and Nan.

Marianne was chronically ill for 5 years before the cancer diagnosis, but she had functioned fairly independently, although with constant medical involvement. In the last 5 years of her life, she was quite ill and depended almost entirely on Allie, and when she went off to college, on Nan for her primary care. Both girls spoke of their mother in glowing terms, describing her as a "perfect mom" who, despite her physical illness, attended to all aspects of her household and the lives of her children. She was particularly concerned that Debbie's needs be addressed, and the two older sisters described many instances in which they discussed this topic with Mom. Mother also named Allie as Debbie's godmother and was explicit in her expectations that Allie would take care of her younger sister when she was no longer around.

Curiously absent from most of the description of Marianne's illness was Dad, who also made few contributions in the session. When the discussion turned to Debbie—the problem that had brought them to me—everyone, including Dad, agreed that she had failed to make a good adjustment after her mother's death. The biggest problem, all agreed, was the constant fighting between Debbie and Dad. Allie began to describe the interaction between the two and commented that Mom had "never really let Dad be a Dad" because she did not believe he was very good at it.

Allie:	You see, Dad has a real bad temper, and Mom knew it was best not to let Debbie and him get too involved with each other.
James:	Well, it's true, she doesn't really take direction very well, and I have a short fuse. Her mother handled her much better so it made sense. . . .
Therapist:	And Debbie? How long is her fuse?
Allie:	Well, if you just try and tell her what to do then she understandably gets really upset. But Debbie is fine if you talk to her calmly and reason with her.
Therapist:	And Mom did that real well?
James:	Well, actually my wife was pretty sick for quite a while, and her sisters did most of that with Debbie. But now, with Allie working and Nan at school, I think Debbie's having some problems. We get into some scrapes, but we understand each other. I think Allie agrees that Deb needs to grow up a bit, and it probably doesn't help to coddle her. If Allie supports me a little more I think Deb and I can work things out.

What struck me as we spoke of the "problem" with Debbie was how much James and Allie sounded like husband and wife, and not father and daughter. I did not express that directly but asked Debbie to describe a typical problem at home. She proceeded to relate a couple of recent incidents in which it was clear that she looked to her sister to intervene when she and her father clashed. She was also tearful when she spoke of her mother and wanted all of us to know how difficult it was for her that her mother was so sick—and how she hardly knew her.

In the second session, I wondered aloud whether anyone thought that perhaps Mom had underestimated Dad's ability to parent. No one, including James, believed she did.

Therapist:	But did you and your wife talk about child rearing with the elder girls—before Debbie came along?
James:	Well, I was more involved then. She wasn't sick, we did a lot more together and she expected me to help out with the kids. And sure, we did talk about what we wanted for the girls and how our parents were and how we wanted to be . . . different, y'know?
Therapist:	When did you stop doing that? After Debbie was born?
James:	[thoughtful, pensive] No, I don't think so. I think it was after her diabetes began to get real bad, and she got pretty sick. I think she kind of gave Debbie over to Allie to take care of.
Therapist:	And Nan?
Nan:	I think I've always taken care of myself. That's just who I am.
Therapist:	[to James] So, if you no longer needed to be a dad, what was your job?
James:	Mmm, I guess to work, make enough money to be sure all the bills would be handled and the kids would be taken care of. Other than that. . . .

This example gives a glimpse of what had happened in the system after Marianne became ill. A strong, competent woman, as she weakened she transferred the mothering of her youngest child to her eldest daughter, naming her the godmother (really, the surrogate mother) and effectively cutting her husband out of the parenting process. In subsequent sessions, it emerged that James was an alcoholic who had been dry since shortly after Allie's birth. Early in their marriage he had lost a great deal of money gambling, and Marianne worried that if he felt undue pressure with her illness and the children, he might begin drinking or gambling again. This information shocked the girls; James was also a bit shocked as he revealed it. But in a sense it was a confession and an explanation, the latter encouraged by questioning whether he was comfortable with being labeled an inadequate father.

As we continued to meet, it also became clear that Debbie, rather than being emotionally disturbed, was constantly testing limits and had learned to play her sisters skillfully (particularly Allie) against their father. What complicated this process was that Allie had a serious boyfriend—they were considering marriage—and both wanted her to leave the house and move in with him. But because of the conflict between Debbie and Dad, Allie was reluctant to leave the house. Debbie intuited all this, and it placed her in a terrible bind. If she was "good," she risked losing her surrogate mom; if she continued to be "bad," her turmoil with her Dad escalated.

How easy it would be to label Debbie a "patient" who needs individual psychotherapy, and how common is this practice. Let us look at Debbie's behavior without recourse to an examination of the context of her family: Her mother has recently died after a long illness, she is frequently weepy, and seems labile and unhappy. She fights constantly with her father, and he finds it nearly impossible to get her to listen or cooperate. She is distractible and fidgety in school, has lost weight, chooses to stay at home rather than go out with friends, and is not, in short, a happy child. It is my contention that such a child is typically referred for individual treatment (Allie, in fact, did call me hoping I would see Debbie) without adequate attention paid to the context of her life and the potential for her family to become a healing resource. This observation does not indicate that Debbie would not have been helped at all in such treatment, but I believe it would have fallen far short of what was necessary.

Treatment with the Howells lasted about 8 months. I most often saw them together as a family, although Nan was away at school and only attended sessions when she was in town. I encouraged Allie to see a counselor who I felt could help her with the difficult process of separating from her family in a healthy way. Although this goal could have been on the agenda of our work as a family, I believe that young adults can benefit greatly from short-term psychotherapy focused on the process of individuation. I did see James a few times separately from the family and was able to suggest ways in which he could reclaim his role of father without Debbie's experiencing it as punitive or his feeling overwhelmed by it.

My primary goal, however, was to encourage all four members of this family to see themselves as having family wounds that needed healing. None of them was truly comfortable with an arrangement that left Dad feeling wholly inadequate, Allie feeling trapped, and Debbie labeled as "bad." The notion of the family as a healing resource includes the important idea that families make their best efforts at achieving stability in the face of crisis, despite their own sense (and often the judgment of others) that things are not going as they should. The Howells, for example, felt that Debbie was behaving abnormally. The larger context of their family's life, however, suggests that, in fact, Debbie was responding reasonably to the situation.

How was she to manage the dilemma that faced her? Try as she might, it is difficult to imagine how she could—on her own—succeed in navigating the delicate balance between her sister and father. Many children are asked to assume this role by family members—and by professionals. Although sympathetic to the child's plight, the tendency to label him or her as having the problem results in expecting that he or she should do what is necessary to solve it. This expectation puts the child in a bind that may ultimately be impossible to resolve.

CONCLUSION

Work with the Howells, and with many other families who have faced life-threatening illness and death, provides ample evidence that the choice made by them and the professionals to whom they turn for help—to treat children as if grief were an illness and the failure to adapt to loss a psychological disability—is often mistaken. In this chapter, the family has consistently been described as a healing resource, but I would further suggest that the family is often the only sensible resource for children. Adults who have suffered the loss of a loved one early in life typically report that the pain of loss was exacerbated by the sense of isolation they experienced afterward. Loving family members who were once their source of guidance and support seemed to disappear into their own grieving, and the memory of being left to heal themselves often remains a prominent legacy of loss. The purpose of this chapter has been to present a paradigm of treatment in which the child's most powerful resource—the family—is used as the source of healing and recovery.

13

Building the Foundation: Preparation Before a Trauma

Margaret M. Metzgar and Barbara C. Zick

This chapter examines what can be done to prepare children to cope with loss before its occurrence. The background for this work includes recognizing the need for such prior preparation; appreciating the value of helping children to "give grief a name" by showing them how to recognize and identify their responses to loss; and acknowledging personal, professional, or cultural factors that may lead adults to resist teaching children about loss and death. Three principal elements in a proactive program of prior preparation are education, communication, and validation. The main section of this chapter shows how to implement the program of prior preparation by describing opportunities that adults can use to talk with children by responding to questions and answers, providing comfort and support, engaging symbolic play, and direct sharing.

THE NEED

In general, our society acknowledges the need to teach children about crosswalk safety, personal safety, safe touching, and drugs. Yet few programs address the need to teach about loss or death. The belief expressed in this chapter is that the best way to help children to understand the concept of "dead" and the process of grief is to begin teaching these explanations long before children are faced with a trauma. The need to talk about grief and giving children tools to cope with loss could easily be compared with any other type of preventive teaching. Helping children build a foundation for understanding grief and loss, before an actual trauma, is the focus of this chapter (Metzgar, 1994).

At some time in their young lives children will be forced, on some level, to deal with grief and loss. Historically, attempts have been made to shield children from grief. When a pet, like a goldfish or hamster, dies, a replacement animal is often purchased almost immediately. When a family member dies, children are frequently left out of planning and participating in the family funeral rituals. Adults commonly seek to insulate and protect children from the pain of the grief process.

This response is complicated because few adults feel confident about how to begin explaining the concept of death to children, either before or after the fact. However, times are changing and the need for dialogue about death is increasing daily. For example, one 9-year-old was feeling forced to make a decision after the deaths of two of her close friends. Each of her friends had been violently murdered, in separate occurrences, on the same day. Her dilemma consisted of trying to decide which funeral to attend because both funerals had been scheduled at the same time! This decision is one that most adults would have a difficult time making.

Another example of the growing need for dialogue about death is an 11-year-old boy who was overheard asking his math teacher how she wanted to die. He followed the question by expressing the hope that he would die in a car accident rather than getting shot like his friends. The frequency of these types of incidents is increasing daily. Death, today, is all too commonly a reality in children's lives. How can adults continue to deny the need for addressing preventively, in healthy ways, topics of grief and loss with children? Children in our society are bombarded daily with images of violence and death, both real and fictitious. A study by the American Psychological Association stated that children who watched 2 to 4 hours of television a day will have witnessed 8,000 murders and 100,000 acts of violence by the time they finish elementary school (Diamant, 1994). Researchers for TV Guide Center for Media and Public Affairs stated that, on the average, an act of violence occurs every 6 minutes on television (Diamant, 1994). Similarly, the National Coalition on Television Violence indicated that 75% of all children's video games contain violent images (Diamant, 1994).

This chapter explores ways to begin the much-needed dialogue about grief, loss, and death before an actual event. Specific strategies are suggested to help build a constructive base to prepare children to handle difficult grief and loss situations effectively. To develop and teach children ways of coping with grief and loss, adults have to explore their own beliefs on the subject. In addition, adults will need to expand their own awareness and understanding of loss beyond illness, death, or divorce. All of the strategies contained in this chapter are intended to be used to help children normalize the experience of loss. In general, this goal is best accomplished by helping children expand their understanding of the continuum of loss, because loss is a universal experience that is not limited to death only.

Note that frequently the strategies mentioned in this chapter do not even address death specifically but instead focus on the exploration of feelings and the processing of a loss experience. Children learn best when adults can help them apply their current experiences to a specific learning. This is what is frequently referred to as capitalizing on a "teachable moment," or taking one of life's daily lessons and using it as a teaching tool.

The experience of loss is a part of our lives from the very moment of our birth when we exchange the safe, dark, protected comfort of our mother's womb for the cold air, bright lights, and noises of the new world. Young children can experience loss in the "simple" acts of starting school, breaking a toy, losing their lunch money, or having a substitute teacher. As children grow, so do the number and variety of their loss experiences. Sadness over the broken toy may now be replaced with the pain of a broken relationship, being rejected by a best friend, or not being chosen for the select team. Frequently now the issue is not losing lunch money but having enough money to buy the latest fad. Then, along the way, many children are also obliged by life events to cope with a variety of major losses, such as the death of a succession of pets, parental divorce, the death of a friend or loved one, abuse, or the chemical dependency of someone in their home. That is life today; it is full of loss.

GIVING GRIEF A NAME

An old Native American belief says: *If you give something a name and a shape, you can have power over it. However, if it remains nameless and shapeless, it will continue to have power over you.* Because loss and grief are such integral parts of life, adults must find ways, not only for ourselves but for our children, to give those experiences a name and shape.

To help children define that name and shape, adults need to help them create a frame or context for understanding grief and loss. That is most easily done by helping children explore their emotional, as well as their physical and cognitive responses, to their everyday experiences. This exploration does not necessarily require an additional curriculum. Instead, it challenges adults to be aware of the daily opportunities life provides to address these topics. Capitalizing on teachable moments, such as those noted throughout this chapter, allows adults to encourage recognition, acknowledgment, and the processing through life's little losses while we are, in fact, helping empower children to build their coping skills. In these ways, adults can assist children to create their own tool chest of strategies for handling the larger losses that they will encounter in the future.

THE HIDDEN POWER OF RESISTANCE

To capitalize on teachable moments and be successful in teaching children about loss, adults must first struggle to overcome their own resistance to this topic. Resistance comes in many forms. Three types of resistance to teaching children about loss and death arise from personal, professional or administrative, and cultural or societal sources.

Personal resistance typically sounds like, "yes, it is important but . . . I wouldn't know what to say. I wouldn't know where to start. I'm afraid I won't be able to find the right words, or I won't be able to express myself clearly. What if I started talking about death and began to cry? I'm too overloaded already, too overwhelmed just trying to keep my home or class in order. There are just too many other demands and expectations on my time. It will be soon enough to teach children about death when we are faced with that reality. How can you expect me to teach about grief and loss when I don't understand it myself?"

Beyond personal resistance, especially in schools, *professional, or administrative, resistance* also exists. That sounds more like, "yes, I know it is really important but . . . what would the parents think about our teaching their children about such a sensitive subject? I know if I talk about death it will be my head on the block. My superiors (administration/school board/voters) will never support discussion of that topic. Why complicate a child's life by making children think about such things? Isn't life difficult enough already? Anyhow, I couldn't talk about grief and loss without talking about God, and that is moving into forbidden territory."

In our society, a pervasive *cultural and societal resistance* to teaching children about death and loss also exists. This sort of resistance can be categorized as another "yes but . . ." response. "Yes, I know it is important, but . . . why ruin a child's youth by making him or her learn about that painful reality? Children are resilient, and they don't understand grief anyway, so why talk about it? Why don't schools just stick to reading, writing, and arithmetic? Talking about suicide will give kids ideas. When something bad happens, that will be soon enough to talk about it. These topics should be left to the parents or to priests, ministers, and rabbis."

Growing beyond resistance requires confronting our own fears first. This growth involves finding, exploring, and giving grief a name in our own world before we try to name it for our children. That might include examining our own feelings about death, educating ourselves about the processes of grief, and expanding our own definitions of loss. Caring adults and parents recognize the need to prepare children to cope with sexuality, drugs, and death. The question is how can this preparation be done best. Programs developed nationally are already established to teach about drugs and sex, but what about loss and death? Teaching about loss and death does not have to be feared or as complicated as it seems, if one will remember just three fundamental rules: educate, communicate, and validate (Metzgar, 1991).

EDUCATE, COMMUNICATE, AND VALIDATE

Education

In helping children increase their sense of competency and mastery over their life experiences, adults need first to *educate children about what is normal.* Loss is a normal part of life. *Lifetimes: A Beautiful Way to Explain Death to Children* (Mellonie & Ingpen, 1983), an excellent book for children about death, makes this point the following way: "There is a beginning and an ending for everything that is alive. In between is living. . . . So, no matter how long they are, or how short, lifetimes are really all the same. They have beginnings, and endings, and there is living in between" (pp. 2 & 36). Insights, such as this one, can offer frameworks within which adults can help to guide children in learning about loss and death. Books designed for child readers (see Corr, 1993a, 1995; Rudman, Gagne, & Bernstein, 1993) can be a good way to help normalize the experience of loss and its many predictable responses, thereby making the concept much less frightening. Adults must learn to teach children about loss and grief just as matter of factly and routinely as we teach them about the pain and potential danger in touching a hot stove (Grollman, 1990).

When educating about loss it is best to share honest, simple explanations that are based in reality and that dispel fantasy. It is important to remember that young children, in particular, live in a concrete reality that may lead them to fail to understand or to misinterpret what is said. If, for example, an adult were to say to a child "we lost Grandma today," the child might legitimately wonder why that adult and others are not out looking for her. Alternatively, if Grandma's death is explained by saying that she has "gone to sleep," children might logically suggest that we should wake her.

Communication

Effective communication means keeping the lines of communication open at all times. This type of communication requires both talking and listening. That includes not only listening to what is said but also to what is not being said, or what is being communicated through the child's behaviors. Many times out of fear or resistance adults seem to talk too much, filling in all of the awkward silences and overwhelming children with too much information. Alternatively, they choose to say nothing. When children believe that it is okay to express their feelings about loss and grief, whenever they are thinking about them, both out loud and through their play, they will do so. But if they receive from the adults in their world a message that this topic is not to be discussed, they will find others to dialogue with—most commonly their friends.

One excellent illustration of that point can be found in a 1989 "Safe Havens" cartoon by Bill Holbrook. This particular cartoon acts as a powerful reminder that just because adults are not talking to children about death does not mean children are not thinking about it. In the cartoon, two children are talking about Halloween. One says that "Halloween is an odd holiday. It's the only time adults openly acknowledge death." The other child agrees, observing that "The rest of the year it never crosses their minds. They don't mention it at all!" The children conclude their exchange in the following way, "Such a happy, carefree existence!" "I can't wait 'til I'm that age." For the astute reader, this cartoon acts as a reminder that children do think about death. It could also easily be used as a springboard or entry point for a discussion with children that might otherwise be avoided.

Validation

Validation is the act of acknowledging an experience as it is, without judgment. In helping children understand loss, adults must help them explore how it feels for them, even when those feelings are confusing. After all, how else is a child to be expected to understand his or her experience of rage at a loved one who just died, especially when this intense anger is intermixed with many other feelings, such as sadness and hurt. All of these mixed and confusing feelings are real. They need to be identified, acknowledged, given appropriate names, brought to understanding, and validated in a child's life.

Many adults find validation difficult because of their understandable desire to want to find a way to take the pain away. This effort is a misdirected one to "fix" or otherwise find some way to eliminate strong feelings—especially those that are thought of as "negative" feelings—in a child's life. As a result, it is not uncommon in our society for a child's grief to be diminished, dismissed, or somehow judged to be inappropriate. But it is not inappropriate for a child to react strongly to the loss of a significant person or treasured object in his or her life. What would be inappropriate, for the child, would be to ignore or fail to react in any way to such a loss.

In the aftermath of an important loss in their lives, when adults tell children "Don't think such bad thoughts," or "Put a smile on your face," they are misunderstanding important realities and needs in a child's life. They are teaching children incorrect lessons about the appropriateness and healthiness of their reactions to loss. Clumsy attempts to "fix" the pain of grief are harmful to children. What children and other grievers need is support and assistance in identifying and validating their grief, a caring supportive context in which grief can be shared, and respect for their "grief work" and the coping that is involved in healthy mourning. Reactions to and coping with loss are not experiences in the lives of children that adults should try to fix or circumvent by denying their existence, rejecting their appropriateness, or looking for the "right" words to make everything better.

Opportunities for discussing loss are all around us. They can be found in children's dialogue with adults and each other, in their play, books, drawings, and writings, and in daily events in a school classroom or in media reports about the larger world around us.

LOSS IN EVERYDAY LANGUAGE

Several strategies are designed to increase children's sense of safety and mastery of their life experiences. The main focus of this discussion is to suggest ideas to help adults support children by addressing and providing outlets for the children's needs, while not adding an extra burden to the existing responsibilities of parents, teachers, or other adult helpers. The assistance children need in coping with loss and death can be provided most effectively by establishing an open, communicative relationship before a crisis occurs. Talking about trauma, whether it is real or imagined, may seem difficult. However, such discussions are actually not as difficult as they may appear at first glance. Education and support can be provided to children by using additional avenues of communication in conjunction with talking. The key is to open the door before a need arises, so that when trauma occurs both adults and children will know ways to work together.

We suggest four primary building blocks that adults can use to provide a foundation for effective communication with children about loss and death.

- Questions and answers
- Comfort and support
- Symbolic play
- Direct sharing

Each of these building blocks promotes productive interactions with children. As children progress in their own developmental processes, these strategies allow for increasing complexity and sophistication in communication. The following discussion examines each of these building blocks individually, and illustrates both their implementation and their interaction in a series of examples spanning age ranges from kindergarten to seventh grade.

Questions and Answers

Listening for the questions and answering them directly is the first basic building block that can be used in helping children construct a foundation for understanding loss, death, and grief. Children's questions will frequently present themselves in ways that seem "out of context," that is, when most adults are least prepared to respond. A good example of how that can happen is the question mentioned earlier in this chapter when an 11-year-old asked his teacher how she wanted to die. That question was asked during the last few minutes of a math class, after all the assignments were done and the class was just waiting for the bell to ring. Clearly, both the question and the child's statement about how he wanted to die showed that this thought was not an isolated one for him. He was sincerely reaching out for someone to discuss with him his fears about life and death.

Unfortunately, as is all too often the case, his teacher did not feel prepared to respond to that kind of question. By her own admission, she was relieved when seconds later the bell rang. That put an end to the discussion and "saved" her from having to answer the child's question. The teacher also admitted that her own fear and anxiety stopped her from doing anything to pursue the conversation later. Clearly, an opportunity was missed for an adult to work with a child in a helpful way.

The questions that children ask change both in purpose and content as the children grow through the normal developmental stages. Young children often ask questions based on their need for reassurance. "Who is going to take care of me?" "Are you going to die?" Or as Big Bird said in *I'll Miss You, Mister Hooper,* "Who is going to make me my birdseed milkshakes?" (Stiles, 1984). Children who pose such questions are most concerned that the response that is offered to them is reassuring and that, whatever it may be, it is reliable and consistent. They are much less concerned with the specific content of the reply. They are not so much seeking "answers" as they are looking for reinforcement of their sense of safety and security.

Questions evolve and change as children mature. By the time a child is starting preschool or kindergarten, it is not uncommon to hear questions that are asking for a little more specific detail. "Where is dead?" "I know they are dead, but when will they come back?" "How do they decide if you get a mommy kind or a daddy kind of divorce?" Children who pose questions of this type are engaging with life and its details, and are trying to formulate queries that will help satisfy their curiosity, uncertainties, perplexity, or insecurities.

One day while visiting a kindergarten class, one of the authors asked a group of 6-year-olds if they would tell her about their worries. After one child clarified the question by saying, "you mean what makes me feel not good inside?" the other children began volunteering their answers. Here is a sampling of their responses.

- "I worry that one day I will be here for lunch but nothing will be in my lunch box."
- "Being left."
- "Those bad people on the other side of the world will hurt all of us."
- "The world will be on fire and a big ucky dragon will come and kill me and pull my dad's head off and eat up my mom."
- "Nothing."
- "Running out of presents."

Then, with a shrug of his shoulders, the last little boy quietly said, "Dying in a car."

Look at all that was learned about what these children's concerns were by asking them that simple question. Through answering this question, these children created an important teachable moment. It was a moment that provided an opportunity to talk with these children about grief and loss, as they were experiencing it or as they feared they might experience it.

As children's cognitive abilities continue to increase, so does their need for more detailed explanation and specific content. By the time children are 7 to 10 years of age, it would not be uncommon to hear any of the following questions:

- "Just how do you know that heaven is up, and hell is down?"
- "Did God make her die?"
- "Was it my fault?"
- "I know they are dead, but just how did they die?"

Or as a student asked after the death of her friend in a house fire, "Do you think he is still burned and hurting in heaven?"

Extensive experience in talking with children about loss and grief has led to the development of a way to assess children's perceptions of loss quickly, before speaking to them on the topics of loss. This technique combines a question with a drawing and writing exercise. It involves asking children to sketch quickly what they think we are going to talk about and what words they think we will use. The words never cease to surprise. Words like "ouch," "dead," "non–life force," "spirit," or "Jesus lifts out spirits," "sadness," and "pain" are commonplace. Almost always, without provocation, the words are connected somehow to death, as if loss was limited to death. This exercise is then used as a springboard to help the children expand their definition and awareness of loss including giving grief a name and discussing predictable grief responses.

As puberty begins, a further shifting of typical questions occur. Now, not only is the content of the questions changing by requiring even more specific information, but it is also important to note who is being asked the questions. At this age, children often search for answers outside their parents' beliefs. After all, it is difficult to be seeking your independence, yet still have to turn to your parents for answers and guidance. That does not mean that significant questions are never put to parents or that parents cannot serve as important sources of guidance for preadolescent children. But questions from this age group are often addressed to peers, teachers, and other adult friends or authority figures.

Many adults find asking questions is easier than being prepared to answer them. The discomfort of answering questions about grief and loss is commonly based in personal insecurity and the resistances that were discussed earlier. Here are some tips to remember to help field those tough questions. First, and foremost, listen to the question. Listen for both the spoken and unspoken content. Be sure you are answering the question that is being asked rather than one for which you conveniently already have a prepackaged answer. If you are not sure what the question is, do not be afraid to acknowledge your lack of understanding or confusion. To do so is to communicate that you respect the child and his or her question, and to indicate that you are seeking to grasp it correctly. For example, one of the authors was once asked if she knew that heaven was in a box. By acknowledging her confusion and encouraging the child to explore the question further, the child was able to articulate clearly that heaven must be in a box, because Daddy had said that Grandma had gone to heaven, and the child had seen Grandma in that box (the casket).

Consider the age and developmental level of the child or children asking the questions. Remember that the unspoken content with young children is frequently a request for reassurance. But also be sensitive to children's needs for specific content in the responses to their questions, especially as their cognitive abilities increase and the range of their life experiences broadens. Keep answers clear, simple, and honest. Avoid the use of clichés, euphemisms, or simple pat answers. Strive for answers that help dispel fantasy and encourage reality. As a general rule, a child's fantasy can and many times is much worse than the reality.

Do not be too verbose. A common mistake that adults make is using too many words, or employing unfamiliar words without explaining what they mean. For example, "dead" is a word that has no context for many young children. When using the word "dead," it needs to be defined. One might say that "dead" means the body does not work anymore. A person who is dead does not breathe. His or her heart does not beat. Dead persons do not laugh or play. They do not feel hurt or pain, and they do not eat.

If religious explanations are to be used, it is important to make distinctions between the body in the box and that part of the person that we call "spirit" or "soul." Thus, when we say that someone is in heaven, and heaven is represented as a place up in the sky, children need to know that when they take an airplane trip to Disneyland they are not going to be flying through heaven and seeing their loved one who died.

It is also critical when answering questions not to promise anything that you cannot make come true. For example, if a child were to say

"Mommy, are you going to die?", it would be wrong to say "no" because we all die. Saying "no" encourages fantasy or magical thinking on the part of a child. Instead, an adult might say, "We will all die someday, but you and Mommy are going to take good care of ourselves and do everything we can to live a very, very long time." This answer helps to provide a sense of being able to do something, when most of life seems so out of control.

Comfort and Support

Providing comfort and support to children includes meeting their needs for physical, emotional, and spiritual support. It is important to recognize that those needs will be manifested differently by various children and are influenced by age, development, and family norms or patterns. Comfort and support are provided to children by adults in subtle and usually quiet ways. It is important that the adults develop a relationship with children before adults can expect the children to feel comfortable enough reveal their true feelings about what is concerning them. That means building a trust level because children need to know that the adult respects and honors their thoughts and their feelings, and will not take this opportunity to lecture or sermonize. A comfortable, trusting relationship can also provide an adult with information about the child's use of language, behavior patterns, and family beliefs. Knowing the common ways children talk and behave before experiencing a trauma will make it easier to provide comfort and support to them in times of need.

Children gain a sense of control and well-being if the comfort and support they receive are consistent and repetitive. Especially in times of trauma when life's events seem so out of control, support is helpful and useful as a counterbalance that serves to regain a sense of control. When children feel scared and unsure of what is happening, either inside their bodies or in their daily relationships, they need someone to ask "Is it okay that I feel this way?" or "Is it normal to feel this way?" Consistent and repeated messages of support by adults allow children to have an adult to turn to as an "anchor" or "safe" place to help normalize their experiences of loss.

Providing comfort and support means being available when children want to talk about concerns and feelings that have arisen for them. It also means being able to recognize children's needs even before the children are able to verbalize what is happening in their world. At times, children may not realize how some of life's event are affecting them. They may just appear worried, have many physical complaints, or seem generally miserable. Frequently, they will feel they are the *only* child who has ever felt this way. In these circumstances, adults can help to normalize what is occurring and assist children to put more clearly into their own words how it feels to them.

Comfort and support can be as simple as giving a supportive hug. Or they can take the form of gently putting your hand on the child's shoulder or knee while sitting alongside and quietly listening to the details of an event. Or it might mean offering Kleenex for tears of pain or sadness. It is always necessary to respect children's boundaries of distance and time, so that the comfort and support that are offered is truly experienced as nurturing and does not add to their discomfort or trauma.

Remember, too, that children will notice how you, as the adult, are listening to them. Do you encouraging dialogue, recognizing their struggle as they try to put words to the events that are occurring in their lives? Do you help them explore their language of grief and loss, or do you search for euphemisms and clichés that, in fact, diminish or minimize their experience? Are you, as the adult, patient in allowing children to sort out what is happening to them, how they feel about it, and what they want to do next? New events, no matter how big or small, can feel traumatic to children, even just the event of entering a new developmental stage. Throughout their lives, adults experience many events, deciding along the way if they feel scary or safe. But for children life is a new adventure; they need time and support to figure it out for themselves.

Children, adolescents, and adults all need to feel safe physically and emotionally before being able to express truthfully how an experience is impacting them. One primary factor in feeling physically safe, beyond food clothing and shelter, is proxemics (Worchel & Cooper, 1983). "Proxemics" is a word coined by Hall (1966) to describe the study of the human use of space. It usually refers to one's personal space or the "bubble of space" humans attempt to keep around them when interacting with others. Children have their own personal space "bubble." Its size varies depending on the child's age. Consistent spatial behavior for children does not begin to be apparent before children are approximately 4 or 5 years old (Worchel & Cooper, 1983).

Close physical support and comfort are especially important for young children. This comfort includes physical touch and reassurance with frequent repetition of the reassurance. It is common to see a young child who is feeling anxious—for whatever reason—search out and attempt to maintain physical contact with the adult who represents security in his or her life. Children's personal space increases in size after age 4 or 5 and continues to vary until they reach approximately age 12 or 13, when it seems to stabilize (Worchel & Cooper, 1983).

Between the ages of 5 and 10, children are more likely to allow an adult to be a "companion" with them through a traumatic experience. At this age, a touch or hug is still generally experienced as comfort and a means to soothe them when they are upset. Older children, however, in the age range of 10 to teens, may experience touching by an adult as an invasion of their personal space. Therefore, before an adult gives a hug or touches an older child, it is important to check out with the child if that would feel comforting or not—and truly listen to the child's reply. Children of this age need to feel a sense of control and choice about how interactions occur. One option for adults working with older children is to acknowledge that hugs are always available whenever the children might ask for them.

A final, important note about comfort and support—one that adults must always remember—is that normal development is interrupted when a child has been touched in a painful or abusive manor by an adult. In those circumstances, any touch by an adult may not feel safe. Because it is so difficult to know if those circumstances exist in the case of a particular child, it is always important for adults to ask permission to touch or check out with the child if it feels okay to be held or touched.

Symbolic Play

Play is one of children's primary "jobs." Symbolic play is when children reenact events, thoughts, or feelings through behavioral or verbal symbols in their play. These symbols may be direct or indirect. Symbolic play is one of the major ways children gain a sense of competence and mastery over their life experiences. Play is a way for children to work out their feelings by using words, sounds, and touch to explore events they do not understand. Through play, children can do and redo an experience repeatedly. This sort of activity often may feel to children like a safer way to express how they feel about an experience and about the adults who may have control over many other aspects of their lives. Play is also a relatively safe way for children to try out the adult world. After all, when they are ready to leave that world and its demands, all they have to do is return to childhood.

Through symbolic play, children can pretend they are Mom or Dad, teacher, firefighter, police officer, doctor, nurse, or any combination they may choose. Play is also a way to practice and master social interactions with their peers, experience relationships, express a full range of emotions, or test their own physical capabilities. Play can be a safe activity that allows children to test their eye-hand coordination in the handling of tools, equipment, or utensils. Allowing and encouraging children to practice relating to and experiencing the traumas in the world around them through symbolic play helps prepare them for when trauma, a major loss, or death actually enter their world. Play provides a safe haven, an environment to which children can turn to work out their feelings, test their words, and explore their behaviors.

Peek-a-boo is an example of symbolic play for young children. Some theorists have even hypothesized that peek-a-boo is a child's first attempt at symbolically understanding separation (Maurer, 1966). When a young child closes his or her eyes, you are gone; when he or she opens them again, you are back. As children grow, even simple symbolic games like peek-a-boo increase in complexity. Separation is played out repeatedly to gain a sense of competence and mastery.

Five- or 6-year-old children often use playhouse settings, costumes, dress-up clothes, role playing, or games to sort out their thoughts, feelings, and the world around them. They experience the social ramifications of personal interactions with peers, as well as themselves, in their pretend settings. It is not uncommon to witness children of this age actually acting out personal experiences in their play, which may include playing divorce, playing dead, playing funeral, or any number of other experiences (Rochlin, 1967). Children of this age are increasing their locomotion and language mastery at the same time. Often, they may initiate but not always complete projects or games. The playhouse setting can give children of this age power or control to decide the outcome of an event. This setting may be used to replace their "real world feeling" of being out of control. By using symbolic play, children can fulfill the developmental task of "taking charge" of some of the normal fears that are developmentally present at this time. Play also gives their vivid imaginations a safe and constructive outlet for expression. Exploring fantasy and make believe can also help children manage the "monsters" and loud spooky noises of childhood.

Stuffed animals and puppet play are important components of this type of activity. It is also helpful to have many realistic toys, such as miniature ambulances, police cars, fire trucks, people, animals, telephones, and furniture. These provide a child opportunities to work out a variety of results for events from the surrounding world.

Large body movement can also be used to bring to life whatever a child might imagine, ranging from wild animals, space creatures, and aircraft to a wish for things to be different. These physical expressions can be an outlet for a child, providing large muscle movements when words or drawings are inadequate vehicles for expression. One child danced around outside while blowing bubbles; with each bubble, a wish was made for more money to pay the bills and have some left over for fun things. Her mother thought that after the death of the father, she had been protecting this child from more trauma arising from their financial predicament. However, the child had sensed and overheard much about the family's financial struggles. Body movement gave this youngster an outlet for expressing her fears, frustration, and tension.

Children of all ages can use creative activities to achieve symbolic expression for the events and emotions in their lives. However, just as with questions and answers, as a child's cognitive ability increases his or her symbolic play can be expected to change, taking on a more detailed nature and greater complexity. Sand-tray play, art work, clay, paints, crayons, felt pens, paper folding, pudding finger painting, photography, writing stories, musical instruments, singing, and dancing are all devices that can provide appropriate outlets for children.

Holiday art is an ideal time to encourage creative expression, especially Halloween. At this time, children can face skeletons, ghosts, and spirits. Making fun of such figures can remove some of their scariness. Halloween is an ideal time to talk about the word "dead." Adults might seize that seasonal opportunity to ask questions like: "What does that word and other words related to death and loss mean to children?" "And what are ghosts, skeletons, and spirits, really?"

Other creative projects can involve children in making a badge or coat of arms that represents something about themselves. It could be a symbol of their own protection, how they comfort themselves, or a way of saying who they are and what is important to them. It could also include assigning a color to an emotion. Some examples appear in our everyday language as we describe emotions: "red with rage" or "green with envy." The point is to demonstrate that emotions are always present in our lives, not just when a crisis occurs.

Story writing is another way to prepare children to express themselves when a trauma occurs. All school-age children can write stories at their grade level, talking about events, whether real or make believe. This vehicle allows children to experience using words about emotions, observations, and people in their lives. Children 7 to 12 years old want to learn and feel successful in school. Such feelings of accomplishment may be severely challenged if a death in a child's life occurs. When children have already developed the skills to write stories, poems, or songs, they have vehicles available to them for addressing loss and grief when a trauma occurs.

Science projects provide wonderful ways to prepare children for understanding the cycle of life and death. Plants and animals that are observed from the beginning of their lives can show children, in a relatively short period of time, how small cells can grow to larger organisms and may eventually die. Children can study specific details more completely as they grow older, so this is a process that can be adapted to the age of the child and that can include all age ranges.

All children need and want to have their questions answered honestly and simply. When adults keep their answers short and truly to the point, children sense those adults are persons who hear them and people who they can trust. The respect that adults show children by answering their questions truthfully comes across to them. When they need answers to difficult questions, they will feel more secure to return to the person who was truthful with them on a previous occasion. A particular child may not be able to put words to a traumatic situation, but the person who was clear and open with them during easier times will be seen as a person of integrity. A child will know that such a person will be able to help in articulating his or her experiences and feelings, and the child will return to that person for support in times of need.

Direct Sharing

The fourth and final building block is direct sharing. Direct sharing is specific and concrete communication with children for the purpose of normalizing both the content and feelings of grief and loss. Astute observers can see that we are surrounded daily with opportunities for direct sharing in art, reading, television, movies, current events, and personal stories. For example, how many hundreds of thousands of children sat mesmerized by *The Lion King* or *My Girl*, both movies based on life and death dramas. In one of the early scenes of *The Lion King*, when Mufasa tells Simba that he will not live forever, Simba responds with an expected child's response, saying something like, "You cannot leave . . . who will take care me?" Mufasa replies with a touching story that his father had told him about how even when the lion kings died, if we looked to the stars we would always feel their presence among us. The rest of the movie is all based on death, examining both Simba's and the community's grief responses. This movie could be considered Walt Disney's gift to reluctant adults to open communication using direct sharing about life and death.

My Girl is yet another example. It is a movie based on the life of a funeral director and his daughter with multiple plot twists that all involve loss, grief, or death. The plot includes the sudden death of the daugh-

ter's close friend, the death of her mother at her birth, her aging grandmother, her broken heart when she discovers that the teacher she
"loves" was already spoken for, and even her own suicidal thoughts. The
point is that children's lives are touched by grief and loss, real or fic-
tion. Adults can capitalize on that to help them build a foundation of
understanding.

Books are another example of direct sharing, including those al-
ready mentioned and ones like *Geranium Morning* (Powell, 1990); *Everett
Anderson's Goodbye* (Clifton, 1983); and *Dinosaurs Divorce* (Brown &
Brown, 1986). Older children might enjoy: *A Begonia for Miss Applebaum*
(Zindel, 1989); *Bridge to Terabithia* (Paterson, 1977); or *Grief Child* (Dar-
mani, 1991). Several classic stories can also be used, along with many
other books designed for child readers (Corr, 1993a, 1995; Rudman,
Gagne, & Bernstein, 1993).

Another resource that is well known to children yet seldom considered for use in teaching about grief and loss is the *TV Guide*. One exercise that is fun to do is have children go through the *TV Guide* and see
how many shows they can find that have to do with loss and then discuss
what they have discovered. This can also be done with the newspaper or
even their favorite compact disks or tapes. All of these exercises are designed to help children understand how normal the experience of loss
is and to help them give grief a name.

Current events are another excellent source of learning. Even as this
chapter was being written, Seattle was mourning the death of four fire-
fighters, killed attempting to extinguish an arson fire. The city sat fixated, starring at their televisions, first waiting for the bodies to be
recovered, then participating in the rituals of their funerals and the celebration of their lives. Being able to watch from a safe distance allowed
many people to share in this painful experience and explore in their
own hearts what it might be like for them if that was their father,
brother, or friend. We might hope that many teachers and parents
across the city took this opportunity to discuss death and grief with their
children.

So many ways are available to initiate direct sharing that entire books
could be written on the subject. Earlier in this chapter, an example was
given of asking kindergartners what they worried about—that was direct sharing. Another conversation opener that we frequently use with
children and adults is to have them break into groups and together see
how many "dead" words or phrases they can come up with that we use
in our everyday language that have nothing to do with death itself, such
as "dead bolt," "dead end," "dead as a door nail," "to scream bloody

murder," "my . . . is killing me." Children or adults can also be asked to list the words we use to avoid death language, when we are actually talking about someone's death. For example, someone "expired," "bit the dust," "kicked the can," "is 6 feet under," "went to heaven," or "was taken home by God." We then discuss why it is so difficult to say "dead" when we mean dead and so easy when we are not talking about dead at all.

Art is yet another avenue. Have you ever had children lie down on a piece of art paper, trace the outline of their body, and then ask them to take crayons or markers and mark where they hide their feelings, good and bad? Or have you ever had children create a "feeling bag"? This exercise allows children to cut pictures out of magazines and paste the feelings that are easy to share on the outside of a paper lunch bag while they put the feelings that are difficult to share on the inside. By doing that exercise, an opportunity has been created to talk about how some feelings are difficult to share. The discussion might also suggest possible ways to make it easier to share those feelings. In addition, if this activity is done as a group exercise, each child has also been shown that other kids have feelings that are difficult to share, too.

Some art projects can represent both symbolic play and direct sharing. Clay sculpturing is a good example. Many children love to create things out of clay and then smash them. That activity can easily be used to help explain the difference between constructive anger and destructive anger. Anger is a normal emotion of grief, yet seldom do adults teach children constructive ways of discharging that energy. The lesson is that it may be constructive to smash your own clay sculpture because you are angry, but it is destructive to hit your playmate. Similarly, it may be constructive to go shoot hoops, but it is destructive to shoot a friend or enemy. Adults need to help children understand this important distinction before they simply react out of pain and trauma.

Exchanging personal stories is another means of direct sharing and another way to educate in advance about normal grief processes. This exchange can be done in simple ways, such as the "magic circle" technique in which children sit in a circle and talk about their experiences or feelings. As children's linguistic skills increase, this kind of direct sharing might include more sophisticated verbal sharing or sentence completion, story writing, journaling, or even poetry. Methods of teaching through direct sharing are restricted only by the limitations we, as adults, create for ourselves out of our own fears, resistance, and limited imaginations.

CONCLUSION

Teaching about grief and loss is not something that should be reserved for the aftermath of a traumatic event. Helping children build a foundation for understanding the concept of death and the processes of grief must begin before an actual trauma. Also, for adults to be really helpful to children, they must first explore their own beliefs as well as their resistance to the subject of death. That includes examining our own feelings about death, educating ourselves about the processes of grief, and expanding our own definitions of loss.

It is crucial for children and adults alike to be able to give grief a name. That can only be done by normalizing the experience. By capitalizing on teachable moments, adults are able to encourage recognition, acknowledgment, and the processing of life's little losses while helping to empower children to build their own coping skills. The key is to open the door before a need arises, so that when a traumatic event does occur, both adults and children will be prepared and know ways to work together in the healing process. That goal is best accomplished by working with the building blocks and strategies described in this chapter.

14

Postvention with Elementary School Children

Antoon A. Leenaars and Susanne Wenckstern

This chapter begins with a brief discussion of the concept of "postvention" and its role in assisting bereaved children, together with experiences of traumatic losses and posttraumatic stress as they apply to school-age children. Subsequently, the chapter describes eight principles for postvention and seven elements that are involved in the implementation of postvention in elementary school settings. Finally, we provide two examples of postvention in a community school setting.

POSTVENTION

Postvention refers to "things done" to address and alleviate actual or potential reactions to trauma, whether homicide, suicide, any other type of unusual death, or catastrophic event that inflict significant pain in survivors. The term *postvention* was first introduced by Shneidman (1973a) in relationship to suicide and was defined as

> Those things done after the dire event has occurred that serve to mollify the aftereffects of the event in a person who has attempted suicide, or to deal with the adverse effects on the survivor-victims of a person who has committed suicide. (p. 385)

Although Shneidman here refers to suicide, the process of postvention can be applied to any trauma. Postvention includes services to all survivors of a dire event who are in need, primarily those immediately affected, but not just those people (Shneidman, 1973b, 1975).

A widely accepted approach to mental health and public health problems was proposed by Caplan (1964), who described a prevention model at three clinical levels: "primary prevention," "secondary prevention," and "tertiary prevention." The more common terms today are *prevention, intervention,* and *postvention,* respectively. That is, "postvention" is the third of three possible ways of interceding in a traumatic situation: *prevention,* which occurs before the fact to forestall or ameliorate that which might happen (e.g., through education); *intervention,* which involves doing something to help during the crisis event (e.g., psychotherapy); and *postvention,* which occurs after the event. In itself, postvention is a synthesis of strategies drawn from and combining education, consultation, crisis intervention, and trauma response in general.

When a tragic event occurs in a school context, it might take the form of a natural disaster (e.g., an earthquake), a catastrophic event (e.g., the crash of an airplane in the community), or the unusual death of a student, teacher, or staff member. In these and other situations in which children are traumatized, schools need to play a key role in postvention. The same principle applies to suicide, a relatively low-frequency, unusual—but not unimportant—death during childhood. Essentially, postvention programs in the schools represent a systematic, model-guided response to address traumatic events and their aftershocks (Leenaars & Wenckstern, 1991). It is a crisis-oriented prevention in the form of a systematic process of addressing the event after it has occurred.

TRAUMATIC LOSSES AND POSTTRAUMATIC STRESS

Many deaths and other significant losses are experienced as traumatic by children and other survivors. This reaction is especially true for deaths and losses that occur suddenly or unusually. At times, the aftershocks of such events become painful—sometimes unbearably so. Experience with child survivors of such deaths in schools and other contexts suggests that this type of bereavement may be associated with a prolonged stress response in some individuals (Gleser, Green, & Wignet, 1981; Horowitz, 1979; Leenaars, 1985; Newman, 1976; Wilson, Smith, & Johnson, 1985). The aftershock results in a significant distress (perturbation). Indeed, the greater the degree of trauma (mild, moderate, or severe on a quantification scale) or its symbolic implications (such as might be experienced in relation to a previous death), the severer the traumatic stress syndrome, similar to a level warranting the label "disaster" or disturbance (pain).

The APA (1980) recognizes PTSD as a series of interrelated manifestations that may follow "a psychologically traumatic event that is generally outside the range of usual human experience" (p. 238). Thus, PTSD has been defined "as a set of conscious and unconscious behaviors and emotions associated with dealing with the memories of the stressors of the catastrophe and immediately afterwards" (Figley, 1985, p. xix).

Manifestations of PTSD often include natural behaviors and emotions such as the following:

- Reexperiencing the trauma (e.g., recurrent recollection or dreams, associations that the event is recurring)
- Numbing of responsiveness leading to a reduced involvement with the external world (e.g., diminished interest, detachment, or constricted affect)
- Experiencing at least two of the following: hyperalertness, sleep disturbance, survivor guilt, problems in concentration or memory, avoidance of events that evoke recall of the trauma, or intensification of symptoms by events that symbolize the traumatic experience

Consider, for example, implications for elementary school children of being present when one student kills himself, herself, or someone else in the classroom, or when a teacher or staff member kills himself or herself in the school corridor. How might children be expected to respond to unusual events like these?

The recognition of psychical trauma resulting from unusual events dates back to Freud's early observations (1974). Subsequently, Janoff-Bulman (1985, p. 17) noted that "much of the psychological trauma produced by victimizing events derives from the shattering of very basic assumptions that victims have held about the operation of the world." We all have constructs or a theory of the world. For example, children, as well as adults, may have assumed that "a 10-year-old does not kill himself"—at least, such an assumption may have been maintained until it is shattered in front of us.

Eth and Pynoos (1985a, 1985b) have presented convincing arguments for applying the concept of PTSD to children. They note that children of trauma have exhibited "deleterious effects on cognition (including memory, school performance, and learning), affect, interpersonal relations, impulse control, and behavior, vegetative function, and the formulations of symptoms" (1985a, p. 41). Posttrauma reactions have been observed in abducted children and in children surviving a disaster, such as the atomic bombing of Hiroshima or other disasters (Leenaars, 1985; Lifton, 1969; Lifton & Olson, 1976; Newman, 1976; Terr, 1979; Wilson, Smith, & Johnson, 1985). Reactions are often negative in these children. Anna Freud (1966), for example, noted that children often rely on various forms of denial, evident in fantasy, action, and affect, all to ease or numb the pain that they are experiencing. Such children simply want to deny the event—and, all too often, so do their caregivers.

A poignant example of PTSD within our own experience involved a school-age child who found his teenage brother hanging: He simply did not believe it; in his mind it did not happen. Months later, he still spoke as if his brother was alive. At a conscious level, he reported no memory of the death. Similarly, another child sat for hours in front of her dead parent without responding. Denial may not be the only reaction to experiences of this sort, however. Aggressiveness, obsessive fantasies (recurrence), anxious arousal, behavioral problems, poor peer relations, school failure, and even imitation have been documented in children after a suicide. For example, one 8-year-old was found scratching himself with a knife in his classroom as a reaction to his teenage brother's serious attempt at suicide by cutting 6 months earlier. As Bowlby (1977) has noted, these reactions may be related to children who experience anxious attachment. Accordingly, the APA (1987) has clarified its definition of PTSD to include children.

Clinical experience has shown that recovery from a traumatic event is difficult. Children who are experiencing aftershocks are often caught in a no-win cycle of events: "To talk about the powerful and overwhelming trauma means risking further stigmatization; the failure to discuss the traumatic episode increases the need for defensive avoidance and thus increases the probability of depression alternating with cycles of intensive imagery and other symptoms of PTSD" (Wilson, Smith, & Johnson, 1985, p. 169). Regrettably, it is all too tempting to adult caregivers—who may themselves be shocked by the traumatic event—to absolve themselves from responsibility to help by urging denial. Such adults are inclined to say things like: "Don't talk about it"; "Discussing this will only make things worse"; "Let's put it behind us and forget the whole thing." In these ways, they themselves exhibit PTSD.

We firmly believe that this approach, as Freud (1974) showed, only exacerbates the trauma. Adults need to foster constructive coping strategies in survivors of traumatic events. Even children who do not appear to be exhibiting reactions to the loss event (e.g., few recognizable overt verbalizations are made), may be reacting in counterproductive ways. Worse yet, they may find themselves encouraged in that reaction by an adult who also wants to deny the loss.

PRINCIPLES FOR POSTVENTION

Shneidman (1975) has provided us with a structure for postvention. He outlined basic principles common to all postvention. Those principles are modified here for application within elementary school settings.

1. *In working with child survivor-victims, it is best to begin as soon as possible after the tragic event, within the first 24 hours if at all feasible.*

Consultation and networking between all concerned personnel at a school (e.g., administrators, teachers, and mental health professionals acting under the direction of a postvention coordinator) are critical at this time. Response must be as prompt as possible; waiting even 24 hours can exacerbate the situation. It is important to compile and share accurate, reliable information about the event as it becomes known. This is desirable to combat hysteria, which often mounts when misinformation, frequently of a sensational nature, proliferates. In these early moments of postvention, it is imperative to strive to establish clear lines of structure and communication as quickly and as effectively as possible.

In the first encounter with survivors, the initial goal is to develop an immediate, active, nonjudgmental rapport. Rapport involves good "object relations." It is characterized by a "strong interest in, affection for another person, a willingness to give up something for another person, a willingness to assume responsibility for another person" (Tarachow, 1963, p. 103). It is the ability to love. It is, in fact, a key to affective response. The postventionist must be willing to express attachment and to work quickly to establish a trusting relationship with children in crisis (Hoff, 1984).

Within the relationship, the postventionist works to alleviate post-traumatic responses. In practice, this amounts to decreasing or mollifying the level of perturbation or psychological disturbance in the survivor (Leenaars, Maltsberger, & Neimeyer, 1994; Shneidman, 1975). "Perturbation" refers to the person's subjective distress (disturbed, agitated, sane/insane) and can be rated as high to moderate to low. Reducing the perturbation is accomplished, for example, through efforts to improve the survivors' immediate external and internal situations. Those situations are centered on the survivors' feelings and other aspects of the posttraumatic state. The postventionist seeks to give survivors realistic transfusions of hope until the intensity of their pain subsides enough to reduce it to a tolerable, bearable level.

2. *Resistance may be met from child survivors; some—but not all—are either willing or eager to have the opportunity to talk to professionally oriented persons.*

The etymological roots of the word "survive" come from two Latin words, *super,* which means "over," and *vivere,* which means "to live" (Hewett, 1980). To review or live through traumatic events a second time in the process of postvention may be painful. Therefore, resistance is understandable and, in fact, is to be expected. Yet surviving is essential for children to go on living, working, and playing after the shocking event.

Individuals often wish to deny the reality of the traumatic event or of its implications. Experience has shown that this resistance may come not only from child survivors but also from a source that is essential in the cooperative effort of postvention: administration and colleagues. For example, people who have experienced a traumatic event may feel angry, injured, or rejected in any or all of the following circumstances: when they have had to wait for help for an excessive period (24 hours; even 1 hour!); when they are offered inadequate rapport, interest, and so on; when they are dealt with too directly; when they are disappointed by a postventionist who forgets important details or who confronts them about an issue too early; when they are offered only an inadequate intervention (e.g., a 1-hour group meeting) or are left feeling "cut off" by premature termination of assistance; when they are referred to others without adequate explanation of the process or the reasons for the referral; when they are approached with procedures that are not age appropriate; or when they are contacted by unfamiliar persons other than those involved in the postvention response.

Similarly, the postventionist must be aware of possible denial in himself or herself. It may be unhelpful or even dangerous, for example, when postventionists: underestimate the seriousness of the trauma; are overwhelmed with their own feelings of guilt, incompetence, anxiety, fear, and anger; are unwilling to discuss posttrauma aftershocks or view cries for help solely as manipulative efforts; allow themselves to be lulled into a false sense of security by statements from survivors that everything is fine (e.g., when a principal denies the impact of the event and refuses to allow a postvention response in the school setting); are unable to identify or access appropriate resources required by a particular event (e.g., a homicide/suicide in the school); or fail to persuade survivors to obtain additional assistance that they need.

3. *Negative emotions about the deceased person or about any aspect of the traumatic event—irritation, anger, envy, shame, guilt, etc.—need to be explored, but not necessarily at the very beginning. Timing is critical.*

Negative emotions are to be expected after an unusual, traumatic event. Despite commonalities in young people's responses to a trauma, studies of children who saw a parent killed revealed differences related to developmental age (Eth & Pynoos, 1985a; Johnson, 1989). A child of five reacts differently than the 12-year-old. Children at these ages express negative emotion in different modes. Their understanding of death and, by implication, of suicide, for example, varies (Leenaars, 1995; Orbach, 1988; Pfeffer, 1986). In adolescence, the posttraumatic reactions increasingly resemble adult reactions (e.g., acting out, truancy, precocious sexual behavior, substance abuse, and delinquency). These reactions are ways of adjusting, often the best they can do in the face of the aftershocks (Leenaars & Wenckstern, 1996).

Moreover, individual children will respond differently to the same event, and the greatest risk of complications may occur in children who identify most closely with the dead person (Nagera, 1970). Some children, in fact, may become at risk for suicide (Leenaars, 1996). Thus, it is important "to specify how the nature and complexity of the stressor event impacts on the unique personality of the survivor" (Wilson, Smith, & Johnson, 1985, pp. 167-168). Child survivors are not all alike; they bring with them their own special ways of adjusting to trauma. It is unreasonable to expect that the distress produced by a traumatic death or loss will produce the same effect in every child. Those who are closest to the experience or to the person who died are most likely to be at risk. In addition, another important variable might be the child survivor's own previous experiences with loss, death, or depression.

In general, however, the severer and more complex the stressful life event, the greater the likelihood that an individual child might have difficulty in coping effectively. In other words, anyone might be at risk.

The critical question in all postvention is whether or not the environment is supportive (Figley, 1983). Not surprisingly, "more supportive environments tend to be associated with better adjustment to stress" (Green, Wilson, & Lindy, 1985, p. 61). It is unfortunate that even in our elementary schools some adults foster denial and unwittingly promote negative adjustment by failing to explore children's reactions to traumatic events or by addressing them at the wrong time or in the wrong way(s). Constructive responses need to begin with the school administration, followed by school staff and other involved adults.

4. *Postventionists should play the important role of reality tester. They are not so much the echo of conscience as the quiet voice of reason.*

Postvention is needed. Our theory of the world should include a sense of responsibility to help people in the face of trauma. People who experience traumatic aftershocks, such as suicide, are in pain and thus need assistance. The person, despite denial, is ambivalent, even the principal who refuses a program at his or her school. Such a principal, to continue this example, may feel hopeless, yet he or she is ambivalent about approach or avoidance. Such a person can be destructive. That is equally true of the suicidal person. A change, a structural plan, a reduction in the level of perturbation is often sufficient to reduce the pain and the level of the traumatic response. It should be the postventionist's duty to help a person recognize this fact and guide that person.

Regrettably, all too often we hear the voice of censure. For example, the claim that postvention ought to be initiated only if a contract among all involved exists. Others assert that a principal can refuse response because it is his or her civil right. We believe, despite the potential for meddling, that one should prevent PTSD or death. If a child survivor becomes at risk for suicide, we should side with life.

5. *Postventionists should be constantly alert for possible decline in physical health and in overall mental well-being, as well as other manifestations of posttraumatic stress disorder (including risk of suicide).*

Risks to physical and mental well-being should not be surprising in the wake of a traumatic death or other unusual event. The possibility of exaggerated responses to trauma, including the potential for life-threatening behavior and suicide, should not be too quickly ruled out, even in children. Postvention programs were first initiated in the early 1980s (Leenaars, 1985) as a response to suicidal behavior and its contagious quality among some youth in the aftermath of a suicide. Suicidal survivors have the strong desire to flee from the pain of the catastrophic event. The pain seems bottomless—an eternal suffering.

Children in these circumstances are likely to feel boxed in, rejected, deprived, forlorn, and distressed. In particular, feelings of hopelessness and helplessness may lead to a sense of painful impotence. The child desperately wants a way out and may find that in aberrant or life-threatening behavior (Orbach, 1988; Pfeffer, 1986). Regression and constriction in thinking may lead the child to fail to recognize constructive alternatives. Suicide may appear to be *the* solution to a problem. The child is insufficiently developed to cope with the pain. He or she is ambivalent. The child's ego—the part of the mind that reacts to reality and has a sense of individuality—is not sufficiently developed. These children lack constructive tendencies. A weakened ego correlates positively with suicide risk.

Suicide is often related to unsatisfied or frustrated needs, often attachment. These needs are frustrated in the wake of the trauma. The child experiences loss and anger. In response to the trauma, such as the suicide of another student, the child's loss results in broken bonds that the child cannot endure. The child wants to deny this and escape. Thus, the child plunges into the abyss.

The role of the postventionist is to anticipate suicide or other undesirable behaviors in the aftermath of a traumatic event, to identify the presence of these tendencies when they actually do occur, to work to mitigate their likelihood or gravity, and to offer constructive alternatives as appropriate. In circumstances when life seems to have rejected a child and caused extreme hurt, the postventionist offers acceptance, care, and love.

6. *Unwarranted optimism or banal platitudes should be avoided in postvention.*

We often hear adults say the following: "Don't talk about the trauma, it will go away"; "Don't worry, we will save you"; "All people respond in the same way, we will tell you how they will react"; "Postvention is the same as prevention"; or "Postvention is only grief counseling." All of these and other similar statements are banal platitudes. Denial will not make the trauma go away. One hour of group counseling with 30 students is not postvention. Unrealistic optimism makes the aftershocks worse. Postvention is complex work requiring sensitivity, imagination, and dedication (Leenaars, 1985; Leenaars & Wenckstern, 1991; Wenckstern & Leenaars, 1993).

7. *Postvention is multifaceted and takes a while, from several months to the end of life.*

The multifaceted character of postvention arises from the potential complexity of traumatic events, on the one hand, as well as the multidimensional character and individuality of human responses to those events, on the other hand. This multifaceted characteristic of postvention is often not understood, even by professionals and researchers. This reality can be illustrated by the recent research of Hazell and

Lewin (1993). These authors sought to evaluate postvention by examining suicide cases in two schools, albeit with limitations. Hazell and Lewin equated postvention with group counseling. Yet, postvention does not simply equal group counseling. Group counseling can be one strategy of postvention, although we strongly believe that individual work is a more appropriate primary mode of treatment. Hazell and Lewin evaluated only increase in risk; however, contagion is only one possible aftershock. They developed a risk index for suicide, which itself is questionable according to a recent review by the National Institute of Mental Health (Garrison, Lewinsohn, Marsteller, Langhinrichsen, & Lann, 1991; Lewinsohn, Garrison, Langhinrichsen, & Marsteller, 1989), to measure the aftershocks. Group counseling in the situations examined by Hazell and Lewin also presents problems because it consisted of seeing 20 to 30 children in a group for 90 minutes. Hazell and Lewin (1993) concluded that postvention does not work and schools should not implement such programs. Regrettably, some people have now argued that postvention is useless.

Postvention must be based on sound research. The same issue has arisen in the field of education in the schools about suicide and death. From a methodologically unsound study, Shaffer, Garland, Vieland, Underwood, and Busner (1991) concluded that there should be *no* primary prevention in schools. However, developing research (Kalafat & Elias, 1994) has shown the value of prevention. We believe the same is true about postvention and we encourage sound research in the field to be able to respond better to trauma in elementary schools—especially since postvention work is multifaceted.

8. *A comprehensive program of health care on the part of a benign and enlightened community should include prevention, intervention, and postvention.*

As a response to its awareness of the complexity of postvention, the Centers for Disease Control (CDC; since renamed Centers for Disease Control and Prevention) in the United States has developed a set of comprehensive guidelines for postvention with special attention to suicide "contagion" or clustering (CDC, 1988). These guidelines incorporate aspects of prevention, intervention, and postvention as equally essential. Among these guidelines, the following points can be adapted to our present discussion.

A community and its schools should develop plans for responding to traumatic events before they occur. These plans should include the following:

- All concerned individuals should be involved in the response, along with leadership from a mental health coordinator, the postventionist.
- The response should be initiated promptly after a traumatic event.
- The response should begin with coordination.
- Constructive relationships should be developed with the media, and efforts should be made to avoid sensationalism in any form.
- Children and others who are at risk for suicide or other complicated responses to the traumatic event should be identified and referred for individual therapy.
- Potentially harmful aspects of the environment should be identified and changed.
- Long-term issues should be addressed.

These suggestions are inherent in any sound program of postvention.

It is apparent from our experience in postvention that no cookbook or common recipe exists for all postvention activities. One can speak of understanding but never with absolute precision. In traumatic situations, we can be no more accurate or scientific than are permitted by the subject matter itself, the individuals involved, and the available ways of responding. It is understandable that a yearning for universal postvention laws persists. But the search for a single postvention response to loss and death is based on a foolish and unrealistic wish. No one method of postvention exists.

The CDC recognizes that no universal rules apply for all postvention situations. Both the principles noted here and the suggestions provided by the CDC are guidelines. They are meant to provide schools and communities with "a conceptual framework for developing their own . . . [postvention] plans, adapted to the particular needs, resources, and cultural characteristics of their communities" (CDC, 1988, p. 2).

Providing postvention services to traumatized children and school communities is best managed by individuals who have no other demands on their time and energies than the trauma response. These situations are demanding on the postventionist's time, energy, and other resources. We can confirm the demands of such procedures from our own experiences. Nevertheless, the potential for being of significant help to the children and to the school communities who are receiving postvention services is great, both in the immediate circumstances and for the long term.

APPLYING POSTVENTION PRINCIPLES IN ELEMENTARY SCHOOL SETTINGS

Seven elements of our model are involved in the application of postvention principles in elementary school settings: consultation, crisis intervention, community linkage, assessment and counseling, education, liaison with the media, and follow-up. We will consider each of these, in turn, in this section and then illustrate their use in concrete examples in the following section.

Consultation

Discussion, coordination, and joint planning must be undertaken at every phase in postvention, beginning with school administration and then followed by school staff and other involved individuals, such as students and parents. These activities should be conducted under the direction of the coordinator (the postventionist), who should be a mental health expert charged with overall structuring and supervision of postvention activities. Community personnel may also need to be included in every aspect of the process, depending on the evaluation of the level of severity (mild/moderate/severe) of the traumatic event and the number of those whom it has impacted. Concurrent peer consultation and review among members of the postvention team are conducted to review plans that were implemented, and to design and coordinate further action. For example, a flexible contingency plan must be preplanned to allow for alternative actions, if needed. Territorial problems between school and community (and their own internal politics) need to be addressed because often these are the elements that raise the traumatic levels of the event.

Crisis Intervention

Emergency or crisis response is provided, using basic problem-solving strategies (Hoff, 1984; Leenaars, Maltsberger, & Neimeyer, 1994). We believe that students and staff of the local school(s) are likely to need support in response to a traumatic event. It is crucial not to underestimate the closeness of relationships or the intensity of reactions of individuals who might be experiencing posttraumatic reactions (Leenaars & Wenckstern, 1991).

Community Linkage

Postvention efforts should assist educational systems to develop a linkage system or network to aid in making referrals to appropriate community services. In addition to resources that are directly available within the school system, this includes exchanging information and coordinating services with appropriate community services as needed. Such a network should be predefined. Being familiar with and updating local community resources before a traumatic event occurs (e.g., knowing which agency or service to contact and preferably the name of the contact person) is highly recommended. In the case of culturally diverse students, having a directory on hand listing local cultural centers and names of translators, with preestablished communications, may be not only helpful but necessary.

Assessment and Counseling

Postvention efforts provide evaluation and therapy as needed or requested by the school administrator. Assessment may be complex in the aftermath of a traumatic event, but can be approximated. Psychotherapy may be equally complicated and often must be long term. Assessment and counseling may lead to referral of some children to other resources for additional attention (Leenaars, 1985; Leenaars, Maltsberger, & Neimeyer, 1994; Maris, Berman, Maltsberger, & Yufit, 1992).

Education

Postvention includes providing information about death, loss, and trauma through discussion, seminars, workshops, and small assemblies (35 to 50 people) at the school and within the community (Leenaars & Wenckstern, 1991). This information should include factual, unsensationalized details about the particular event; general knowledge about death, loss, and trauma; and practical guidance for self-help and help by others (e.g., clues to problematic reactions and their causes, misleading or unfounded myths, what to do, or where to go for help).

Liaison with the Media

Information about a traumatic event in the form of publicity, especially that which tends to sensationalize or glamorize the event, should be avoided. It is not and should not be the school's responsibility to provide information about the specific details of the trauma to the media. This responsibility falls within the jurisdiction of the police department, coroner's office, or other authorities. However, our experience has shown that (a) a media spokesperson for the school must be appointed at the outset of the crisis; and (b) this role should be filled by the postvention coordinator rather than by a school administrator (e.g., the principal). Not only does this ensure the accuracy and consistency of information being given out, but, most important, it ensures that this information is being provided by someone who understands the postvention procedures and the positive impact of the program. It is these procedures and their impact that should be emphasized to the media.

Follow-Up

Periodic follow-ups are undertaken as a part of the postvention process with children, parents, the school administrators, school staff, and mental health professionals. A formal final consultation is provided several months after the traumatic event to facilitate explicit closure to the program. However, every attempt is made to let all concerned know that the postventionists are available on request for further follow-up if the need arises. We have, for example, even been involved 5 years later to address a latent aftershock.

TWO EXAMPLES OF POSTVENTION IN AN ELEMENTARY SCHOOL SETTING

We will next illustrate the foregoing principles and strategies by providing two cases of postvention in elementary school settings: a case of completed suicide of a seventh-grade boy, age 14; and a case of attempted suicide of a sixth-grade girl, age 13. These youngsters are a bit older than the children discussed elsewhere in this book and both cases involve behaviors related to suicide. But the basic principles emerging from these examples apply to all postvention with children and to all situations of traumatic death and loss. In particular, both cases highlight the need to evaluate the degree of trauma of the survivors; here it is moderate/severe in the first case but low in the second. Equally, these examples show that our suggestions are primarily of heuristic value. There is no cookbook in postvention. One must evaluate the needs and strategies for each trauma, not rigidly, which itself would be a sign of PTSD in the postventionist.

Case 1

1. The postventionist was notified by the school superintendent of a seventh-grade pupil's suicide on the evening of the day that the pupil died. Telephone consultations were undertaken that evening with the administration, the school principal, the crisis response team, and the classroom teacher to plan a cooperative effort at the school the next day.

2. The following morning, the principal, the postventionist, and the response team met the entire school staff, including teachers, teacher's aides, secretaries, janitors, and so on, to discuss appropriate responses to possible questions and to children's reactions because many children and parents were aware of the incident before school started. All were urged to be open about the death and about suicide without in any way being sensational, in the hope of providing sound models for the children. Individual support and encouragement were provided to the pupil's classroom teacher, who was in shock and was feeling somewhat guilty about whether he had missed any clues before the event as to what might be about to happen. The postventionist and team members held individual discussions with other school staff, being careful to discuss with the school secretaries their responses on the telephone—an important detail that can easily be overlooked. Further direct consultations by crisis services staff were provided to school staff during the day following the death and in the next few months as requested or as a need was perceived.

3. The postventionist was assigned to address all media calls. A suicide in a child, for example, may be of interest to many in a community. In this case, only one call was received from a local newspaper reporter. The reporter was informed about the constructive aspects of the efforts at the school.

4. Involved personnel of the school district's crisis services staff undertook a group consultation the day after the death to review actions that had been taken and to coordinate further action. Further peer consultations were undertaken by staff as the postvention continued because it is our belief that such postvention should not be undertaken by one individual alone. Sharing the responsibility helps to prevent stress overload, to provide alternative perspectives and information, and to provide ongoing assistance—as well as multiple contacts and supports—for the individual(s) in crisis. Our experience has shown that such consultations and reviews should be supportive in character (e.g., "What did you do?"; "What other things might have been considered?"; "What can we do next?"; etc.) rather than "assaultive" or overly critical (e.g., "Did you do _____?"; "Why did/didn't you do _____?"; etc.). A supportive approach is helpful to the providers of the service and to the entire postvention program.

5. The postventionist contacted the deceased pupil's parents to inform them of the program and arranged a consultation at their request. Time was spent discussing their feelings, thoughts, and behavior as well as the reactions of their other children. Therapy was recommended for one daughter who appeared to be overly denying the death until the first "family outing," during which she cried uncontrollably and expressed verbal anger towards her parents. The recommendation for counseling was subsequently followed, and counseling assistance was provided by our own staff at the girl's school. The parents were also referred to a support group for survivors that is fortunately available in our community. We believe it is imperative that family members who experience a significant death or other loss should be provided with appropriate support, and we help these individuals obtain such support. At their request, additional contacts have occurred with family members after the pupil's death, and they are aware that further consultations are available.

6. In addition to the preceding, special attention was paid to the children at the dead pupil's school, and several postvention services were offered to them directly. For example, members of the response team visited identified classrooms at the school and talked with children both in groups and individually as judged appropriate. This approach follows our desire to take care not to underestimate either the closeness of relations within the school community or the intensity of traumatic reactions among children. One such pupil was a first-grade student who had developed a close relation to the deceased; he exhibited an overly hyper reaction. We were striving to ensure that pupils and staff at the school in question would receive the support that they needed in response to this traumatic event.

7. In addition, members of the team undertook consultations with the parents of several classmates when asked. As a result, some children were assessed individually and several referrals were made to the school's services and other community agencies. We believe that such supportive services are essential. For example, one classmate continued to have disturbing dreams about the death 6 months after the event.

8. Also, during the week after the death the postventionist organized and presented an educational workshop for the school staff to provide information about suicide and responses to death in elementary school children as well as about helpful services that are available in our school system and community.

9. In addition, staff organized and presented a workshop about "death, dying, and suicide" for the children and the teacher in the pupil's classroom, approximately 3 weeks after the death. All parents were informed about the workshop and its general purpose. Happily and perhaps a bit surprisingly, all parents consented to have their children included in the program. The purposes of the workshop included the following: to deal with the children's reactions to suicide, death, and loss generally; to address any specific feelings of guilt, previous unresolved grief, or other reaction patterns that might be present; and to give the children an opportunity to discuss this traumatic experi-

ence openly and frankly in a supportive atmosphere. An evening program for parents was also provided at the school.

10. Furthermore, periodic follow-up contacts were undertaken with the principal, school staff, and support staff. The postventionist conducted a final consultation 4 months after the death with the principal, classroom teacher, and crisis response staff to provide formal closure to the postvention program, although "the doors were left open" for further requests for assistance from and contacts with the school. We strongly believe that the potential for contact for an indefinite, extended period should be included in any postvention program. PTSD symptoms are sometimes not seen until 6 months (or later) after the event. We found this final consultation to be important as a review of the effectiveness of the postvention efforts, as a basis for planning responses to future traumatic events, and as a contribution to our own professional development.

Case 2

1. The postventionist was notified by school administration of a sixth-grade pupil's suicide attempt of the night before. The vice-principal reported that "everything is quiet" with students, but that the pupil's teacher was upset. In consultation with the principal, the postventionist and one other mental health professional met to process the event and outline a plan of action.

2. Next, that same day, the team met with teachers/staff (e.g., school secretary). Staff expressed shock and concern about the attempt, and especially over the parents' request that their child's suicide attempt "be kept quiet." In addition, on that very day, a school/community program on terminal illness was occurring. Many of the adults related their mixed emotions on the two events, as one teacher put it, "of one child fighting to live and another child fighting to die."

Issues, such as how much to reveal to pupils and their families, arose at the outset. People struggled with the need to meet their pupils' needs and those of the immediate family. It was explained to staff that although we understand and empathize with the immediate family's concerns and wish to respect their wishes, once such information is in any way made public (e.g., whispered among pupils on the playground), we need to be responsive to the needs of all survivors. Because information tends to surface quickly, usually within a matter of hours after a traumatic event, the school must be ready to respond despite request for denial (and other symptoms of PTSD) by caregivers.

3. The remainder of the first day was spent evaluating the level of the traumatic event and organizing a postvention response. Indeed, as would be predicted, "the news broke" later that day. No media calls were received, however.

4. *The school's greatest concern the next morning was for the close-knit circle of five friends who were clustered around the principal's office, in obvious distress. Evaluation and assistive responses were undertaken by the postvention team. This small group of pupils met as a group (because they identified themselves as a group) and individually. They were encouraged to talk about their feelings, fears, and so on, with a supportive, nonjudgmental rapport. Many of the pupils expressed concern and guilt feelings over "not listening to her anymore." The young attempter had relied heavily on her friends for support, and they had all faithfully "kept her secret." Further, several of these pupils expressed feeling bad because they had, indeed, told someone at school against the expressed wishes of the family. Regrettably, secrecy produces PTSD. The pupils' emphasis was slowly shifted to a more positive direction (e.g., what they could do to support one another; how to relate to their friend if and when she was released from hospital).*

5. *Following consultation, teachers from the sixth grade and adjacent grade levels, with a member of the postvention team present, told their pupils within their homeroom, familiar atmosphere about the suicide attempt. Questions and concerns were addressed, and accurate information was provided. Unlike postvention for a completed suicide, considerable time was allotted to both teachers' and pupils' anxieties related to "how to treat" the girl when she returned to school (e.g., "what to say" and "what to do").*

6. *Parents were also informed about the event and about postvention efforts, and they were invited to call, come to the school, meet with the postventionist, and so on. As usual, several parents took advantage of these efforts to assist (e.g., how to talk about the attempt with their children). Those children who were suspected to be depressed or suicidal themselves, who knew someone who was dying, and so on were identified as in need of possible additional support and referred within the school/community.*

7. *As planned, 2 weeks after the event, the suicide prevention aspect of the program was presented. In the intervening weeks, close contact was kept with school staff and pupils as various individual needs arose.*

8. *After the suicide prevention workshop, an informal follow-up was held with all those involved in the postvention to obtain feedback and help us to identify future needs.*

CONCLUSION

Postvention has an important place in elementary schools and local communities. Staff in schools and members of local communities must act as "reasonably prudent persons." Traumatic deaths and other catastrophic events will occur and can have a powerful impact on children, their schools, and their communities. It would be imprudent to think that traumatic losses will never occur, to believe that their impact on children will not be significant, or to fail to be prepared to respond to such losses. Postvention programs can provide an effective response to assist children who are experiencing traumatic loss and to minimize unfortunate consequences. The principles outlined in this chapter provide the foundation upon which to design and implement postvention programs in elementary school settings.

15

Support Groups for Bereaved Children

Joan B. Bacon

This chapter sets forth a set of principles for establishing and operating support groups for bereaved children. It does so, first, by explaining that such groups arise because many parents encounter difficulties in helping their children cope with bereavement and because most bereaved children find great value in support from their peers. On that basis, bereavement support groups are designed to normalize children's experiences of loss and grief, and to assist them in their tasks of coping with mourning. Such groups may take many forms, may address different types of bereavement experiences, and may take children in at different points in their bereavement. In all cases, however, support groups for bereaved children, concurrent groups for bereaved parents and other adult caretakers, and leaders of both groups focus primarily on what members have in common in their experiences of loss. Typically, that is addressed through talking, sharing, and a program of activities designed to help members confront aspects of their grief in gentle and caring ways.

A RATIONALE FOR SUPPORT GROUPS FOR BEREAVED CHILDREN

Support groups for bereaved children are founded on two basic principles: a recognition that parents or other adult caretakers may find it difficult to function effectively in helping bereaved children cope with loss and grief; and the value of peer support.

Parental Functioning

At every stage of their development, children are dependent on their parents, to varying degrees, for a sense of well-being. In addition to protection and security, parents provide children with emotional and psychological support, soothing and tension regulation, and empathy (Altschul, 1988). Each of these influences a child's ability to cope with a death: psychological protection guards against more stimulation than the child's ego can tolerate; soothing and tension regulation help children to tolerate the many changes brought on by a death; and empathy serves to validate the intense feelings that the child is experiencing and to facilitate a continued relationship to the parent. Each of these is necessary for any child to grieve in a healthy way.

At a time of increased stress, children turn to the parental figures who have supported them in the past. In such situations, the parent-child relationship is critical to the child's ability to begin the tasks of grieving and look toward adapting to a life without the loved one who has died. Thus, during this vulnerable time, professionals should focus on strengthening the parent-child relationship (Martinson, Davies, & McClowry, 1987).

However, the availability of the surviving parent(s) can be problematic after the death of a parent, sibling, or other important person in the child's life (Fleming, 1985). Parents may exhibit either lack of affection or insufficient energy to show affection to the bereaved child. Parenting in these circumstances is frequently marked by a distinct lack of involvement. Communication between parent and child may be impaired in a context of bereavement. In short, at a time when a child is increasingly dependent on a parent to be accessible and supportive, a parent is often less available. The adult's own grief process may take much of his or her emotional energy, leaving little to expend on the child.

This situation is further complicated by the inability of many bereaved children to deal with their own intense emotions. Changes in the children's behavior and the difficulty most children have communicating their feelings verbally make parenting even more difficult. Many adults do not understand children's grief processes and have unrealistic ideas of how bereaved children experience grief. Coping with uncharacteristic behavioral changes, such as acting out, withdrawal, or regression, may be overwhelming for bereaved adults who can barely deal with their own intense pain.

In families where a parent has died, the surviving parent may be the target of children's anger. Fleming (1985) suggested that much anger may be directed at the surviving parent both for allowing the other parent to die and for not being adequately available to the child emotionally since the death. This anger is not only painful to the parent but scary to the child. A child will often find such anger difficult both to tolerate and express.

In addition, children are perceptive and are almost universally aware of the pain that their parents are going through after a death. To protect their parents and spare them further anguish, children will often refuse to discuss their own feelings. Acting on the recognition that the parent is necessary for the child's own survival, a child may relinquish his or her own integrity to protect a parent's well-being (Piper, McCallum, & Azim, 1992). As a result, communication may become even more difficult. Even parents who approach their children in an effort to comfort them may find the children will not openly share their own feelings of loss.

When children need to have emotionally available parents, but parents experience difficulty in meeting those needs, other avenues of support for both child and parent are required. A bereavement support group model that includes a companion group for parents addresses the needs of all concerned. Children gain support not only from other grieving children but also from facilitators who understand their pain and are emotionally available to support them. At the same time, parents receive support for their own grief and learn to understand the grief of their children better.

Peer Support

The importance of peer relationships to children is another issue at the heart of bereavement support groups. Children have a need to be like other children, to feel that they fit in somehow with their peers. Bereaved children often feel "different" because they have had a family member die (Raphael, 1993). Older children face this problem in a heightened way because their sense of identity has become increasingly peer oriented.

Children desire not only to be with peers, but to appear competent and feel accepted (Lonetto, 1980). An important task in the developmental process for children is to become less adult oriented and more peer oriented; in attaching more to children of his or her own age, the process of a child's becoming an individual is enhanced. How other children perceive and respond to a bereaved child will often greatly affect that child's self-concept.

Preserving peer relationships is, therefore, critical to a bereaved child. In an effort to maintain these relationships, a child might deny his or her own pain and sense of fear, and replace those feelings with an outward display of competence or even lack of concern about the recent loss. Peers and classmates, who often have limited experience with this kind of loss, may themselves not know how to respond. Betz (1985) noted that well-meaning friends may be oversolicitous, which may embarrass the child. Children who have not been bereaved may ask pointed and personal questions, or respond with thoughtless remarks. The once-predictable pattern of peer relationships has been altered by the death and each child's response to it.

One other important factor to consider is the bereaved child's typical behavioral changes after a death. Even a child who attempts to hide the depth of his or her pain, anger, or sadness is still clearly a different child from the one he or she was before the death. An inability to focus and concentrate may interfere with classwork. Unexpressed anger may unexpectedly flare up in situations that a child would formerly have been able to handle without difficulty. Children may withdraw or become clingy; either pattern makes an impact on peers. Finally, bereaved children may feel that no one understands what they have experienced and become frustrated with their friends. These feelings, coupled with the need to deal with other grieving family members, can constitute a great burden for a bereaved child.

Supportive peer relationships are central to a child's sense of competence and positive self-esteem. The bereavement support group provides children with the unique opportunity to be with peers who have also experienced the death of a close family member. The shared group experience can help children come to accept their feelings, rather than deny them, and receive support from others who can understand their complex grief processes. Within the bereavement support group, children feel that they are neither alone nor different. As a result, an affirmation of self is an important by-product of the peer group experience. The normalization process also helps children to come to a better understanding of the reactions of other friends and to develop ways to cope with changes in peer relationships.

FUNCTIONS OF SUPPORT GROUPS FOR BEREAVED CHILDREN

After the death of a loved one, children often feel a sense of isolation and even abandonment. The world for them is irrevocably changed; what formerly was familiar and predictable has now often become an unpredictable and unsafe place. Even those that care for them will have changed, and they may be consumed with their own grief. Friends often do not understand or appreciate the depth of their loss. All of these factors suggest the importance of a establishing a system that can help address some of these changes and feelings, and that is able to provide much needed support. Bereavement support groups can serve this role in four basic ways: (a) groups with peers who share similar losses can help to normalize feelings and experiences; (b) groups provide much-needed peer support; (c) these groups also dispel the sense of isolation that bereaved children often experience; and (d) a well-functioning group creates a safe place to deal with scary issues and feelings (Tait & Depta, 1993).

Corr (1992b) agreed that bereavement support groups decrease a sense of isolation and provide valuable peer support. Groups impart important information even as they also establish a medium for understanding both death and grieving better. Groups also offer opportunities to discover ways to remember and commemorate the person who died. Through these shared experiences, bereaved children can begin to make sense of life without the deceased.

Rutter (1987) suggested that four protective mechanisms serve to counter risk after a major change in a person's life. These include decreasing the risk impact, interrupting the negative chain of events, establishing a system designed to foster self-esteem as well as a sense of adequacy, and providing new opportunities. Bereavement support groups for children can address these four protective mechanisms to help a child adapt after the death of a loved one (Zambelli & DeRosa, 1992). For example, risk impact is reduced through group activities that allow children to cope with intense emotions through activities and play. Support groups also facilitate symbolic communication of feelings of anger, sadness, confusion, and fear, and they help children express these feelings in a safe and receptive setting. The group leader also promotes verbal expression of feelings, which is further supported by the shared experience with other bereaved children.

If the parents of bereaved children are struggling with their own grief and may not be able to provide consistent support, the children will still need a trusted adult to validate their feelings and to support them in their struggle to understand what has happened. The group leader can serve as a supportive, empathetic adult figure who can assist the family in this role. This approach may help prevent further complications resulting from unexpressed grief.

Finally, bereavement support groups help children validate their sense of self. They provide unique opportunities for peer relationships and shared experiences that explore a common loss. Although adult support is necessary, the bereaved child's need to feel accepted by other children despite his or her loss is an important developmental issue addressed by the support group. The peer group support may help make participants more resilient in dealing with children who do not understand the bereaved child's experience.

The focus of children's bereavement support groups should be on helping children cope with death. Activities and discussions should be centered on addressing the four basic psychological tasks of mourning described by Fox (1988): (a) understanding the death, (b) grieving or responding to the death, (c) commemorating the life of the one who has died, and (d) learning to go on with living and loving without the deceased (see Table 15.1).

Of particular importance are three complicating factors that Fox suggested might interfere with children's understanding of death. How the death was explained to the child should be explored in the group to determine if the child understands the concept of death. If concrete terms have not been used, increased difficulty often exists in grasping the difficult meaning of death. The developmental level of the child greatly influences the understanding of death. As each child matures, his or her understanding of death changes and is reworked at each new developmental level. Assessing the current level of understanding and working with the child at the appropriate stage is most important in providing optimal support from the group. Finally, the concept of magical thinking influences how a child perceives a death. Children often feel responsible for what happens in their world; it can seem to them that thoughts may have magical powers to either make something happen or prevent an event. Children are frequently afraid to share these thoughts with family members and may blame themselves for years for something that had nothing to do with the death. The group can be a safe place to explore magical thinking. Within the group, the concept of magical thinking can be introduced in nonthreatening ways through stories, puppets, or role play, and then followed up by group discussion.

SETTING UP A BEREAVEMENT SUPPORT GROUP

Open Versus Closed Format

The group organizer must determine whether the support group for bereaved children is to be open or closed. The difference is that open groups may admit new members at any time, whereas closed groups work with an established group of children for a specified period of time. Often, the decision between these two types of groups is based on

TABLE 15.1 Examples of Group Activities Corresponding to Tasks

Understanding the death	Responding to the death	Commemorating the life	Moving on with life
Group circle time sharing topics Share a favorite picture of the person who died; explain why this picture was chosen Tell a story about how the person died Share the story of the funeral Share family's beliefs about what happens to a person after death	Share highs and lows of the week Express feelings through movement, music, drawing, role play Ongoing opportunities to share feelings throughout group participation Discuss dreams Incorporate issues of magical thinking and somatization in discussion and sharing times	Share favorite picture or memory of the person who died Share memory boxes; why include different decorations; what special things might be placed in the box?	Identify people who are special to me, ways others let me know I am special Why I am special? What are changes in my family since the death? Look at hopes, dreams for the future Share feelings about group ending
Related activities Plant seeds or bulbs Share understanding through drawings, stories, puppets, etc.	Trace body outline on a large sheet of paper; have child use colors to illustrate where different feelings are felt Write different feelings on small pieces of paper; put in balloons and inflate; have a game in which each child gets to catch and pop a balloon; read feeling found inside and share a time when child felt that feeling Make an anger collage Make a happiness collage Act out feelings charades Make "dream catchers"	Decorate memory boxes Make memory books or scrapbooks that tell the story of the person's life and death Decorate picture frame for favorite picture of person who died Make beeswax candles for family to light on special remembering days	Balloon lift-off Take group picture; share addresses or telephone numbers for those who want to keep in touch Sign each other's memory books; share one thing about each person that each will remember Discuss future group reunion

For additional activities, see Heegaard, 1992; Reynolds, 1992.

practical issues such as the availability of staff and setting for the group. For example, hospitals and hospices may offer ongoing groups that meet two evenings a month, whereas a school-sponsored group may meet only during a designated academic term.

The open format permits the greatest flexibility for group participants. Participants can join the group at their initiative, attend when possible, and return to the group as desired. Group membership changes, offering a variety of perspectives as new members join and others who have participated longer move on. This format gives children an opportunity to experience other children at different stages of the grief process. Furthermore, participants are exposed to a greater number of other children who share a common experience. Open groups also provide a chance to experience saying good-bye to some members while still having the support of the group structure.

In a well-established open group, continuity can be maintained by those who become regular attendees and who welcome new participants. Schwab (1986) cited the advantages of an open format that allows a family to come to the group several times without having to make an ongoing commitment. Further, members who have participated in such groups know that they have the option of returning to the group during especially difficult times, such as holidays or anniversaries. The group can remain a safe and supportive resource in their lives for as long as the participants choose. Finally, the open group that provides ongoing service offers the benefit of a continuing program to the community; this may not be possible for a closed, time-limited group.

Nevertheless, the open format may encounter greater difficulty in promoting group cohesiveness. An inconsistent attendance pattern coupled with the unpredictability of membership may make creating a cohesive group more difficult. Roy and Sumpter (1983) addressed this issue and focused on the importance of cohesiveness in a positive group experience. However, the common experience of loss often creates a bond between members that leads to feelings of acceptance and unity despite varied and changing membership.

The closed format is offered in many settings that focus on time-limited, structured groups. In these programs, participants generally make a commitment to attend for a certain period of time (such as eight sessions), and the group is limited to those members. Trotzer (1977) indicated that continuity of membership coupled with frequent contacts helps maximize effectiveness by encouraging cohesiveness within the group. The level of trust and sharing is enhanced by continuity of membership. In this format, children have the opportunity to get to know each other better and to depend on the other children in the group. A sense of community often develops.

A closed format allows leaders to plan specific activities based on the interests and issues of the children currently participating. The group focus can be designed to fit the needs of that specific group of children. Further, activities or discussions begun at one session can be continued at a following session. When children complete one "series" of group meetings, the schedule can be extended for a session or two, or the children can be enrolled in a subsequent series if the leaders and family feel that this would be helpful and feasible (Zambelli, Clark, Barile, & de Jong, 1988).

One intrinsic drawback of a closed group is that a family must make a commitment to attend consistently for a defined period. This requirement may pose problems for some families whose lives are already stressed. Such a commitment may appear to be another burden during a difficult period of their lives. Also, families who wish to enroll a child in a closed group program may have to wait until one series of meetings ends and a new group convenes. This waiting period may be difficult for those who have already acknowledged that a support group is needed. Some programs provide a general, monthly support group for those who are waiting to participate in the upcoming series.

Screening

The issue of screening children for group participation is of interest to many group organizers. In part, screening may reflect a self-selection process, whereby potential members either choose not to participate or to discontinue involvement if their needs are not being met by the group (Schwab, 1986). If referrals are made by professionals, they will often redirect those who cannot be helped by a support group to other more suitable resources.

In organizing support groups for bereaved children, however, one must consider the appropriateness of each child for the group process. Reynolds (1992) highlighted the importance of an intake-assessment session for each family that is interested in participating in the bereavement program. The intake questionnaire for both parent and child provides the group leader with valuable information that includes attitudes, behaviors, and feelings of the child since the death. Physical problems, changes in eating and sleeping patterns, and school performance are also explored. If the family has sought professional counseling, this information will give the coordinators a better sense of the family's issues at this time. The intake assessment process provides the group leader with an opportunity to meet directly with the family and to assess briefly the family's level of functioning both before and since the death.

Through the gathering of this information and the interactive interview process, the interviewer should be able to determine if a child is appropriate for group support. For some children, individual or family therapy may be a more appropriate choice at that particular time. This referral can be made, and the family will have been well served by offering them a more appropriate support system. As Moody and Moody (1991) indicated, a family with a history of continuous unresolved conflicts or maladaptive coping patterns may need professional help beyond the scope of the bereavement support model. Tait and Depta (1993) underscored the importance of screening to identify the best possible service mode for each child.

Another positive aspect of the intake-assessment process is that it allows the family to meet directly with those who will be leading the groups, perhaps within the safety of their own homes. If the intake can occur where the groups will be held, the children can become acquainted with the setting. This arrangement will make the first session less threatening. The children also have the opportunity to meet separately with the leader and ask any questions that they might have. A scrapbook of activities that former groups have worked on might be shared with potential participants to help them to understand better the overall program and how its sessions are structured. The more the children understand, the less anxious they seem to be about participating in the bereavement program.

Finally, through the assessment process, the leader will be able to determine each child's developmental level. Because most groups are divided by age cluster (i.e., 5 to 8 years and 9 to 12 years), placing a child in the proper group is most important. If a child falls between two age groupings, the personal interview will help to assign him or her to the most appropriate group.

Timing for Participation in the Group

One issue that also needs to be considered is what is the appropriate time after a death to participate in a bereavement support group. Soricelli and Utech (1985) reported that participating in an adult support group less than 6 weeks after the death was too soon for most parents to be able to process their grief. In their experience, the optimal time for a bereaved parents' group was between 6 weeks to 8 months after the death. Many agree that joining a group early in one's bereavement may not be helpful to most children and families. Schwab (1986) emphasized that it is only after the intense support from friends, relatives, and other natural or informal support systems begins to diminish that the reality of the loss begins to set in. A bereavement support group can be of particular help at this time. However, many children and families have also found it helpful to participate at 1 year or 2 years after the death. At this later time, children and other family members may be struggling with reorganizing the family system and coping with the reality that the deceased will not return.

FOCUS OF SUPPORT GROUPS

Roy and Sumpter (1983) proposed that children attending a support group need not be in the same stage of bereavement. In fact, those who are at an earlier stage in the grief process can learn from those who are further along, whereas those in later stages can appreciate how far they have come and perhaps gain satisfaction in sharing with those at an earlier stage. One of the most beneficial aspects of a bereavement group is the opportunity for individuals at different stages of the grief process to share and support each other. This can help normalize feelings as well as provide encouragement for those striving to discover ways to cope with their loss.

The issue of combining in one support group those who have experienced different kinds of death is often debated. Schwab (1986) noted that similarity of loss is important to the bereaved. If so, ideally children who have had a parent die would be in a separate group from those who had lost a sibling. Programs that are well established with an adequate referral system can offer separate groups for each kind of loss. However, those programs that cannot provide separate groups are faced with a dilemma: exclude those with a different kind of loss or combine loss experiences within one group.

Fleming (1985) indicated that initially he sought to differentiate between the death of a parent and the death of a sibling based on the uniqueness of each relationship. However, Fleming reported similar responses when death occurs to either a parent or a sibling. The tasks of grieving are the same and children often share similar feelings about either type of death. In general, the kind of death experienced does not appear to be a barrier to a cohesive group for children. However, some problems have been noted in concurrent adult groups, where members are more apt to compare types of loss.

One drawback to a homogeneous group where everyone has experienced the same kind of loss (i.e., death of a parent from cancer) is that there may be a tendency to focus on issues of treatment and the disease process rather than on the tasks of coping with the death. It has been reported that a group for parents whose children died of a variety of illnesses was more productive than one for parents whose children died of the same illness (Soricelli & Utech, 1985). In the latter situation, a group leader may find that he or she must strive to keep the tasks of grieving central to the process rather than allowing discussion to focus on details of the dying process.

Families who are coping with death from violence may need special consideration. Miller, Moore, and Lexius (1985) suggested two particular goals that must be addressed after a death from homicide: (a) to help families understand their feelings of isolation; and (b) to help families regain a sense of control and mastery over their lives. The loss of someone through violence often leaves surviving family members feeling vulnerable and powerless. Peach and Klass (1987) also recommended that group members who had experienced a murder had special needs arising from the manner of their loved one's death. Typically, their grief included overwhelming anger as well as a sense of vengeance against the murderer. A group designed with these factors in mind would be appropriate for these families. Children may need activities designed to acknowledge the intensity of their anger, validate their intense feelings, and help express this anger in appropriate ways.

Combining children from different socioeconomic and ethnic backgrounds in a single bereavement group has proved to be successful in many situations. The common bond of a shared experience seems to minimize differences that might otherwise dominate (Hickey, 1993). The expressive quality of children's support groups, where activities are used to demonstrate feelings, lends itself to a varied group membership. Music, art, movement, and storytelling are all ways to deal with the children's feelings that can help children relate in spite of their differences. A variety of perspectives, lifestyles, and family traditions can add to the group experience for children.

LEADERSHIP

Almost all children's bereavement support programs acknowledge the importance of trained leaders. Leadership varies to include such professionals as trained social workers and counselors, art therapists, teachers and educators, and pastoral care personnel. All of these professionals should have in common an understanding of the grief process, children's distinctive reactions to bereavement, and an ability to work in a supportive way with children. Wolfelt (1991b) highlighted the importance of surrounding children with feelings of warmth, acceptance, and understanding after a death has occurred. The group leaders serve as an important dimension of this support. Zambelli and DeRosa (1992) also discussed the importance of the group leaders providing not only this consistent support but emotional holding as well. This may help children contain the anxiety associated with their grief.

Another model of bereavement program uses volunteer facilitators as group leaders. At the Dougy Center for Grieving Children in Portland, Oregon, volunteer facilitators are screened and interviewed, and then provided with 35 hours of facilitator training (Corr & the Staff of The Dougy Center, 1991; Whitney, 1992). The training, designed to teach volunteers to help children and adults cope with their grief, includes several objectives. These are (a) to provide an intellectual understanding of the grief process experienced by children and adults; (b) to offer practical tips for working as a grief support person, including communication skills and limit setting; (c) to explore personal beliefs about death and the dying process; and (d) to experience facilitation in a support group. A professional group coordinator is on site during the support groups, and may circulate in and out of different groups.

Haasl and Marnocha (1990) suggested some particular characteristics that are important for bereavement group facilitators. These include comfort with and interest in children; comfort with and knowledge of the grief process; empathy, sensitivity, and warmth; a nonjudgmental attitude; and flexibility. In addition, a facilitator needs to be able to tolerate the pain that grieving children and their parents feel and express. The purpose of the groups is to help children move towards grief and not away from it. It is necessary, therefore, for facilitators to be able to tolerate the expression of grief, and to encourage participants to express their painful feelings.

Heegaard (1992) noted that it is important for facilitators to acknowledge and share their own personal grief issues for them to be most effective in supporting bereaved children. Exploring one's own history of losses, including ways of coping, can give a leader insight into a child's current feelings. Further, remembering earlier childhood experiences of loss or death helps put one in touch again with the unique childhood perspective of such experiences. According to Heegaard (1992), the facilitator's role focuses on six basic tasks: (a) teach basic concepts; (b) help children recognize, accept, and express feelings; (c) provide opportunities for risks and problem solving; (d) encourage open communication and opportunities to learn from each other; (e) give support and encouragement; and (f) discover unhealthy misconceptions. Each of these can be addressed through children's activities, sharing times, and the dynamics of group process.

For children who are grieving the death of a parent, the Widowed Information and Consultation Services Program of Seattle (Widowed Information and Consultation Service, 1986; 15417 First Avenue, S., Seattle, WA 98148; tel. (206) 246-6142) has urged that a leadership team consisting of both a male and a female leader is most effective. This model allows children to express their feelings about their parent's death with a leader of the same sex as the deceased parent. Furthermore, it provides the children with a role model that may now be missing in their lives.

Almost all programs acknowledge the importance of cofacilitation of groups. Tait and Depta (1993) proposed that the ratio between supportive adults and children be as low as possible. Having at least two facilitators per group allows one person to attend to the needs of a specific child while the other facilitator continues with the group process. Anschuetz (1990) also suggested that cofacilitators together share the intensity of the emotions that such groups express (and evoke). The importance of having another leader to help plan, process, and evaluate the groups is self-evident. Additional facilitators also provide the children with different role models, as well as sources and styles of support.

Providing at least two cofacilitators for all groups is suggested. For younger children (ages 5 to 8), one facilitator for every two children is best. This ratio can be reduced when the group is composed of older children, although a ratio of greater than one facilitator to five children is not recommended. In the context of the bereavement group, children need to receive both group support and individual attention, when the latter is needed. Often, children share the most when they are working on individualized activities, such as art or drawing. If each child has a facilitator's undivided attention for a period of time, the opportunity to explore feelings in some detail is enhanced. This also gives the facilitator the chance to follow up on statements shared by the child in talking about his work. Special individual time with an adult who cares, supports, and can listen nonjudgmentally is invaluable to children. Often, this is the one place that they can share their feelings without worrying how it will affect the person they are talking to; at home, discussing such feelings may elicit reactions of sorrow, anger, or inability to deal with the child's emotions.

CONCURRENT GROUPS FOR PARENTS AND OTHER CARETAKING ADULTS

A support system model that provides concurrent support groups for both children and parents or other adult parental figures who take part in caring for the bereaved child is one that looks at bereavement as a family process (Shapiro, 1994). Thus, Moody and Moody (1991) suggested that the ideal approach would be to support children and their parents simultaneously in the bereavement process. Siegel, Mesagno, and Christ (1990) reported that children's adjustment to a death is greatly influenced by the ability of the parents to remain stable and consistent, facilitate parent-child communication, and maintain a sense of competence. Thus, a concurrent group for parents that provides a forum for supporting parents in these parenting tasks as well as in their understanding of the family's grief process can play an important role in helping both parents and children. As the parents begin to understand better the dimensions of children's grief and how it is expressed, they can perhaps become more effective in addressing their children's emotional and behavioral responses to the death. As the parents' sense of competence increases, their anxiety about their children may simultaneously decrease. The parents' group may also help members learn new ways to deal with challenging situations, and normalize the difficulty that parents often experience in dealing with their own grief as well as that of their children.

Fleming (1985) viewed the parental bereavement group as a tool in the prevention of future bereavement complications. Through this support system, parents have opportunities to cope with their own expressions of grief and to begin to understand and help their children with their grief processes. Serious problems in the family system can develop if neither grief is dealt with adequately. McGoldrick and Walsh (1983) noted that if a death is not dealt with by the entire family, communication patterns within the family system can become maladaptive. A structure that provides both a children's support group and a concurrent parent's group helps to enhance communication between family members and to encourage the entire family to work together in coping with a death.

Supporting and nurturing the parent-child relationship is an important goal of bereavement support groups. Siegel, Mesagno, and Christ (1990) suggested that the parents' own needs must first be met before they can focus effectively on the needs of their children. Through a concurrent parents' support group, parents can be affirmed in their struggles, talk with other parents who share common experiences, and work on their own grief issues. Within the group, parents are also supported in their parenting role. A parent's sense of self is often related to how that parent feels he or she is functioning as a parent. Improving one's sense of perceived competence as a parent can contribute to a feeling of well being during this stressful time.

Roy and Sumpter (1983) proposed that some of the issues to be addressed in the parents' group might include the parents' personal feelings of grief, discussion of how the family is coping as a system with the death, how the parents' roles may have changed since the death, and general supportive information that deals with both adult and children's bereavement processes. In Zambelli and DeRosa's (1992) model, the parent's companion group included both didactic and discussion activities. The overall impact of a support group program for bereaved children can only be enhanced by the participation of parents in a companion group; the family as a system is working together on the grief process.

Martinson, Davies, and McClowry (1987) addressed a special issue for families that have experienced the death of a child. The strength of the parent-child relationship is key in the ways in which surviving children will cope with the death of their sibling. Support groups provide opportunities to strengthen the parent-child relationship by increasing the potential for mutual support and understanding. Further, the child's support group should provide the children with a forum to share their special ideas and talents with their parents. Art activities and special memorial crafts, such as candles and memory boxes, are brought by the children to the adult group at the end of each session. This provides opportunities to share these special activities with the parents and receive positive feedback from the parents in the support group setting.

CHILDREN'S GROUP INTERVENTION TECHNIQUES: RATIONALE

The children's support group process is often one that is activity based (see Table 15.1). Moody and Moody (1991) addressed the importance of providing a place for children that feels safe so that they can express their feelings. However, inherent in each child's developmental process is often the inability to recognize, let alone express, such feelings. Even if feelings are recognized, children often feel uncomfortable expressing them directly. Zambelli and DeRosa (1992) attributed this to children's short-term defenses against remembering the pain, as well as their inability to express such powerful feelings in words. The combination of these attributes provides a basis for activity-based support groups.

Activity-based bereavement support groups provide children with ways of coping with loss and grief which go beyond just talking. For example, emotions may be addressed through art, music, movement, and role play. This provides a less threatening means to deal with powerful feelings. Zambelli and DeRosa (1992) drew attention to group activities as a way of redirecting mental energy from intense grief emotions to dealing with the activity. Through these activities, during which children can express different aspects of their grief, the children are supported, encouraged, and have the benefit of sharing their experiences with other children who have experienced a death. The activity model decreases anxiety and tension that may be associated with dealing with these emotions. Heegaard (1992) noted that children often respond positively to art therapy because of their need to express both grief emotions and death-related fears. Art counterbalances the children's natural tendency to repress intense and painful feelings.

Through activities, such as music, art, and body movement, symbolic communication can become the means for confronting and expressing grief. It is important to remember that play is children's work. Through play and activity, children confront and rework their special person's death. The support group provides a constructive, safe environment in which this can take place. Opportunities to express feelings verbally and to share personal stories are also an important part of the group process. The affirmation of feelings and the chance to share them with peers and supportive adults is an important part of the healing process. Haasl and Marnocha (1990) suggested that activities themselves may stimulate verbal expression in a reluctant child as the activities are shared and discussed in the group.

Heegaard (1992) emphasized that through art activities and play, children experience the freedom to express impulses and feelings without worrying about real-life consequences. Through a structured environment, children can struggle with their issues, experiment with wishes and fantasies, and work towards accepting reality. An important component of art activities is encouraging each child to clarify what is happening in the picture, and to explore feelings that are shared. This process helps move the child toward a greater ability to identify and accept his or her feelings.

Segal (1984) highlighted the importance of the expressive arts in helping children express grief. Children who are dealing with intense and scary emotions often expend a great deal of energy in trying to repress their feelings. The nonthreatening, spontaneous, and creative atmosphere created through art, music, and movement facilitates the safe expression of such feelings. Through structured and guided activity, the group experience can provide children with a medium for beginning to deal with anxieties, conflict, and fears that they have been unable to resolve. A peer modeling situation is created as children in the group participate in specially designed activities.

One of the major factors in healing is having an opportunity to tell and retell one's story. Children's stories are told through many different media as well as verbally in sharing with the group. One of the main palliative features of bereavement support groups is the retelling of each person's story—in multidimensional ways—to a group of trusted peers and leaders who listen, understand, and validate one's feelings (Hickey, 1993).

REFERRALS FOR COMPLICATED MOURNING

An important characteristic of bereavement support groups is that they are designed to provide support, not therapy. By screening participants at the outset, children who need individual or family therapy will be referred for appropriate interventions before beginning a group experience. Some referrals, however, will be made either during or after participation in bereavement support groups.

Although every child grieves in an individual manner, basic similarities of content and timing exist within the grief process (Fox, 1985). Those who interact with recently bereaved children may find them exhibiting any of the following behaviors: (a) changes in appetite or sleep patterns; (b) withdrawal; (c) difficulty in concentrating; (d) regression to an earlier developmental stage; (e) increased dependency; (f) restlessness; and (g) anger, anxiety, sadness, and aggression (Osterweis, Solomon, & Green, 1984). Many children will exhibit a combination of these experiences in reacting to the death of a loved one. This reaction is a part of the normal grief process.

Some children, however, exhibit signs that suggest that they are having an especially difficult time coping. One cue is the intensity and duration of the factors listed earlier; those children who cannot seem to move beyond these initial adaptive behavioral responses and seem "stuck" can be helped by therapy. Fox (1985) noted seven specific behaviors that indicate the need for a referral for individual therapeutic intervention: (a) a child gives even a hint of being at risk for suicide; (b) psychosomatic problems; (c) a prolonged period of time during which the child cannot concentrate on schoolwork, daydreams consistently, and is unable to complete assignments; (d) persistent sleep disorders, nightmares, or severe changes in eating patterns; (e) prolonged regression to an earlier developmental level that may seem safer; (f) attempts to act like the deceased person to bring him or her back or to gain favor with parents; and (g) fear of illness or mimicking symptoms of the deceased. Bereavement groups can support children in their grief; professional counseling may be needed to help a child who is especially troubled to cope with these additional factors.

Denial and guilt are two additional responses to a death that may be of particular concern. Many children will initially deny that the loved person has actually died. For a period of time, they may hold on to the belief that the person will return. Gradual acceptance of the reality of the death is necessary to proceed with the grief process. Those children that remain in denial for an extended period may require professional help. A sense of guilt is also common to many bereaved children. They look back and revisit times when they could have been kinder to the deceased, or think of ways that they might have been able to alter their actions and perhaps to prevent the death altogether. Children who remain trapped in the guilt cycle need help in moving on. Unresolved guilt in bereaved children has been known to lead to subsequent depression (Raphael, 1983).

Therapists working with grieving children usually find themselves addressing issues of withdrawal, denial, and repression (Segal, 1984; see chapter 16 in this book). These responses may lead to a sense of confusion, helplessness, and depression. Segal recommended the use of expressive arts, such as music, art, and body movement, to facilitate dealing with these issues.

Making the referral itself need not be a difficult process. Initially, one must share with the parents what has been observed in the child (or reported to the leader during the intake interview or during group time) that merits special concern. Clarify first if the child is currently, or has been previously, in therapy. If not, be prepared to offer several referral options. Once a parent has made the initial call for individual intervention, offer to share your insights with the professional if the parent has signed a release of information form. In these circumstances, the group leader must emphasize to participants that the group is not a therapy group and that additional resources may be needed by some people (Schwab, 1986).

CONCLUSION

Establishing support groups for bereaved children is a challenge, but one that can also be rewarding in important ways. It is a rare privilege to be allowed into the life of a child at a time when he or she is challenged by a death and its surrounding losses, as well as by his or her grief responses. Bereaved children and their parents turn to support groups for assistance in coping with unusual challenges that appear to exceed their resources. In turn, support groups provide unique opportunities to assist these children and their families, and to help them develop their own ways of coping. Bereaved children and their families who have experienced support groups consistently respond positively to their experiences. The groups recreate small communities of care in which individual children and their family members can find peers who have encountered similar experiences of loss and grief.

16

Individual Treatment of the Bereaved Child

Corinne Masur

The child who faces the death of a loved one, whether a parent, grand-parent, sibling, or friend does so at great potential risk to his or her future development. Only in childhood can death deprive an individual of so much opportunity to love and be loved by confronting the child with so difficult a task of adaptation (Furman, 1974; Richter, 1986). After a significant loss, children may encounter difficulties in experiencing grief and in mourning. Such difficulties may take a variety of forms and are generally associated with a child's problems in tolerating the feelings associated with mourning, his or her immature understanding of death, the traumatically overwhelming nature of the loss, and lack of support for the child in his or her mourning. Responses to loss will also be affected by the child's age and stage of development, level of intelligence, personality makeup, and the availability of external and internal resources.

The danger to a child's development posed by significant loss can be averted, however, if the child is helped to mourn as fully as possible. Children from toddlerhood on can be assisted in this difficult task by those who work with children as part of their professional lives. Professionals can identify children who have suffered recent loss; select out those children who are having difficulty or who are at risk for difficulty; assess each child's level and type of need; and, when necessary, refer such children for appropriate treatment to facilitate healthy mourning and normal developmental processes (Crenshaw, 1991; Cook & Dworkin, 1992; Rando, 1993). This chapter describes the identification, assessment, and treatment of the bereaved child.

IDENTIFYING AND ASSESSING
THE BEREAVED CHILD

Identifying Bereaved Children Who Need
Professional Assistance

It is critical that recently bereaved children be identified and assessed as to their ability to cope with the loss (Cook & Dworkin, 1992; Webb, 1993b). It is equally important in each case that the child's family be evaluated as to the ability to support and care for the child after the loss (Walsh & McGoldrick, 1991b). Those who are most crucial for the early identification of children who have suffered a significant loss are the professionals who are at the scene at the time of a loss or illness, or those who work with children on a daily basis. These professionals include emergency room nurses and physicians, oncology nurses and physicians, hospice workers, police, members of the clergy, day care workers, teachers, and social workers.

Especially in the case of sudden or violent deaths, or in the case of the death of a parent, it is important that children be referred for immediate psychological evaluation. However, all children who have suffered a recent significant loss may appropriately be referred for the assessment of both their mourning and the adequacy of their ongoing development.

Assessing Bereaved Children

It is important to evaluate whether or not a bereaved child is experiencing difficulty in coping with the death of a loved one. Such difficulty may take many forms including an inability to experience the affects associated with grief and mourning, an inability to do the work of mourning, or the development of a complicated or pathological grief process. More simply, the child may need support in initiating and continuing a normal mourning process. To understand the nature of an individual child's loss, grief, and mourning, a careful assessment process must occur (Cook & Dworkin, 1992; Masur, 1991; Webb, 1993b).

Baker, Sedney, and Gross (1992; see also chapter 6 in this book) described a series of mourning tasks for children. Following their example, the tasks of a social worker, psychologist, psychiatrist, or other professional in evaluating the bereaved child can also be described. Early tasks in assessing the bereaved child are as follows:

1. The clinician must gather the facts as to what has happened. These include specific details about the death, the way in which it occurred, who was present at the time, what the child or children saw, or, if they were not present, what they were told. It is also important to find out who has been taking care of the child since the death (especially in the case of the death of a parent), what changes in routine have occurred, whether the child attended the funeral, who accompanied the child during the funeral, and the like.
2. The clinician must assess the family concerning their ability to support the child both materially and emotionally. It is important to note the personality characteristics of the family members and to evaluate the mourning processes of those family members who are close to the child.
3. The clinician must learn what the child's understandings of and experiences with death were before this loss.
4. The clinician must learn what the child's understanding is of this particular death including the child's theories regarding the cause of the death and any feelings of responsibility for the death.
5. The clinician must assess the child's emotional reaction to the death. To do this, one must compare the child's current level of functioning to his or her previous level of functioning, and learn if the child has experienced any regressions in functioning or has developed any symptomatic behavior.
6. The clinician must assess the child's ability to tolerate the emotions involved in experiencing the grief associated with mourning, especially the sadness, yearning, and anger.
7. The clinician must assess the child's ability to do the work of mourning, that is, to review memories of the lost loved one, to experience the feelings associated with the lost loved one, and to gradually reinvest in other relationships the feelings that had been associated with the person who died. The child's ability to do this work will depend on his or her age, stage of development, personality, intellectual ability, and the availability within the child's environment of external supports for the mourning process.

Undertaking the Assessment

An assessment, such as that outlined here, is a complicated and detailed process. It will be best accomplished by interviewing the adults involved first, except in the case of bereavement resulting from violent death for which it has been suggested that the child be seen immediately (Pynoos & Eth, 1986). In the case of the death of a parent, the surviving parent can be interviewed and grandparents or other relatives or caretakers important to the child can also be included in the assessment process. Several sessions may be spent with these adults to accomplish the tasks described. In so doing, the clinician will talk to the adults about their own feelings regarding the death, assess the adults' ability to cope with and mourn the loss, and evaluate the adults' ability to support the child's mourning processes emotionally. This last involves being able to talk with the child about the loss, to comfort the child when necessary, and to model for the child the ability to experience and display feelings appropriate to the loss. During the assessment process, it will also be necessary to glean developmental and current information about the child as described earlier.

This portion of the assessment should not be rushed. Even though the adults' anxiety about the child may be considerable, it is important to take the time to get to know them, not only to acquire the needed information but also to establish a relationship with them which will later be helpful in supporting the child's treatment should psychotherapy be recommended.

Following the gathering of information from the adults, the child may be seen in a play therapy evaluation. The child will be brought to the clinician by his or her current caretakers. Depending on the child's wishes, he or she may come alone into the playroom or may be accompanied by one or more of the adults who are functioning as his or her caretakers.

Although the goal of the evaluation is to gain as much information as possible, sessions are best kept nondirective. At the time of the first session, the evaluating clinician seeing a child 10 years old or younger may introduce himself or herself as the kind of doctor (or person) who helps children with their worries. Using the name of the deceased person, the clinician may explain that he or she knows that individual has died. Awareness of some of the circumstances around the death can also be reported as a result of conversations with the child's parent or other caretaker. However, it will also be important for the clinician to indicate a desire to know what the experience has been like for the child and what the child's feelings are. The clinician can then offer to talk with the child and play together as a means of sharing information, insights, and feelings. The child can then be shown where the toys and art supplies are kept. From this point on, communication and activity can be spontaneous. A great deal can be learned about a child's experience of the loss, thoughts, feelings, and concerns from his or her free play and artistic productions.

Case Examples

A three-year-old boy was evaluated following the suicide of his mother. The child's father told the treating clinician that the boy had been told that his mommy had gone "up there," as the father pointed toward the sky. Although the family was not particularly religious, this explanation was the best they had been able to think of in the moment. At the time of the first evaluation session, the child entered the playroom and went immediately to the doll house. He picked up the adult woman doll and tossed it behind the house. When the clinician asked, "Where's the mommy?" the little boy retrieved the doll, put it on the roof of the doll house, and said, "The mommy's on the roof!" In this way the clinician learned what the child had understood by the father's gesturing toward the sky in telling his son what had happened to Mommy. This was extremely important as it was later understood that this little boy felt that Mommy was not dead but living in a new location, and, if he were only good enough, she might return.

Another child, 11 years old, was seen for what her mother described as "bad behavior." During the evaluation sessions with the mother, it was learned that the girl's parents had divorced 5 years ago and that the father had suicided 3 years ago. The mother reported, however, that the child had not suffered any negative reactions at all either at the time of the divorce or at the time of the father's death. The mother said that, in fact, the child had behaved like a "model child" in all regards until recently.

It was not until the child sat down in the first evaluation session and drew a colorful heart, split down the middle with a rainbow coming out of both sides that either the clinician or the mother had any indication of what was bothering the girl. In asking about each element of the picture, the clinician inquired about the rainbow. The child replied that the last rainbow she had seen had been at the house she had lived in with her mother and father while they were still married. She then reported that she and her mother had recently moved from that house to a new neighborhood. When the clinician asked if leaving the house had made the girl sad, she said, "yes." When asked if the house reminded her of her father because they had lived there together years ago, the girl also said, "yes." When the clinician noted that the heart was split down the middle, the girl said that it was a "broken heart."

When the clinician suggested that perhaps the girl was sad and broken-hearted because she missed her dad and that leaving the house had made her begin to feel these feelings, she sadly nodded that this observation was true. So in response to an opportunity to draw or make whatever she wanted this 11-year-old immediately disclosed the meaning of what her mother had called her "bad behavior" by revealing that she had recently started to mourn the loss of her father for the first time in 3 years. Consequently, she no longer had the energy or motivation to help her mother and achieve straight As in school.

Circumstances Bearing on Assessment

During the evaluation, the child's appointments may be scheduled once, twice, or three times in a week depending on the needs of the family. It is not recommended that the child be seen less often than once per week as it is important to establish some continuity in the child's work with the clinician and to allow the child and the clinician the opportunity to begin to develop a relationship. During these sessions it is the clinician's job to take note of (a) the child's ability or inability to acknowledge the loss, to discuss it, and to demonstrate feelings about it; (b) the child's ability or inability to separate from the caretakers who brought him or her for the evaluation; and (c) the derivatives in the play indicating the child's thoughts, concerns, feelings, and understanding of the death.

With children who demonstrate anxiety about separating from the adult who brings them for the evaluation, the adult may be invited into the playroom to accompany the child. The context of the evaluation must be one in which the child feels sufficiently relaxed to talk and play freely, and thereby to demonstrate his or her concerns. The nature of the anxiety may be addressed at this point simply by stating how difficult it is for the child to leave Daddy (or whomever) and by the clinician's accepting this for the moment. However, information regarding the child's relative ease or difficulty in separating will be regarded as important. Throughout the evaluation the clinician will make preliminary comments to the child regarding his or her feelings (or the lack thereof), as well as thoughts and theories about the death (or the lack thereof). In general, during this process the clinician will attempt to make sense of the child's play activities in an effort to assess the child's current level of functioning and his or her status regarding mourning.

In the case of a child closely related to someone who has experienced a violent death or in the case of a child who has witnessed such a violent event occurring to an unrelated person, it is recommended by knowledgeable experts (Nader & Pynoos, 1991; Pynoos & Eth, 1986; see also Chapter 11 in this book) that the child be seen immediately for evaluation and intervention. These experts have studied child victims of violence and have designed an emergency intervention strategy which they recommend instituting 24 to 48 hours following the event. Pynoos and Eth (1986) described an evaluation format that allows a child to discuss his or her impressions, and to release feelings regarding the event. The interview in and of itself can ameliorate the symptoms of posttraumatic stress disorder, which may result from witnessing a violent death or being related to the victim of violence.

RESULTS OF THE ASSESSMENT: INDICATIONS FOR TREATMENT

Once the clinician has met with the adults and child as many times as are deemed necessary to gather the information described earlier, it must be decided whether this child and family require further help. For this assessment, the clinician must differentiate between a child's internal difficulties in proceeding with a healthy mourning process and difficulties in the family that may interfere with the child's ability to proceed.

When it is clear that the primary caretaker or other adult close to the child is having significant difficulty coping with the loss, that adult may be referred for individual treatment. When it seems that the child's primary caretaker is able to mourn but is either so involved in his or her mourning as to be unavailable to the child or so devastated by his or her own feelings as to be unable to support expression of the child's feelings, both the adult caretaker and the child will be in need of help. When the caretakers seem to be doing well, but the child is experiencing difficulties with grief and mourning, then the child can be referred for individual treatment.

Following a significant loss, the types of difficulty commonly seen in children which require treatment include the absence of grief; a denial that the death has occurred; inhibitions in the expression and experiencing of sadness and grief; persistent feelings of anger toward the lost loved one; and fantasies of reunion with the lost loved one. However, other specific factors predispose the child to difficulties in mourning and adaptation. These include the following:

1. The death occurred as a result of murder or violent accident.
2. The death occurred as a result of suicide (especially when the lost loved one is a parent or sibling).
3. The child is under the age of 5 years at the time of the death of a parent or sibling.
4. The death occurred unexpectedly or abruptly.

5. The parent or sibling died following a painful or prolonged illness.
6. The parent died of cancer that involved the reproductive organs.
7. The personality of the child before the loss was either temperamental or withdrawn (Elizur & Kaffman, 1983).
8. The child had adjustment difficulties before the loss (Elizur & Kaffman, 1983).
9. In the case of parental death, marital discord or divorce preceded the death.
10. A conflictual relationship with the deceased person existed before the death.
11. In the case of the death of a parent, a poor relationship existed between the child and the surviving parent.
12. The person who died was mentally ill and resided with the family (Kliman, 1968).
13. In the case of parental death, the remaining parent is mentally ill.
14. In the case of parental death, the surviving parent is unable to function "normally" after 6 months following the loss (Elizur & Kaffman, 1983).

Every child to whom one or more of these factors applies will not necessarily be in need of individual psychotherapy. Nevertheless, such children will need to be evaluated especially carefully as to their potential for experiencing difficulty in the mourning process.

INTERVENTION: APPROACHES AND GOALS

Help for the bereaved child and for that child's family may take a variety of forms (Crenshaw, 1991; Cook & Dworkin, 1992; Masur, 1991; Webb, 1993c). As noted earlier, when parents are experiencing difficulty in their own mourning and adaptation to loss, they may be referred for their own treatment both to help them toward recovery and to aid them in being more available to their child or children. For parents who are functioning well and whose children are younger than the age of 2 years or seem to be experiencing little in the way of disruption in normal functioning, some educative sessions with a clinician may be sufficient to help them to know how to support their child's grief and mourning. For older children who are experiencing little in the way of disruption, school or clinic-based grief support groups may also be helpful in order to allow them to communicate their feelings with other children who have experienced a similar loss and to feel less alone with their experience. However, for children who are experiencing significant difficulty in progressing with the mourning process and for those who have developed an absent, inhibited, delayed, or otherwise complicated response to loss, intensive individual psychotherapy is indicated.

Three main goals in treating the bereaved child are (a) to ensure that the family is able to care for the child following the loss by providing for daily material needs, understanding special needs for comfort and emotional support after the loss, and supporting the expression of the child's thoughts and feelings regarding the loss; (b) to facilitate the mourning process; and (c) to prevent the development of a disturbed grief response when possible or to treat such a response once it has occurred. When treatment is indicated, these goals can be attained in one of two ways: either by treatment of a child through his or her caretakers, or by individual treatment of the child directly.

TREATING A CHILD THROUGH THE PARENT OR CARETAKER

When treatment is to be undertaken through the parent or other adult caretaker, the adult can be seen once weekly, biweekly, or on an as-needed basis to report on the child's progress. Such an adult can be helped to know how to understand the child's behavior, how to understand the child's experience of the loss, and how to facilitate the mourning process.

Children younger than the age of 2 years, as well as less affected older children, may be treated through parent guidance. For the young infant who has suffered the death of a primary caretaker, his or her needs are immediate and critical. Infants' needs at the time of the loss of a parent or other significant caretaker are for the most seamless continuity of care possible. For infants up to 6 months of age, the loss of a mother or full-time caretaking father or grandparent will result in the infant's experiencing the discomfort of disruption in daily routines and familiarity with the feel, smell, rhythms, and voice of the beloved caretaker. Those taking over the care of the young bereaved infant may be helped to understand the necessity of preserving as many of the previous rituals and routines as possible. For a baby who must be moved to a new home, it is important to educate the new caretakers as to the need to take along familiar furniture, toys, clothing, towels, blankets, and the like. If the child had a transitional object such as a particular stuffed toy or "blankey," it is particularly important to make sure that the infant is allowed to keep that object. At moments of family crisis, it is easy for adults, particularly those not intimately familiar with the infant, to overlook the importance of such items.

For the older infant (older than 7 months) and toddler, it is the task of professionals to help the caretakers of these young children to continue the familiar rituals and routines to which these children are accustomed, to talk to them about the loved one who has died, and to be prepared for disruptions in the child's previously established emotional organization. Regressions may be expected. Recently acquired skills may be lost. For example, a child who previously was able to sleep through the night may begin to wake. A 14-month-old who fed himself may demand to be fed. A gregarious 2-year-old may withdraw or become angry and belligerent. Young children of this type must be provided with a stable home and reassurance that they are loved and will be well cared for before they can begin to progress again in their development.

The surviving parent or caretaker must be helped to understand the needs of the infant and the profound disruption that the infant experiences. Many adults, in their wish to deny the impact of loss on one so young, are tempted to underestimate the effects of loss at this age. Sensitive support for these adults, open-ended discussions of their own experience of the loss, and gradual education as to the infant's needs will be helpful.

Starting at $2\frac{1}{2}$ or 3 years of age, children can begin to discuss their concepts of death, express ideas and feelings about death verbally, and understand more fully explanations that are offered about death (as well as other matters). At this age, children begin to demonstrate a capacity to mourn if they are supported by the adults in their environment. In this context, support means that all of the child's questions are answered, the child is helped to remember the lost loved one, feelings are validated, labeled, and respectfully accepted, and the child is helped to manage feelings when they become overwhelming. It is at the age of $2\frac{1}{2}$ to 3 years that a child can be helped by surrounding adults to understand and process loss more fully. At this age, a child who has suffered a significant loss and does not seem to be experiencing extreme disruption in functioning may also be treated through the parent or other caretaker.

Older children may also be treated by way of the parent, although frequently the child can be invited into the office for more direct help.

INDIVIDUAL TREATMENT

Therapeutic Strategies and Mourning Tasks

The purpose of individual therapy with any child, and specifically with a bereaved child, is to allow the expression of the child's full range of feelings, thoughts, and fantasies in a place where it is safe to do so, and within the context of a relationship with an understanding, empathic ally.

For children younger than the age of 13 or 14 years, play therapy is recommended (Masur, 1991; Webb, 1991). In play therapy, the child is encouraged to play, fantasize, work on artistic projects, and engage in other similar activities as part of a process of understanding with the therapist what the child's concerns and worries may be. In introducing the child to the therapy, it is important for the therapist to indicate awareness that the child has experienced some difficult times, to enumerate these, and to tell the child that the therapist knows that the child has worries and feelings about all that has happened. The therapist will then go on to explain that he or she and the child will work on understanding the nature of the child's feelings in order to help the child to feel better.

Adolescents usually prefer to talk rather than to play, although some will feel most comfortable if, when they experience difficulty talking, they are invited to play cards, draw, or engage in some other activity while they talk to the therapist. With adolescents, however, the goal is the same as for younger children—to allow for full expression of their thoughts and feelings.

Baker, Sedney, and Gross (1992), Bowlby (1980), Furman (1974), and others have described tasks of mourning for children which can inform their treatment. Although it is an oversimplification to imagine that such a complex and individual process as mourning can be broken into a single set of specific tasks for all bereaved children, those that have been described can serve as general guidelines for goals in psychotherapy and as markers of change if applied flexibly. Baker, Sedney, and Gross (1992) described the following tasks:

1. To begin to grieve, children must know that someone has died.
2. They must accept and emotionally acknowledge the reality of the loss.
3. They must explore and reevaluate the relationship to the lost loved one.

4. They must face and bear the psychological pain that accompanies the loss.
5. They must know that their own personal safety is assured.
6. They must reorganize their individual sense of identity.
7. They must return wholeheartedly to age-appropriate developmental tasks and activities.
8. They must be able to cope with periodic resurgence of pain.

The role of a therapist is to try to help a bereaved child to mourn or cope effectively with his or her loss and grief. This role may be described as helping the child to complete the tasks identified by Baker, Sedney, and Gross (1992). In practice, although it is common for children to experience shock and numbing (denial), as well as yearning and searching (Bowlby, 1980), children often have particular difficulty in accepting the fact that someone has died, understanding the irreversibility of this fact, facing the painful feelings associated with this understanding, reevaluating their relationship to the deceased person, and reorganizing their own sense of personal identity.

Accepting the Fact that Someone Has Died

Children often have problems relinquishing the conscious or unconscious belief that the lost loved one continues to exist. Bereaved children may, therefore, continue to yearn and to search for the loved one rather than proceeding with the work of mourning in which they reevaluate the relationship with the lost loved one and review memories of that person as compared to the reality of the person's absence.

For example, Lopez and Kliman (1979) described a case in which 19-month-old Diane was repeatedly told the facts of her mother's suicide. Although Diane verbally acknowledged these facts for the first 2 weeks after her mother's death, she also continually asked about her mother's whereabouts and when she would return.

As a result of her age and stage of development, Diane did not have the intrapsychic capacity or the cognitive ability to understand the permanence of death. In treatment, she was helped to learn about death and gently reminded that her mother could not return even if she had wanted to. In describing how this was done, Lopez and Kliman elucidated the first task of mourning noted previously. That is, they brought to Diane's awareness the reality of the loss. In the first 4 weeks of treatment, which occurred when Diane was 4 years old, the death of Diane's mother was not acknowledged at all. Only when a game of losing toys was interpreted by the therapist as being like losing the painful feelings that we do not want to feel did Diane provide any material at all demonstrating her concerns about her mother's death.

For the following 10 weeks of treatment themes of searching for the mother were played out, thus bringing into the treatment Diane's fantasy of her mother's continued existence. Lopez and Kliman described the therapist's efforts during this time as gentle repudiation of Diane's denial of the loss of her mother and her denial of her painful feelings about the loss. To Diane's barely veiled negation of her belief in ghosts (that is, the ongoing existence of her mother), the therapist stated that perhaps at times she did believe in such ghosts. To her wishes of reunion with her mother, the therapist communicated that he understood that she very much wanted to be with her mother again. It was through this clarification and interpretation of her feelings, coupled with empathically expressed reminders of reality, that Diane was able, by the end of her therapy, to come to the conscious and unconscious acceptance of the fact that her mother no longer existed.

Even in treating older children and adolescents it is common to discover through a child's play, dreams, or fantasies that he or she believes that the lost loved one continues to exist. With older children, it is important to help them to understand that this is their wish rather than a representation of reality. The therapist may need to stress this interpretation of the situation repeatedly in order to assist the bereaved youngster.

Facing and Bearing the Pain of Loss

In psychotherapy, a child may also need help with another important task of mourning—facing, bearing, and expressing the psychological pain associated with the loss. Typically, children have particular difficulty with anger (Jewett, 1982). It is common for children to assign responsibility for the death to themselves or an inappropriate third party. Rather than being angry with the person who died for leaving them or rather than accepting the painful reality that we all must die, children often turn their anger elsewhere. Often children feel that the abandonment by the person who died was brought on by the child's own misbehavior, innate badness, or hostile thoughts or wishes.

For example, Davids (1993) beautifully described difficulties experienced by her young patient, Alfredo, regarding the sudden death of his baby brother. She stated that work with Alfredo "revealed that death was equated with hostile wishes in his mind. Believing in the power of his destructive impulses, Alfredo unconsciously believed that he had killed his baby brother" (p. 284). Davids also described an incident that occurred one day when Alfredo was on his way to his appointment with her. As he was riding in the car with his mother, they stopped at a traffic light. Posted on a pole where Alfredo could see it was a wanted poster which read "Alfredo ———, wanted for murder." Evidently, Alfredo became frightened and pale. He begged his mother to go back home protesting that he had not murdered anyone. Interestingly, shortly before this incident Alfredo had admitted to having been angry with his baby brother when he would scream and cry.

The therapist must also help a bereaved child to tolerate his or her own pain and sadness. The loss of a loved one involves the loss of all that the relationship held for the child—whether in reality or in the child's fantasy. In the case of the death of a parent, the child loses the love and nurturance that is so badly needed from that parent. Also lost are the attention that that parent would pay to the child in daily life and in each successive developmental stage. Further, the child loses opportunities to please that parent in ways that the child imagines might formerly have been possible. Bowlby (1980) stated that one of the therapist's main jobs in treating the bereaved child is to interpret the meaning of the child's pathological escapes from mourning. Often these escapes take the form of attempts to ward off pain.

Robert Furman (1964b) described this in the case of Billy, a 6-year-old boy. Following the death of his mother, Billy experienced many angry, anxious, and out-of-control feelings. After working together for some time, Billy and his therapist came to understand that these feelings were caused by what he named "mommy missing feelings" (Furman, 1964b, p. 394). Furman stated that his young patient experienced these in every situation that one would expect a first-grader to need his mother and want her to be with him—in getting dressed, going to school for the first day, coming home for lunch, and the like. Furman noted that each episode of mommy missing feelings had to take its turn in a process that could not be accelerated. By talking about the meaning of his angry, anxious, out-of-control feelings and labeling them, Furman allowed Billy to understand his upsets around these daily routines and to experience the sad feelings consciously.

Reevaluating the Relationship and Reorganizing One's Sense of Personal Identity

In exploring and reevaluating the relationship with the lost loved one, it is important for the therapist to uncover and understand the nature of the child's feelings toward the person who has died. Initially, a tendency may exist to idealize the lost loved one. The child may remember only the good things about that person or the fun times that were had. Gradually, based on the therapist's own understanding of the relationship (from information supplied by the child and by the family), the therapist can suggest that the child may have experienced other feelings regarding the lost loved one. In Alfredo's case, as he became more able to accept and express his jealousy of his baby brother who had died, he also became more able to accept and enjoy his mother's current attention.

Another aspect of mourning that is closely related to reevaluating the relationship is the need for the child to reorganize his or her sense of personal identity. For example, a child who has lost a sibling loses the opportunity to be a brother or sister to that sibling. A child who loses a parent loses the sense of being a son or daughter to that person and becomes a child who does not have a mother or father. These are difficult realizations and the child may need help to face them. Moreover, it is crucial to separate the child's fate from that of the lost loved one. Following a death, it is common for children to develop fears of death and to believe that they are also going to die. Frequently, children and adolescents believe they will die in the same way that the lost loved one died.

In the case of Alfredo, Davids (1993) reported that Alfredo believed that his baby brother died as a result of being too hot. Alfredo then worried that if he went on the family vacation to Italy he also would become too hot and die. Davids said to Alfredo that he seemed to be "very afraid something disastrous would happen to him in Italy and that his baby brother's sudden death made him extra scared for his own safety, life, and health, so scared that he would suffer a similar fate to his brother" (1993, p. 283). After this interpretation, the trip to Italy went better than expected although on his return Alfredo remarked that he did prefer his home city's rainy weather to the hot weather in Italy.

The Relationship with the Therapist

In the course of psychotherapy, a child develops a most important relationship with a therapist. The therapist serves a variety of functions regarding the bereaved child: he or she is a real person, genuinely and uniquely interested in the child at a time of crisis in the child's life; he or she is an auxiliary ego who helps the child to face and tolerate difficult thoughts and feelings; and he or she is also a target for some of these very feelings. For example, a child who is angry at having been abandoned by a beloved relative who has died may very well transfer that anger onto the therapist. The child will feel that valid reasons exist for this anger with the therapist and will need help to understand the true origins of these feelings.

In other cases or at other moments with the same child, the child may form an intense and loving relationship with the therapist, allowing the child to feel for the therapist what had previously been felt for the lost loved one. In this case as well, the child will need to be helped to remember that he or she loved the person who died, and that he or she misses the opportunity to show such love for that person in real life.

The degree to which the therapist is able or willing to use the child's feelings addressed toward the therapist in the course of the therapeutic process will depend on the therapist's orientation toward psychotherapy. More psychodynamically oriented therapists who see the child in intensive individual work will use these feelings, also referred to as the transference, more extensively.

Ongoing Involvement with the Child's Caretakers

During the process of individual psychotherapy with a bereaved child, it is important to maintain active involvement with the child's caretakers. Although the child's specific communications with the therapist must be kept confidential, the therapist may meet with the caretakers on a regular basis in order to learn how the child is doing at home and at school. It is important to learn what the child is feeling and talking about at home regarding the loss. It is also important to know about the child's general mood, activities, and relationships outside of the office. It is crucial that the therapist know about any disruptions in the child's behavior, the development of new symptoms, or any improvements that may be occurring. The child's careretakers will also want to have some feedback regarding the child's work in therapy and it is often most helpful to their understanding of the child to be provided with general information regarding the child's feelings.

Finally, it is important to discuss the way in which the child, the child's caretakers, and the therapist can decide when to bring the child's therapy to an end. Given that the goal of psychotherapy for the bereaved child is the facilitation of his or her mourning process and given that the goal of mourning is to allow the bereaved child to be able to reattach to new loved ones, the child can begin to terminate work with the therapist when he or she is able to begin to reinvest in friends, family, and new caretakers, and to proceed with normal development. The goal of psychotherapy is to learn to manage in a healthy way challenges and tasks arising from the situational crisis associated with death and loss to be able to return wholeheartedly to age-appropriate developmental tasks. The therapy may be expected to last anywhere from several months to years based on the individual needs of the child. Despite external demands for short-term psychotherapy, a bereaved child's mourning process, its facilitation, and his or her return to forward development cannot be rushed.

CONCLUSION

Although the death of a loved one is difficult for anyone of any age, it is clear that it is an especially difficult experience for children and adolescents. However, children of all ages can be helped to accomplish the mourning process. Whether through the love and support of their families, or through professional intervention, children from the earliest years on can be helped to manage both the internal and the external difficulties associated with loss. When individual psychotherapy is required to help with an absent, delayed, or disturbed mourning process, both the child and the therapist have the unique opportunity to explore and understand the wealth of feelings that the child has about loss, separation, and death as well as about life, attachment, and love. In this process, the child and the therapist share an intense and important experience, working together to help the child to remember the lost loved one, to clearly understand the death, to mourn, and to reinvest in life and all the pleasures and ongoing relationships that it holds.

References

Adams, B. (1972). *Kinship in an urban setting.* Chicago: Markham.

Adams, D. W., & Deveau, E. J. (1987). When a brother or sister is dying of cancer: The vulnerability of the adolescent sibling. *Death Studies, 11,* 279–295.

Adams, D. W., & Deveau, E. J. (1993). *Coping with childhood cancer: Where do we go from here?* (rev. ed.). Hamilton, Ontario: Kinbridge.

Adams-Tucker, C. (1982). Proximate effects of sexual abuse in childhood: A report on 28 children. *American Journal of Psychiatry, 139,* 1252–1256.

Ainsworth, M. D. S. (1979). Attachment as related to mother-infant interaction. In J. Rosenblatt, R. Hinde, C. Beer, & M-C. Busnel (Eds.), *Advances in the study of behavior* (pp. 2–51). New York: Academic Press.

Altschul, S. (Ed.). (1988). *Childhood bereavement and its aftermath.* Madison, CT: International University Press.

Ambrosini, P. J., Metz, C., Prabucki, K., & Lee, J. (1989). Video-tape reliability of the third revised edition of the K-SADS. *Journal of the American Academy of Child and Adolescent Psychiatry, 28,* 723–728.

American Psychiatric Association. (1980). *Diagnostic and statistical manual of mental disorders* (3rd ed.). Washington, DC: Author.

American Psychiatric Association. (1987). *Diagnostic and statistical manual of mental disorders* (3rd ed., rev.). Washington, DC: Author.

American Psychiatric Association. (1994). *Diagnostic and statistical manual of mental disorders* (4th ed.). Washington, DC: Author.

Anderson, G. R. (1986). *Children and AIDS: The challenge for child welfare.* Washington, DC: Child Welfare League of America.

Anderson, R. (1968). *I never sang for my father.* New York: Dramatists Play Service.

Andrews, E. J., Bennet, B. T., Clark, J. D., Houpt, K. A., Pascoe, P. J., Robinson, G. W., & Boyce, J. R. (1993). 1993 Report of the AVMA Panel on Euthanasia. *Journal of the American Veterinary Medical Association, 202,* 229–249.

Andrews, S., Williams, A., & Neil K. (1993). The mother-child relationship in the HIV-1 positive family. *Image: Journal of Nursing Scholarship, 25,* 193–198.

Anschuetz, B. L. (1990). *Bereavement counseling group for adolescents: Training manual.* Queensville, Ontario, Canada: Author

Anthony, S. (1939). A study of the development of the concept of death [abstract]. *British Journal of Educational Psychology, 9,* 276–277.

Anthony, S. (1940). *The child's discovery of death.* New York: Harcourt, Brace.

Anthony, S. (1972). *The discovery of death in childhood and after* (rev. ed.). New York: Basic Books.

Anthony, Z., & Bhana, K. (1988). An exploratory study of Muslim girls' understanding of death. *Omega, 19,* 215–227.

Apter, A., Orvaschel, H., Laseg, M., Moses, T., & Tyano, S. (1989). Psychometric properties of K-SADS-P in Israeli adolescent inpatient population. *Journal of the American Academy of Child and Adolescent Psychiatry, 28,* 61–65.

Arena, C., Hermann, J., & Hoffman, T. (1984). Helping children deal with the death of a classmate: A crisis intervention model. *Elementary School Guidance & Counseling, 19,* 107–115.

Armstrong-Dailey, A., & Goltzer, S. Z. (Eds.). (1993). *Hospice care for children.* New York: Oxford University Press.

Armsworth, M. W., & Holaday, M. (1993). The effects of psychological trauma on children and adolescents. *Journal of Counseling & Development, 72,* 49–56.

Arnold, J. H., & Gemma, P. B. (1984). *A child dies: A portrait of family grief* (2nd ed.). Philadelphia: Charles Press.

Arthur, B., & Kemme, M. L. (1964). Bereavement in childhood. *Journal of Child Psychology and Psychiatry, 5,* 37–49.

Asarnow, J. R. (1992). Suicidal ideation and attempts during middle childhood: Associations with perceived family stress and depression among child psychiatric inpatients. *Journal of Clinical Child Psychology, 21,* 35–40.

Asarnow, J. R., & Carlson, G. (1988). Suicide attempts in preadolescent child psychiatry inpatients. *Suicide and Life-Threatening Behavior, 18,* 129–136.

Asarnow, J. R., Carlson, G. A., & Guthrie, D. (1987). Coping strategies, self-perceptions, hopelessness, and perceived family environments in depressed and suicidal children. *Journal of Consulting and Clinical Psychology, 55,* 361–366.

Asarnow, J. R., & Guthrie, D. (1989). Suicidal behavior, depression, and hopelessness in child psychiatric inpatients: A replication and extension. *Journal of Clinical Child Psychology, 18,* 129–136.

Asher, S. R., & Coie, J. D. (1990). *Peer rejection in childhood.* Cambridge, MA: Cambridge University Press.

Attig, T. (1991). The importance of conceiving of grief as an active process. *Death Studies, 15,* 385–393.

Atwood, V. A. (1984). Children's concepts of death: A descriptive study. *Child Study Journal, 14,* 11–29.

Babensee, B. A., & Pequette, J. R. (1982). *Perspectives on loss: A manual for educators.* Evergreen, CO: Authors (P.O. Box 1352).

Baker, J. E. (in press). Helping the parents of the bereaved child: Improving the family environment. In C. R. Figley, B. E. Bride, & N. Mazza (Eds.), *Death and trauma: The traumatology of surviving.* Washington, DC: Taylor & Francis.

Baker, J. E., Sedney, M. A., & Gross, E. (1992). Psychological tasks for bereaved children. *American Journal of Orthopsychiatry, 62,* 105–116.

Baltes, P. B., Reese, H. W., & Lipsitt, L. P. (1980). Life-span developmental psychology. *Annual Review of Psychology, 31,* 65–110.

Beauchamp, N. W. (1974). The young child's perception of death. Doctoral dissertation, Purdue University. *Dissertation Abstracts International, 35,* 3288A.

Beck, A. T., Kovacs, M., & Weissman, M. (1979). Assessment of suicide ideation: The Scale for Suicide Ideation. *Journal of Consulting and Clinical Psychology, 47,* 343–352.

Becker, E. (1973). *The denial of death.* New York: Free Press.

Berk, L. E. (1991). *Child development.* Boston: Allyn & Bacon.

Berlinsky, E. B., & Biller, H. B. (1982). *Parental death and psychological development.* Lexington, MA: D. C. Heath.

Berndt, T. J. (1983). Social cognition, social behavior, and children's friendships. In E. T. Higgins, D. N. Ruble, & W. W. Hartup (Eds.), *Social cognition and social development: A sociocultural perspective* (pp. 158–192). Cambridge, MA: Cambridge University Press.

Berndt, T. J. (1986). Children's comments about their friendships. In M. Perlmutter (Ed.), *Cognitive perspectives on children's social, and behavioral development: Minnesota Symposia on Child Psychology* (Vol. 18, pp. 189–212). Hillsdale, NJ: Erlbaum.

Berndt, T. J., & Perry, T. B. (1986). Children's perceptions of friendships as supportive relationships. *Developmental Psychology, 22,* 640–648.

Bertoia, J., & Allan, J. (1988). School management of the bereaved child. *Elementary School Guidance & Counseling, 23,* 30–38.

Berzonsky, M. D. (1987). A preliminary investigation of children's conceptions of life and death. *Merrill Palmer Quarterly, 33,* 505–513.

Bettes, B. A., & Walker, E. W. (1986). Symptoms associated with suicidal behavior in childhood and adolescence. *Journal of Abnormal Child Psychology, 14,* 591–604.

Betz, C. (1985). Helping children cope with the death of a sibling. *Child Care Newsletter, 3*(2).

Betz, C. (1987). Death, dying and bereavement: A review of the literature, 1970–1985. In T. Krulik, B. Holaday, & I. M. Martinson (Eds.), *The child and family facing life-threatening illness* (pp. 32–49). New York: J. B. Lippincott.

Bilu, Y. (1989). The other as a nightmare: The Israeli-Arab encounter as reflected in children's dreams in Israel and the West Bank. *Political Psychology, 10,* 365–387.

Binger, C. M. (1973). Childhood leukemia: Emotional impact on siblings. In E. J. Anthony & C. Koupernik (Eds.), *The child in his family: The impact of disease and death* (Vol. 2, pp. 195–209). New York: Wiley.

Binger, C. M., Ablin, A. T., Feuerstein, R. C., Kushner, J. H., Zoger, S., & Mikkelsen, C. (1969). Childhood leukemia: Emotional impact on patient and family. *New England Journal of Medicine, 280,* 414–418.

Black, C. F. P. (1979). Young children's understandings about death as perceived by parents, teachers, and a recorder. Doctoral dissertation, Texas Woman's University. *Dissertation Abstracts International, 40,* 157B.

Blinder, B. (1972). Sibling death in childhood. *Child Psychiatry and Human Development, 2,* 169–175.

Bluebond-Langner, M. (1978). *The private worlds of dying children.* Princeton: Princeton University Press.

Bluebond-Langner, M. (1989). Worlds of dying children and their well siblings. *Death Studies, 13,* 1–16.

Bluebond-Langner, M. (1991). Living with cystic fibrosis: The well sibling's perspective. *Medical Anthropology Quarterly, 5*(2), 133–152.

Blum, A. H. (1976). Children's conceptions of death and an after-life. Doctoral dissertation, State University of New York at Buffalo. *Dissertation Abstracts International, 36,* 5248B.

Blume, J. (1981). *Tiger eyes.* Scarsdale, NY: Bradbury.

Blumenthal, S. J., & Kupfer, D. J. (1988). Overview of early detection and treatment strategies for suicidal behavior in young people. *Journal of Youth and Adolescence, 17,* 1–23.

Bolduc, J. (1972). A developmental study of the relationship between experiences of death and age and development of the concept of death. Doctoral dissertation, Columbia University. *Dissertation Abstracts International, 33,* 2758A.

Bowen, M. (1976). Family reaction to death. In P. Guerin (Ed.), *Family therapy: Theory and practice* (pp. 335–348). New York: Gardner.

Bowlby, J. (1977). The making and breaking of affectional bonds: 1. Aetiology and psychopathology in the light of attachment theory. *British Journal of Psychiatry, 130,* 201–210, 421–431.

Bowlby, J. (1980). *Attachment and loss, Vol. 3: Loss—Sadness and depression.* New York: Basic Books.

Bowlby, J. (1982). *Attachment and loss, Vol. 1: Attachment* (2nd ed.). New York: Basic Books. (Original work published 1969)

Boyd, J. H., & Moscicki, E. K. (1986). Firearms and youth suicide. *American Journal of Public Health, 76,* 1240–1242.

Boyd-Franklin, N., Steiner, G. L., & Boland, M. G. (Eds.). (1995). *Children, families, and HIV/AIDS: Psychosocial and therapeutic issues.* New York: Guilford.

Brent, S. B., & Speece, M. W. (1993). "Adult" conceptualization of irreversibility: Implications for the development of the concept of death. *Death Studies, 17,* 203–224.

Brent, S. B., Speece, M. W., Lin, C., Dong, Q., & Yang, C. (in press). The development of the concept of death among Chinese and U.S. children 3–17 years of age: From binary to "fuzzy" concepts? *Omega.*

Brown, G. W., Harris, T. O., & Bifulco, A. (1986). Long term effects of early loss of parent. In M. Rutter, C. E. Izard, & P. Read (Eds.), *Depression in young people: Developmental and clinical perspectives* (pp. 251–297). New York: Guilford.

Brown, L., & Brown, M. (1986). *Dinosaurs divorce: A guide for changing families.* New York: Atlantic Monthly Press.

Brun, J. A. (1981). An investigation into the adolescent's conception of death. Doctoral dissertation, The Southern Baptist Theological Seminary. *Dissertation Abstracts International, 42,* 2518B.

Bryant, B. (1987, October). *Characterizing the family life and social-emotional development of children who are highly involved with pets.* Paper presented at the annual meeting of the Delta Society, Vancouver, Canada.

Bryant, B. (1990). The richness of the child-pet relationship: A consideration of both benefits and costs of pets to children. *Anthrozoos, 3,* 253–261.

Burr, C. K. (1985). Impact on the family of a chronically-ill child. In N. Hobbs & J. Perrin (Eds.), *Issues in the care of children with chronic illness* (pp. 24–40). San Francisco: Jossey-Bass.

Burton, L. (1974). The family coping with a heavy treatment regimen. In L. Burton (Ed.), *Care of the child facing death* (pp. 74–86). London: Routledge & Kegan Paul.

Busher, P. (1995). Principal of Cleveland Elementary School, Stockton, California, personal communication, January 24 & 30.

Cain, A. C., & Cain, B. S. (1964). On replacing a child. *Journal of the American Academy of Child Psychiatry, 3,* 433–456.

Cain, A. C., Fast, I., & Erickson, M. E. (1964). Children's disturbed reactions to the death of a sibling. *American Journal of Orthopsychiatry, 34,* 741–752.

Cairns, R. B. (1966). Attachment behavior in mammals. *Psychological Review, 73,* 409–429.

Campbell, N. B., Milling, L., Laughlin, A., & Bush, E. (1993). The psychosocial climate of families with suicidal pre-adolescent children. *American Journal of Psychiatry, 63,* 142–145.

Canda, E. (1989). Religious content in social work education: A comparative approach. *Journal of Social Work Education, 25*, 36–45.

Canda, E., & Phaobtong, T. (1992). Buddhism as a support system for Southeast Asian refugees. *Social Work, 37*, 61–66.

Candy-Gibbs, S. E., Sharp, K. C., & Petrun, C. J. (1985). The effects of age, object, and cultural/religious background on children's concepts of death. *Omega, 15*, 329–346.

Caplan, G. (1964). *Principles of preventive psychiatry.* New York: Basic Books.

Carey, S. (1985). *Conceptual changes in childhood.* Cambridge, MA: MIT Press.

Carlson, G. A., Asarnow, J. R., & Orbach, I. (1987). Developmental aspects of suicidal behavior in children: I. *Journal of the American Academy of Child and Adolescent Psychiatry, 26*, 186–192.

Carson, U. (1984). Teachable moments occasioned by "small deaths." In H. Wass & C. A. Corr (Eds.), *Childhood and death* (pp. 315–343). Washington, DC: Hemisphere.

Carter, B., & McGoldrick, M. (Eds.) (1988). *The changing family life cycle: A framework for family therapy* (2nd ed.). New York: Gardner.

Cates, J. A., Graham, L. L., Boeglin, D., & Tielker, S. (1990). The effect of AIDS on the family system. *Families in Society, 71*, 195–201.

Centers for Disease Control. (1988). Recommendations for the community plan for the prevention and containment of suicide clusters. *Morbidity and Mortality Weekly Report, 37*(Suppl. 5–6). Washington, DC: Author.

Centers for Disease Control and Prevention. (1992). *HIV/AIDS surveillance report, 4*(1). Atlanta: Centers for Disease Control and Prevention.

Centers for Disease Control and Prevention. (1994). *HIV/AIDS surveillance report, 6*(2). Atlanta: Centers for Disease Control and Prevention.

Childers, P., & Wimmer, M. (1971). The concept of death in early childhood. *Child Development, 42*, 1299–1301.

Chodoff, P. (1985). Psychiatric aspects of the Nazi persecutions. In S. Arieti (Ed.), *American handbook of psychiatry.* New York: Basic Books.

Christ, G. H., & Wiener, L. S. (1985). Psychosocial issues in AIDS. In V. T. DeVita, S. Hellman, & S. Rosenberg (Eds.), *AIDS: Etiology, diagnosis, treatment, and prevention* (pp. 275–297). Philadelphia: J. B. Lippincott.

Cicirelli, V. (1980). Sibling relationships in adulthood: A lifespan perspective. In L. Poon (Ed.), *Aging in the 1980s: Psychological Issues* (pp. 455–462). Washington, DC: American Psychological Association.

Cicirelli, V. (1982). Sibling influence throughout the lifespan. In M. Lamb & B. Sutton-Smith (Eds.), *Sibling relationships* (pp. 267–284). Hillsdale, NJ: Erlbaum.

Cleaver, V., & Cleaver, B. (1970). *Grover.* Philadelphia: J. B. Lippincott.

Clifton, L. (1983). *Everett Anderson's goodbye.* New York: Henry Holt.

Clunies-Ross, C., & Lansdown, R. (1988). Concepts of death, illness and isolation found in children with leukaemia. *Child: Care, Health & Development, 14,* 373–386.

Cole, D. A. (1988). Hopelessness, social desirability, depression, and parasuicide in two college student samples. *Journal of Consulting and Clinical Psychology, 56,* 131–136.

Coleman, F. W., & Coleman, W. A. (1984). Helping siblings and other peers cope with dying. In H. Wass & C. A. Corr (Eds.), *Childhood and death* (pp. 129–150). Washington, DC: Hemisphere.

Coles, R. (1990). *The spiritual life of children.* Boston: Houghton Mifflin.

Cook, A. S., & Dworkin, D. S. (1992). *Helping the bereaved: Therapeutic interventions for children, adolescents, and adults.* New York: Basic Books.

Cook, A. S., & Oltjenbruns, K. A. (1989). *Dying and grieving: Lifespan and family perspectives.* New York: Holt, Rinehart, & Winston.

Corr, C. A. (1991). Should young children attend funerals? What constitutes reliable advice? *Thanatos, 16*(4), 19–21.

Corr, C. A. (1992a). A task-based approach to coping with dying. *Omega, 24,* 81–94.

Corr, C. A. (1992b, March 3). *Support groups for bereaved adolescents: Principles and purposes.* Paper presented at the meeting of the Association for Death Education and Counseling, Boston.

Corr, C. A. (1993a). Children's literature on death. In A. Armstrong-Dailey & S. Z. Goltzer (Eds.), *Hospice care for children* (pp. 266–284). New York: Oxford University Press.

Corr, C. A. (1993b). Coping with dying: Lessons that we should and should not learn from the work of Elisabeth Kübler-Ross. *Death Studies, 17,* 69–83.

Corr, C. A. (1995). A sampler of literature for young readers: Death, dying, and bereavement. In K. J. Doka (Ed.), *Children mourning, mourning children* (pp. 163–171). Washington, DC: Hospice Foundation of America.

Corr, C. A., & Balk, D. E. (Eds.). (1996). *Handbook of adolescent death and bereavement.* New York: Springer Publishing Co.

Corr, C. A., & Corr, D. M. (Eds.). (1985). *Hospice approaches to pediatric care.* New York: Springer Publishing Co.

Corr, C. A., & Doka, K. J. (1994). Current models of death, dying, and bereavement. *Critical-Care Nursing Clinics of North America, 6,* 545–552.

Corr, C. A., Fuller, H. H., Barnickol, C. A., & Corr, D. M. (Eds.). (1991). *Sudden Infant Death Syndrome: Who can help and how.* New York: Springer Publishing Co.

Corr, C. A., and the Staff of The Dougy Center. (1991). Support for grieving children: The Dougy Center and the hospice philosophy. *The American Journal of Hospice and Palliative Care, 8*(4), 23–27.

Costanzo, P. R. (1970). Conformity development as a function of self-blame. *Journal of Personality and Social Psychology, 14,* 366–374.

Cotton, C. R., Peters, D. K., & Range, L. M. (1995). Psychometric proper-
    ties of the Suicidal Behaviors Questionnaire. *Death Studies, 19,* 391–397.
Cotton, C. R., & Range, L. M. (1990). Children's death concepts: Relation-
    ship to cognitive functioning, age, experience with death, fear of
    death, and hopelessness. *Journal of Clinical Child Psychology, 19,* 123–
    127.
Cotton, C. R., & Range, L. M. (1993). Suicidality, hopelessness, and atti-
    tudes toward life and death in children. *Death Studies, 17,* 185–191.
Crenshaw, D. (1991). *Bereavement: Counseling the grieving throughout the life
    cycle.* New York: Continuum.
Cullinan, A. L. (1990). Teachers' death anxiety, ability to cope with death,
    and perceived ability to aid bereaved students. *Death Studies, 14,* 147–
    160.
Cytryn, L., Moore, P. V., & Robinson, M. (1973). Psychological adjustment
    of children with cystic fibrosis. In E. J. Anthony & C. Koupernik (Eds.),
    The child in his family: The impact of disease and death (Vol. 2, pp. 37–47).
    New York: Wiley.
Damon, W. (1977). *The social world of the child.* San Francisco: Jossey-Bass.
Dane, B. O. (1989). New beginnings for AIDS patients. *Social Casework, 70,*
    305–309.
Dane, B. O. (1993). Mourning in secret: How youngsters experience a fam-
    ily death from AIDS. In C. Levine (Ed.), *A death in the family: Orphans of
    the HIV epidemic* (pp. 60–68). New York: United Hospital Fund of New
    York.
Dane, B. O., & Levine, C. (Eds.). (1994). *AIDS and the new orphans: Coping
    with death.* Westport, CT: Auburn House.
Dane, B. O., & Miller, S. (1992). *AIDS: Intervening with hidden grievers.* West-
    port, CT: Auburn House.
Danieli, Y. (1985). The treatment and prevention of long-term effects and
    intergenerational transmission of victimization: A lesson from Holo-
    caust survivors and their children. In C. Figley (Ed.), *Trauma and its
    wake* (pp. 295–313). New York: Brunner/Mazel.
Darmani, L. (1991). *Grief child.* Illinois: Lion.
Davids, J. (1993). The reaction of an early latency boy to the sudden death
    of his baby brother. *Psychoanalytic Study of the Child, 48,* 277–292.
Davidson, M. W., & Wagner, W. G. (1994, March). *"No-suicide" agreements/
    contracts: Clinicians' attitudes and the standard of care.* Poster at South-
    eastern Psychological Association, New Orleans, LA.
Davies, E. M. B. (1983). *Behavioral responses of children to a sibling's death.* Un-
    published doctoral dissertation. University of Washington, Seattle, WA.
Davies, B. (1985, April 9–11). *Predictors of behavior outcomes in bereaved sib-
    lings.* Paper presented at the 10th National Research Conference:
    Nursing Research, "Science for Quality Care," Toronto, Ontario.

Davies, B. (1988a). Shared life space and sibling bereavement responses. *Cancer Nursing, 11,* 339–347.

Davies, B. (1988b). The family environment in bereaved families and its relationship to surviving sibling behavior. *Children's Health Care, 17*(1), 22–31.

Davies, B. (1995). Long-term effects of siblings death in childhood. In D. W. Adams & E. J. Deveau (Eds.), *Beyond the innocence of childhood: Helping children and adolescents cope with death, and bereavement* (Vol. 3, pp. 89–98). Amityville, NY: Baywood.

Davies, D. (1991). Intervention with male toddlers who have witnessed parental violence. *Families in Society: The Journal of Contemporary Human Services, 72,* 515–524.

Dawes, A., Tredoux, C., & Feinstein, A. (1989). Political violence in South Africa: Some effects on children of the violent destruction of their community. *International Journal of Mental Health, 18*(2), 16–43.

DeFrain, J., Ernst, L., Jakub, D., & Taylor, J. (1991). *Sudden infant death: Enduring the loss.* Lexington, MA: Lexington Books.

Demmin, H. S. (1986). Death concept formation. Doctoral dissertation, Texas Tech University. *Dissertation Abstracts International, 47,* 2610B.

Denenberg, R. (1995). Special concerns for women with HIV and AIDS. In W. Odets & M. Shernoff (Eds.), *The second decade of AIDS: A mental health practice handbook* (pp. 115–135). New York: Hatherleigh Press.

Derry, S. M. (1979). *An empirical investigation of the concept of death in children.* Doctoral dissertation, University of Ottawa, Ottawa, Canada.

Devereux, W. C. (1984). Children's understanding of the physical realities of death. Doctoral dissertation, The University of North Dakota. *Dissertation Abstracts International, 44,* 3523B.

de Wilde, E. J., Kienhorst, I., Diekstra, R., & Wolters, W. (1992). The relationship between adolescent suicidal behavior and life events in childhood and adolescence. *American Journal of Psychiatry, 149,* 45–51.

Deykin, E. Y., Hsieh, C., Neela, J., & McNamarra, J. (1986). Adolescent suicidal and self-destructive behavior: Results of an intervention study. *Journal of Adolescent Health Care, 7,* 88–95.

Diamant, A. (1994, October). Special report: Media violence. *Parents Magazine,* pp. 40–41, 45.

Diamond, G. W. (1989). Developmental problems in children with HIV infection. *Mental Retardation, 27,* 213–217.

Doka, K. J. (1982). The social organization of terminal care in the pediatric hospitals. *Omega, 12,* 345–354.

Doka, K. J. (Ed.). (1989). *Disenfranchised grief: Recognizing hidden sorrow.* Lexington, MA: Lexington Books.

Doka, K. J. (1993). *Living with life-threatening illness: A Guide for patients, their families, and caregivers.* Lexington, MA: Lexington Books.

Donders, J. (1993). Bereavement and mourning in pediatric rehabilitation settings. *Death Studies, 17,* 517–527.

Dudley, R. G. (1993). All alike but each one different: Orphans of the HIV epidemic. In C. Levine (Ed.), *A death in the family: Orphans of the HIV epidemic* (pp. 55–59). New York: United Hospital Fund of New York.

Dunn, J. (1993). *Young children's close relationships beyond attachment.* Newbury Park, CA: Sage.

Edelman, H. (1994). *Motherless daughters: The legacy of loss.* Reading, MA: Addison-Wesley.

Elizur, E., & Kaffman, M. (1982). Children's bereavement reactions following death of the father: II. *Journal of the American Academy of Child Psychiatry, 21,* 474–480.

Elizur, E., & Kaffman, M. (1983). Factors influencing the severity of childhood bereavement reactions. *American Journal of Orthopsychiatry, 53,* 668–676.

Emerson, R. W. (1970). In W. H. Gilman & J. E. Parsons (Eds.), *The journals and miscellaneous notebooks of Ralph Waldo Emerson* (Vol. 8, 1841–1843). Cambridge, MA: The Belknap Press of Harvard University Press.

Engel, B. A. (1981). Children's attitudes toward death. Doctoral dissertation, University of Florida. *Dissertation Abstracts International, 42,* 2571A.

Erikson, E. H. (1950). *Childhood and society.* New York: Norton.

Erikson, E. (1963). *Childhood and society* (2nd ed.). New York: Norton.

Erikson, E. (1968). *Identity: Youth and crisis.* New York: Norton.

Erikson, E. (1975). *Life history and the historical moment.* New York: Norton.

Eskow, K. (1980). The conceptions of children regarding death as assessed by the Eskow death conception test. Doctoral dissertation, Indiana State University. *Dissertation Abstracts International, 41,* 2296B.

Eth, S., & Pynoos, R. (1985a). Developmental perspectives on psychic trauma in childhood. In C. Figley (Ed.), *Trauma and its wake* (pp. 36–52). New York: Brunner/Mazel.

Eth, S., & Pynoos, R. (1985b). Interaction of trauma and grief in childhood. In S. Eth & R. Pynoos (Eds.), *Post-traumatic stress disorder in children* (pp. 171–186). Washington, DC: American Psychiatric Press.

Eth, S., & Pynoos, R. (1985c). *Post-traumatic stress disorder in children.* Washington, DC: American Psychiatric Press.

Famularo, R., Kinscherff, R., & Fenton, T. (1991). Posttraumatic stress disorder among children clinically diagnosed as borderline personality disorder. *The Journal of Nervous and Mental Disease, 179,* 428–431.

Fassler, J. (1971). *My grandpa died today.* New York: Human Sciences Press.

Fetsch, S. H. (1984). The 7- to 10-year-old child's conceptualization of death. *Oncology Nursing Forum, 11*(6), 52–56.

Figley, C. (1983). Catastrophes: An overview of family reactions. In C. Figley & H. Cubbin (Eds.), *Stress and the family, Vol. 2. Coping with catastrophes* (pp. 137–139). New York: Brunner/Mazel.

Figley, C. (Ed.). (1985). Introduction. In C. Figley (Ed.), *Trauma and its wake* (pp. xvii–xxvi). New York: Brunner/Mazel.

Fine, G. A. (1980). The natural history of pre-adolescent friendship groups. In H. C. Foot, A. J. Chapman, & J. R. Smith (Eds.), *Friendship and social relations in children* (pp. 293–320). Chichester, England: Wiley.

Fink, R. W. (1976). Death as conceptualized by adolescents. Doctoral dissertation, University of Maryland College Park. *Dissertation Abstracts International, 37*, 3046B.

Fitzgerald, H. (1992). *The grieving child: A parent's guide.* New York: Simon & Schuster.

Flavell, J. H. (1985). *Cognitive development* (2nd ed.). Englewood Cliffs, NJ: Prentice Hall.

Fleming, S. J. (1985). Children's grief: Individual and family dynamics. In C. A. Corr & D. M. Corr (Eds.), *Hospice approaches to pediatric care* (pp. 197–218). New York: Springer Publishing Co.

Fleming, S. J., & Adolph, R. (1986). Helping bereaved adolescents: Needs and responses. In C. A. Corr & J. N. McNeil (Eds.), *Adolescence and death* (pp. 97–118). New York: Springer Publishing Co.

Fleming, S., & Balmer, L. (1991). Group intervention with bereaved children. In D. Papadatou & C. Papadatos (Eds.), *Children and death* (pp. 105–124). Washington, DC: Hemisphere.

Florian, V. (1985). Children's concept of death: An empirical study of a cognitive and environmental approach. *Death Studies, 9*, 133–141.

Florian, V., & Kravetz, S. (1985). Children's concepts of death: A cross-cultural comparison among Muslims, Druze, Christians, and Jews in Israel. *Journal of Cross Cultural Psychology, 16*, 174–189.

Fogle, B. (1981). Attachment—euthanasia—grieving. In B. Fogle (Ed.), *Interrelations between people and pets* (pp. 331–343). Springfield, IL: Charles C Thomas.

Foster, Z. (1988). The treatment of people with AIDS: Psychosocial considerations. In I. B. Corless & M. Pittman-Lindemann (Eds.), *AIDS: Principles, practice and politics* (pp. 33–45). Washington, DC: Hemisphere.

Fox, S. S. (1985). *Good grief: Helping groups of children when a friend dies.* Boston: New England Association for the Education of Young Children.

Fox, S. S. (1988, August). Helping child deal with death teaches valuable skills. *The Psychiatric Times,* pp. 10–11.

Fremouw, W. J., Perczel, M., & Ellis, T. E. (1990). *Suicide risk: Assessment and response guidelines.* New York: Pergamon.

Freud, A. (1966). *Ego and mechanisms of defense.* New York: International Universities Press.

Freud, S. (1974). Mourning and melancholia. In L. Strachey (Ed. & Trans.), *The standard edition of the complete psychological works of Sigmund Freud* (Vol. 14. London: Hogarth Press. (Original work published 1917)

Friedland, G., Kahl, P., Saltzman, B., Rogers, M., Feiner, C., Mayers, M., Schable, C., & Klein, R. S. (1990). Additional evidence for lack of transmission of HIV infection by close interpersonal (casual) contact. *AIDS, 4*, 639–644.

Friedman, R. C., Corn, R., Hurt, W. S., Fibel, B., Schulick, J., & Swirsky, S. (1984). Family history of illness in the seriously suicidal adolescent: A life-cycle approach. *American Journal of Orthopsychiatry, 54*, 390–397.

Fulton, R. (1988). Death and the funeral in contemporary society. In H. Wass (Ed.), *Dying: Facing the facts* (pp. 257–277). Washington, DC: Hemisphere.

Furman, E. (1974). *A child's parent dies: Studies in childhood bereavement.* New Haven: Yale University Press.

Furman, E. (1984). Children's patterns in mourning the death of a loved one. In H. Wass & C. A. Corr (Eds.), *Childhood and death* (pp. 185–203). Washington, DC: Hemisphere.

Furman, R. A. (1964a). Death and the young child: Some preliminary considerations. *Psychoanalytic Study of the Child, 19*, 321–333.

Furman, R. A. (1964b). The death of a 6 year old's mother during his analysis. *Psychoanalytic Study of the Child, 19*, 377–397.

Furman, R. A. (1973). A child's capacity for mourning. In E. J. Anthony & C. Koupernik (Eds.). *The child in his family: The impact of disease and death* (Vol. 2, pp. 225–231). New York: Wiley.

Furman, W., & Bierman, K. L. (1984). Children's conceptions of friendship: A multimethod study of developmental changes. *Developmental Psychology, 20*, 925–931.

Gage, G., & Holcomb, R. (1991). Couples' perceptions of the stressfulness of the death of the family pet. *Family Relations, 40*, 103–105.

Garbarino, J., Kostelny, K., & Dubrow, N. (1991). What children can tell us about living in danger. *American Psychologist, 46*, 376–383.

Gardner, R. A. (1979). Death of a parent. In J. D. Noshpitz (Ed.), *Basic handbook of child psychiatry*, 4 vols. (Vol. 4, pp. 270–283). New York: Basic Books.

Garfinkel, B. D., Froese, A., & Hood, J. (1982). Suicide attempts in children and adolescents. *American Journal of Psychiatry, 139*, 1257–1261.

Garrison, C., Lewinsohn, P. Marsteller, F., Langhinrichsen, J., & Lann, I. (1991). The assessment of suicidal behavior in adolescents. *Suicide and Life-Threatening Behavior, 21*, 217–330.

Gartley, W., & Bernasconi, M. (1967). The concept of death in children. *Journal of Genetic Psychology, 110*, 71–85.

Gellman, R., & Baillargeon, R. (1983). A review of some Piagetian concepts. In J. H. Flavell & E. M. Markman (Eds.), *Carmichael's manual of child psychology: Cognitive development* (pp. 167–230). New York: Wiley.

Gibbons, M. B. (1992). A child dies, a child survives: The impact of sibling loss. *Journal of Pediatric Health Care, 6*, 65–72.

Gleser, G., Green, B., & Wignet, C. (1981). *Buffalo Creek revisited: Prolonged psychosocial effects of disaster.* New York: Simon & Schuster.

Glick, I. O., Weiss, R. S., & Parkes, C. M. (1974). *The first year of bereavement.* New York: Wiley.

Goffman, E. (1963). *Stigma: Notes on the management of spoiled identity.* Upper Saddle River, NJ: Prentice Hall.

Gogan, J., Koocher, G., Foster, D., & O'Malley, J. (1977). Childhood cancer and siblings. *Health and Social Work, 2,* 42–57.

Goldstone, R., & Gamble, W. (1969). On borrowed time: Observation on children with implanted cardiac pacemakers and their families. *American Journal of Psychiatry, 126,* 104.

Goodman, R. F. (1990). Development of the concept of death in children: The cognitive and affective components. Doctoral dissertation, Adelphi University, The Institute of Advanced Psychological Studies. *Dissertation Abstracts International, 51,* 452B.

Goodwin, J. (1981). Suicide attempts in sexual abuse victims and their mothers. *Child Abuse and Neglect, 5,* 217–221.

Goodwin, J. (1985). Post-traumatic symptoms in incest victims. In S. Eth & R. Pynoos (Eds.), *Post-traumatic stress disorder in children* (pp. 157–168). Washington, DC: American Psychiatric Press.

Gordon, A. K. (1986). The tattered cloak of immortality. In C. A. Corr & J. N. McNeil (Eds.), *Adolescence and death* (pp. 16–31). New York: Springer Publishing Co.

Gorman, M. C. T. (1983). Children's concepts of death and animistic thinking. Doctoral dissertation, York University. *Dissertation Abstracts International, 44,* 2540B.

Gould, M. S., & Shaffer, D. (1986). The impact of suicide in television movies: Evidence of imitation. *New England Journal of Medicine, 315,* 690–694.

Gould, M. S., Shaffer, D., & Kleinman, M. (1988). The impact of suicide in television movies: Replication and commentary. *Suicide and Life-Threatening Behavior, 18,* 90–99.

Green, A. (1993). Childhood sexual and physical abuse. In J. P. Wilson & B. Raphael (Eds.), *International handbook of traumatic stress syndromes* (pp. 577–592). New York: Plenum Press.

Green, G., Wilson, J., & Lindy, J. (1985). Conceptualizing post-traumatic stress disorders: A psychosocial framework. In C. Figley (Ed.), *Trauma and its wake* (pp. 53–69). New York: Brunner/Mazel.

Grollman, E. A. (Ed.). (1967). *Explaining death to children.* Boston: Beacon Press.

Grollman, E. A. (1990). *Talking about death: A dialogue between parent and child* (3rd ed.). Boston: Beacon Press.

Grollman, E. A. (Ed.). (1995). *Bereaved children and teens: A support guide for parents and professionals.* Boston: Beacon Press.

Gullo, S., & Plimpton, G. (1985). On understanding and coping with death during childhood. In S. Gullo, P. Patterson, J. Schowalter, M. Tallner, A. Kutscher, & P. Brachman (Eds.), *Death and children: A guide for educating parents and caregivers* (pp. 79–92). Dobbs Ferry, NY: Tappen Press.

Gunther, J. (1949). *Death be not proud: A memoir.* New York: Harper & Row.

Guy, T. (1993). Exploratory study of elementary-aged children's conceptions of death through the use of story. *Death Studies, 17,* 27–54.

Gyulay, J. (1978). *The dying child.* New York: McGraw-Hill.

Haasl, B., & Marnocha, J. (1990). *Bereavement support group program for children: Leader manual.* Muncie, IN: Accelerated Development.

Hafen, B. Q., & Frandsen, K. J. (1983). *Faces of death.* Englewood, CO: Morton.

Hagey, S. L. (1991). A developmental study of terminally-ill, chronically-ill and physically-healthy children's concern with and cognitive evaluation of death. Doctoral dissertation, The University of Texas at Austin. *Dissertation Abstracts International, 51,* 3363A.

Haley, J. (1976). *Problem solving therapy.* San Francisco: Jossey-Bass.

Hall, E. T. (1966). *The hidden dimension.* Garden City, NY: Doubleday.

Hansen, Y. F. (1973). Development of the concept of death: Cognitive aspects. Doctoral dissertation, California School of Professional Psychology—Los Angeles. *Dissertation Abstracts International, 34,* 853B.

Hargrove, E. L. (1979). An exploratory study of children's ideas about death, with a view toward developing an explanatory model. Doctoral dissertation, University of North Texas. *Dissertation Abstracts International, 40,* 1688A.

Harkness, L. L. (1993). Transgenerational transmission of war-related trauma. In J. P. Wilson & B. Raphael (Eds.), *International handbook of traumatic stress syndromes* (pp. 635–643). New York: Plenum Press.

Hart, L. A., Hart, B. L., & Mader, B. (1990). Humane euthanasia and companion animal death: Caring for the animal, the client, and the veterinarian. Special commentary. *Journal of the American Veterinary Medical Association, 197,* 1292–1299.

Hartup, W. W. (1986). On relationships and development. In W. W. Hartup & Z. Rubin (Eds.), *Relationships and development* (pp. 1–26). Hillsdale, NJ: Erlbaum.

Hazell, P., & Lewin, T. (1993). Postvention following adolescent suicide. *Suicide and Life-Threatening Behavior, 23,* 101–109.

Heegaard, M. (1992). *Facilitator guide for drawing out feelings.* Minneapolis: Woodland Press.

Herman, J., Perry, J. C., & van der Kolk, B. A. (1989). Childhood trauma in borderline personality disorder. *American Journal of Psychiatry, 22,* 231–237.

Herz Brown, F. (1988). The impact of death and serious illness on the family life cycle. In B. Carter & M. McGoldrick (Eds.), *The changing family life cycle: A framework for family therapy* (2nd ed.; pp. 457–482). New York: Gardner.

Herz Brown, F. (1991). *Reweaving the family tapestry.* New York: Norton.

Hewett, J. (1980). *After suicide.* Philadelphia: Westminster Press.

Hickey, L. O. (1993). Death of a counselor: A bereavement group for junior high school students. In N. B. Webb (Ed.), *Helping bereaved children: A handbook for practitioners* (pp. 239–266). New York: Guilford.

Hilgard, J. (1969). Depressive and psychotic states as anniversaries to sibling death in childhood. *International Psychiatry Clinics, 6,* 197–211.

Hirsch, D. A., & Enlow, R. W. (1984). The effects of the acquired immune deficiency syndrome on gay life style and the gay individual. *Annals of the New York Academy of Sciences, 437,* 273–282.

Hobbs, N., Perrin, J., & Irays, H. (1985). *Chronically-ill children and their families.* San Francisco: Jossey-Bass.

Hoff, L. (1984). *People in crisis* (2nd ed.). Reading, MA: Addison-Wesley.

Hoffman, L. (1988). The family life cycle and discontinuous change. In B. Carter & M. McGoldrick (Eds.), *The changing family life cycle: A framework for family therapy* (2nd ed., pp. 91–105). New York: Gardner.

Hoffman, S. I., & Strauss, S. (1985). The development of children's concepts of death. *Death Studies, 9,* 469–482.

Hollingsworth, C., & Pasnau, R. (1977). Parents' reactions to the death of their child. In C. Hollingsworth & R. Pasnau (Eds.), *The family in mourning: A guide for health professionals* (pp. 63–67). New York: Grune and Stratton.

Holmes, T. H., & Rahe, R. H. (1967). The social readjustment scale. *Journal of Psychosomatic Research, 39,* 413–431.

Hornblum, J. N. (1978). Death concepts in childhood and their relationship to concepts of time and conservation. Doctoral dissertation, Temple University. *Dissertation Abstracts International, 39,* 2146A.

Horowitz, M. (1976). *Stress response syndromes.* New York: Jason Aronson.

Horowitz, M. (1979). Psychological response to serious life events. In V. Hamilton & D. Warburton (Eds.), *Human stress and cognition* (pp. 542–545). New York: Wiley.

Horowitz, M., & Kaltreider, N. (1980). Brief treatment of post-traumatic stress disorders. *New Directions for Mental Health Services, 6,* 67–79.

Hui, C., Chan, I. S., & Chan, J. (1989). Death cognition among Chinese teenagers: Beliefs about consequences of death. *Journal of Research in Personality, 23,* 99–117.

Hurst, P. E. (1980). A comparison of death concept development in emotionally disturbed and non-disturbed children. Doctoral dissertation, University of Toronto. *Dissertation Abstracts International, 41,* 2516A.

Hutman, S. (1990, August). The current status of pediatric AIDS: Diagnosis, treatment, prevention, and research. *AIDS Patient Care,* pp. 7–11.

Ibrahim, Y. M. (1992, August 4). Iraqis left coarse scars on the psyche of Kuwait. *The New York Times,* p. A3.

Imber-Black, E. (1993). Ghosts in the therapy room. *The Family Therapy Networker,* 17(3), 18–29.

Jaffe, P., Wolfe, D., Wilson, S. K., & Zak, L. (1986). Family violence and child adjustment: A comparative analysis of girls and boys behavioral symptoms. *American Journal of Psychiatry, 143,* 74–76.

Janoff-Bulman, R. (1985). The aftermath of victimization: Rebuilding shattered assumptions. In C. Figley (Ed.), *Trauma and its wake* (pp. 15–35). New York: Brunner/Mazel.

Jay, S. M., Green, V., Johnson, S., Caldwell, S., & Nitschke, R. (1987). Differences in death concepts between children with cancer and physically healthy children. *Journal of Clinical Child Psychology, 16,* 301–306.

Jenkins, R. A., & Cavanaugh, J. C. (1985). Examining the relationship between the development of the concept of death and overall cognitive development. *Omega, 16,* 193–199.

Jesse, P. O., Strickland, M. P., & Ladewig, B. H. (1992). The after effects of a hostage situation on children's behavior. *American Journal of Orthopsychiatry, 62,* 309–324.

Jewett, C. L. (1982). *Helping children cope with separation and loss.* Harvard, MA: Harvard Common Press.

Johnson, K. (1989). *Trauma in the lives of children.* Claremont, CA: Hunter House.

Johnson, M. K., & Foley, M. A. (1984). Differentiating fact from fantasy: The reliability of children's memory. *Journal of Social Issues, 40,* 33–50.

Kaffman, M., & Elizur, E. (1979). Children's bereavement reactions following the death of the father. *International Journal of Family Therapy, 1,* 203–229.

Kalafat, J., & Elias, M. (1994). An evaluation of a school-based suicide awareness intervention. *Suicide and Life-Threatening Behavior, 24,* 224–233.

Kalmbach, C. A. (1979). The relationship between the cognitive level of the child and his/her conception of death. Doctoral dissertation, The Florida State University. *Dissertation Abstracts International, 39,* 5518B.

Kammeyer, K. (1967). Birth order as a research variable. *Social Forces, 46,* 71–80.

Kane, B. (1979). Children's concepts of death. *Journal of Genetic Psychology, 134,* 141–153.

Kaplan, C. (1988). The biological children of foster parents in the foster family. *Child and Adolescent Social Work, 5*(4), 281–299.

Kaplan, D. M., Grobstein, R., & Smith, A. (1976). Predicting the impact of severe illness in families. *Health and Social Work, 1,* 71–82.

Karpas, R. J. (1986). Concept of death and suicidal behavior in children and adolescents. Doctoral dissertation, Pace University. *Dissertation Abstracts International, 47,* 3136B.

Karthas, N. P., & Chanock, S. (1990). Clinical management of HIV infection in infants and children. *Family and Community Health, 13*(2), 8–20.

Kastenbaum, R. (1967). The child's understanding of death: How does it develop? In E. A. Grollman (Ed.), *Explaining death to children* (pp. 89–109). Boston: Beacon Press.

Kastenbaum, R. (1992). *The psychology of death* (2nd ed.). New York: Springer.

Katzenbach, J. (1986). *The traveler.* New York: G. P. Putnam's Sons.

Kazdin, A. E. (1985). *Suicide assessment battery.* Unpublished test, University of Pittsburgh School of Medicine.

Kazdin, A. E., French, N. H., Unis, A. S., Esveldt-Dawson, K., & Sherick, R. B. (1983). Hopelessness, depression, and suicidal intent among psychiatrically disturbed inpatient children. *Journal of Consulting and Clinical Psychology, 51,* 504–510.

Kazdin, A. E., Rodgers, A., & Colbus, D. (1986). The Hopelessness Scale for Children: Psychometric characteristics and concurrent validity. *Journal of Consulting and Clinical Psychology, 54,* 241–245.

Kellermann, A. L., Frederick, P. R., Somes, G., Reay, D. T., Francisco, J., Banton, J. G., Prodzinski, J., Fligner, C., & Hackman, B. B. (1992). Suicide in the home in relation to gun ownership. *New England Journal of Medicine, 327,* 467–472.

Kidd, A. H., & Kidd, R. M. (1985). children's attitudes towards their pets. *Psychological Reports, 57,* 15–31.

Kienhorst, C. W. M., Wolters, W. H. G., Diekstra, R. F. W., & Otte, E. (1987). A study of the frequency of suicidal behavior in children aged 5 to 14. *Journal of Child Psychology and Psychiatry, 28,* 153–165.

Klass, D. (1988). *Parental grief: Solace and resolution.* New York: Springer Publishing Co.

Klatt, H. (1991). In search of a mature concept of death. *Death Studies, 15,* 177–187.

Kleck, G. (1988). Miscounting suicides. *Suicide and Life-Threatening Behavior, 13,* 219–236.

Kliman, G. (1968). *Psychological emergencies of childhood.* New York: Grune & Stratton.

Klingman, A. (1985). Responding to a bereaved classmate: Comparison of two strategies for death education in the classroom. *Death Studies, 9,* 449–454.

Kochanek, K. D., & Hudson, B. L. (1994). Advance report of final mortality statistics, 1992. *Monthly Vital Statistics Report, 43*(6)(Suppl). Hyattsville, MD: National Center for Health Statistics.

Kohly, M. (1994). Reported child abuse and neglect victims during the flood months of 1993. St. Louis, MO: Missouri Department of Social Services, Division of Family Services, Research and Development Unit.

Koocher, G. P. (1973). Childhood, death and cognitive development. *Developmental Psychology, 9,* 369–375.

Koocher, G. P. (1974). Talking with children about death. *American Journal of Orthopsychiatry, 44,* 404–411.

Koocher, G. P. (1983). Grief and loss in childhood. In C. E. Walker & M. C. Roberts (Eds.), *Handbook of clinical child psychology* (pp. 1273–1284). New York: Wiley.

Koocher, G. P., & O'Malley J. E. (1981). *The Damocles syndrome: Psychological consequences of surviving childhood cancer.* New York: McGraw-Hill.

Kosko, B., & Sartoru, I. (1993). Fuzzy logic. *Scientific American, 267,* 76–81.

Kosky, R. (1983). Childhood suicidal behavior. *Journal of Child Psychology and Psychiatry, 24,* 457–468.

Kosky, R., Silburn, S., & Zubrick, S. A. (1990). Are children and adolescents who have suicidal thoughts different from those who attempted suicide? *Journal of Nervous and Mental Disease, 178,* 38–43.

Kovacs, M. (1981). Rating scales to assess depression in school aged children. *Acta Paedopsychiatrica, 46,* 305–315.

Kovacs, M., Goldston, D., & Gatsonis, C. (1993). Suicidal behavior and childhood-onset depressive disorders: A longitudinal investigation. *Journal of the American Academy of Child and Adolescent Psychiatry, 32,* 8–20.

Krasnow, J. E. (1993). The impact of experience on children's conceptions of death. Doctoral dissertation, State University of New York at Buffalo. *Dissertation Abstracts International, 53,* 4976B.

Krell, R., & Rabkin, L. (1979). The effects of sibling death on the surviving child: A family perspective. *Family Process, 18,* 471–477.

Krementz, J. (1981). *How it feels when a parent dies.* New York: Knopf.

Krupnick, J. L. (1984). Bereavement during childhood and adolescence. In M. Osterweis, F. Solomon, & M. Green (Eds.), *Bereavement: Reactions, consequences, and care* (pp. 99–141). Washington, DC: National Academy Press.

Labouvie-Vief, G., & Hakim-Larsen, J. (1989). Developmental shifts in adult thought. In S. Hunter & M. Sundel (Eds.), *Midlife myths: Issues, findings and practice implications* (pp. 69–96). Newbury Park, CA: Sage.

Lagoni, L., & Butler, C. (1994). Facilitating companion animal death. *Compendium on Continuing Education, 16,* 70–76.

Lagoni, L., Butler, C., & Hetts, S. (1994). *The human-animal bond and grief.* Philadelphia: W. B. Saunders.

Lansdown, R., & Benjamin, G. (1985). The development of the concept of death in children aged 5–9 years. *Child: Care, Health and Development, 11,* 13–20.

Lazar, A., & Torney-Purta, J. (1991). The development of the subconcepts of death in young children: A short-term longitudinal study. *Child Development, 62,* 1321–1333.

Lebovits, R. W. (1980). Parental influences in the development of the child's concept of human and personal death. Doctoral dissertation, Case Western Reserve University. *Dissertation Abstracts International, 41,* 1513B.

Leder, S. N. (1992). Life events, social support, and children's competence after parent and sibling death. *Journal of Pediatric Nursing, 7,* 110–119.

Lee, W. (1987). Children's conceptions of death: A study on age and gender as factors in concept development. Doctoral dissertation, Harvard University. *Dissertation Abstracts International, 48,* 2119B.

Leenaars, A. A. (1985). Suicide postvention in a school system. *Canada's Mental Health, 33*(4), 29–30.

Leenaars, A. A. (1996). Justin. In A. A. Leenaars & D. Lester (Eds.), *Suicide and the unconscious* (pp. 139–174). Northvale, NJ: Jason Aronson.

Leenaars, A. A., Maltsberger, J., & Neimeyer, R. (1994). *Treatment of suicidal people.* London: Taylor & Francis.

Leenaars, A. A., & Wenckstern, S. (Eds.). (1991). *Suicide prevention in schools.* Washington, DC: Hemisphere.

LeShan E. (1976). *Learning to say good-by: When a parent dies.* New York: Macmillan.

Lester, D. (1988). Research note: Gun control, gun ownership, and suicide prevention. *Suicide and Life-Threatening Behavior, 18,* 176–180.

Levenson, M., & Neuringer, C. (1971). Intropunitiveness in suicidal adolescents. *Journal of Projective Techniques and Personality Assessment, 34,* 409–411.

Levine, C. (Ed.). (1993). *A death in the family: Orphans of the HIV epidemic.* New York: United Hospital Fund of New York.

Lewert, G. (1988). Children and AIDS. *Social Casework, 69,* 348–354.

Lewinsohn, P., Garrison, C., Langhinrichsen, J., & Marsteller, F. (1989). *The assessment of suicidal behavior in adolescents: A review of scales suitable for epidemiological and clinical research.* Rockville, MD: National Institute of Mental Health.

Lifton, R. J. (1969). *Death in life: Survivors of Hiroshima.* New York: Vintage.

Lifton, R. J., & Olson, E. (1976). The human meaning of total disaster: The Buffalo Creek experience. *Psychiatry, 39,* 1–18.

Lindemann, E. (1944). The symptomatology and management of acute grief. *American Journal of Psychiatry, 101,* 141–148.

Linehan, M. M. (1981). *Suicidal Behaviors Questionnaire.* Unpublished inventory, University of Washington, Seattle, WA.

Little, J. (1984). *Mama's going to buy you a mockingbird.* New York: Viking Kestrel.

Lofland, L. H. (1982). Loss and human connection: An exploration into the nature of the social bond. In W. Ickes & E. S. Knowles (Eds.), *Personality, roles, and social behavior* (pp. 219–242). New York: Springer-Verlag.

Lomax, G. L., & Sandler, J. (1988). Psychotherapy and consultation with persons with AIDS. *Psychiatric Annals, 18,* 253–259.

Lonetto, R. (1980). *Children's conceptions of death.* New York: Springer Publishing Co.

Lopez, T., & Kliman, G. (1979). Memory, reconstruction, and mourning in the analysis of a four year old child. *Psychoanalytic Study of the Child, 34,* 235–271.

Lowenberg, F. (1988). *Religion and social work practice in contemporary American society.* New York: Columbia University Press.

Mahler, M. S., Pine, F., & Bergman, A. (1975). *The psychological birth of the human infant.* New York: Basic Books.

Mahon, M. M. (1992). The relationship between the experience of sibling death from trauma and acquisition of an accurate concept of death. Doctoral dissertation, University of Pennsylvania. *Dissertation Abstracts International, 53,* 2248B.

Malinosky-Rummell, R., & Hansen, D. J. (1993). Long-term consequences of childhood physical abuse. *Psychological Bulletin, 114,* 68–79.

Malmquist, C. P. (1986). Children who witness parental murder: Posttraumatic aspects. *Journal of the American Academy of Child Psychiatry, 25,* 320–325.

Marciano, P. L., & Kazdin, A. E. (1994). Self-esteem, depression, hopelessness, and suicidal intent among psychiatrically disturbed inpatient children. *Journal of Clinical Child Psychology, 23,* 151–160.

Maris, R., Berman, A., Maltsberger, J., & Yufit, R. (Eds.). (1992). *Assessment and prediction of suicide.* New York: Guilford.

Marris, P. (1991). The social construction of uncertainty. In C. M. Parkes, J. Stevenson-Hinde, & P. Marris (Eds), *Attachment across the life cycle* (pp. 82–84). New York: Routledge.

Martinson, I. M., Davies, E. B., & McClowry, S. G. (1987). The long-term effects of sibling death on self-concept. *Journal of Pediatric Nursing, 2,* 227–235.

Masur, C. (1991). Alternative approaches in the treatment of the bereaved child. In J. D. Morgan (Ed.), *Young people and death* (pp. 108–118). Philadelphia: Charles Press.

Maurer, A. (1966). Maturation of the conception of death. *Journal of Medical Psychology, 39,* 35–41.

McBride, M. M. (1987). The well child's concept of death during a sibling's life-threatening illness. Doctoral dissertation, Case Western Reserve University. *Dissertation Abstracts International, 48,* 1642B.

McClowry, S. G., Davies, E. B., May, K. A., Kulenkamp, E. J., & Martinson, I. M. (1987). The empty space phenomenon: The process of grief in the bereaved family. *Death Studies, 11,* 361–374.

McCown, D. E. (1983). *Selected factors related to children's adjustment following sibling death.* Doctoral dissertation. Portland State University, Portland, Oregon.

McCown, D. E. (1987). Factors relating to bereaved children's behavior. *Recent Advances in Nursing, 16,* 85–93.

McCown, D. E., & Davies, B. (1995). Patterns of grief in young children following the death of a sibling. *Death Studies, 19,* 41–53.

McGoldrick, M., & Walsh, F. (1983). A systemic view of family history and loss. In L. R. Wolberg & M. L. Aronson (Eds.), *Group and family therapy* (pp. 252–270). New York: Brunner/Mazel.

McIntire, M. S., Angle, C. R., & Struempler, L. J. (1972). The concept of death in Midwestern children and youth. *American Journal of Diseases of Children, 123,* 527–532.

McKelvy, L. (1995). Counseling children who have a parent with AIDS or have lost a parent to AIDS. In W. Odets & M. Shernoff (Eds.), *The second decade of AIDS: A mental health practice handbook* (pp. 137–159). New York: Hatherleigh Press.

McWhirter, L., Young, V., & Majury, J. (1983). Belfast children's awareness of violent death. *British Journal of Social Psychology, 22,* 81–92.

Mellonie, B., & Ingpen, R. (1983). *Lifetimes: A beautiful way to explain death to children.* New York: Bantam.

Melson, G. F. (1988). Availability of and involvement with pets by children: Determinants and correlates. *Anthrozoos, 2,* 45–52.

Melson, G. F., Sparks, C., & Peet, S. (1989, November). *Children's ideas about pets and their care.* Paper presented at the annual meeting of the Delta Society, Parsipanny, NJ.

Melson, G. F, & Taylor, S. (1990, October). *Pet ownership and attachment in young children: Relations to behavior problems and social competence.* Paper presented at the annual meeting of the Delta Society, Houston, TX.

Meneese, W. B., & Yutrzenka, B. A. (1990). Correlates of suicidal ideation among rural adolescents. *Suicide and Life-Threatening Behavior, 20,* 206–211.

Menig-Peterson, C., & McCabe, A. (1978). Children talk about death. *Omega, 8,* 305–317.

Metzgar, M. (1991). *Little ears, big issues: Children and loss.* Seattle, WA: Author.

Metzgar, M. (1994). Preparing schools for crisis management. In R. G. Stevenson (Ed.), *What will we do? Preparing a school community to cope with crises* (pp. 17–35). Amityville, NY: Baywood.

Miles, M. S., & Demi, A. S. (1984). Toward the development of a theory of bereavement guilt: Sources of guilt in bereaved parents. *Omega, 14,* 299–314.

Millay, E. St. V. (1956). *Collected poems.* New York: Harper.

Miller, J. B. M. (1971). Children's reactions to the death of a parent: A review of the psychoanalytic literature. *Journal of the American Psychoanalytic Association, 19,* 697–719.

Miller, K., Moore, N., & Lexius, C. (1985). A group for families of homicide victims: An evaluation. *Social Casework, 66,* 432–437.

Miller, S. (1988). *The acquisition and evolution of the death concept in school-age children.* Doctoral dissertation, University of Montreal, Montreal, Canada.

Minuchin, S. (1974). *Families and family therapy.* Cambridge, MA.: Harvard University Press.

Montalbano, P. (1990). Consequents of divorce on death attitudes and death concepts: A comparison between children of divorced families and children of intact families. Doctoral dissertation, Adelphi University, The Institute of Advanced Psychological Studies. *Dissertation Abstracts International, 51,* 3141B.

Moody, R. A. (1975). *Life after life.* New York: Bantam.

Moody, R. A., & Moody, C. P. (1991). A family perspective: Helping children acknowledge and express grief following the death of a parent. *Death Studies, 15,* 587–602.

Moseley, P. A. (1974). Selected child beliefs about death: Toward the development of instruments to measure the source of these beliefs. Doctoral dissertation, George Peabody College for Teachers of Vanderbilt University. *Dissertation Abstracts International, 35,* 3577A.

Moss, M., & Moss, S. (1986). Death of an adult sibling. *International Journal of Family Psychiatry, 7,* 397–418.

Munsch, M. (1993). School-based intervention following violent death in a classmate's family. In N. B. Webb (Ed.), *Helping bereaved children: A handbook for practitioners* (pp. 267–285). New York: Guilford.

Murphy, G. E., & Wetzel, R. D. (1982). Family history of suicidal behavior among suicide attempters. *Journal of Nervous and Mental Disease, 170,* 86–90.

Myers, E. (1986). *When parents die.* New York: Viking.

Myers, K., Burke, P., & McCauley, E. (1985). Suicidal behavior by hospitalized preadolescent children on a psychiatric unit. *Journal of the American Academy of Child Psychiatry, 24,* 474–480.

Myers, K., McCauley, E., Calderon, R., Mitchell, J., Burke, P., & Schloredt, K. (1991). Risks for suicidality in major depressive disorders. *Journal of the American Academy of Child and Adolescent Psychiatry, 1,* 86–94.

Nader, K. (1994a). Countertransference in treating trauma and victimization in childhood. In J. Wilson & J. Lindy (Eds.), *Countertransference in the treatment of Post-traumatic Stress Disorder* (pp. 179–205). New York: Guilford.

Nader, K. (1994b, November 6). *The impact of a parent's trauma on children exposed to catastrophic events: A school shooting and a public suicide.* In Intergenerational Effects of Trauma, a Pre-meeting Institute, International Society for Traumatic Stress Studies 10th Annual Meeting, Chicago, Illinois.

Nader, K. (in press a). Childhood traumatic loss: The interaction of trauma and grief. In C. R. Figley, B. E. Bride, & N. Mazza (Eds.), *Death and trauma: The traumatology of surviving.* Washington, DC: Taylor & Francis.

Nader, K. (in press b). Treating traumatic grief in systems. In C. R. Figley, B. E. Bride, & N. Mazza (Eds.), *Death and trauma: The traumatology of surviving.* Washington, DC: Taylor & Francis.

Nader, K. (in press c). Children's traumatic dreams. In D. Barrett (Ed.), *Trauma and dreams.* Cambridge, MA: Harvard University Press.

Nader, K. O., Blake, D. D., & Kriegler, J. A. (1994). *Instruction Manual: Clinician-Administered PTSD Scale, Child and Adolescent Version (CAPS-C).* White River Junction, VT: National Center for PTSD.

Nader, K., & Fairbanks, L. (1994). The suppression of reexperiencing: Impulse control and somatic symptoms in children following traumatic exposure. *Anxiety, Stress and Coping: An International Journal, 7,* 229–239.

Nader, K., & Pynoos, R. (1991). Play and drawing as tools for interviewing traumatized children. In C. Schaeffer, K. Gitlan, & A. Sandgrund (Eds.), *Play, diagnosis and assessment* (pp. 375–389). New York: Wiley.

Nader, K., & Pynoos, R. (1993). School disaster: Planning and initial interventions. *Journal of Social Behavior and Personality, 8*(5), 299–320.

Nader, K., Pynoos, R., Fairbanks, L., Al-Ajeel, M., & Al-Asfour, A. (1993). Acute post-traumatic stress reactions among Kuwait children following the Gulf Crisis. *British Journal of Clinical Psychology, 32,* 407–416.

Nader, K., Pynoos, R., Fairbanks, L., & Frederick, C. (1990). Children's PTSD reactions one year after a sniper attack at their school. *American Journal of Psychiatry, 147,* 1526–1530.

Nader, K., & Stuber, M. (1992, October 23). *Catastrophic events vs. catastrophic illness: A comparison of traumatized children.* A workshop presented at the annual meeting of the International Society for Traumatic Stress Studies.

Nagera, H. (1970). Children's reactions to the death of important objects: A developmental approach. *Psychoanalytic Study of the Child, 25,* 360–400.

Nagy, M. (1948). The child's theories concerning death. *Journal of Genetic Psychology, 73,* 3–27.

National Center for Health Statistics. (1994). Annual summary of births, marriages, divorces, and deaths: United Stattes, 1993. *Monthly Vital Statistics Report, 42*(13). Hyattsville, MD: Public Health Service.

Newman, C. F. (1976). Children of disaster: Clinical observations at Buffalo Creek. *American Journal of Psychiatry, 133,* 306–312.

Niederland, W. G. (1981). The survivor syndrome: Further observations and dimensions. *Journal of the American Psychoanalytic Association, 29,* 413–426.

Noppe, L. D., & Noppe, I. C. (1991). Dialectical themes in adolescent conceptions of death. *Journal of Adolescent Research, 6,* 28–42.

Normand, C. L., & Mishara, B. L. (1992). The development of the concept of suicide in children. *Omega, 25,* 183–203.

Norris-Shortle, C., Young, P. A., Williams, M. A. (1993). Understanding death and grief for children three and younger. *Social Work, 38,* 736–742.

Oltjenbruns, K. A. (1996). Death of a friend during adolescence: Issues and impacts. In C. A. Corr and D. E. Balk, (Eds.), *Handbook of adolescent death and bereavement* (pp. 196–215). New York: Springer Publishing Co.

Orbach, I. (1988). *Children who don't want to live: Understanding and treating the suicidal child.* San Francisco: Jossey-Bass.

Orbach, I., Feshbach, S., Carlson, G., & Ellenberg, L. (1984). Attitudes toward life and death in suicidal, normal, and chronically ill children: An extended replication. *Journal of Consulting and Clinical Psychology, 52,* 1020–1027.

Orbach, I., Feshbach, S., Carlson, G., Glaubman, H., & Gross, Y. (1983). Attraction and repulsion by life and death in suicidal and in normal children. *Journal of Consulting and Clinical Psychology, 51,* 661–670.

Orbach, I., Gross, Y., Glaubman, H., & Berman, D. (1985). Children's perception of death in humans and animals as a function of age, anxiety and cognitive ability. *Journal of Child Psychology and Psychiatry and Allied Disciplines, 26,* 453–463.

Orbach, I., Gross, Y., Glaubman, H., & Berman, D. (1986). Children's perception of various determinants of the death concept as a function of intelligence, age, and anxiety. *Journal of Clinical Child Psychology, 15,* 120–126.

Orbach, I., Rosenheim, E., & Hary, E. (1987). Some aspects of cognitive functioning in suicidal children. *Journal of the American Academy of Child and Adolescent Psychiatry, 26,* 181–185.

Orbach, I., Talmon, O., Kedem, P., & Har-Even, D. (1987). Sequential patterns of five subconcepts of human and animal death in children. *Journal of the American Academy of Child and Adolescent Psychiatry, 26,* 578–582.

Osterweis, M., Solomon, F., & Green, M. (Eds.). (1984). *Bereavement: Reactions, consequences, and care.* Washington, DC: National Academy Press.

Papalia, D. E., & Olds, S. W. (1996). *A child's world: Infancy through adolescence* (7th ed.). New York: McGraw-Hill.

Park, K. A. (1992). Preschoolers' reactions to loss of a best friend: Developmental trends and individual differences. *Child Study Journal, 22,* 233–252.

Park, K. A., Lay, K. L., & Ramsay, L. (1993). Individual differences and developmental changes in preschoolers' friendships. *Developmental Psychology, 29,* 264–270.

Parker, J. G., & Asher, S. R. (1987). Peer acceptance and later personal adjustment: Are low-accepted children "at risk?" *Psychological Bulletin, 102,* 357–389.

Parker, J. G., & Asher, S. R. (1993). Friendship and friendship quality in middle childhood: Links with peer group acceptance and feelings of loneliness and social dissatisfaction. *Developmental Psychology, 29,* 611–621.

Parkes, C. M. (1987). *Bereavement: Studies of grief in adult life* (2nd ed.). Madison, CT: International Universities Press.

Parkes, C. M., & Weiss, R. (1983). *Recovery from bereavement.* New York: Basic Books.

Paterson, K. (1977). *Bridge to Terabithia.* New York: Avon Books

Pattison, E. M. (1969). Help in the dying process. *Voices, 5,* 6–14.

Pattison, E. M. (1978). The living-dying process. In C. Garfield (Ed.), *Psychological care of the dying patient* (pp. 163–168). New York: McGraw-Hill.

Payne, J. S., Goff, J. R., & Paulson, M. A. (1980). Psychosocial adjustment of families following the death of a child. In J. L. Schulman & M. J. Kupst (Eds.), *The child with cancer: Clinical approaches to psychosocial care—research in psychosocial aspects* (pp. 183–193). Springfield, IL: Charles C Thomas.

Payne, B., & Range, L. M. (1994). *Internal consistency of the children's Suicidal Behaviors Questionnaire.* Unpublished manuscript.

Peach, M. R., & Klass, D. (1987). Special issues in the grief of parents of murdered children. *Death Studies, 11,* 81–88.

Peck, R. (1966). The development of the concept of death in selected male children: An experimental investigation of the development of the concept of death in selected children from the point of no concept to the point where a fully developed concept is attained with an investigation of some factors which may affect the course of concept development. Doctoral dissertation, New York University, 1966. *Dissertation Abstracts International, 27,* 1294B.

Peters, D. K., & Range, L. M. (1995). Childhood sexual abuse and current suicidality in college women and men. *Child Abuse and Neglect, 19,* 335–341.

Pfeffer, C. R. (1981). The family system of suicidal children. *American Journal of Psychotherapy, 35,* 330–341.

Pfeffer, C. R. (1985). Observations of ego functioning of suicidal latency-age children. In M. L. Peck, N. L. Farberow, & R. E. Litman (Eds.), *Youth suicide* (pp. 39–47). New York: Springer Publishing Co.

Pfeffer, C. R. (1986). *The suicidal child.* New York: Guilford.

Pfeffer, C. R. (1990). Preoccupations with death in "normal" children: The relationship to suicidal behavior. *Omega, 20,* 205–212.

Pfeffer, C. R., Conte, H. R., Plutchik, R., & Jerrett, I. (1980). Suicidal behavior in latency-age children: An outpatient population. *Journal of the American Academy of Child Psychiatry, 19,* 703–710.

Pfeffer, C. R., Plutchik, R., & Mizruchi, M. S. (1983). Suicidal and assaultive behavior in children: Classification, measurement, and interrelations. *American Journal of Psychiatry, 140,* 154–157.

Pfeffer, C. R., Plutchik, R., Mizruchi, M. S., & Lipkins, R. (1986). Suicidal behavior in child psychiatric inpatients and outpatients an din nonpatients. *American Journal of Psychiatry, 143,* 733–738.

Pfeffer, C. R., Solomon, G., Plutchik, R., Mizruchi, M. S., & Weiner, A. (1982). Suicidal behavior in latency-age psychiatric patients: A replication and cross validation. *Journal of the American Academy of Child Psychiatry, 21,* 564–569.

Pfeffer, C. R., Zuckerman, S., Plutchik, R., & Mizruchi, M. S. (1984). Suicidal behavior in normal school children: A comparison with child psychiatric inpatients. *Journal of the American Academy of Child Psychiatry, 23,* 416–423.

Phillips, D. P., & Carstensen, L. L. (1986). Clustering of teenage suicides after television news stories about suicide. *New England Journal of Medicine, 315,* 685–689.

Phillips, D. P., & Paight, D. J. (1987). The impact of televised movies about suicide: A replicative study. *New England Journal of Medicine, 317,* 809–811.

Piaget, J. (1929). *The child's conception of the world.* London: Routledge & Kegan Paul.

Piaget, J. (1932). *The moral judgment of the child.* New York: Harcourt, Brace.

Piaget, J. (1965). *The moral judgment of the child.* New York: Free Press.

Pincus, L. (1974). *Death and the family: The importance of mourning.* New York: Pantheon.

Piper, W., McCallum, M., & Azim, H. (1992). *Adaptation to loss through short-term group psychotherapy.* New York: Guilford.

Pitcher, E. G., & Prelinger, E. (1963). *Children tell stories: An analysis of fantasy.* New York: International Universities Press.

Pizzo, P. (1990). Pediatric AIDS: Problems within problems, AIDS commentary. *Journal of Infectious Diseases, 161,* 316–328.

Plotkin, D. R. (1983). Children's anniversary reactions following the death of a family member. *Canada's Mental Health, 31*(2), 13–15.

Pohlman, J. C. (1984). Illness and death of a peer in a group of three-year-olds. *Death Education, 8,* 123–136.

Poland, S. (1989). *Suicide intervention in the schools.* New York: Guilford.

Polombo, J. (1978). *Parent loss and childhood bereavement.* Conference on Children and Death. University of Chicago.

Portz, A. T. (1965). The meaning of death to children. Doctoral dissertation, The University of Michigan. *Dissertation Abstracts International, 25,* 7383

Powell, E. S. (1990). *Geranium morning.* Minneapolis: CarolRhoda Books.

Public Health Service. (1987). *Secretary's task force report on youth suicide.* Bethesda, MD: National Institute of Mental Health.

Puig-Antich, J., & Ryan, N. (1986). *Schedule for Affective Disorders and Schizophrenia for School-Age Children (6018 years)—Kiddie SADS (K-SADS).* Unpublished manuscript, Western Psychiatric Institute, Pittsburg.

Pynoos, R., & Eth, S. (1986). Witness to violence: The child interview. *Journal of the American Academy of Child Psychiatry, 25,* 306–319.

Pynoos, R., Frederick, C., Nader, K., Arroyo, W., Eth, S., Nunez, W., Steinberg, A., & Fairbanks, L. (1987). Life threat and posttraumatic stress in school age children. *Archives of General Psychiatry, 44,* 1057–1063.

Pynoos, R., & Nader, K. (1988). Psychological first aid and treatment approach for children exposed to community violence: Research implications. *Journal of Traumatic Stress, 1*(4), 445–473.

Pynoos, R., & Nader, K. (1989). Children's memory and proximity to violence. *Journal of the American Academy of Child and Adolescent Psychiatry, 28*(2), 236–241.

Pynoos, R., & Nader, K. (1990). Mental health disturbances in children exposed to disaster: Prevention intervention strategies. In S. Goldston, J. Yaeger, C. Heinecke, & R. Pynoos (Eds.), *Prevention of mental health disturbances in children* (pp. 211–234). Washington, DC: American Psychiatric Association Press.

Pynoos, R., & Nader, K. (1993). Issues in the treatment of posttraumatic stress in children and adolescents. In J. P. Wilson & B. Raphael (Eds.), *International Handbook of Traumatic Stress Syndromes* (pp. 535–549). New York: Plenum Press.

Ramsay, R. F., Cooke, M. A., & Lang, W. A. (1990). Alberta's Suicide Prevention Training Programs: A retrospective comparison with Rothman's Developmental Research Model. *Suicide and Life-Threatening Behavior, 20,* 335–351.

Ramsey, V. O. (1986). The relationship of age, sex, experience, religion, and culture to children's concepts of death: A study of American and Palestinian children. Doctoral dissertation, Texas Woman's University. *Dissertation Abstracts International, 47,* 2881A.

Rando, T. A. (1984). *Grief, dying, and death: Clinical interventions for caregivers.* Champaign, IL: Research Press.

Rando, T. A. (Ed.). (1986). *Loss and anticipatory grief.* Lexington, MA: Lexington Books.

Rando, T. A. (1988). *How to go on living when someone you love dies.* New York: Bantam.

Rando, T. A. (1993). *Treatment of complicated mourning.* Champaign, IL: Research Press.

Range, L. M. (1993). Suicide prevention: Guidelines for schools. *Educational Psychology Review, 5,* 135–154.

Rao, U., Weissman, M. M., Martin, J. A., & Hammond, R. W. (1993). Childhood depression and risk of suicide: A preliminary report of a longitudinal study. *Journal of the American Academy of Child and Adolescent Psychiatry, 32,* 21–27.

Raphael, B. (1982). The young child and the death of a parent. In C. M. Parkes & J. Stevenson-Hinde (Eds.), *The place of attachment in human behavior* (pp. 131–150). London: Tavistock.

Raphael, B. (1983). *The anatomy of bereavement.* New York: Basic Books.

Reilly, T. P., Hasazi, J. E., & Bond, L. A. (1983). Children's conceptions of death and personal mortality. *Journal of Pediatric Psychology, 8,* 21–31.

Reynolds, S. (1992). *Endings to beginnings: A grief support group for children and adolescents.* Minneapolis: HRG Press.

Richter, E. (1986). *Losing someone you love: When a brother or sister dies.* New York: G. P. Putnam's Sons.

Richters, J. E., & Martinez, P. (1991). Community violence project: I Children as victims or witnesses to violence. *Psychiatry, 56,* 7–21.

Robinson, R. A. (1977). The development of a concept of death in selected groups of Mexican-American and Anglo-American children. Doctoral dissertation, California School of Professional Psychology—San Diego. *Dissertation Abstracts International, 38,* 4478B.

Rochlin, G. (1967). How younger children view death and themselves. In E. A. Grollman (Ed.), *Explaining death to children* (pp. 51–85). Boston: Beacon Press.

Rosen, E. J. (1987). Teaching family therapy concepts to the hospice team. *The American Journal of Hospice Care, 4*(4), 39–44.

Rosen, E. J. (1988a). Family therapy in cases of interminable grief for the loss of a child. *Omega, 19,* 187–202.

Rosen, E. J. (1988b). The ethnic and cultural dimensions of work with hospice families. *The American Journal of Hospice Care, 5*(4), 16–21.

Rosen, E. J. (1990). *Families facing death: Family dynamics of terminal illness.* Lexington, MA: Lexington Books.

Rosen, E. J. (1991). Families facing terminal illness. In F. Herz Brown (Ed.), *Reweaving the family tapestry: A multigenerational approach to families* (pp. 262–285). New York: Norton.

Rosen, E. J., McGoldrick, M., Almeida, R., Moore-Hines, P., Garcia-Preto, N., & Lee, E. (1991). Mourning in different cultures. In F. Walsh & M.

McGoldrick (Eds.), *Living beyond loss: Death in the family* (pp. 176–206). New York: Norton.

Rosen, H. (1986). *Unspoken grief: Coping with childhood sibling loss.* Lexington, MA: Lexington Books.

Rosen, H., & Cohen, H. (1981). Children's reactions to sibling loss. *Clinical Social Work, 9,* 211–219.

Rosenberg, G., & Anspach, D. F. (1973). Sibling solidarity in the working class. *Journal of Marriage and the Family, 35,* 108–113.

Rosenthal, P. A., & Rosenthal, S. (1984). Suicidal behavior by preschool children. *American Journal of Psychiatry, 141,* 520–525.

Ross, C. P. (1985). Teaching children the facts of life and death: Suicide prevention in the schools. In M. L. Peck, N. L. Farberow, & R. E. Litman (Eds.), *Youth suicide* (pp. 147–169). New York: Springer Publishing Co.

Rotheram-Borus, M. (1993). Suicidal behavior and risk factors among runaway youths. *American Journal of Psychiatry, 150,* 103–107.

Rotheram-Borus, M., Trautman, P., Dopkins, S., & Shrout, P. (1990). Cognitive style and pleasant activities among female adolescent suicide attempters. *Journal of Consulting and Clinical Psychology, 58,* 554–561.

Roy, P., & Sumpter, H. (1983). Family support and a child's adjustment to death. *Family Relations, 32,* 43–49.

Rubin, Z. (1980). *Children's friendships.* Cambridge, MA: Harvard University Press.

Rudman, M. K., Gagne, K. D., & Bernstein, J. E. (1993). *Books to help children cope with separation and loss* (4th ed.). Providence, NJ: Bowker.

Rutter, M. (1987). Psychosocial resilience and protective mechanisms. *American Journal of Orthopsychiatry, 57,* 316–331.

Rylant, C. (1992). *Missing May.* New York: Orchard Books.

Safier, G. (1964). A study in relationships between life and death concepts in children. *Journal of Genetic Psychology, 105,* 283–294.

Salasin, S. E., & Rich, R. F. (1993). Mental health policy for victims of violence. In J. P. Wilson & B. Raphael (Eds.), *International handbook of traumatic stress syndromes* (pp. 948–951). New York: Plenum Press.

Saylor, C. F., Finch, A. J., Spirito, A., & Bennett, B. (1984). The Children's Depression Inventory: A systematic evaluation of psychometric properties. *Journal of Consulting and Clinical Psychology, 52,* 955–967.

Saylor, C. F., Swenson, C. C., & Powell, P. (1992). Hurricane Hugo blows down the broccoli: Preschoolers' post-disaster play and adjustment. *Child Psychiatry and Human Development, 22,* 139–149.

Schaefer, D., & Lyons, C. (1993). *How do we tell the children?* (2nd ed.). New York: Newmarket Press.

Schilder, P., & Wechsler, D. (1934). The attitude of children towards death. *Journal of Genetic Psychology, 45,* 406–451.

Schneider, J. (1984). *Stress, loss and grief.* Baltimore: University Press.

Schonfeld, D. J., & Kappelman, M. (1990). The impact of school-based education on the young child's understanding of death. *Journal of Developmental & Behavioral Pediatrics, 11,* 247–252.

Schonfeld, D. J., & Smilansky, S. (1989). A cross-cultural comparison of
Israeli and American children's death concepts. *Death Studies, 13,*
593–604.

Schwab, J. J., Chalmers, J. M., Conroy, S. J., Ferris, P. B., & Markush, R. E.
(1965). Studies in grief: A preliminary report. In B. Schoenberg, L.
Gerber, A. Wiener, A. H. Kutscher, D. Peretz, & A. Carr (Eds.), *Bereavement: Its psychosocial aspects* (pp. 78–87). New York: Columbia University
Press.

Schwab, R. (1986). Support groups for the bereaved. *Journal for Specialists in
Group Work, 11,* 100–106.

Sedney, M. A., Baker, J. E., & Gross, E. (1994). "The story" of a death: Therapeutic considerations with bereaved families. *Journal of Marital and
Family Therapy, 20,* 287–296.

Segal, R. (1984). Helping children express grief through symbolic communication. *Social Casework, 65,* 590–599.

Seide, J. H. (1983). The effect of experience with death on children's understanding of death. Doctoral dissertation, Boston College. *Dissertation Abstracts International, 44,* 627B.

Sekaer, C. (1987). Toward a definition of "childhood mourning." *American
Journal of Psychotherapy, 41,* 201–219.

Selman, R. L. (1980). *The growth of interpersonal understanding: Developmental
and clinical analysis.* New York: Academic Press.

Selman, R. L. (1981). The child as a friendship philosopher. In S. R. Asher
& J. M. Gottman (Eds.), *The development of children's friendships* (pp.
242–272). New York: Cambridge University Press.

Selvini Palazzoli, M., Boscolo, L., Cecchin, G., & Prata, G. (1974). The treatment of children through brief therapy of their parents. *Family Process,
13*(4), 55–67.

Shaffer, D., Garland, A., Gould, M., Fisher, P., & Trautman, P. (1988). Preventing teenage suicide: A critical review. *Journal of the American Academy of Child and Adolescent Psychiatry, 27,* 675–687.

Shaffer, D., Garland, A., Vieland, O., Underwood, M., & Busner, C. (1991).
The impact of curriculum based prevention programs for teenagers.
Journal of the American Academy of Child and Adolescent Psychiatry, 30,
588–596.

Shaffer, D., Vieland, V., Garland, A., Rojas, M., Underwood, M., & Busner,
C. (1990). Adolescent suicide attempters: Response to suicide-preven-
tion programs. *Journal of the American Medical Association, 264,*
3151–3155.

Shafii, M., Steitz-Lenarsky, J., Derrick, A. M., Beckner, C., & Whittinghill, J.
R. (1988). Comorbidity of mental disorders in the post-mortem diag-

nosis of completed suicide in children and adolescents. *Journal of Affective Disorders, 15*, 227–233.

Shapiro, E. R. (1994). *Grief as a family process; A developmental approach to clinical practice.* New York: Guilford.

Shernoff, M. (1995). Counseling chemically dependent clients with HIV infection. In W. Odets & M. Shernoff (Eds.), *The second decade of AIDS: A mental health practice handbook* (pp. 27–46). New York: Hatherleigh Press.

Shneidman, E. (1973a). Suicide. *Encyclopedia Britannica* (14th ed., Vol. 21, pp. 383–385). Chicago: William Benton. (Reprinted in E. Shneidman, *Suicide thoughts and reflections, 1960–1980* [pp. 6–28]. New York: Human Sciences Press, 1981.)

Shneidman, E. S. (1973b). Postvention and the survivor-victim. In E. Shneidman, *Deaths of man* (pp. 33–41). New York: Quadrangle.

Shneidman, E. S. (1975). Postvention: The care of the bereaved. In R. O. Pasnau (Ed.), *Consultation-liaison psychiatry* (pp. 245–256). New York: Grune and Stratton. (Reprinted in E. Shneidman, *Suicide thoughts and reflections, 1960–1980* [pp. 157–167]. New York: Human Sciences Press, 1981.)

Siegel, K., Mesagno, F., & Christ, G. (1990). A prevention program for bereaved children. *American Journal of Orthopsychiatry, 60*, 168–175.

Silverman, P. R., Nickman, S., & Worden, J. W. (1992). Detachment revisited: The child's reconstruction of a dead parent. *American Journal of Orthopsychiatry, 62*, 494–503.

Silverman, P. R., & Worden, J. W. (1992a). Children's reactions in the early months after the death of a parent. *American Journal of Orthopsychiatry, 62*, 93–104.

Silverman, P. R., & Worden, J. W. (1992b). Children's understanding of funeral ritual. *Omega, 24*, 319–331.

Silverman, S. M., & Silverman, P. R. (1979). Parent-child communication in widowed families. *American Journal of Psychotherapy, 33*, 428–441.

Simpson, J. A., & Weiner, E. S. C. (1989). *The Oxford English dictionary* (2nd ed.; 20 vols.). Oxford: Clarendon Press.

Sinclair, R. (1989). The impact on children whose parents or loved ones have HIV disease. *International Conference on AIDS, 5*, 886 #E.504.

Sisson, P. (1987). Children's conceptions of death: The influence of cognitive development and death related experience. Doctoral dissertation, University of Northern Colorado. *Dissertation Abstracts International, 48*, 2805B.

Sklar, F., & Hartley, S. F. (1990). Close friends as survivors: Bereavement patterns in a hidden population. *Omega, 21*, 103–112.

Smeets, P. M. (1974). The influence of MA and CA on the attribution of life and life traits to animate and inanimate objects. *Journal of Genetic Psychology, 124*, 17–27.

Smilansky, S. (1981). *Manual for questionnaire of the development of death conceptualization.* Unpublished manuscript, Tel Aviv University, Department of Psychology, Tel Aviv, Israel.

Smilansky, S. (1987). *On death: Helping children understand and cope.* New York: Peter Lang.

Smilansky, S., & Weissman, T. (1978). *A guide for rehabilitation workers with orphans of war casualties and their mothers.* Jerusalem: Henrietta Szold Institute.

Smith, B. J. (1992). The concept of death among children between the ages of 4 and 14 who have threatened or attempted suicide. Doctoral dissertation, Adelphi University, The Institute of Advanced Psychological Studies. *Dissertation Abstracts International, 52,* 4481B.

Smith, D. B. (1973). *A taste of blackberries.* New York: Harper Collins.

Smith, R. P. (1957). *"Where did you go?" "Out." "What did you do?" "Nothing."* New York: Norton.

Solomon, M., & Hersch, L. B. (1979). Death in the family: Implications for family development. *Journal of Marriage and Family Therapy, 5*(2), 43–49.

Soricelli, B., & Utech, C. (1985). Mourning the death of a child: The family and group process. *Social Work, 30,* 429–434.

Sourkes, B. M. (1980). Siblings of the pediatric cancer patient. In J. Kellerman (Ed.), *Psychological aspects of childhood cancer* (pp. 47–49). Springfield, IL: Charles C Thomas.

Speece, M. W. (1994). *Compendium of studies of children's concepts of death.* Manuscript in preparation, Wayne State University.

Speece, M. W., & Brent, S. B. (1984). Children's understanding of death: A review of three components of a death concept. *Child Development, 55,* 1671–1686.

Speece, M. W., & Brent, S. B. (1992). The acquisition of a mature understanding of three components of the concept of death. *Death Studies, 16,* 211–229.

Spinetta, J. J. (1981). The sibling of the child with cancer. In J. J. Spinetta & P. Deasy-Spinetta (Eds.), *Living with childhood cancer* (pp. 133–142). St. Louis: C. V. Mosby.

Spinetta, J. J., & Deasy-Spinetta, P. (Eds.). (1981). *Living with childhood cancer.* St. Louis: C. V. Mosby.

Spinetta, J. J., McLaren, H. H., Fox, R. W., & Sparta, S. N. (1981). The kinetic family drawing in childhood cancer: A revised application of an age independent measure. In J. J. Spinetta & P. Deasy-Spinetta (Eds.), *Living with childhood cancer* (pp. 86–126). St. Louis: C. V. Mosby.

Spirito, A., Williams, C. A., Stark, L. J., & Hart, K. J. (1988). The Hopelessness Scale for Children: Psychometric properties with normal and emotionally disturbed adolescents. *Journal of Abnormal Child Psychology, 16,* 445–458.

Stack, S. (1987). Celebrities and suicide: A taxonomy and analysis, 1948–1983. *American Sociological Review, 52,* 401–412.

Stahlman, S. D. (1993). *Adult sibling loss: Family dynamics and individual characteristics.* Doctoral dissertation. Virginia Commonwealth University, Richmond.

Stambrook, M., & Parker, K. C. (1987). The development of the concept of death in childhood: A review of the literature. *Merrill Palmalmer Quarterly, 33,* 133–157.

Steiner, G. L. (1965). *Children's concepts of life and death: A developmental study.* Doctoral dissertation, Columbia University. *Dissertation Abstracts International, 26,* 1164.

Sternberg, K. J., Lamb, M. E., Greenbaum, C., Cicchetti, D., Dawud, S., Cortes, R. M., Krispin, O., & Lorey, F. (1993). Effects of domestic violence on children's behavior problems and depression. *Developmental Psychology, 29,* 44–52.

Stewart, M. (1983). Loss of a pet—loss of a person: A comparison study of bereavement. In A. Katcher & A. Beck (Eds.), *New perspectives on our lives with companion animals* (pp. 390–404). Philadelphia: University of Pennsylvania Press.

Stiles, N. (1984). *I'll miss you, Mister Hooper.* New York: Random House/Children's Television Workshop.

Stuber, M., & Nader, K. (1995). Psychiatric sequelae in adolescent bone marrow transplant survivors: Implications for psychotherapy. *The Journal of Psychotherapy Practice and Research, 4*(1), 30–42.

Sullivan, H. S. (1953). *The interpersonal theory of psychiatry.* New York: Norton.

Swain, H. L. (1979). Childhood views of death. *Death Education, 2,* 341–358.

Tait, D. C., & Depta, J.-L. (1993). Play therapy group for bereaved children. In N. B. Webb (Ed.), *Helping bereaved children: A handbook for practitioners* (pp. 169–185). New York: Guilford.

Tallmer, M., Formanek, R., & Tallmer, J. (1974). Factors influencing children's concepts of death. *Journal of Clinical Child Psychology, 3,* 17–19.

Tarachow, S. (1963). *An introduction to psychotherapy.* New York: International Universities Press.

Terr, L. (1979). Children of Chowchilla: Study of psychic trauma. *Psychoanalytic Study of the Child, 34,* 547–623.

Terr, L. (1981). Psychic trauma in children: Observations following the Chowchilla schoolbus kidnaping. *Journal of Psychiatry, 138,* 14–19.

Terr, L. (1983). Chowchilla revisited: The effects of psychic trauma four years after a schoolbus kidnaping. *American Journal of Psychiatry, 140,* 1542–1550.

Terr, L. C. (1991). Childhood traumas: An outline and overview. *American Journal of Psychiatry, 148,* 10–20.

The unyielding AIDS epidemic (1994, August 6). *The New York Times*, Editorial, p. 28.

Thunberg, U. (1977). Death and the dying adult. In R. C. Simmons & H. Pardes (Eds.), *Understanding human behavior in health and illness* (pp. 387–394). Baltimore: Williams & Wilkins.

Townley, K., & Thornburg, K. (1980). Maturation of the concept of death in elementary school children. *Educational Research Quarterly, 5,* 17–24.

Trotzer, J. P. (1977). *The counselor and the group: Integrating theory, training, and practice.* Monterey, CA: Brooks/Cole.

United States Bureau of the Census. (1993). *Statistical abstract of the United States* (113th ed.). Washington, DC: U.S. Government Printing Office.

Vachon, M. L. S., & Stylianos, S. K. (1988). The role of social support in bereavement. *Journal of Social Issues, 44,* 175–190.

Vaillant, G. E. (1977). *Adaptation to life.* Boston: Little, Brown.

Vandell, D. L., & Mueller, E. C. (1980). Peer play and friendships during the first two years. In H. C. Foot, A. J. Chapman, & J. R. Smith (Eds.), *Friendships and social relations in children* (pp. 181–208). New York: Wiley.

van der Kolk, B. A., Perry, J. C., & Herman, J. L. (1991). Childhood origins of self-destructive behavior. *American Journal of Psychiatry, 148,* 1665–1671.

van der Kolk, B. A., Roth, S., Pelcovitz, D., & Mandel, F.S. (1992). *Disorders of extreme stress: Results from the DSM IV field trials for PTSD.* An unpublished manuscript.

van der Kolk, B., & Saporta, J. (1991). The biological response to psychic trauma: Mechanisms and treatment of intrusion and numbing. *Anxiety Research, 4,* 199–212.

Van Dexter, J. D. (1986). Anticipatory grief: Strategies for the classroom. In T. A. Rando (Ed.), *Loss and anticipatory grief* (pp. 115–173). Lexington, MA: Lexington Books.

Van Eerdewegh, M. M., Bieri, M. D., Parilla, R. H., & Clayton, P. J. (1982). The bereaved child. *British Journal of Psychiatry, 140,* 23–29.

Van Eerdewegh, M. M., Clayton, P. J., & Van Eerdewegh, P. (1985). The bereaved child: Variables influencing early psychopathology. *British Journal of Psychiatry, 147,* 188–194.

Vess, J., Moreland, J., & Schwebel, A. I. (1985). Understanding family role allocation following a death: A theoretical framework. *Omega, 16,* 115–128.

Vianello, R., & Marin, M. L. (1989). Children's understanding of death. *Early Child Development and Care, 46,* 97–104.

Vida, S., & Grizenko, N. (1989). DSM-III-R and the phenomenology of childhood bereavement. *Canadian Journal of Psychiatry, 34,* 148–155.

Viorst, J. (1971). *The tenth good thing about Barney.* New York: Atheneum.

Volkan, V., & Zintl, E. (1993). *Life after loss.* New York: Macmillan.

Waechter, E. H. (1971). Children's awareness of fatal illness. *American Journal of Nursing, 71,* 1168–1172.

Waechter, E. H. (1984). Dying children: Patterns of coping. In H. Wass & C. A. Corr (Eds.), *Childhood and death* (pp. 51–68). Washington, DC: Hemisphere.

Wainwright, A. (1987). *Australian children's thinking about death: A Sydney-based study.* Kensington, Australia: Foundation for Child and Youth Studies (ERIC Document Reproduction Service No. ED294657).

Walco, G. A. (1982). *Children's concepts of death: a cognitive training study* (ERIC Document Reproduction Service No. ED222282). Columbus: Ohio State University.

Walco, G. A. (1984). Fatally ill children's comprehension of death. Doctoral dissertation, The Ohio State University. *Dissertation Abstracts International, 45,* 2706B.

Walsh, F., & McGoldrick, M. (1988). Loss and the family life cycle. In C. J. Falicov (Ed.), *Family transitions: Continuity and change over the life cycle* (pp. 311–336). New York: Guilford.

Walsh, F., & McGoldrick, M. (Eds.). (1991a). *Living beyond loss: Death in the family.* New York: Norton.

Walsh, F., & McGoldrick, M. (1991b). Loss and the family: A systemic perspective. In F. Walsh & M. McGoldrick (Eds.), *Living beyond loss: Death in the family* (pp. 1–29). New York: Norton.

Wass, H. (1984a). Concepts of death: A developmental perspective. In H. Wass & C. A. Corr (Eds.), *Childhood and death* (pp. 3–24). Washington, DC: Hemisphere.

Wass, H. (1984b). Parents, teachers, and health professionals as helpers. In H. Wass & C. A. Corr (Eds.), *Helping children cope with death: Guidelines and resources* (2nd ed.; pp. 75–130). Washington, DC: Hemisphere.

Wass, H., Guenther, Z. C., & Towry, B. J. (1979). United States and Brazilian children's concepts of death. *Death Education, 3,* 41–55.

Wass, H., Dinklage, R., Gordon, S. L., Russo, G., Sparks, C. W., & Tatum, J. (1983a). Young children's death concepts revisited. *Death Education, 7,* 385–394.

Wass, H., Dinklage, R., Gordon, S. L., Russo, G., Sparks, C. W., & Tatum, J. (1983b). Use of play for assessing children's death concepts: A reexamination. *Psychological Reports, 53,* 799–803.

Wass, H., & Scott, M. (1978). Middle school students' death concepts and concerns. *Middle School Journal, 9,* 10–12.

Wass, H., & Towry, B. J. (1980). Children's death concepts and ethnicity. *Death Education, 4,* 83–87.

Webb, N. B. (Ed.) (1991). *Play therapy with children in crisis: A casebook for practitioners.* New York: Guilford.

Webb, N. B. (Ed.) (1993a). *Helping bereaved children: A handbook for practitioners.* New York: Guilford.

Webb, N. B. (1993b). Assessment of the bereaved child. In N. B. Webb (Ed.), *Helping bereaved children: A handbook for practitioners* (pp. 19–42). New York: Guilford.

Webb, N. B. (1993c). Counseling and therapy for the bereaved child. In N. B. Webb (Ed.), *Helping bereaved children: A handbook for practitioners* (pp. 43–58). New York: Guilford.

Webb, N. B. (1993d). Death of grandparent—family therapy to assist bereavement, Case of the Silver family—siblings, ages 11, 9, and 5. In N. B. Webb (Ed.), *Helping bereaved children: A handbook for practitioners* (pp. 61–80). New York: Guilford.

Weber, J. A. (1981). Family dynamics and the child's concept of death. Doctoral dissertation, Oklahoma State University. *Dissertation Abstracts International, 42,* 2318A.

Weber, J. A., & Fournier, D. G. (1985). Family support and a child's adjustment to death. Special Issue: The family and health care. *Family Relations Journal of Applied Family and Child Studies, 34,* 43–49.

Wegman, M. E. (1994). Annual summary of vital statistics—1993. *Pediatrics, 94,* 792–803.

Weininger, O. (1979). Young children's concepts of dying and dead. *Psychological Reports, 44,* 395–407.

Weisman, A. (1980). Thanatology. In H. I. Kaplan, A. M. Freedman, & B. J. Sadock (Eds.), *Comprehensive textbook of psychiatry* (3 vols., Vol. 2, pp. 2042–2056). Baltimore: Williams & Williams.

Weissman, M. (1979). Depressed parents and their children: Implications for prevention. In I. Berlin & L. Stone (Eds.), *Basic handbook of child psychiatry,* Vol. 4 (pp. 292–299). New York: Basic Books.

Weller, R. A., Weller, E. B., Fristad, M. A., & Bowes, J. M. (1991). Depression in recently bereaved prepubertal children. *American Journal of Psychiatry, 148,* 1536–1540.

Weller, E. B., Weller, R. A., Fristad, M. A., Cain, S. E., & Bowes, J. M. (1988). Should children attend their parent's funeral? *Journal of the American Academy of Child and Adolescent Psychiatry, 27,* 559–562.

Wenckstern, S., & Leenaars, A. A. (1993). Trauma and suicide in our schools. *Death Studies, 17,* 151–171.

Wenestam, C. G. (1984). Qualitative age-related differences in the meaning of the word "death" to children. *Death Education, 8,* 333–347.

Wenestam, C. G., & Wass, H. (1987). Swedish and U.S. children's thinking about death: A qualitative study and cross-cultural comparison. *Death Studies, 11,* 99–121.

White, E. A., Elsom, B., & Prawat, R. (1978). Children's conceptions of death. *Child Development, 49,* 307–310.

White, E. B. (1952). *Charlotte's web.* New York: Harper.

Whitehead, R. (1971). *The mother tree.* New York: Seabury.

Whitney, S. (1992). *Volunteer facilitator training instructor's manual.* Portland, OR: The Dougy Center for Grieving Children.

Widowed Information and Consultation Services. (1986). *Children grieving the death of a parent: A discussion series curriculum.* Seattle, WA: Widowed Information and Consultation Services.

Wiener, L., Best, H., & Pizzo, P. (1994). *Be a friend: Children who live with HIV speak.* Illinois: Albert Whitman.

Wiener, L., Fair, C., & Garcia, A. (1995). AIDS: Pediatric. *Encyclopedia of social work* (19th ed., Vol. 9, pp. 28–33). Washington, DC: National Association of Social Work.

Wilson, J., Smith, W., & Johnson, S. (1985). A comparative analysis of PTSD among various survivor groups. In C. Figley (Ed.), *Trauma and its wake* (pp. 142–172). New York: Brunner/Mazel.

Wolfelt, A. D. (1983). *Helping children cope with grief.* Muncie, IN: Accelerated Development.

Wolfelt, A. D. (1991a). Children. *Bereavement Magazine, 5*(1), 38–39.

Wolfelt, A. D. (1991b). Helping children cope with grief. *Thanatos, 16*(3), 17–18.

Wolfelt, A. D. (1993). Why I feel this way: Factors influencing the grief of children: 2. *Bereavement Magazine, 7*(6), 36–36.

Wolfenstein, M. (1966). How is mourning possible? *Psychoanalytic Study of the Child, 21,* 93–123.

Wolfenstein, M. (1969). Loss, rage, and repetition. *Psychoanalytic Study of the Child, 24,* 432–460.

Worchel, S., & Cooper, J. (1983). *Understanding social psychology* (3rd ed.). Homewood, IL: Dorsey Press.

Worden, J. W. (1982). *Grief counseling and grief therapy: A handbook for the mental health practitioner.* New York: Springer Publishing Co.

Worden, J. W. (1991). *Grief counseling and grief therapy: A handbook for the mental health practitioner* (2nd ed.). New York: Springer Publishing Co.

Wortman, C. B., & Silver, R. C. (1989). The myths of coping with loss. *Journal of Consulting and Clinical Psychology, 57,* 349–357.

Youniss, J. (1980). *Parents and peers in social development: A Sullivan-Piaget perspective.* Chicago: University of Chicago Press.

Zambelli, G. C., Clark, E. J., Barile, L., & de Jong, A. F. (1988). An interdisciplinary approach to clinical intervention for childhood bereavement. *Death Studies, 12,* 41–50.

Zambelli, G. C., & DeRosa, A. P. (1992). Bereavement support groups for school-age children: Theory, intervention, and case example. *American Journal of Orthopsychiatry, 62,* 481–492.

Zayas, L., & Romano, K. (1994). Adolescents and parental death from AIDS. In B. O. Dane & C. Levine (Eds.), *AIDS and the new orphans* (pp. 59–76). Westport, CT: Auburn House.

Zeanah, C. H., & Zeanah, P. D. (1989). Intergenerational transmission of maltreatment: Insights from attachment theory and research. *Psychiatry, 52,* 177–196.

Zigler, E. F., & Stevenson, M. F. (1993). *Children in a changing world: Development and social issues* (2nd ed.). Pacific Grove, CA: Brooks/Cole.

Zindel, P. (1989). *A begonia for Miss Applebaum.* New York: Bantam.

Zisook, S. & DeVaul, R. (1985). Unresolved grief. *American Journal of Psychoanalysis, 45,* 370–379.

Zweig, A. R. (1977). Children's attitudes towards death. Doctoral dissertation, Northwestern University. *Dissertation Abstracts International, 37,* 4249A.

Author Index

Subject Index

A

Abuse, implications of, 74. *See also specific types of abuse*
Acceptance, *see* Acknowledgment
  of death, 316–317
  emotional, 122
  pain of loss, 317–318
Accidents, as cause of death, 12–15
Acknowledgment:
  of death, family grief, 229–232
  of illness, 97
  significance of, 250–251
Acting-out, 118–119
Administrative resistance, 248
Adolescents:
  bereavement reactions in, 118–119
  cognitive development, 116
  defense mechanisms in, 117
  suicidal, 79
  suicidality measurement in, 82
  trial mourning, 111
  understanding of death, 116
Aftershocks, of trauma. *See* Postvention
Age factor:
  sibling death and, 152
  understanding of death, 43
Aggression, child suicide and, 77. *See also* Anger

AIDS:
  complications of:
    disclosure, 57–58
    multiple loss and, 58–60
    secrecy, 56–57
    shame, 55–56
    stigmatization of, 54–56
    survivor's guilt, 60–62
  parental death, 66–68
  pediatric, *see* Pediatric AIDS
  practice and policy implications, 69–70
  significant other with, 64–66
All inclusiveness, 32
Ambivalence, 123
Anemias, 13
Anger:
  child suicide and, 77
  domestic violence and, 207
  parental death, 286–287
  projection of, 319–320
  traumatic grief and, 214, 219
Antisocial behavior, 66
Art therapy, 176, 260, 301, 303
Assessment, of bereaved child:
  case examples, 309–310
  circumstances of, 310–311
  function of, 306–307
  needs evaluation, 306
  outline of, 307–309

𝕊 *Springer Publishing Company*

LOGOTHERAPY FOR THE HELPING PROFESSIONAL
Meaningful Social Work

David Guttmann, DSW

In this useful resource, the author explains the pioneering work of Dr. Viktor Frankl and his theories of logotherapy. This volume will enable helping professionals to supplement traditional methods of psychotherapy with logotherapy techniques in order to improve their effectiveness through clearer understanding of their clients' problems. Professionals can then derive greater personal meaning and satisfaction from their work, thereby lessening the potential for stress and burnout. This volume addresses therapists, clinical social workers, and counselors.

Contents:

I: Major Concepts in Logotherapy. The Development of Logotherapy • Logotherapy and Psychoanalysis: Similarities and Differences • The Noetic or Spiritual Dimension • The "Tragic Triad": Logotherapy's Attitude to Guilt, Suffering, and Death

II: Logotherapeutic Treatment and Application. Paradoxical Intention as a Special Logotherapeutic Technique • "Dereflection" as Counteracting Behavior • Other Logotherapeutic Techniques • The "Socratic Dialogue" Logotherapy's Main Tool in Helping Seekers Search for Meaning

III. Research in the Service of Logotherapy. Research on Major Logotherapeutic Concepts • Further Developments in Logotherapeutic Research

1995   320pp   0-8261-9020-0   hardcover

536 Broadway, New York, NY 10012-3955 • (212) 431-4370 • Fax (212) 941-7842